I'm nocturnal!!

池田晃久
AKIHISA IKEDA

I've loved vampires ever since I was a kid.
I'm crazy about all those other monsters too.
That's why I made this manga. I love doing
whatever I want with it. I still have a lot to
learn, but I'd be so happy if you'd cheer me on
and watch over me on this journey of mine.
Oh, and watch over Moka, too!

Akihisa Ikeda was born in 1977 in Miyazaki. He debuted as a
mangaka with the four-volume magical warrior fantasy series
Kiruto in 1999, which was serialized in *Monthly Shonen Jump*.
Rosario+Vampire debuted in *Monthly Shonen Jump* in March
of 2002, and is continuing in the new magazine *Jump Square*
(Jump SQ). In Japan, *Rosario+Vampire* is also available as a dram
CD. In 2008, the story was released as an anime.

Ikeda has been a huge fan of vampires and monsters since h
was a little kid.

He says one of the perks of being a manga artist is being able
to go for walks during the day when everybody else is stuck in
the office.

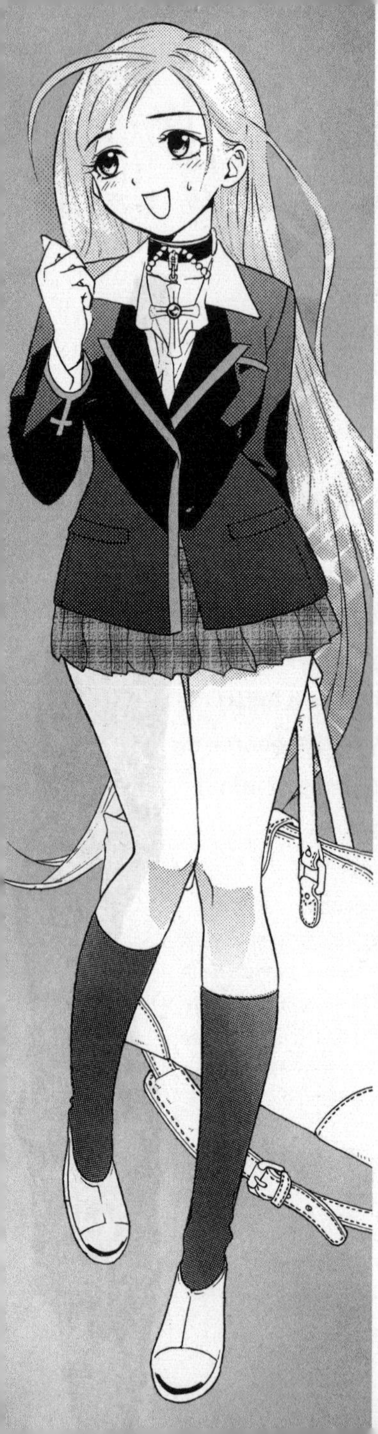

ROSARIO+VAMPIRE 1

SHONEN JUMP ADVANCED Manga Edition

STORY & ART BY AKIHISA IKEDA

Translation/Kaori Inoue
English Adaptation/Gerard Jones
Touch-up Art & Lettering/Stephen Dutro
Cover & Interior Design/Hidemi Dunn
Editor/Annette Roman

Printed in the U.S.A.

Published by VIZ Media, LLC
P.O. Box 77010
San Francisco, CA 94107

10 9
First printing, June 2008
Ninth printing, July 2013

www.viz.com

ADVANCED
www.shonenjump.com

RATED T+ FOR OLDER TEEN

PARENTAL ADVISORY
ROSARIO+VAMPIRE is rated T+ for Older Teen and is recommended for ages 16 and up. It contains suggestive situations.

ratings.viz.com

ROSARIO+VAMPIRE

1

VAMPIRES

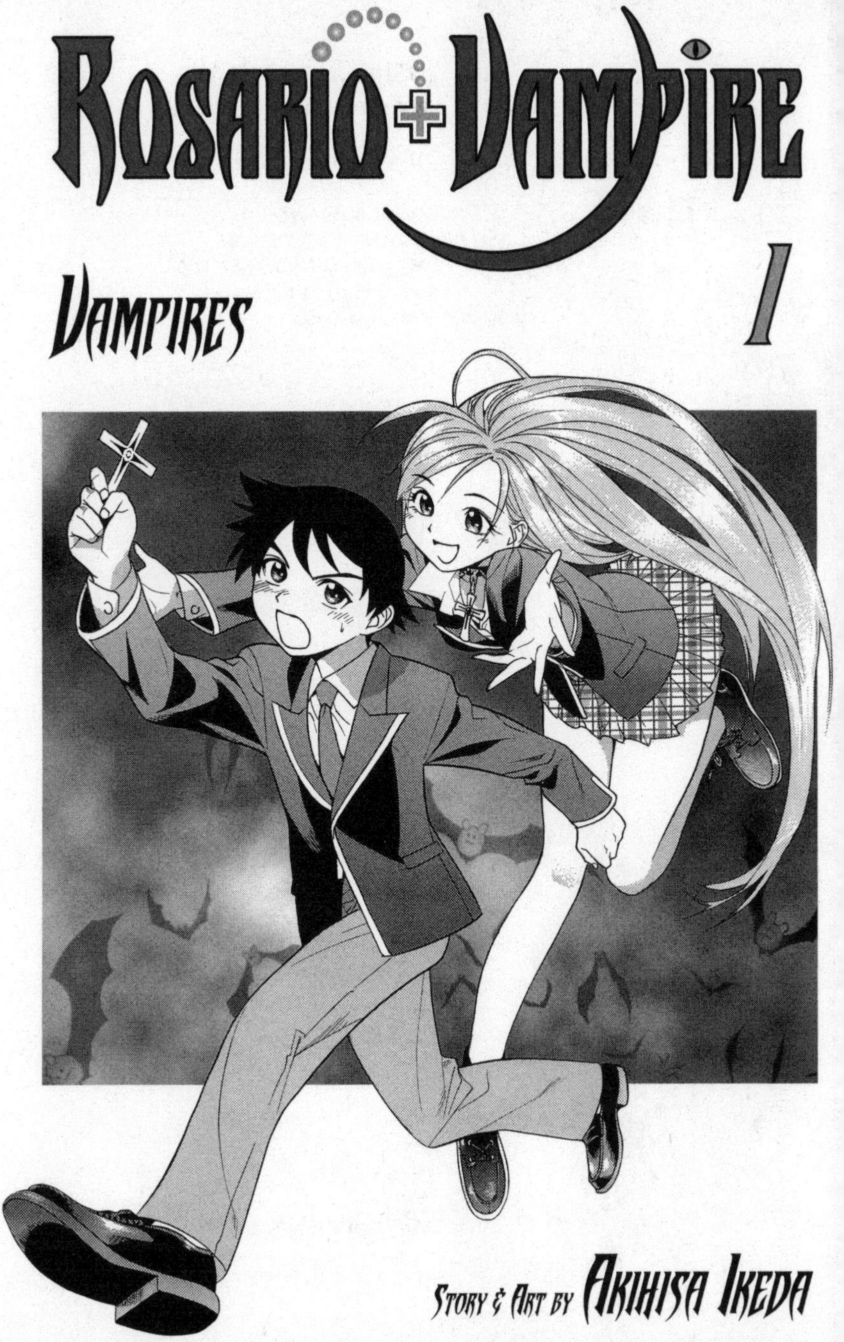

STORY & ART BY AKIHISA IKEDA

CONTENTS

Volume 1: Vampires

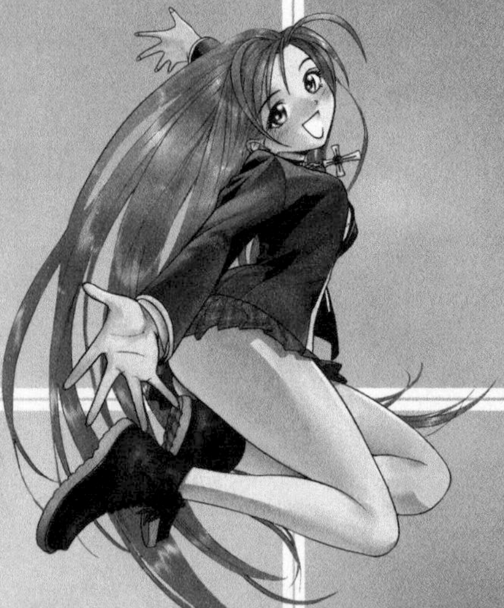

1: The School Vampire

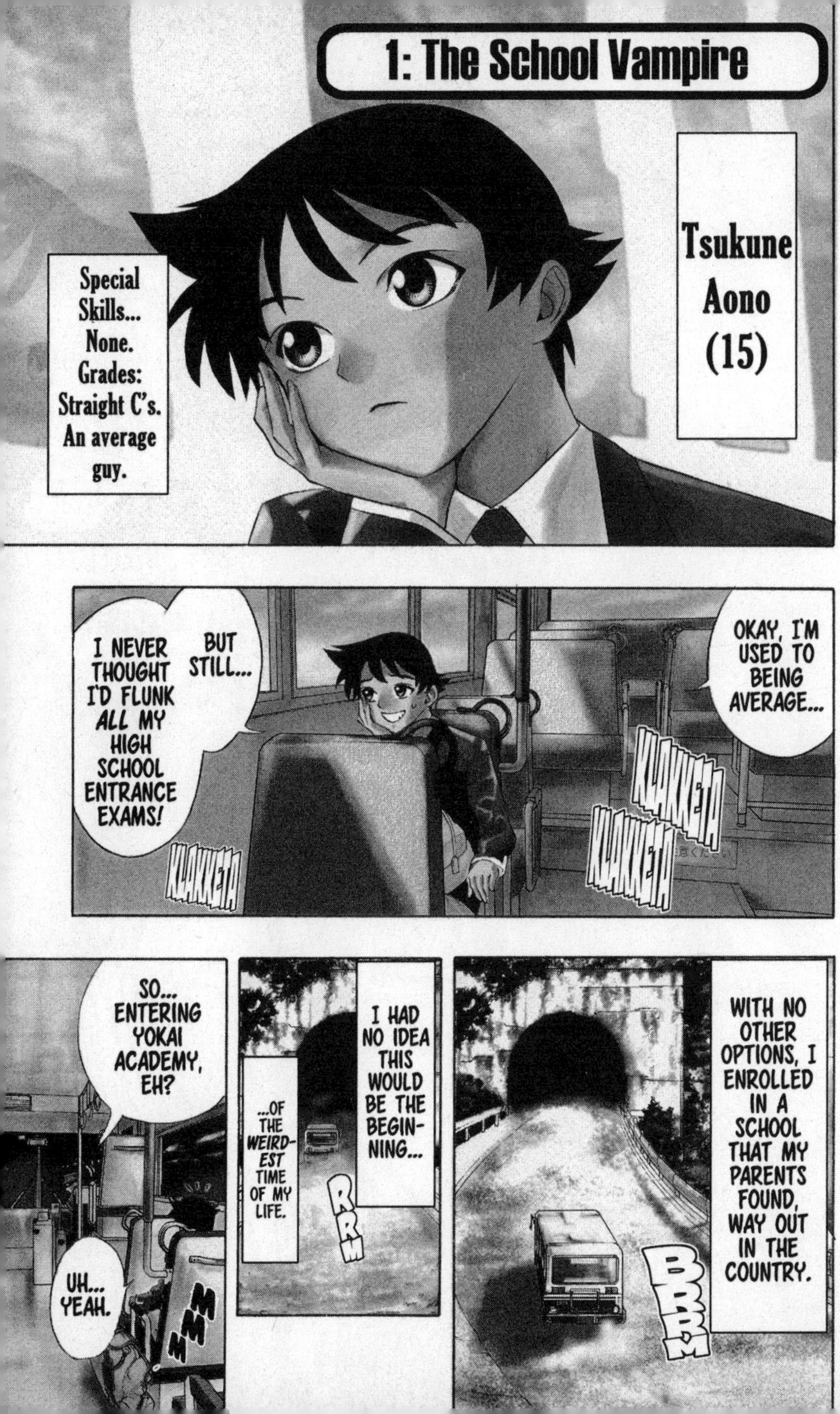

Tsukune Aono (15)
Special Skills... None. Grades: Straight C's. An average guy.
OKAY, I'M USED TO BEING AVERAGE...
BUT STILL...
I NEVER THOUGHT I'D FLUNK *ALL* MY HIGH SCHOOL ENTRANCE EXAMS!
KLAKKETA
KLAKKETA
KLAKKETA
WITH NO OTHER OPTIONS, I ENROLLED IN A SCHOOL THAT MY PARENTS FOUND, WAY OUT IN THE COUNTRY.
BRRRM
I HAD NO IDEA THIS WOULD BE THE BEGINNING...
...OF THE *WEIRDEST* TIME OF MY LIFE.
RRM
SO... ENTERING YOKAI ACADEMY, EH?
UH... YEAH.
MMMM

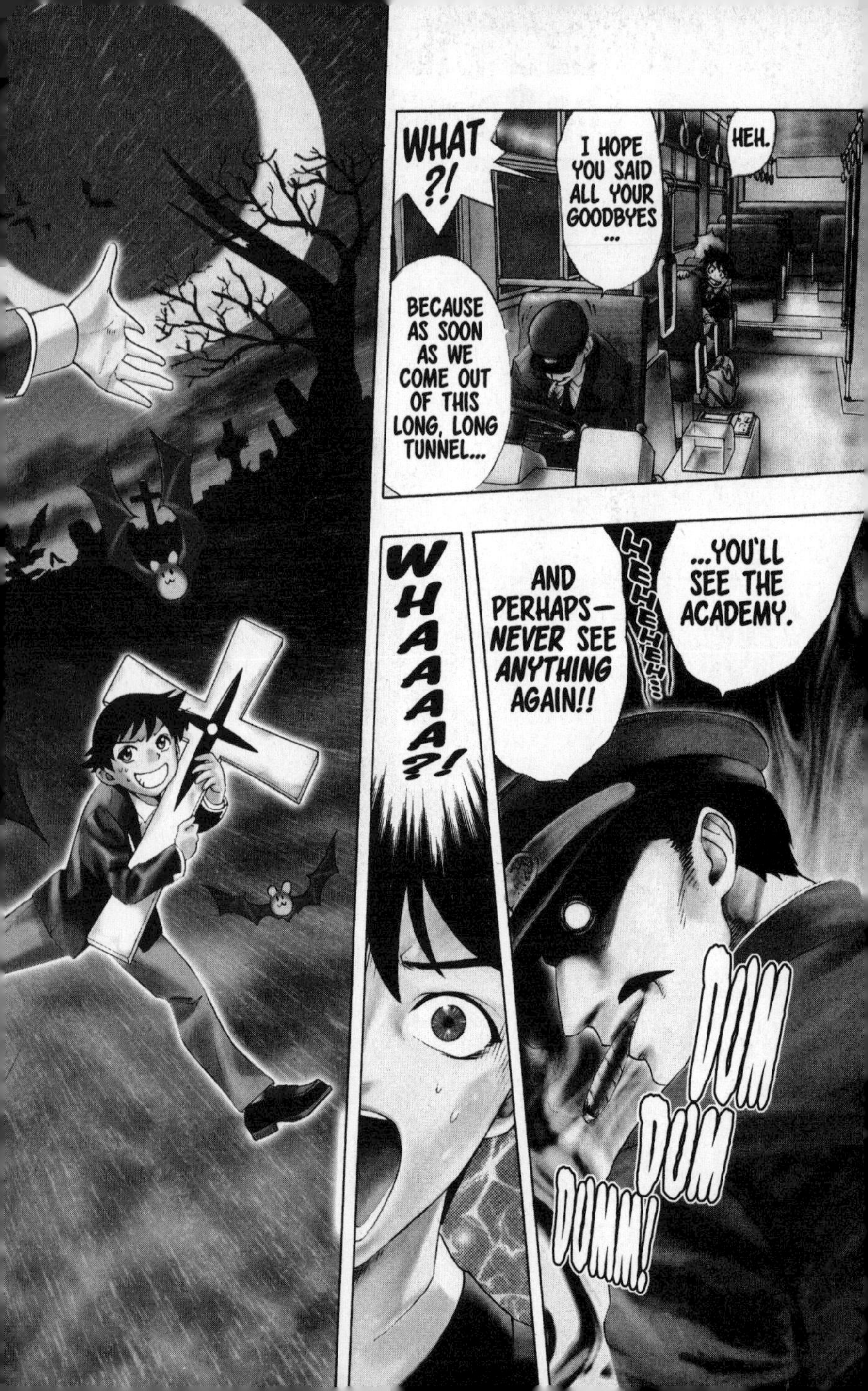
HEH.
I HOPE YOU SAID ALL YOUR GOODBYES ...
WHAT ?!
BECAUSE AS SOON AS WE COME OUT OF THIS LONG, LONG TUNNEL...
...YOU'LL SEE THE ACADEMY.
HEHEHEH...
AND PERHAPS— NEVER SEE ANYTHING AGAIN!!
WHAAAAA?!
DUM
DUM
DUMM!

1: The School Vampire

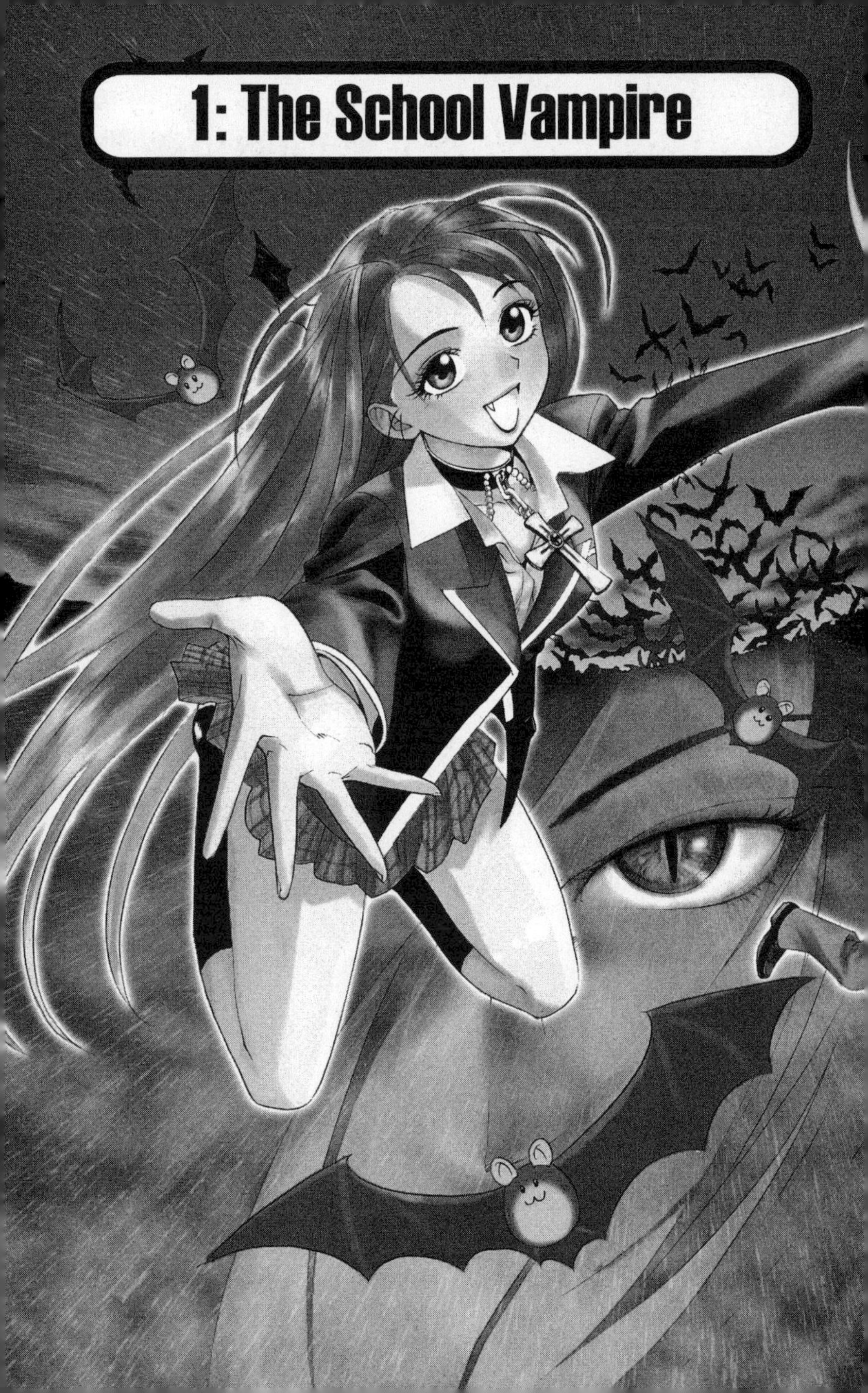

ROSARIO+VAMPIRE

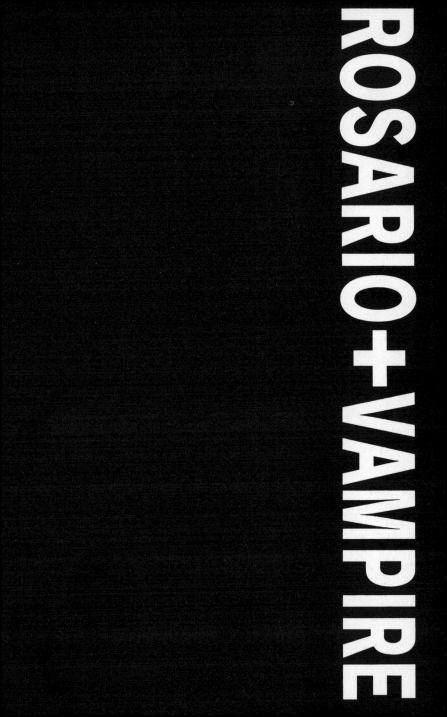

READ THIS WAY

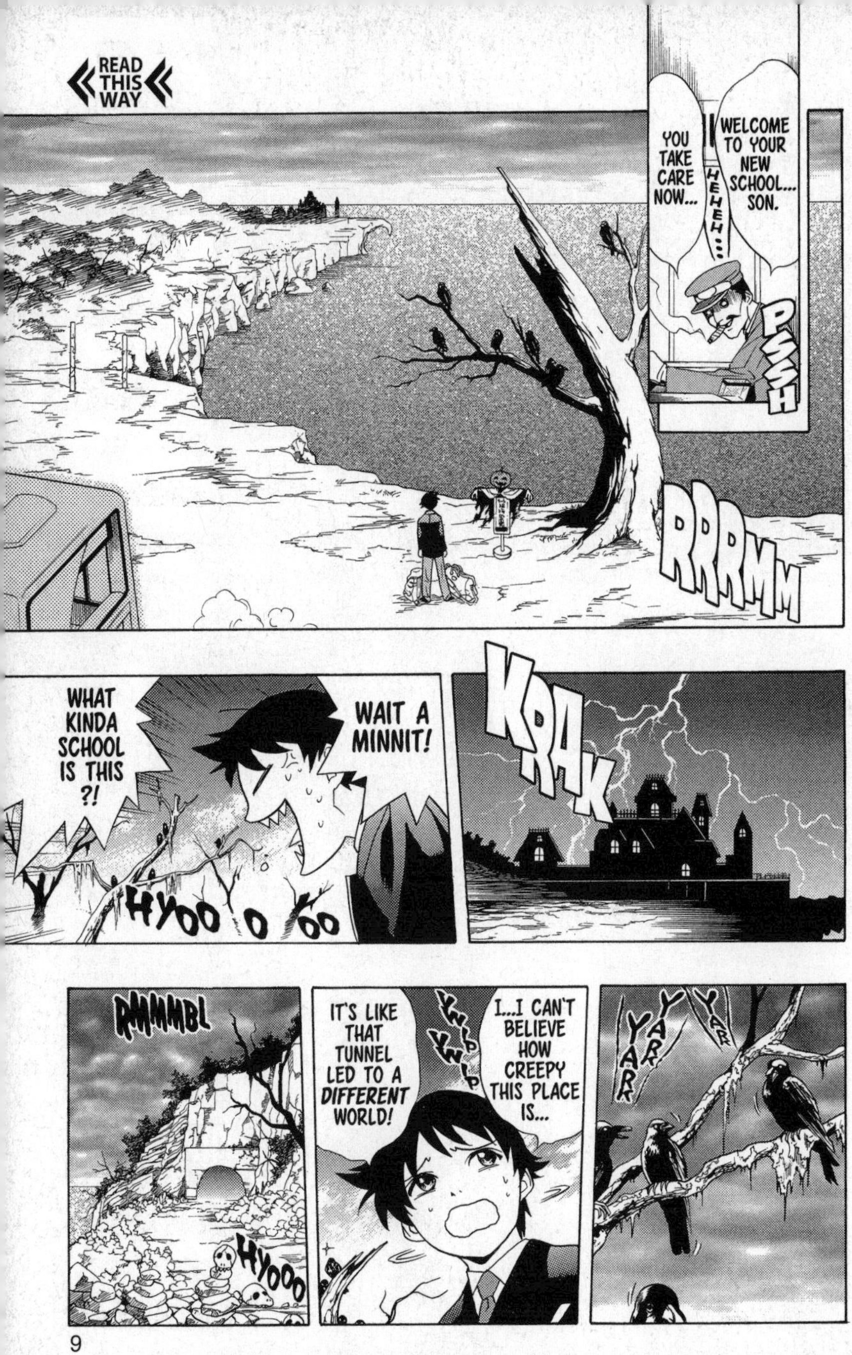
WELCOME TO YOUR NEW SCHOOL... SON.
HEHEH...
YOU TAKE CARE NOW...
PSSH
RRRMM
KRAK
WAIT A MINNIT!
WHAT KINDA SCHOOL IS THIS ?!
HYOO O OO
YAR YAR
YARK YARK
I...I CAN'T BELIEVE HOW CREEPY THIS PLACE IS...
YWIP YWIP
IT'S LIKE THAT TUNNEL LED TO A *DIFFERENT* WORLD!
RMMMBL
HYOOO

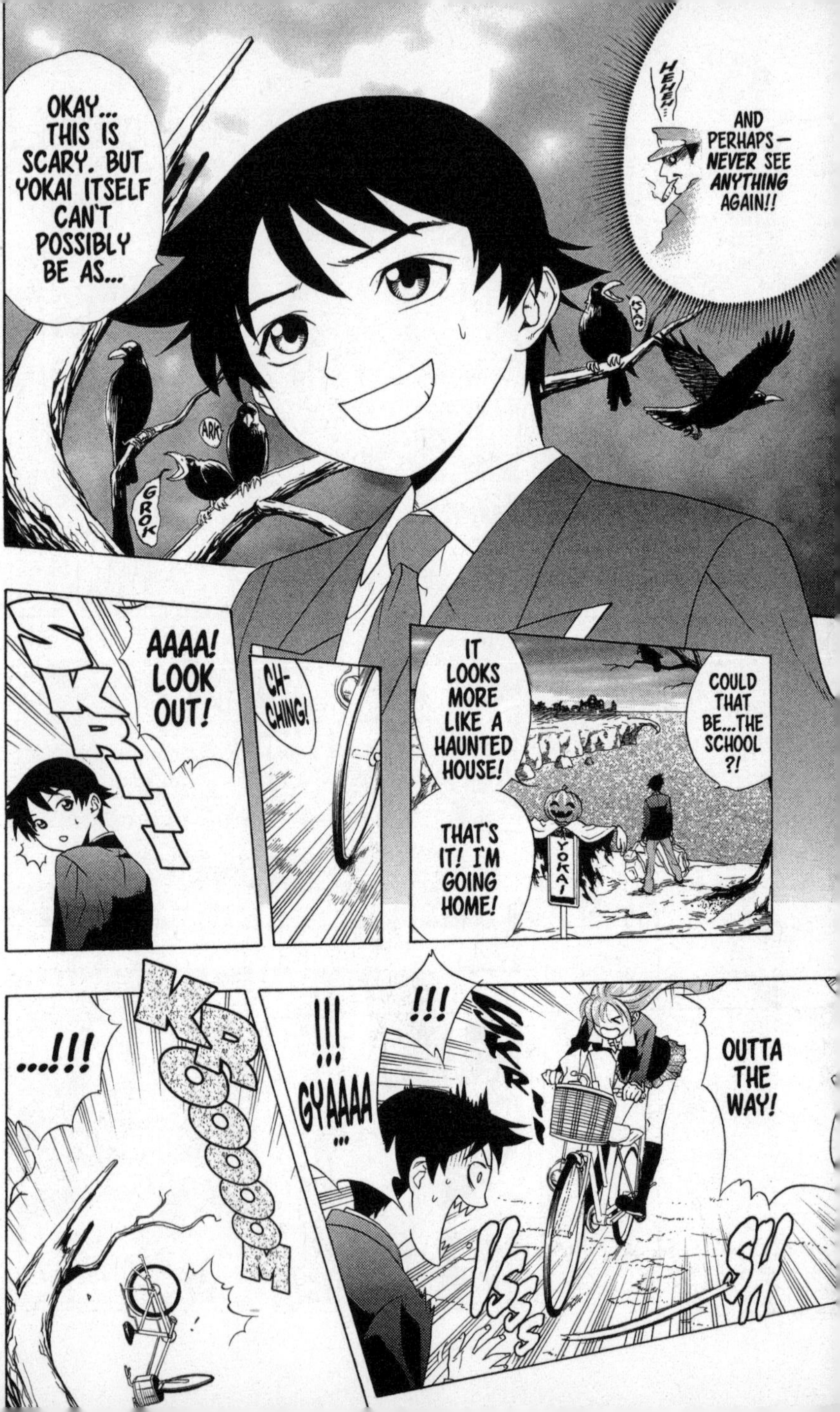
HEHEH...
AND PERHAPS— NEVER SEE ANYTHING AGAIN!!
KYAH
OKAY... THIS IS SCARY. BUT YOKAI ITSELF CAN'T POSSIBLY BE AS...
ARK
GROK
COULD THAT BE...THE SCHOOL?!
IT LOOKS MORE LIKE A HAUNTED HOUSE!
THAT'S IT! I'M GOING HOME!
YOKAI
CH-CHING!
AAAA! LOOK OUT!
SKRIIII
OUTTA THE WAY!
SKR!!
!!!
!!! GYAAAA...
SH
VSSS
...!!!
KROOOOOOM

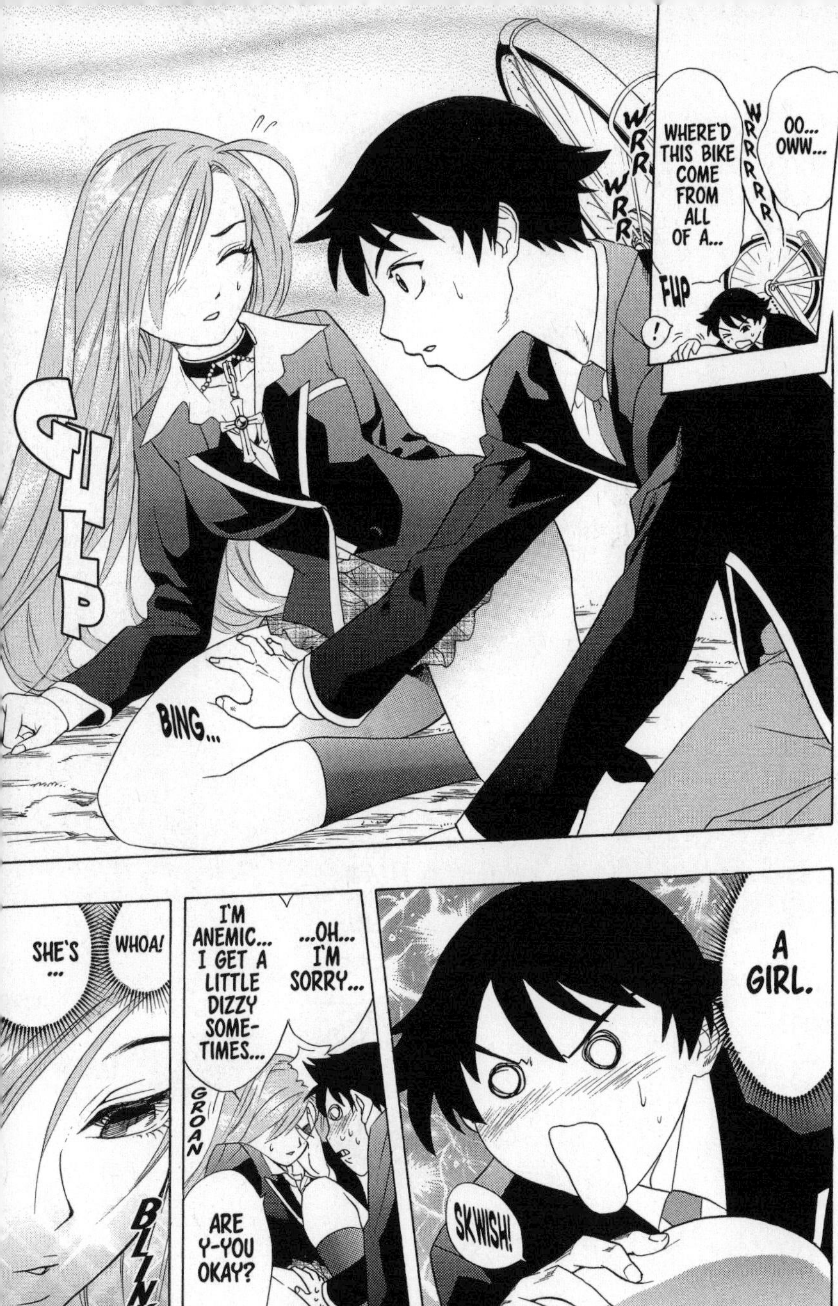
OO... OWW...
WHERE'D THIS BIKE COME FROM ALL OF A...
WRRRRRR
FUP
!
WRR WRR
GULP
BING...
A GIRL.
SKWISH!
...OH... I'M SORRY...
I'M ANEMIC... I GET A LITTLE DIZZY SOME-TIMES...
GROAN
ARE Y-YOU OKAY?
WHOA!
SHE'S ...
BLINK

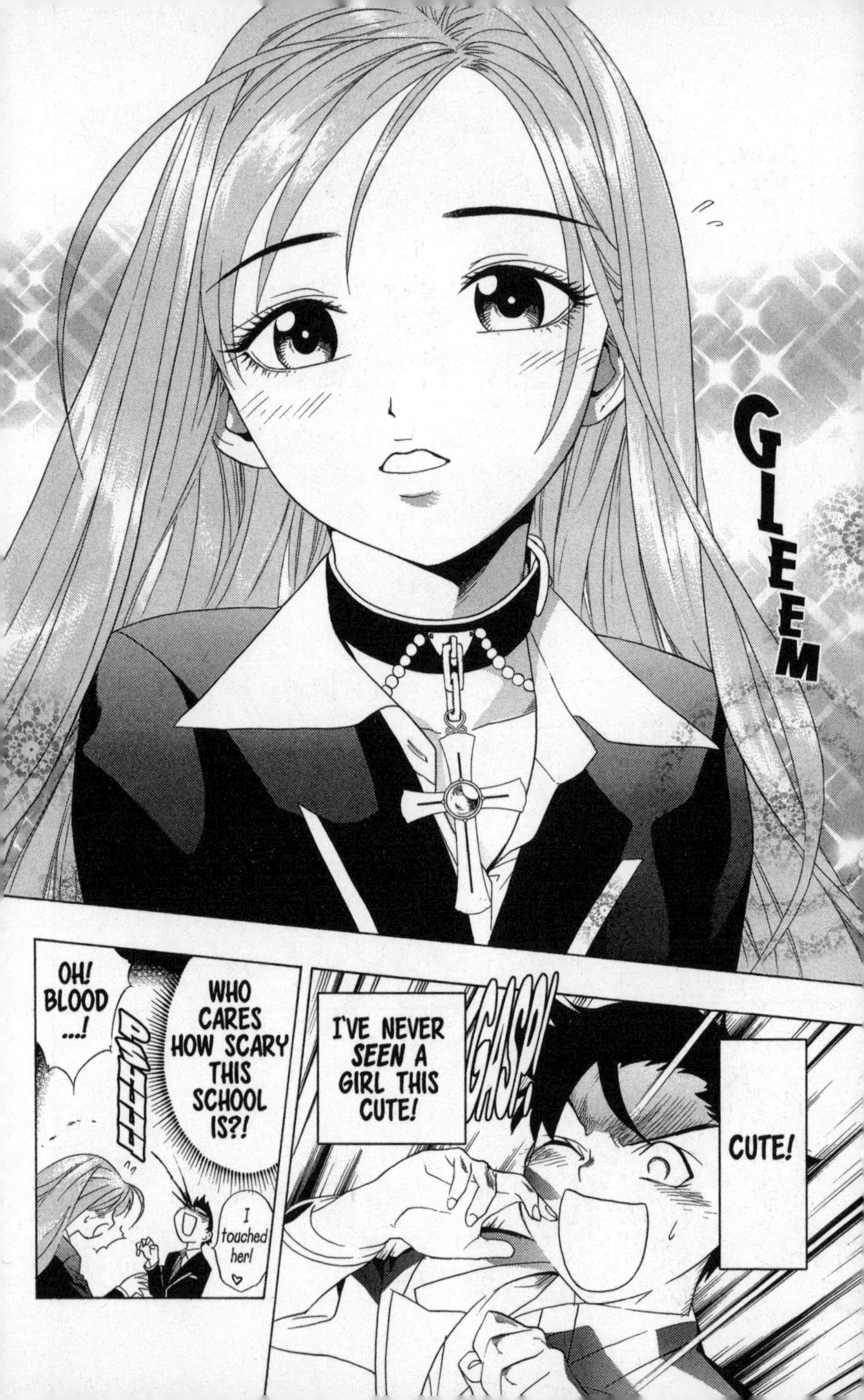
GLEEM
CUTE!
I'VE NEVER SEEN A GIRL THIS CUTE!
GASP!
WHO CARES HOW SCARY THIS SCHOOL IS?!
OH! BLOOD ...!
I touched her!

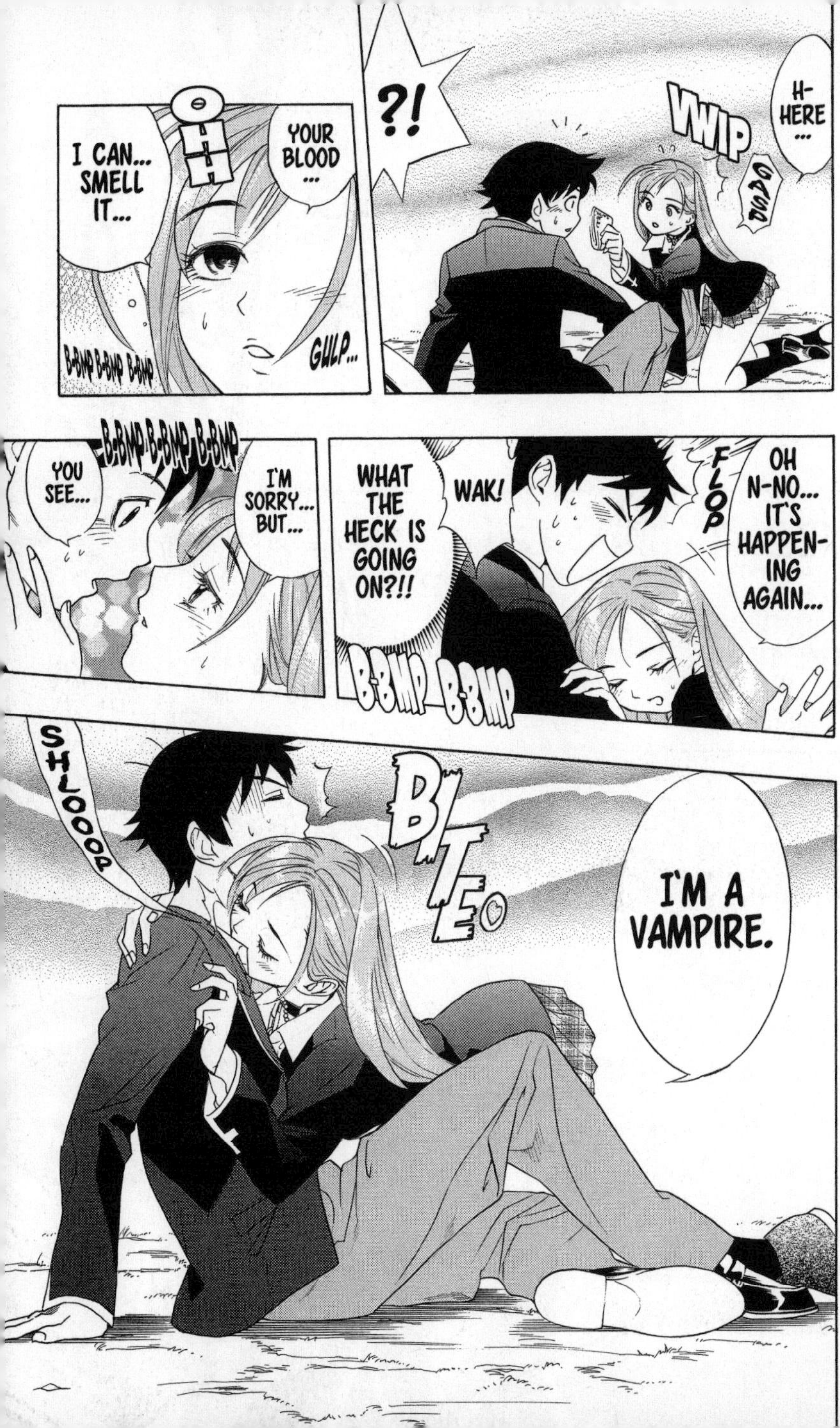
H-HERE...
VWIP
GASP
?!
YOUR BLOOD...
OHHH
I CAN... SMELL IT...
GULP...
B-BMP B-BMP B-BMP
OH N-NO... IT'S HAPPENING AGAIN...
FLOP
WAK!
WHAT THE HECK IS GOING ON?!!
B-BMP B-BMP
I'M SORRY... BUT...
B-BMP B-BMP B-BMP
YOU SEE...
I'M A VAMPIRE.
BITE
SHLOOOOP

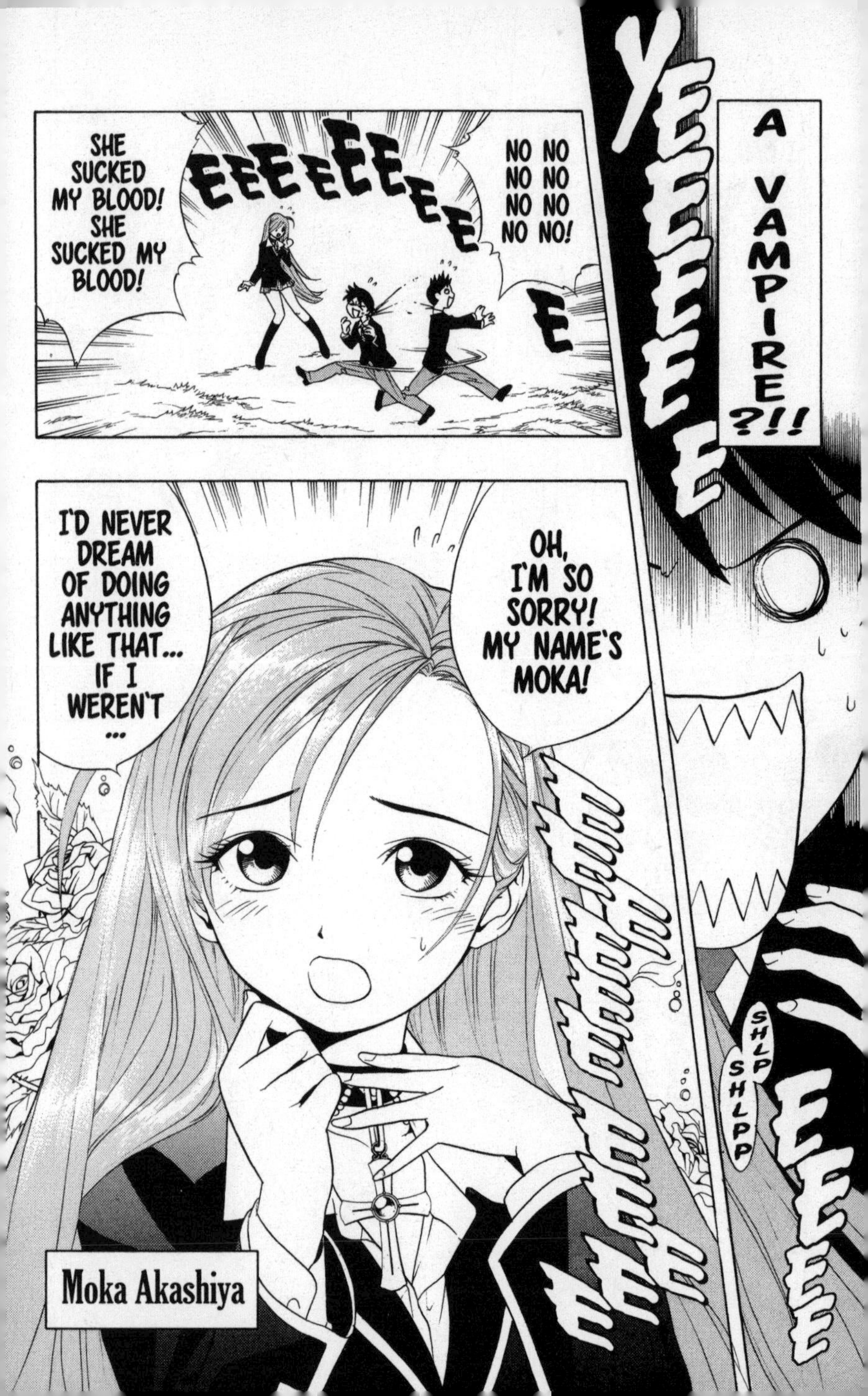
YEEEEEEE
A VAMPIRE?!!
SHLP SHLPP
EEEE
NO NO NO NO NO NO NO NO!
EEEEEEEEEE
SHE SUCKED MY BLOOD! SHE SUCKED MY BLOOD!
OH, I'M SO SORRY! MY NAME'S MOKA!
I'D NEVER DREAM OF DOING ANYTHING LIKE THAT... IF I WEREN'T ...
EEEEEEEEE
Moka Akashiya

READ THIS WAY

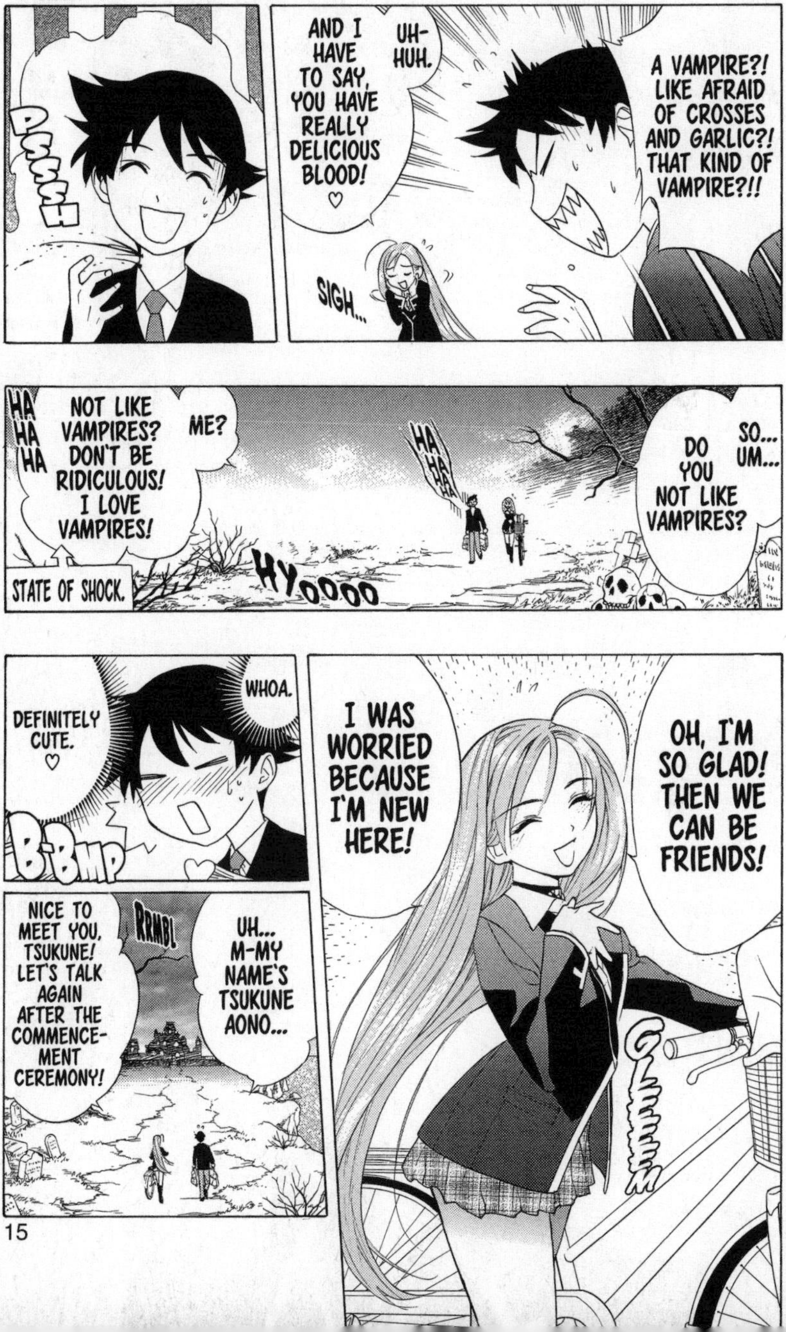
A VAMPIRE?! LIKE AFRAID OF CROSSES AND GARLIC?! THAT KIND OF VAMPIRE?!!
UH-HUH.
AND I HAVE TO SAY, YOU HAVE REALLY DELICIOUS BLOOD! ♡
SIGH...
PSSSH
SO... UM...
DO YOU NOT LIKE VAMPIRES?
HA HA HA HA
HYOOOO
ME?
NOT LIKE VAMPIRES? DON'T BE RIDICULOUS! I LOVE VAMPIRES!
HA HA HA
STATE OF SHOCK.
OH, I'M SO GLAD! THEN WE CAN BE FRIENDS!
I WAS WORRIED BECAUSE I'M NEW HERE!
WHOA.
DEFINITELY CUTE. ♡
B-BMP
UH... M-MY NAME'S TSUKUNE AONO...
RRMBL
NICE TO MEET YOU, TSUKUNE! LET'S TALK AGAIN AFTER THE COMMENCEMENT CEREMONY!

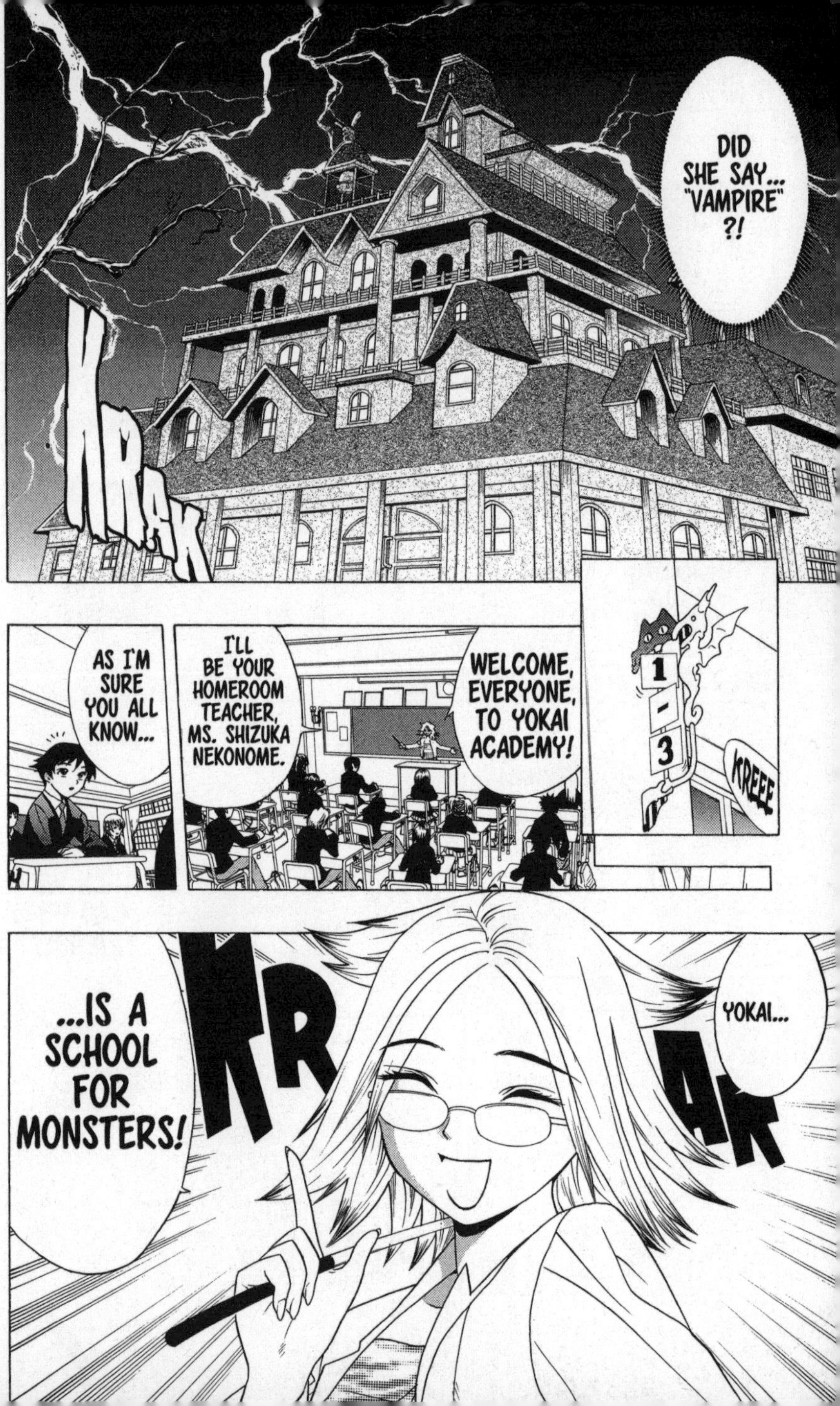
DID SHE SAY... "VAMPIRE" ?!
KRRAK
KREEE
1-3
WELCOME, EVERYONE, TO YOKAI ACADEMY!
I'LL BE YOUR HOMEROOM TEACHER, MS. SHIZUKA NEKONOME.
AS I'M SURE YOU ALL KNOW...
YOKAI...
KRAK
...IS A SCHOOL FOR MONSTERS!

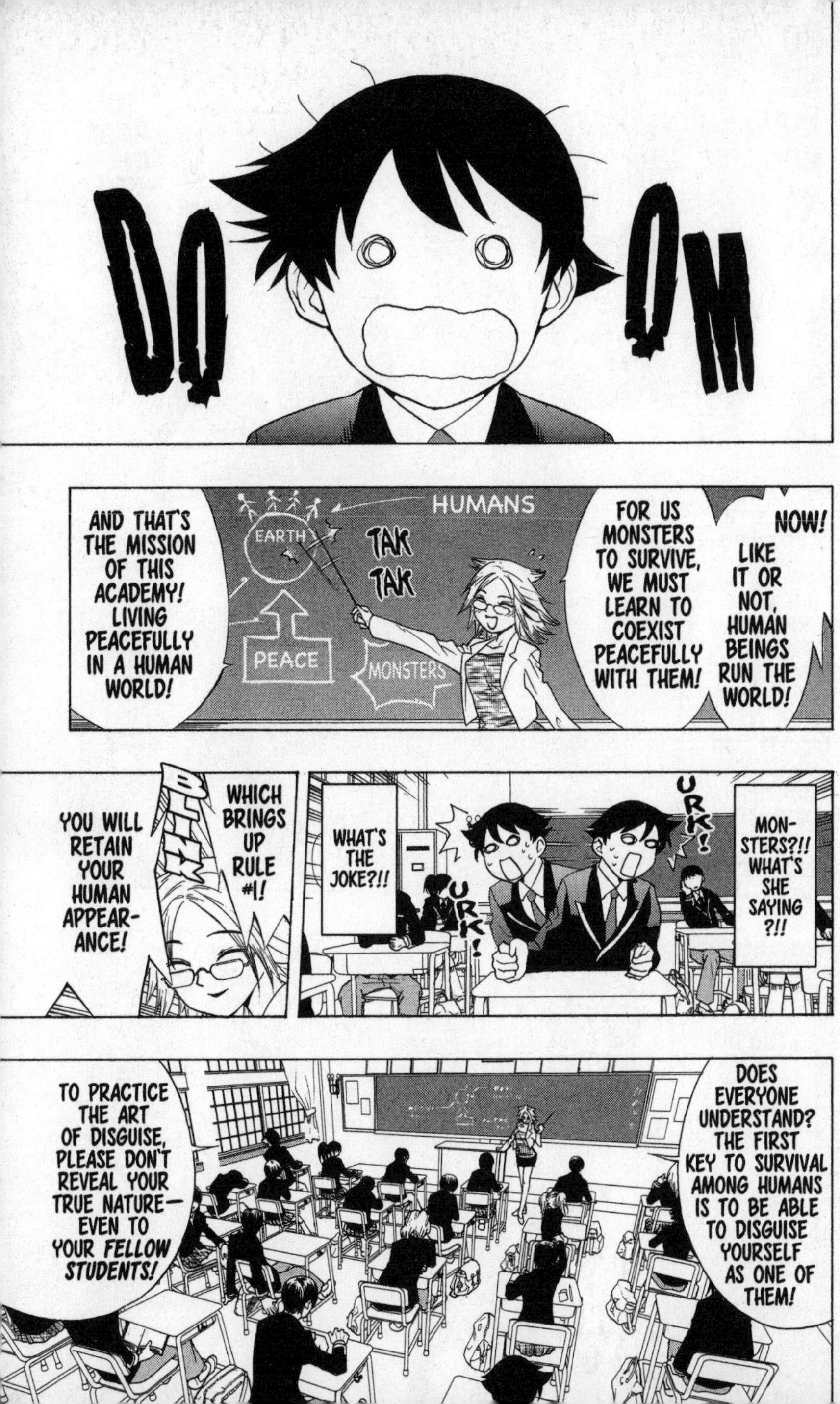
DOOM
NOW! LIKE IT OR NOT, HUMAN BEINGS RUN THE WORLD!
FOR US MONSTERS TO SURVIVE, WE MUST LEARN TO COEXIST PEACEFULLY WITH THEM!
TAK TAK
HUMANS
EARTH
PEACE
MONSTERS
AND THAT'S THE MISSION OF THIS ACADEMY! LIVING PEACEFULLY IN A HUMAN WORLD!
MON-STERS?!! WHAT'S SHE SAYING ?!!
URK!
URK!
WHAT'S THE JOKE?!!
WHICH BRINGS UP RULE #1!
BLINK
YOU WILL RETAIN YOUR HUMAN APPEAR-ANCE!
DOES EVERYONE UNDERSTAND? THE FIRST KEY TO SURVIVAL AMONG HUMANS IS TO BE ABLE TO DISGUISE YOURSELF AS ONE OF THEM!
TO PRACTICE THE ART OF DISGUISE, PLEASE DON'T REVEAL YOUR TRUE NATURE—EVEN TO YOUR FELLOW STUDENTS!

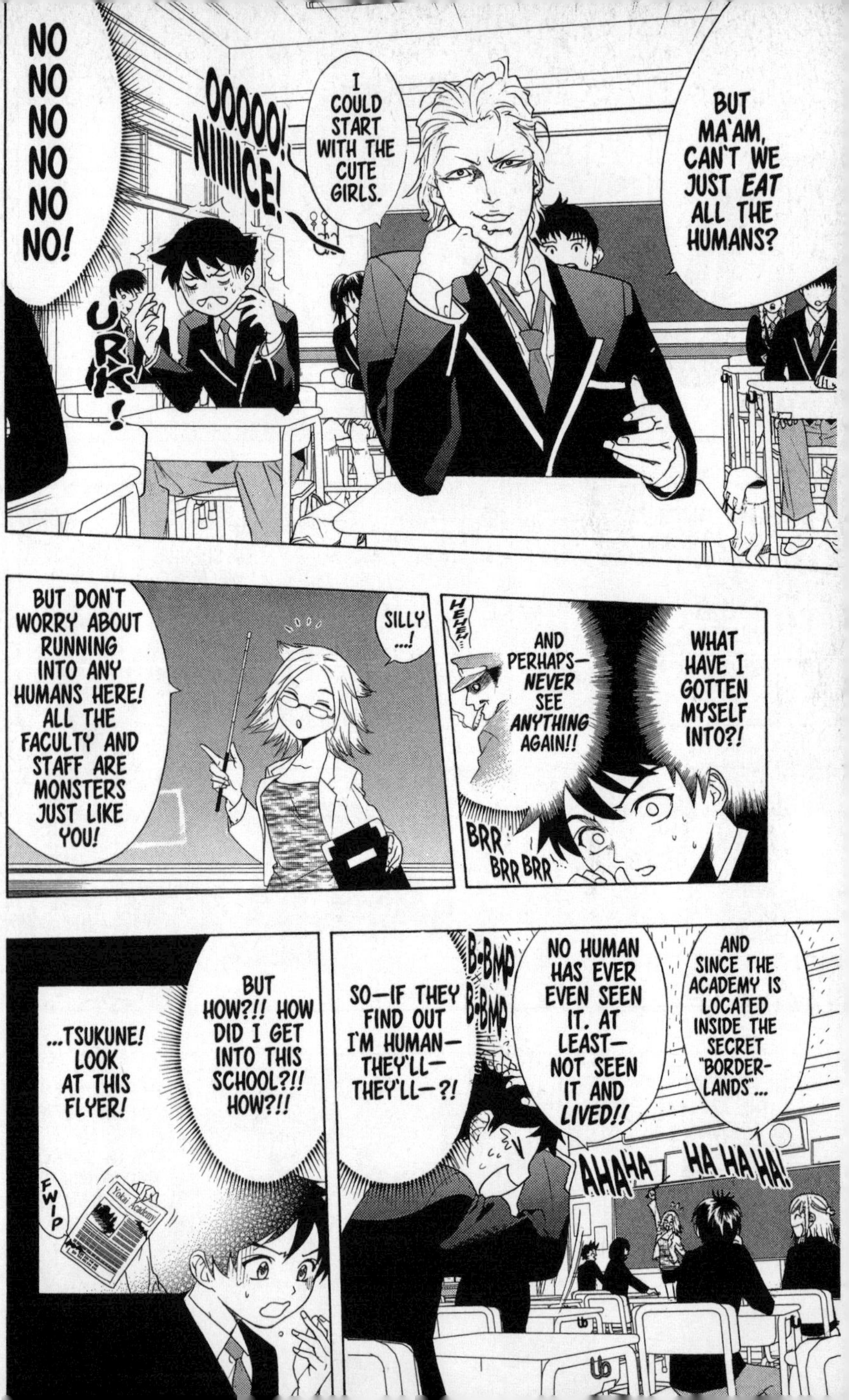
BUT MA'AM, CAN'T WE JUST *EAT* ALL THE HUMANS?
I COULD START WITH THE CUTE GIRLS.
OOOOO! NIIIIICE!
NO NO NO NO NO NO!
URK!
WHAT HAVE I GOTTEN MYSELF INTO?!
HEHEH
AND PERHAPS— *NEVER* SEE *ANYTHING* AGAIN!!
BRR BRR BRR
SILLY ...!
BUT DON'T WORRY ABOUT RUNNING INTO ANY HUMANS HERE! ALL THE FACULTY AND STAFF ARE MONSTERS JUST LIKE YOU!
AND SINCE THE ACADEMY IS LOCATED INSIDE THE SECRET "BORDER-LANDS"...
NO HUMAN HAS EVER EVEN SEEN IT. AT LEAST— NOT SEEN IT AND *LIVED!!*
B-BMP B-BMP
SO—IF THEY FIND OUT I'M HUMAN— THEY'LL— THEY'LL—?!
AHAHA HA HA HA!
BUT HOW?!! HOW DID I GET INTO THIS SCHOOL?!! HOW?!!
...TSUKUNE! LOOK AT THIS FLYER!
FWIP
Yokai Academy

READ THIS WAY

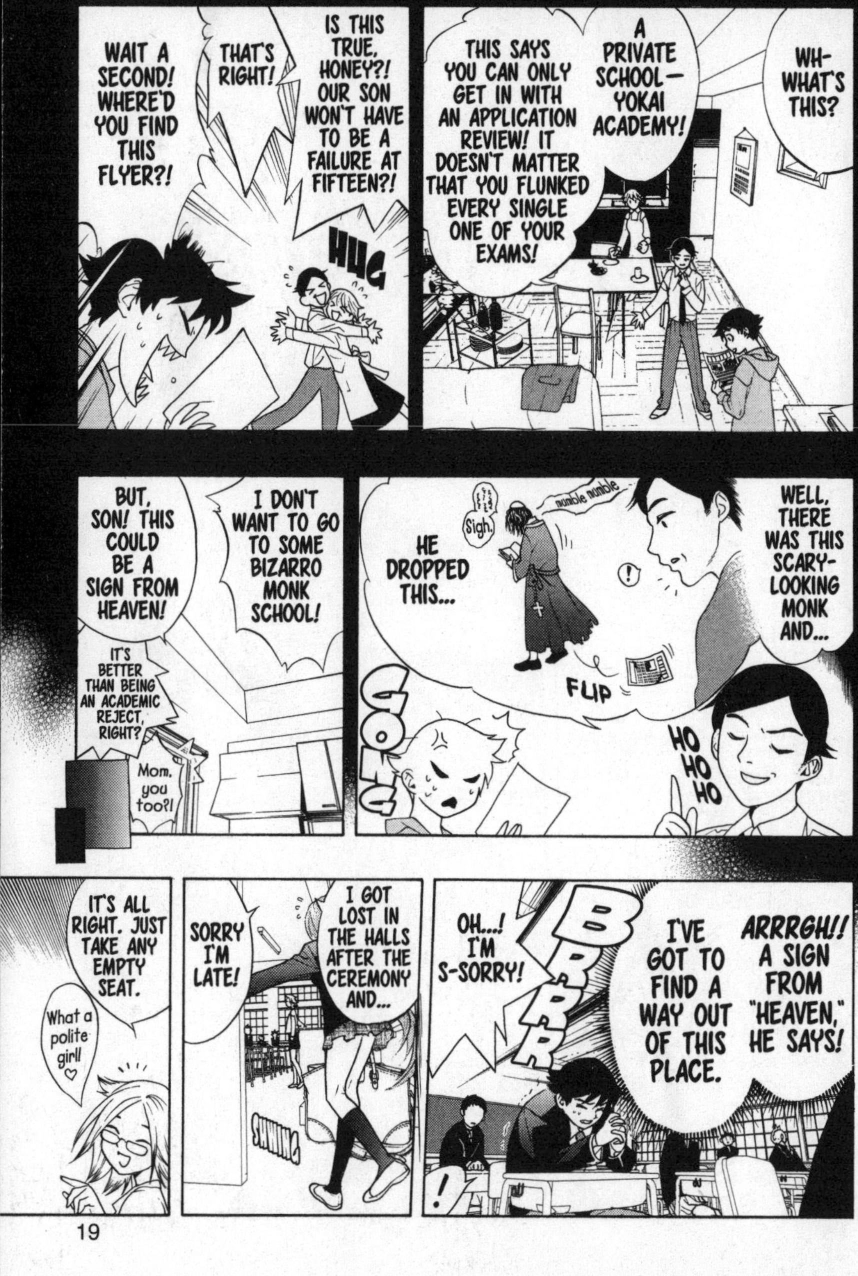
WH- WHAT'S THIS?
A PRIVATE SCHOOL— YOKAI ACADEMY!
THIS SAYS YOU CAN ONLY GET IN WITH AN APPLICATION REVIEW! IT DOESN'T MATTER THAT YOU FLUNKED EVERY SINGLE ONE OF YOUR EXAMS!
IS THIS TRUE, HONEY?! OUR SON WON'T HAVE TO BE A FAILURE AT FIFTEEN?!
THAT'S RIGHT!
HUG
WAIT A SECOND! WHERE'D YOU FIND THIS FLYER?!
WELL, THERE WAS THIS SCARY-LOOKING MONK AND...
mumble mumble
Sigh.
HE DROPPED THIS...
FLIP
HO HO HO
I DON'T WANT TO GO TO SOME BIZARRO MONK SCHOOL!
BUT, SON! THIS COULD BE A SIGN FROM HEAVEN!
IT'S BETTER THAN BEING AN ACADEMIC REJECT, RIGHT?
Mom, you too?!
ARRRGH!! A SIGN FROM "HEAVEN," HE SAYS!
I'VE GOT TO FIND A WAY OUT OF THIS PLACE.
BRRRR
OH...! I'M S-SORRY!
I GOT LOST IN THE HALLS AFTER THE CEREMONY AND...
SORRY I'M LATE!
IT'S ALL RIGHT. JUST TAKE ANY EMPTY SEAT.
What a polite girl! ♡

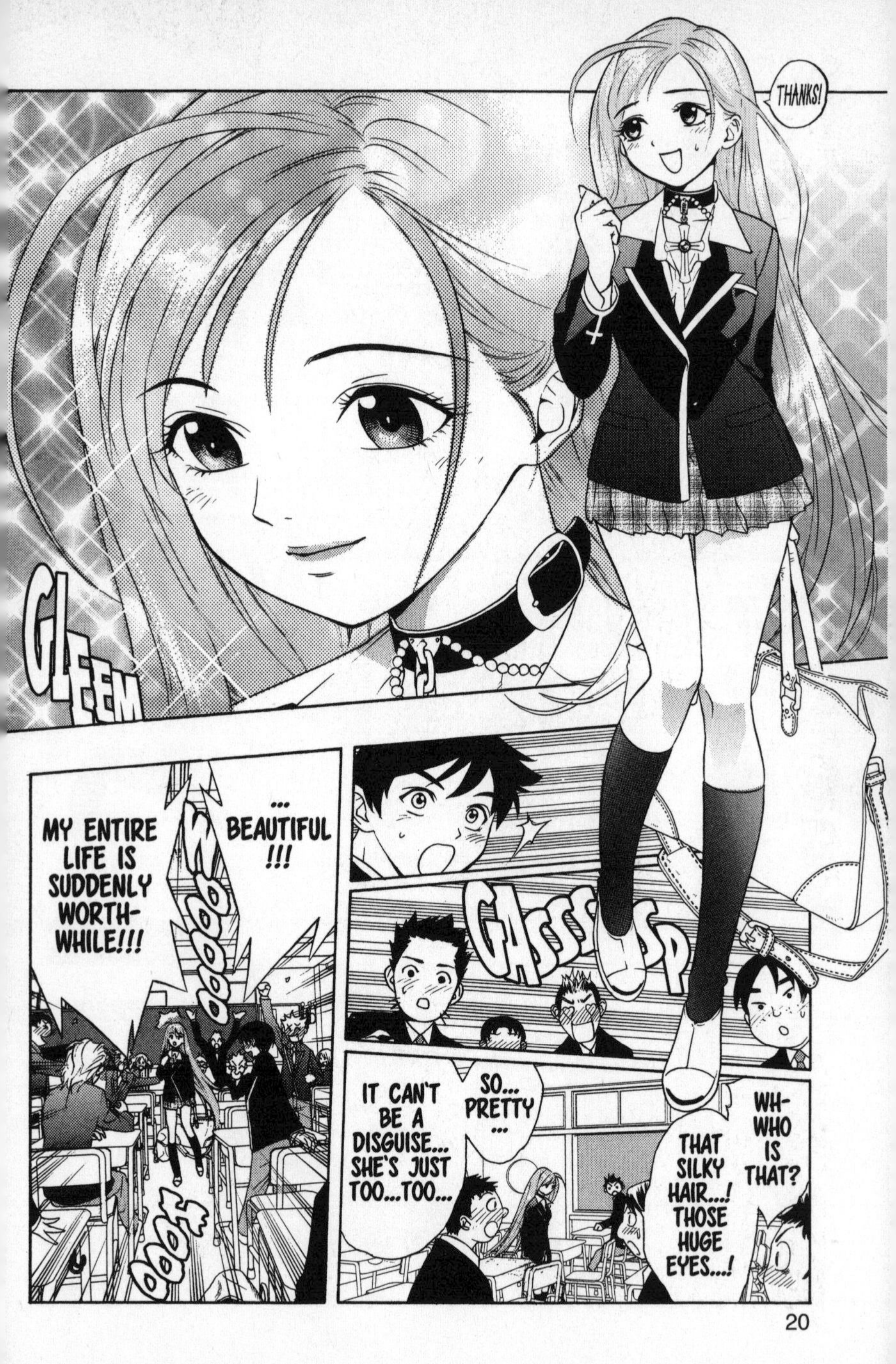
THANKS!
GLEEM
GASSSSP
WH-WHO IS THAT?
THAT SILKY HAIR...! THOSE HUGE EYES...!
SO... PRETTY...
IT CAN'T BE A DISGUISE... SHE'S JUST TOO...TOO...
...BEAUTIFUL!!!
MY ENTIRE LIFE IS SUDDENLY WORTH-WHILE!!!
WOOOOOOO
HOOO

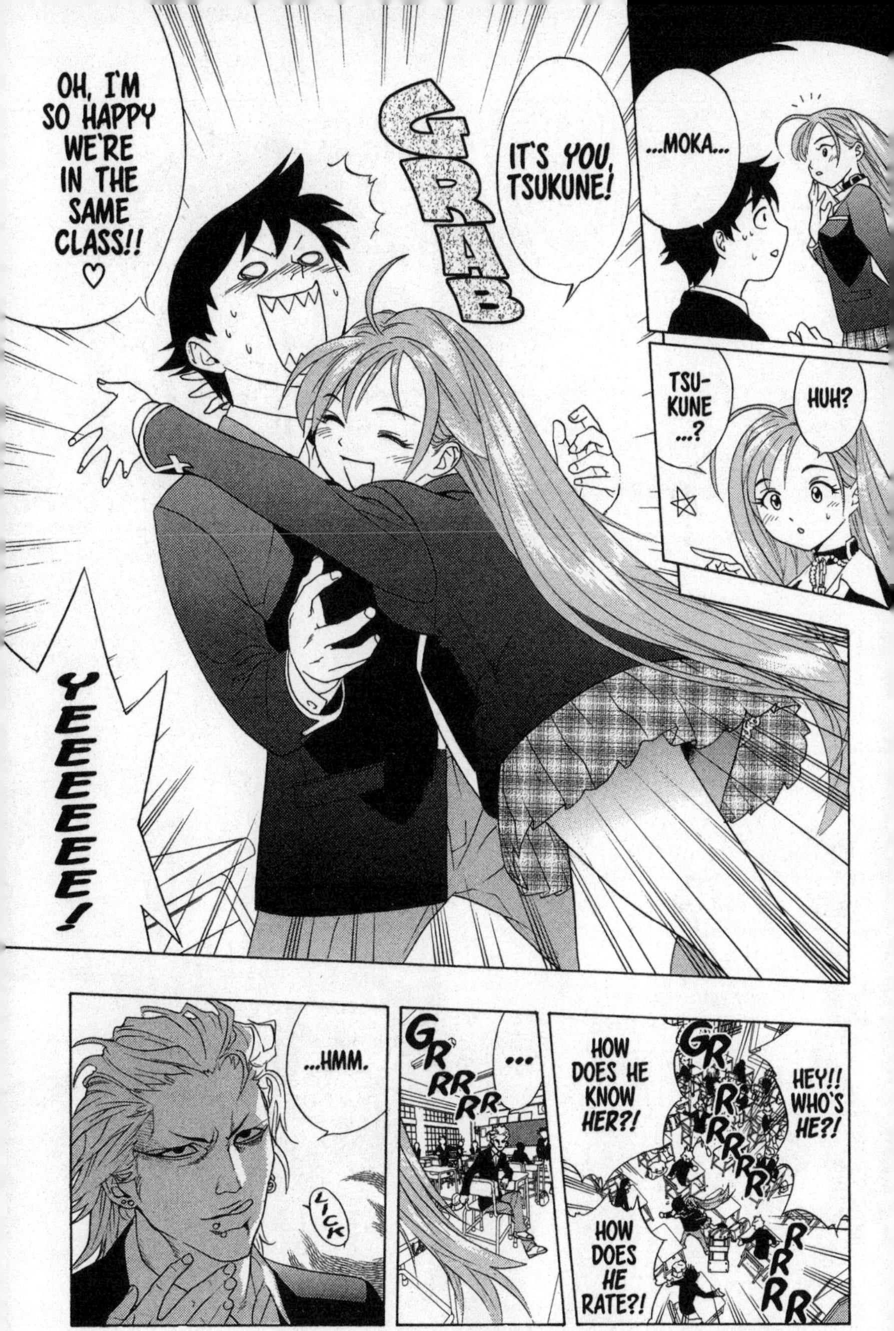
...MOKA...
HUH?
TSU-KUNE...?
IT'S YOU, TSUKUNE!
GRAB
OH, I'M SO HAPPY WE'RE IN THE SAME CLASS!! ♡
YEEEEEEEE!
HEY!! WHO'S HE?!
GRRRRRRRRR
HOW DOES HE KNOW HER?!
HOW DOES HE RATE?!
...
GRRRR
...HMM.
LICK

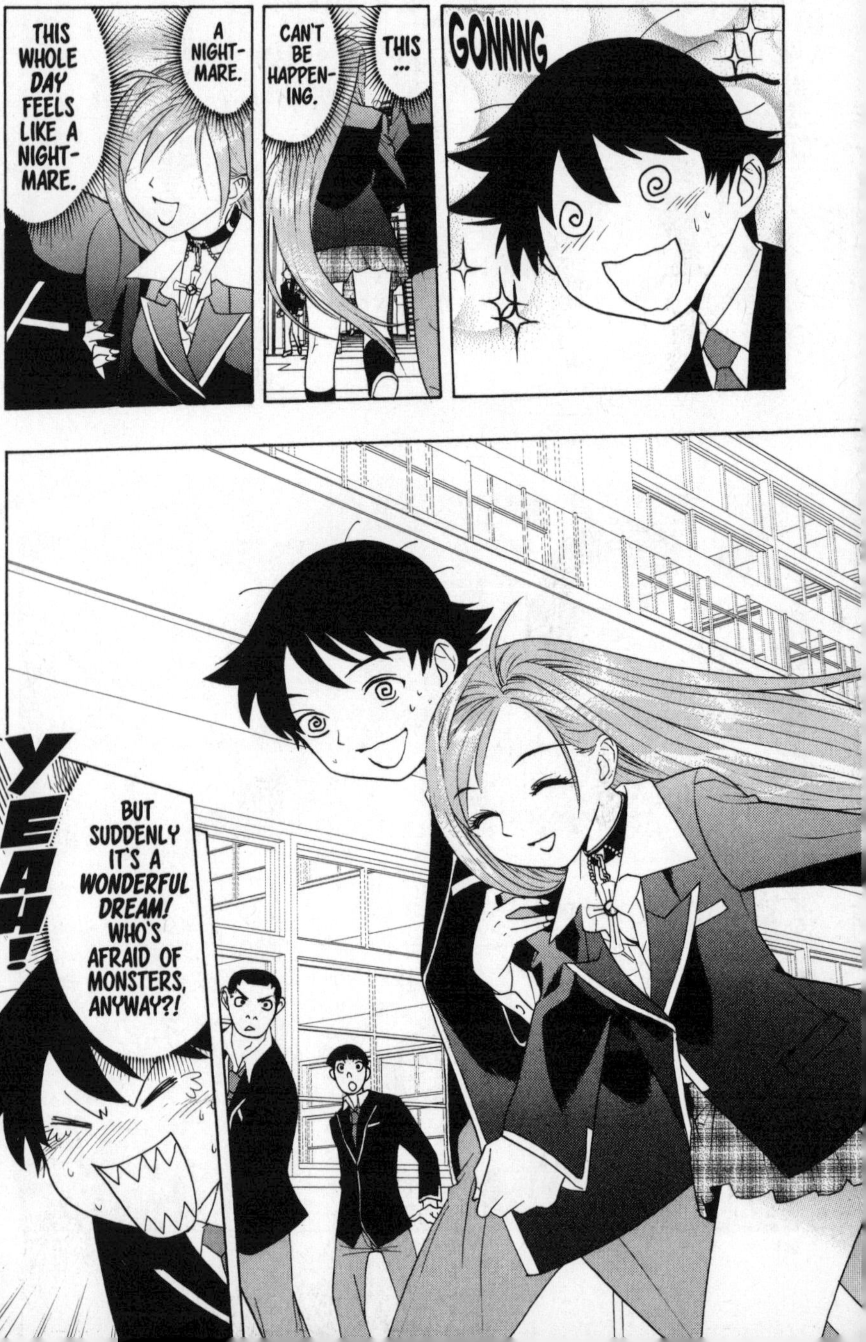
GONNNG
THIS ...
CAN'T BE HAPPENING.
A NIGHTMARE.
THIS WHOLE DAY FEELS LIKE A NIGHTMARE.
YEAH!
BUT SUDDENLY IT'S A WONDERFUL DREAM! WHO'S AFRAID OF MONSTERS, ANYWAY?!

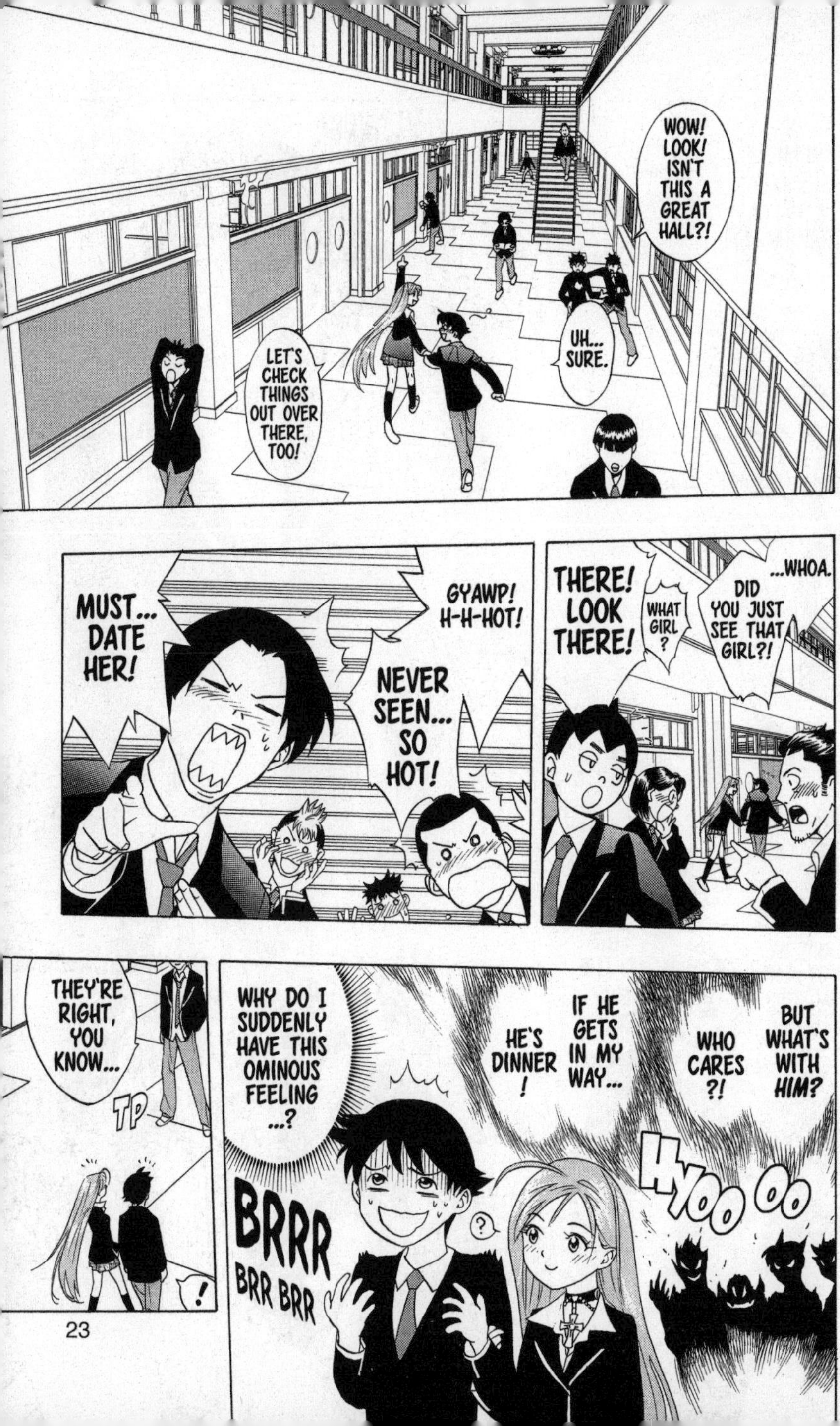

WOW! LOOK! ISN'T THIS A GREAT HALL?!
UH... SURE.
LET'S CHECK THINGS OUT OVER THERE, TOO!
...WHOA.
DID YOU JUST SEE THAT GIRL?!
WHAT GIRL?
THERE! LOOK THERE!
GYAWP! H-H-HOT!
NEVER SEEN... SO HOT!
MUST... DATE HER!
BUT WHAT'S WITH HIM?
WHO CARES?!
IF HE GETS IN MY WAY...
HE'S DINNER!
WHY DO I SUDDENLY HAVE THIS OMINOUS FEELING...?
HYOOOO
?
BRRR BRR BRR
THEY'RE RIGHT, YOU KNOW...
TP
!

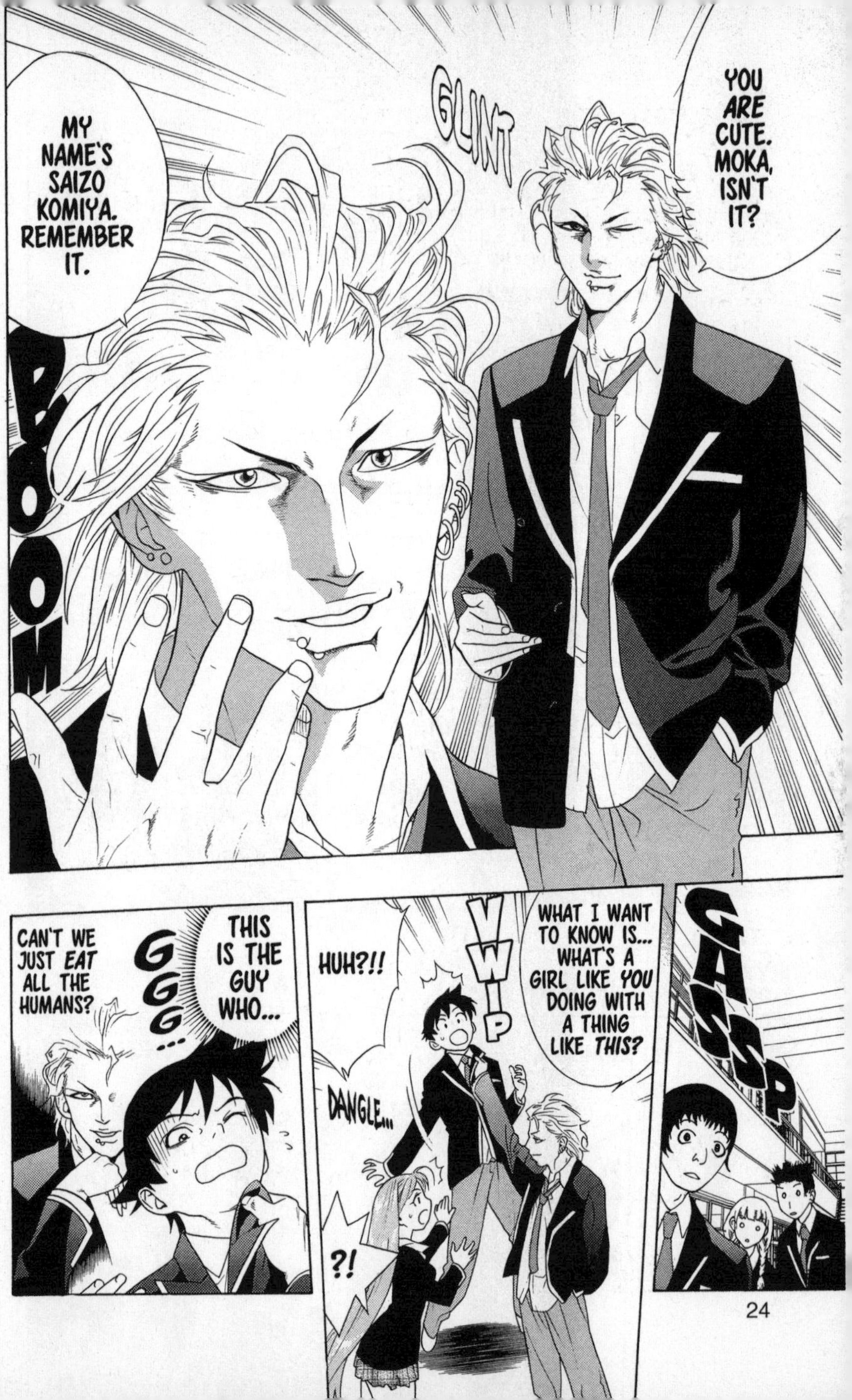
YOU ARE CUTE. MOKA, ISN'T IT?
GLINT
MY NAME'S SAIZO KOMIYA. REMEMBER IT.
BOOM
GASSP
WHAT I WANT TO KNOW IS... WHAT'S A GIRL LIKE YOU DOING WITH A THING LIKE THIS?
VWIP
HUH?!!
DANGLE...
?!
THIS IS THE GUY WHO...
GGG...
CAN'T WE JUST EAT ALL THE HUMANS?

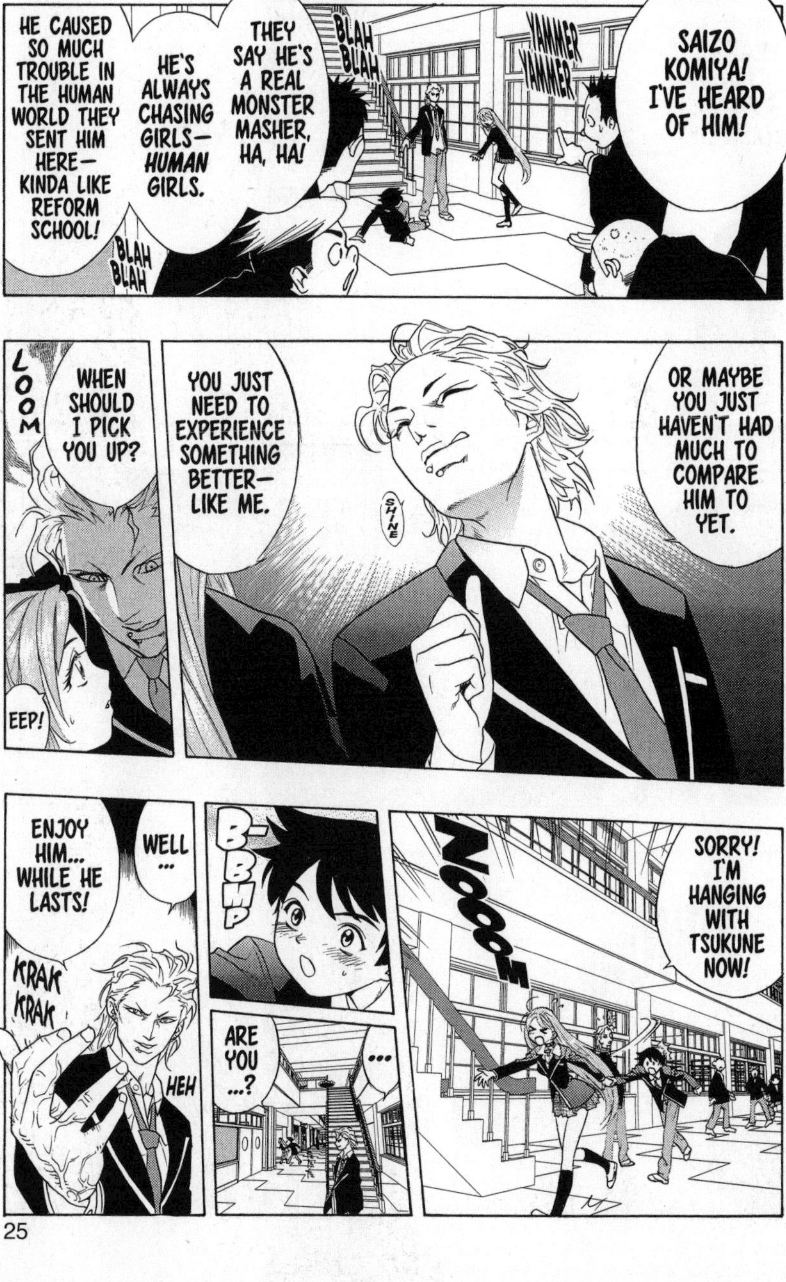
SAIZO KOMIYA! I'VE HEARD OF HIM!
YAMMER YAMMER
THEY SAY HE'S A REAL MONSTER MASHER, HA, HA!
BLAH BLAH
HE'S ALWAYS CHASING GIRLS—*HUMAN* GIRLS.
HE CAUSED SO MUCH TROUBLE IN THE HUMAN WORLD THEY SENT HIM HERE—KINDA LIKE REFORM SCHOOL!
BLAH BLAH
OR MAYBE YOU JUST HAVEN'T HAD MUCH TO COMPARE HIM TO YET.
SHINE
YOU JUST NEED TO EXPERIENCE SOMETHING BETTER—LIKE ME.
LOOM
WHEN SHOULD I PICK YOU UP?
EEP!
SORRY! I'M HANGING WITH TSUKUNE NOW!
NOOOM
B-BMP
...
ARE YOU ...?
WELL ...
ENJOY HIM... WHILE HE LASTS!
KRAK KRAK
HEH

HUF
HF HF
WHOO! THAT WAS KINDA SCARY, HUH?
ARE YOU ALL RIGHT, TSU-KUNE?
UH... YEAH! I'M FINE!
BUT...WHY ARE YOU BEING SO FRIENDLY TO ME, MOKA?
I MEAN... I'M JUST AN AVERAGE GUY...
ONE WHO'S NEVER HAD A REAL CONVERSATION WITH A GIRL BEFORE!
DON'T SAY THAT! YOU'RE HARDLY AVERAGE TO ME, TSUKUNE!
HUH?
B-BMP
BE-SIDES...
BLUSH
YOU...
...
ALREADY LET ME SUCK YOUR BLOOD!
BLUSH
GIGGLE
FWOMP

READ THIS WAY

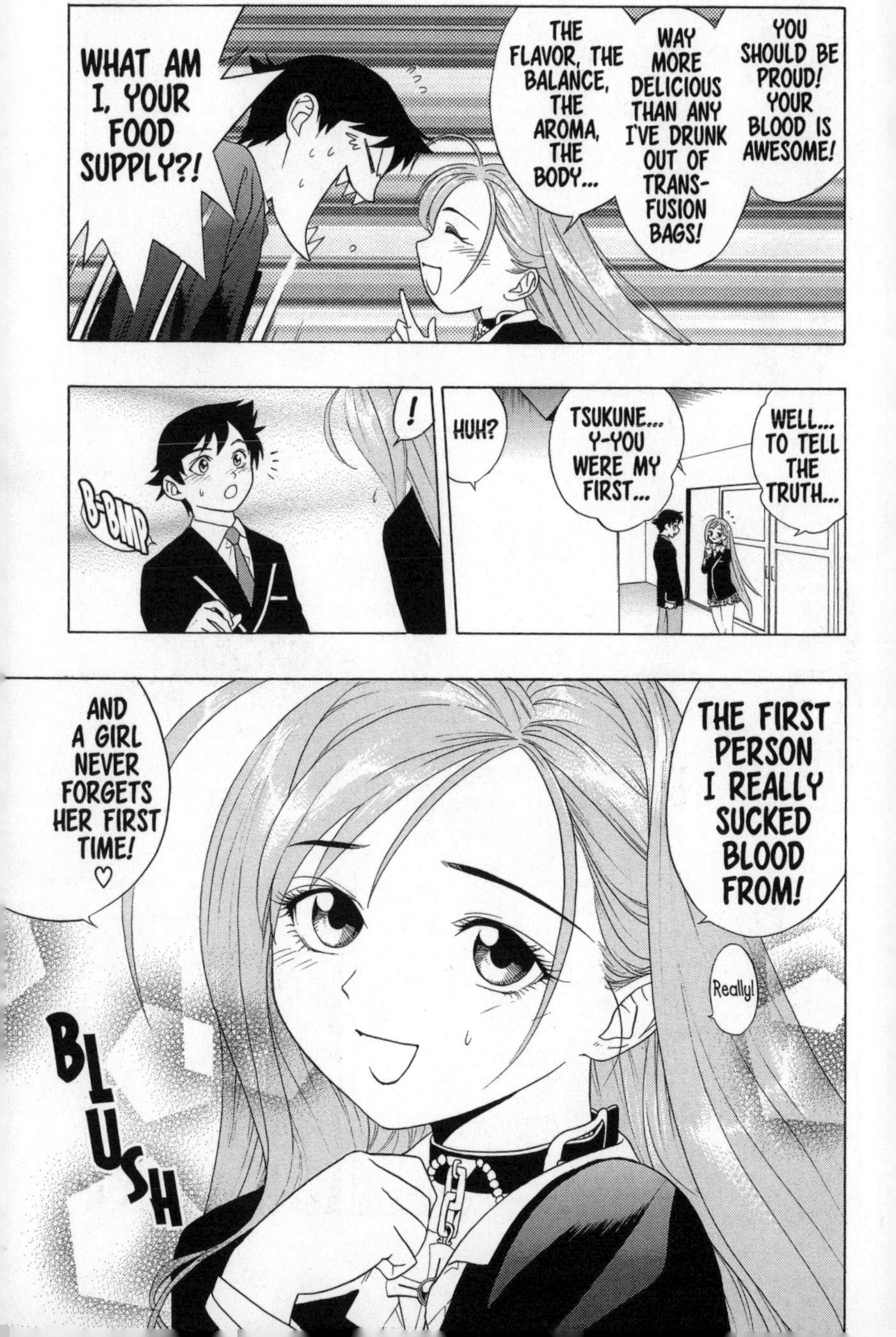
YOU SHOULD BE PROUD! YOUR BLOOD IS AWESOME!
WAY MORE DELICIOUS THAN ANY I'VE DRUNK OUT OF TRANS-FUSION BAGS!
THE FLAVOR, THE BALANCE, THE AROMA, THE BODY...
WHAT AM I, YOUR FOOD SUPPLY?!
WELL... TO TELL THE TRUTH...
TSUKUNE... Y-YOU WERE MY FIRST...
HUH?
!
B-BMP
THE FIRST PERSON I REALLY SUCKED BLOOD FROM!
Really!
AND A GIRL NEVER FORGETS HER FIRST TIME! ♡
BLUSH

READ THIS WAY

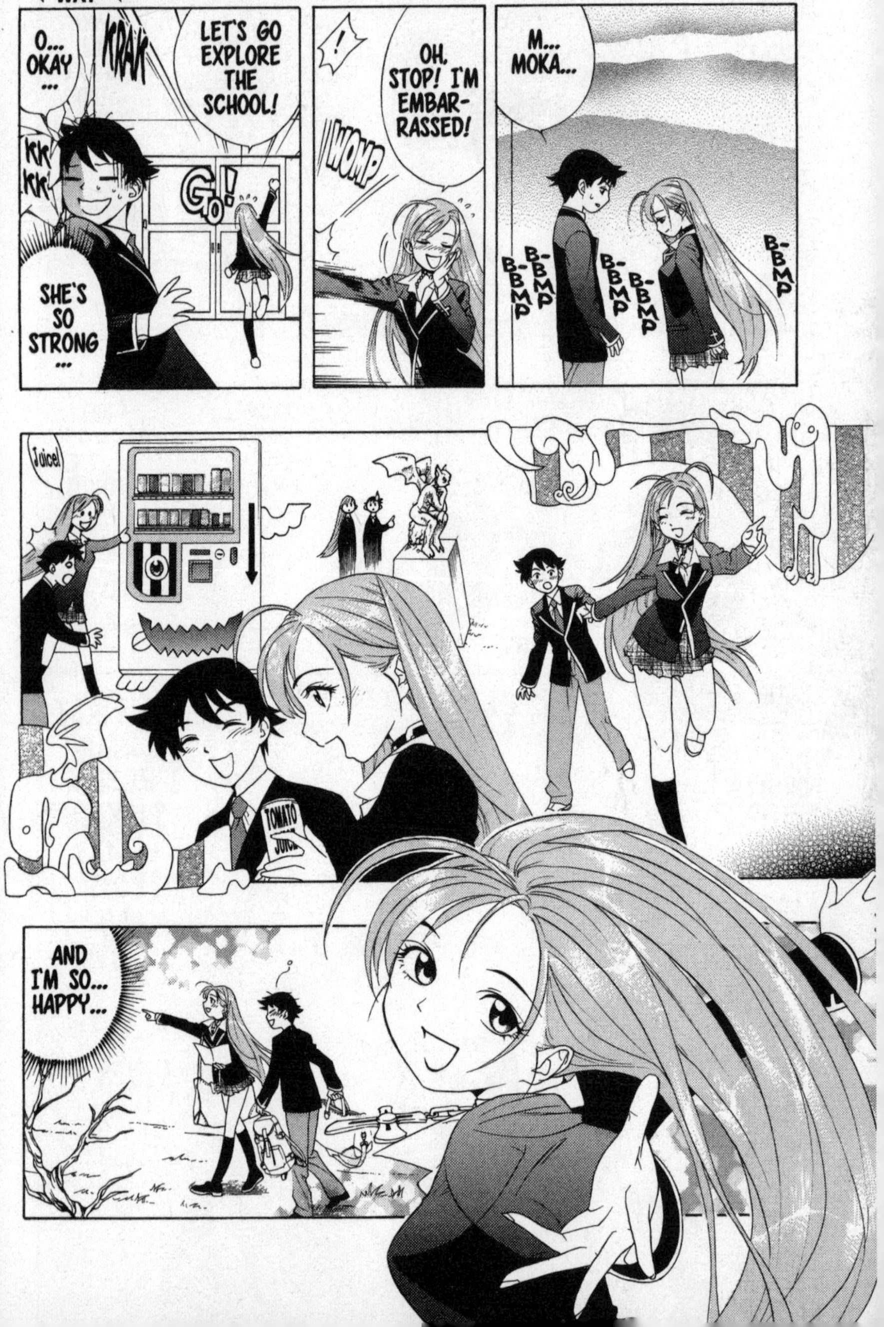
M... MOKA...
B-BMP
B-BMP
B-BMP
B-BMP
B-BMP
!
OH, STOP! I'M EMBARRASSED!
WOMP
LET'S GO EXPLORE THE SCHOOL!
KRAK
O... OKAY...
KK KK
GO!
SHE'S SO STRONG...
Juice!
TOMATO JUICE
AND I'M SO... HAPPY...

READ THIS WAY

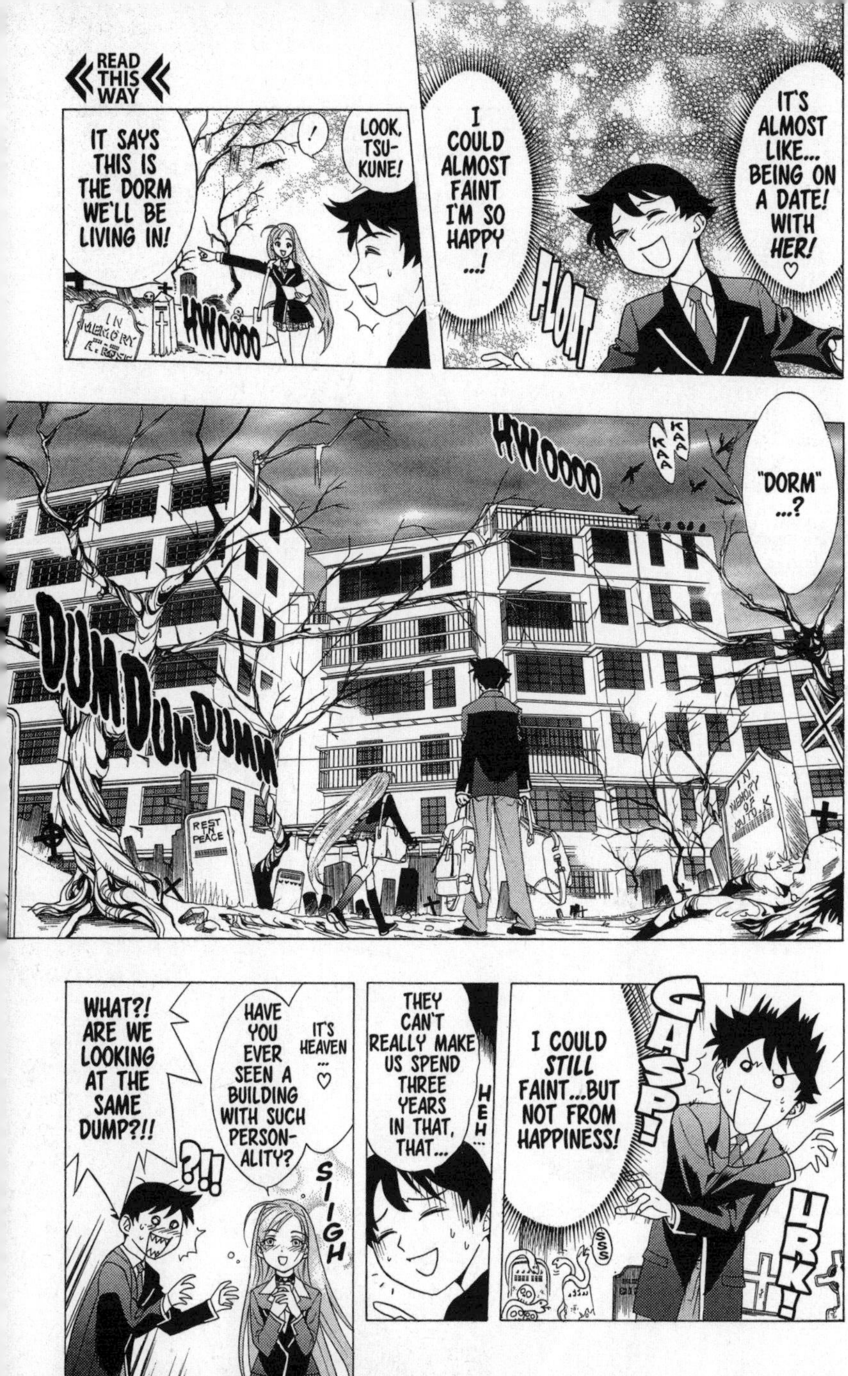
IT'S ALMOST LIKE... BEING ON A DATE! WITH HER! ♡
FLOAT
I COULD ALMOST FAINT I'M SO HAPPY ...!
LOOK, TSU-KUNE!
!
IT SAYS THIS IS THE DORM WE'LL BE LIVING IN!
HWOOOO
IN MEMORY
"DORM" ...?
KAA KAA
HWOOOO
DUM DUM DUMM
REST IN PEACE
IN MEMORY
GASP!
I COULD STILL FAINT...BUT NOT FROM HAPPINESS!
SSS
URK!
THEY CAN'T REALLY MAKE US SPEND THREE YEARS IN THAT, THAT...
HEH...
IT'S HEAVEN ... ♡
HAVE YOU EVER SEEN A BUILDING WITH SUCH PERSON-ALITY?
SIGH
WHAT?! ARE WE LOOKING AT THE SAME DUMP?!!
?!!

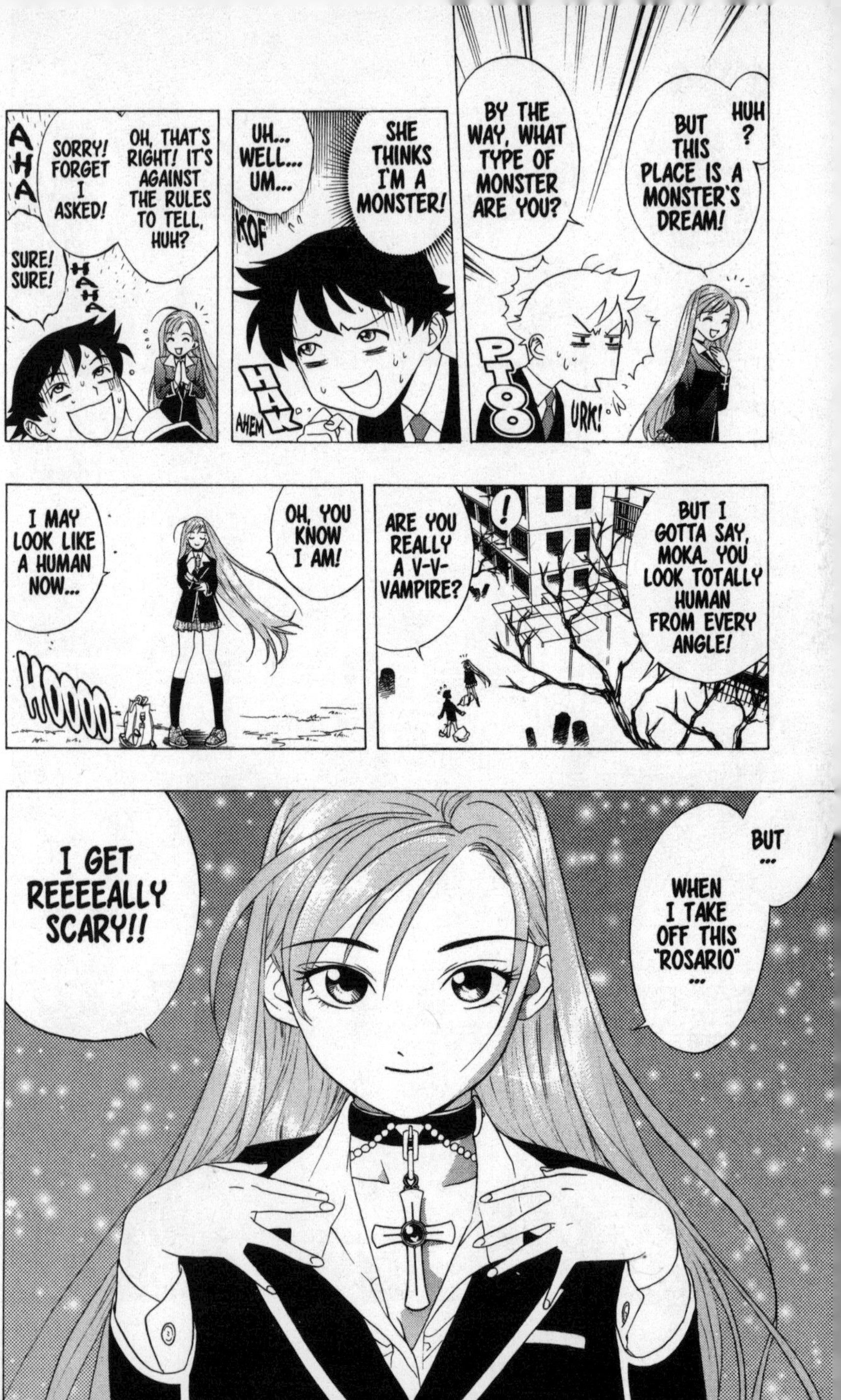
HUH?
BUT THIS PLACE IS A MONSTER'S DREAM!
BY THE WAY, WHAT TYPE OF MONSTER ARE YOU?
PTOO
URK!
SHE THINKS I'M A MONSTER!
UH... WELL... UM...
KOF
HAK
AHEM
OH, THAT'S RIGHT! IT'S AGAINST THE RULES TO TELL, HUH?
SORRY! FORGET I ASKED!
AHAHA
SURE! SURE!
HAHAHA
BUT I GOTTA SAY, MOKA. YOU LOOK TOTALLY HUMAN FROM EVERY ANGLE!
!
ARE YOU REALLY A V-V-VAMPIRE?
OH, YOU KNOW I AM!
I MAY LOOK LIKE A HUMAN NOW...
HOOOO
BUT... WHEN I TAKE OFF THIS "ROSARIO"...
I GET REEEEALLY SCARY!!

READ THIS WAY

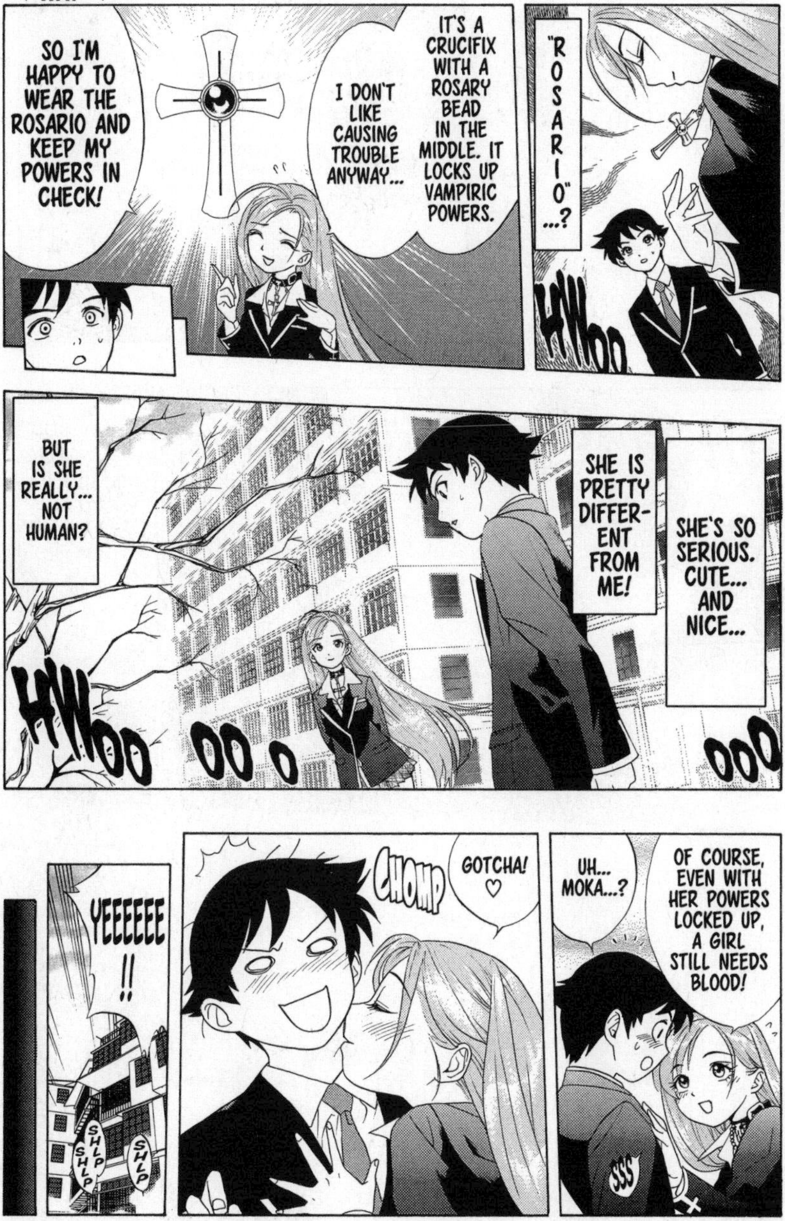

"ROSARIO"...?
HWOO
IT'S A CRUCIFIX WITH A ROSARY BEAD IN THE MIDDLE. IT LOCKS UP VAMPIRIC POWERS.
I DON'T LIKE CAUSING TROUBLE ANYWAY...
SO I'M HAPPY TO WEAR THE ROSARIO AND KEEP MY POWERS IN CHECK!
SHE'S SO SERIOUS. CUTE... AND NICE...
SHE IS PRETTY DIFFER-ENT FROM ME!
BUT IS SHE REALLY... NOT HUMAN?
OOO
HWOOOO OO O
OF COURSE, EVEN WITH HER POWERS LOCKED UP, A GIRL STILL NEEDS BLOOD!
UH... MOKA...?
SSS
GOTCHA! ♡
CHOMP
YEEEEEE !!
SHLP
SHLP
SHLP

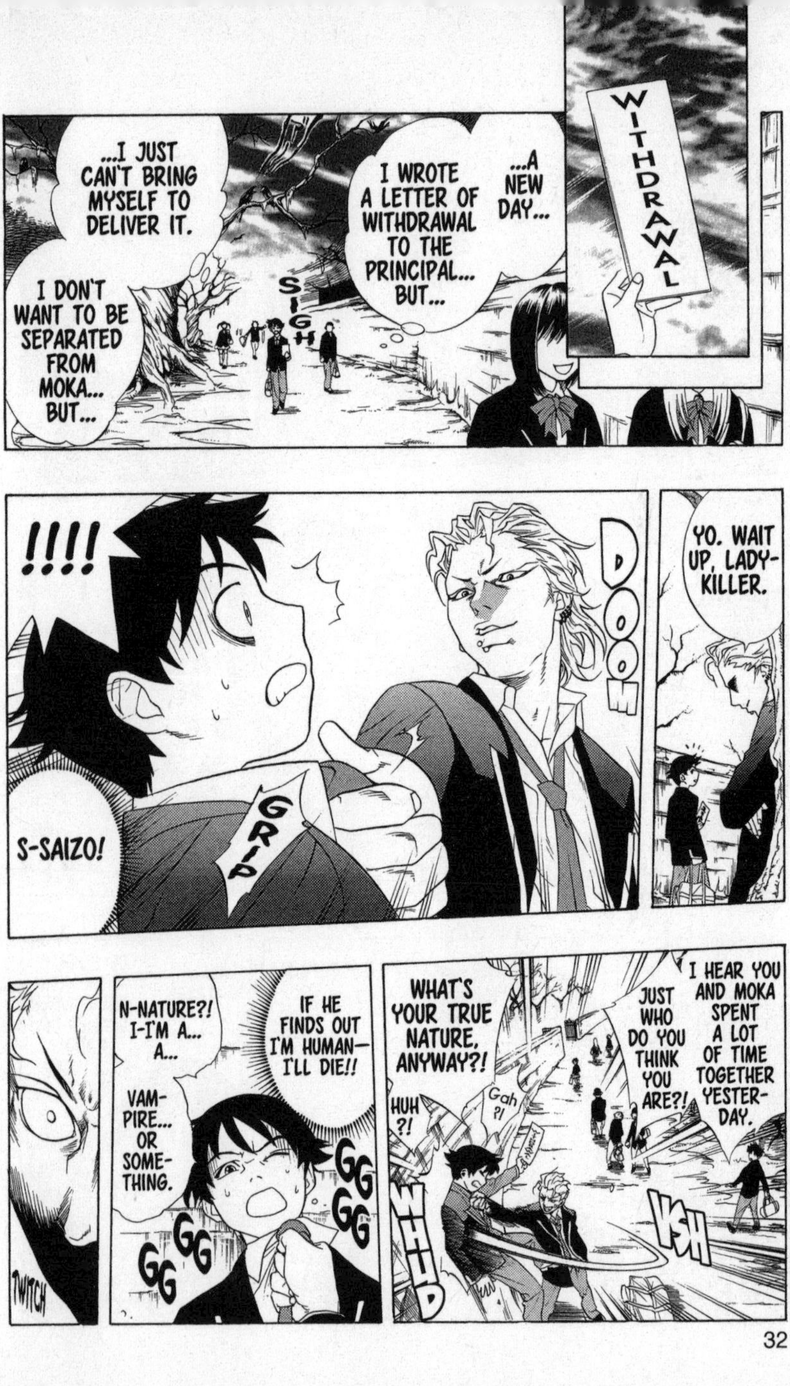
WITHDRAWAL
...A NEW DAY...
I WROTE A LETTER OF WITHDRAWAL TO THE PRINCIPAL... BUT...
SIGH
...I JUST CAN'T BRING MYSELF TO DELIVER IT.
I DON'T WANT TO BE SEPARATED FROM MOKA... BUT...
YO. WAIT UP, LADY-KILLER.
DOOOM
!!!!
GRIP
S-SAIZO!
I HEAR YOU AND MOKA SPENT A LOT OF TIME TOGETHER YESTERDAY.
JUST WHO DO YOU THINK YOU ARE?!
VSH
WHAT'S YOUR TRUE NATURE, ANYWAY?!
Gah ?!
HUH ?!
WHUD
IF HE FINDS OUT I'M HUMAN—I'LL DIE!!
N-NATURE?! I-I'M A... A...
VAMPIRE... OR SOMETHING.
GG GG GG GG
TWITCH

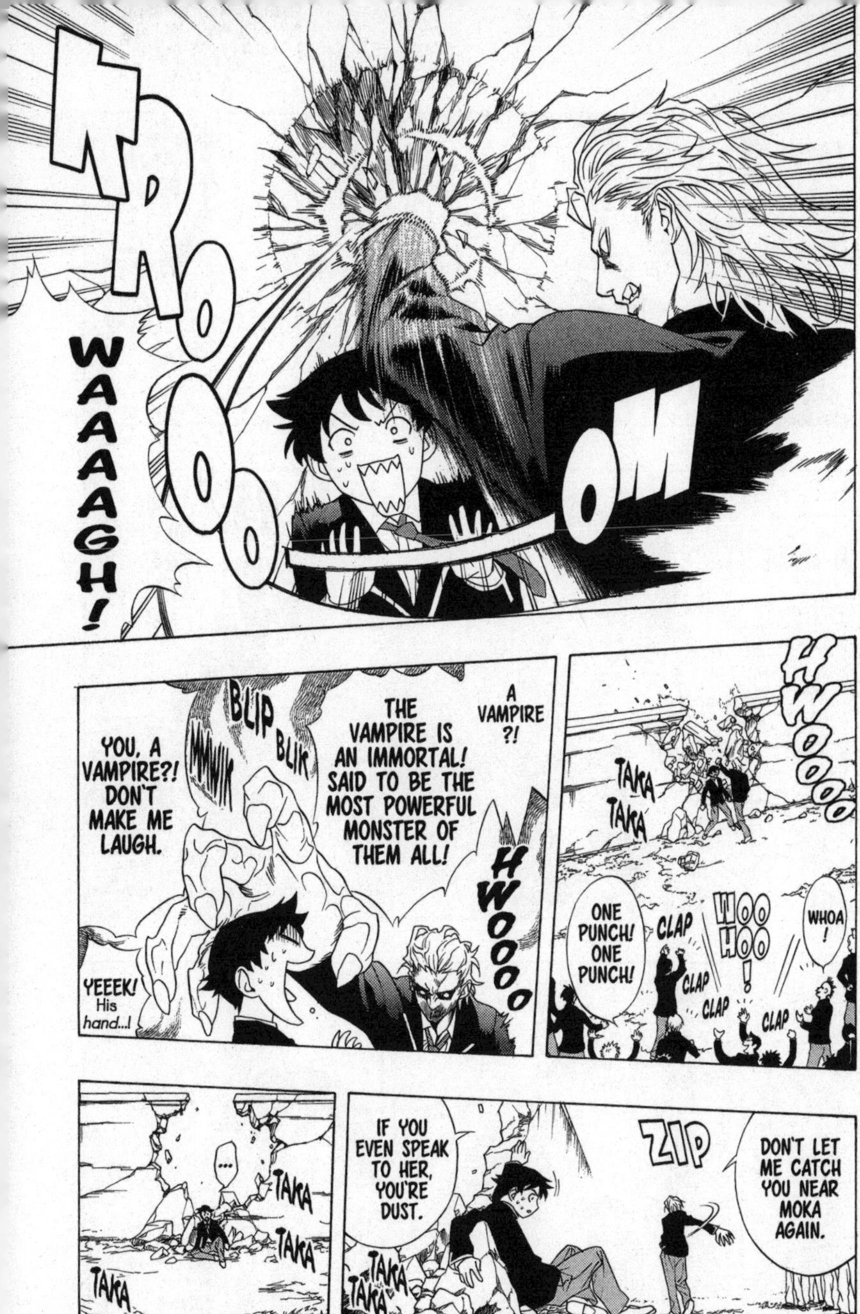
KROOOOOM
WAAAAAGH!
HWOOOOO
TAKA TAKA
WHOA!
WOO HOO!
CLAP
ONE PUNCH! ONE PUNCH!
CLAP
CLAP
CLAP
A VAMPIRE?!
THE VAMPIRE IS AN IMMORTAL! SAID TO BE THE MOST POWERFUL MONSTER OF THEM ALL!
BLIP BLIK
MWIK
YOU, A VAMPIRE?! DON'T MAKE ME LAUGH.
HWOOOO
YEEEK! His hand...!
DON'T LET ME CATCH YOU NEAR MOKA AGAIN.
ZIP
IF YOU EVEN SPEAK TO HER, YOU'RE DUST.
TAKA TAKA
...
TAKA
TAKA
TAKA

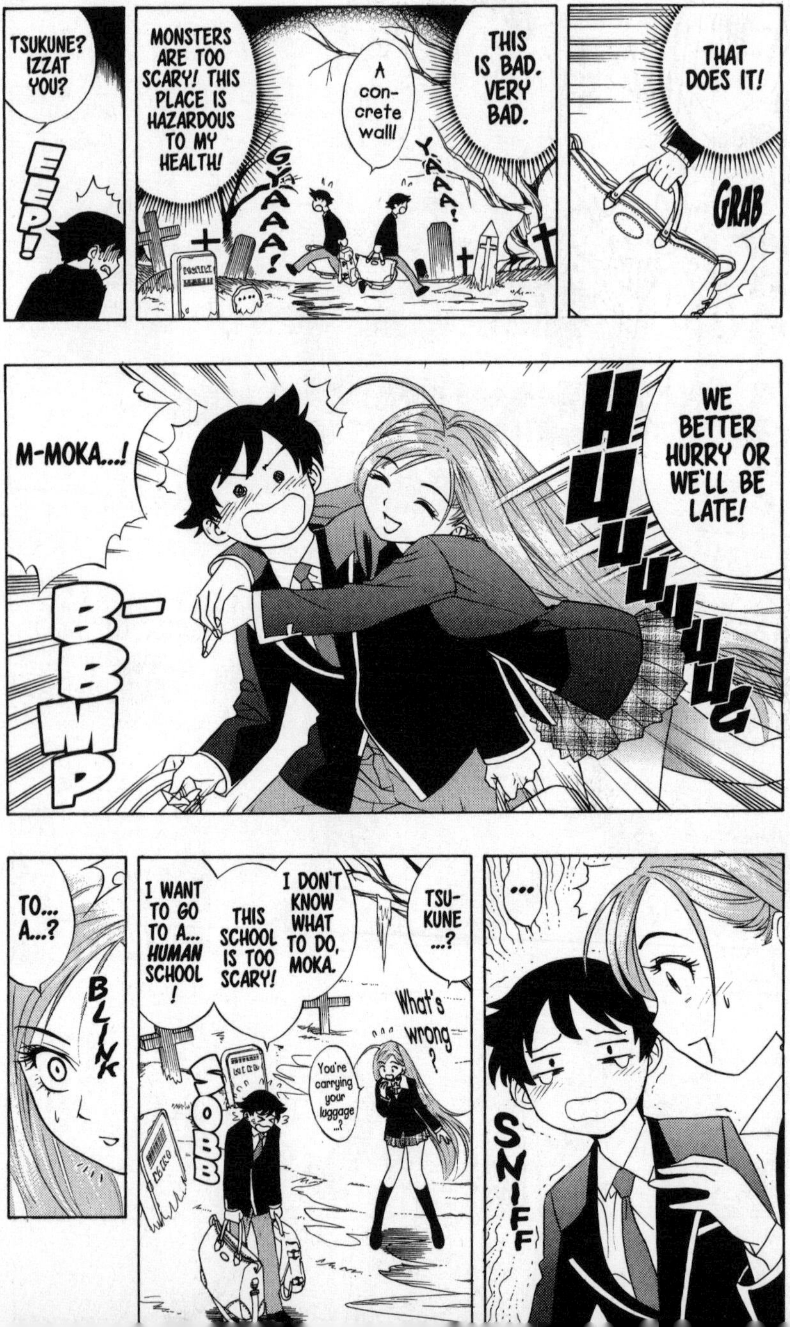
THAT DOES IT!
GRAB
THIS IS BAD. VERY BAD.
A concrete wall!
YAAAA!
GYAAAA!
MONSTERS ARE TOO SCARY! THIS PLACE IS HAZARDOUS TO MY HEALTH!
TSUKUNE? IZZAT YOU?
EEEP!
WE BETTER HURRY OR WE'LL BE LATE!
HUUUUUUUG
M-MOKA...!
B-BBMP
...
SNIFF
TSU-KUNE ...?
I DON'T KNOW WHAT TO DO, MOKA.
THIS SCHOOL IS TOO SCARY!
I WANT TO GO TO A... HUMAN SCHOOL!
What's wrong?
You're carrying your luggage ...?
SOBB
TO... A...?
BLINK

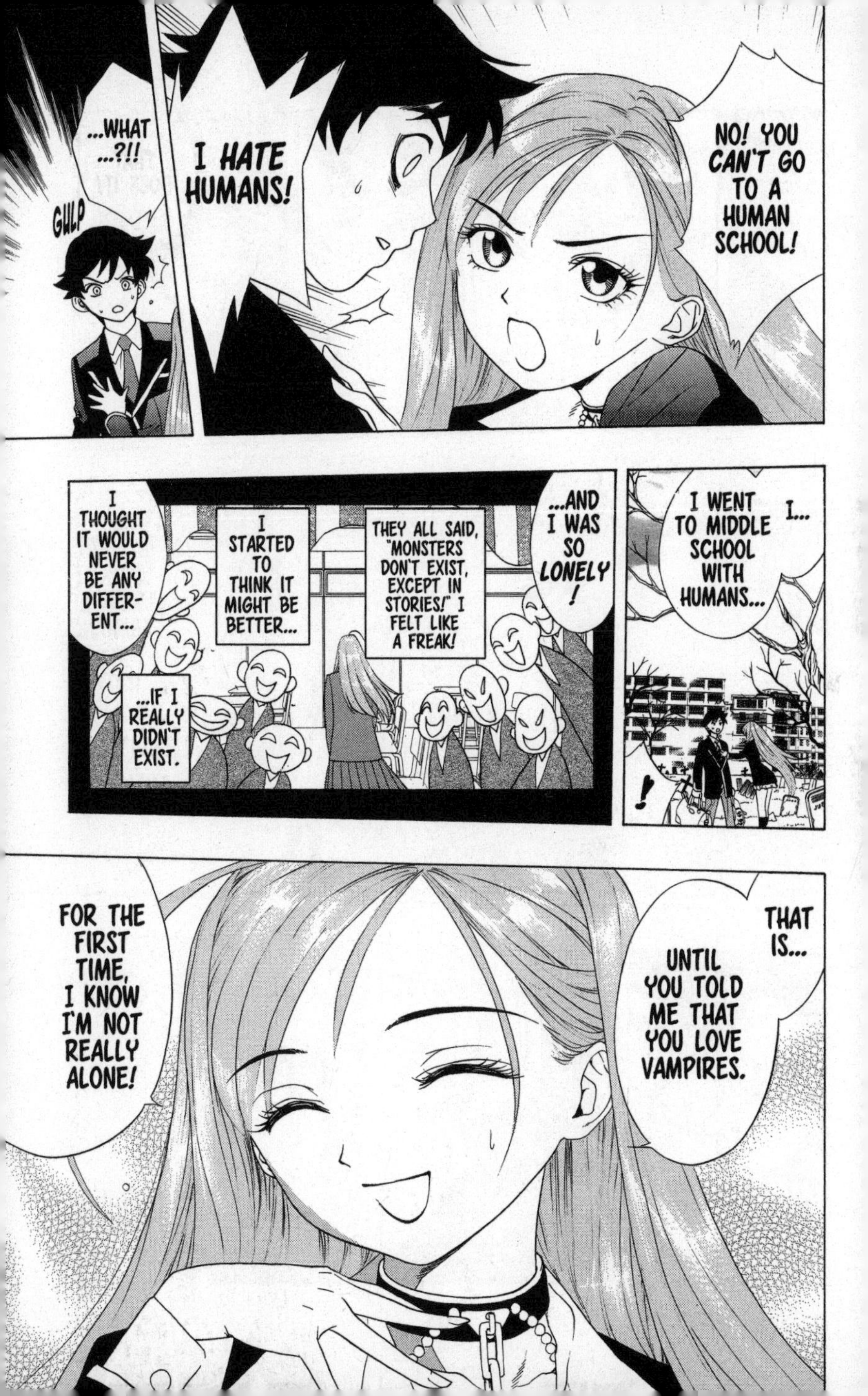
NO! YOU CAN'T GO TO A HUMAN SCHOOL!
I HATE HUMANS!
...WHAT ...?!!
GULP
I...
I WENT TO MIDDLE SCHOOL WITH HUMANS...
!
...AND I WAS SO LONELY!
THEY ALL SAID, "MONSTERS DON'T EXIST, EXCEPT IN STORIES!" I FELT LIKE A FREAK!
I STARTED TO THINK IT MIGHT BE BETTER...
...IF I REALLY DIDN'T EXIST.
I THOUGHT IT WOULD NEVER BE ANY DIFFERENT...
THAT IS...
UNTIL YOU TOLD ME THAT YOU LOVE VAMPIRES.
FOR THE FIRST TIME, I KNOW I'M NOT REALLY ALONE!

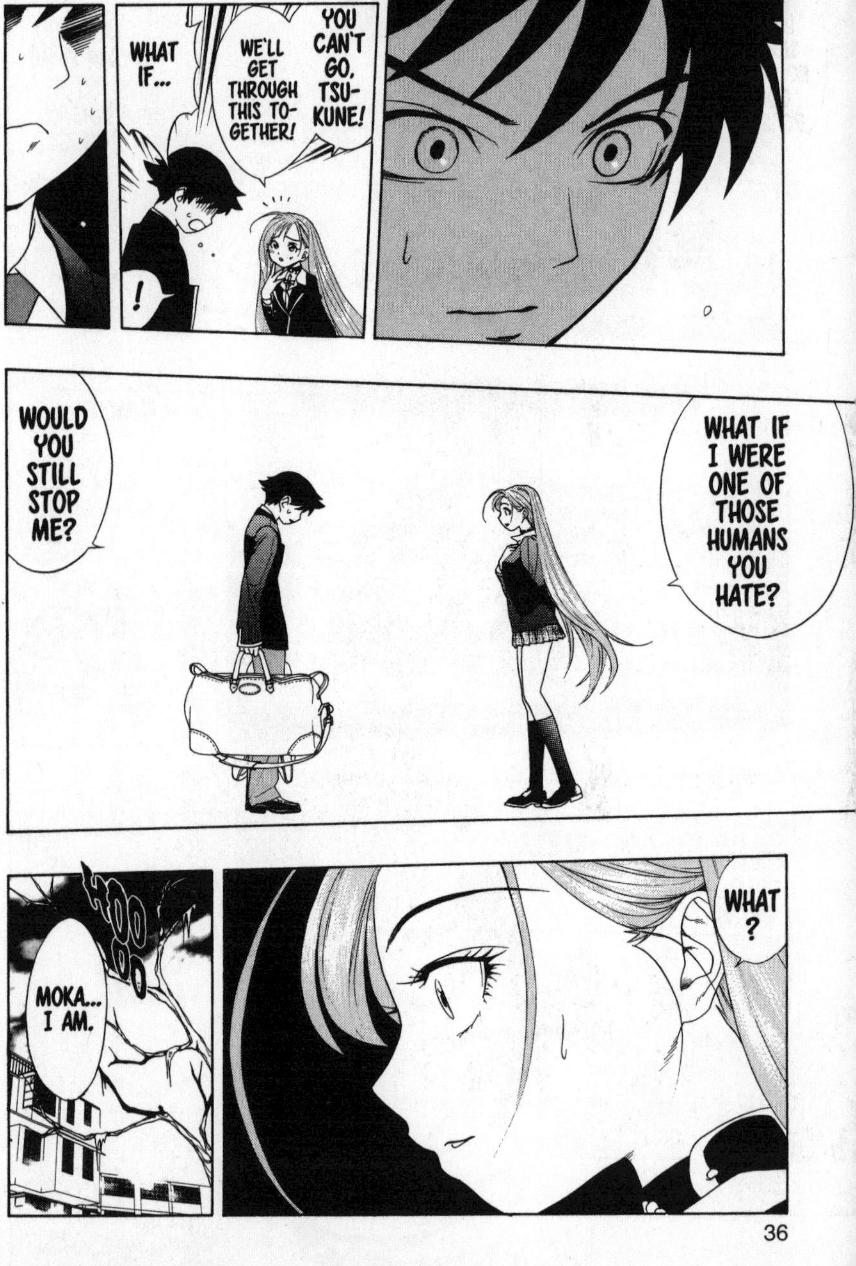
YOU CAN'T GO, TSUKUNE!
WE'LL GET THROUGH THIS TOGETHER!
WHAT IF...
!
WHAT IF I WERE ONE OF THOSE HUMANS YOU HATE?
WOULD YOU STILL STOP ME?
WHAT?
HOO HOO
MOKA... I AM.

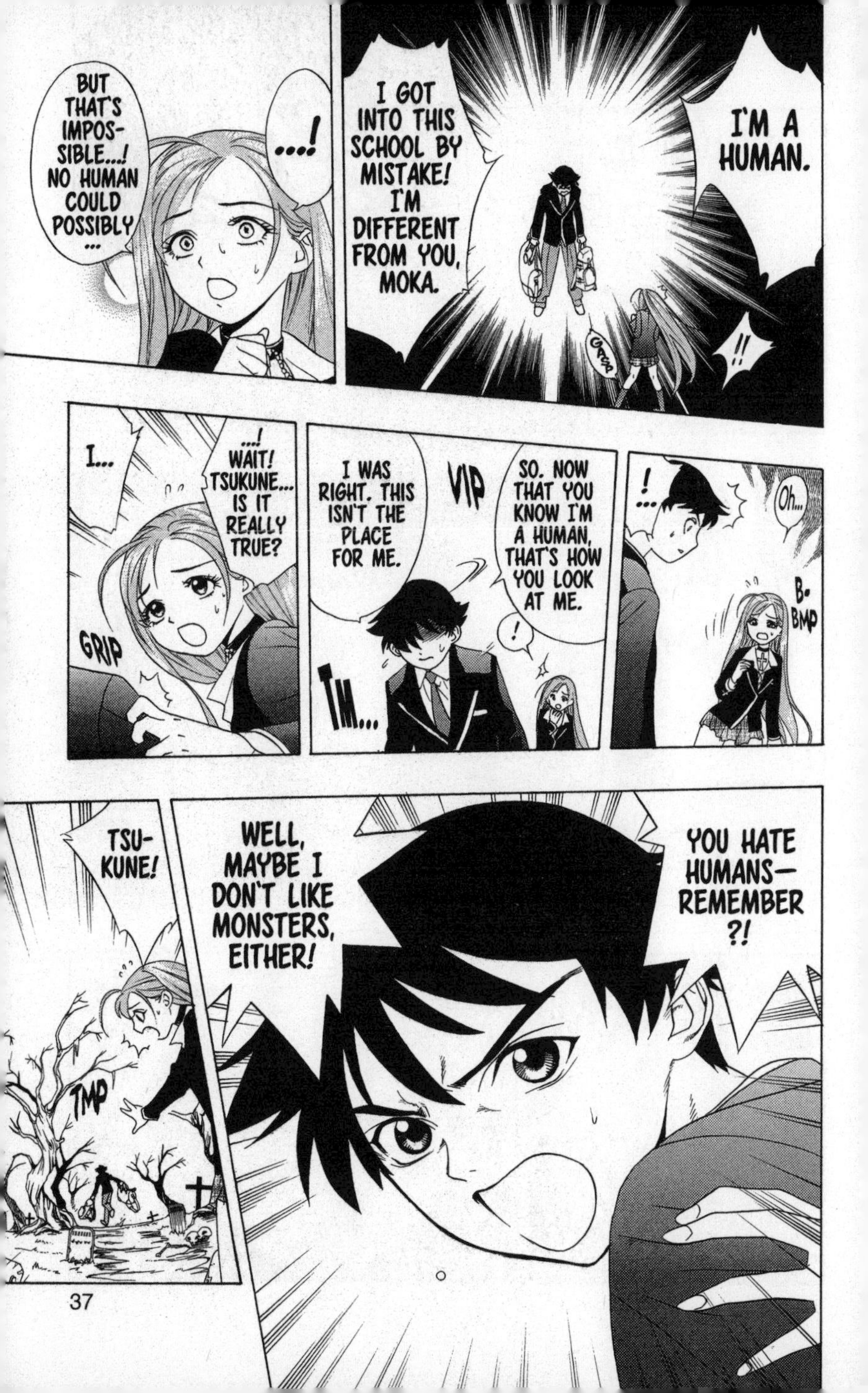
I'M A HUMAN.
I GOT INTO THIS SCHOOL BY MISTAKE! I'M DIFFERENT FROM YOU, MOKA.
!!
GASP
...!
BUT THAT'S IMPOS-SIBLE...! NO HUMAN COULD POSSIBLY...
Oh...
!...
B-BMP
SO. NOW THAT YOU KNOW I'M A HUMAN, THAT'S HOW YOU LOOK AT ME.
VIP
I WAS RIGHT. THIS ISN'T THE PLACE FOR ME.
!
TM...
...! WAIT! TSUKUNE... IS IT REALLY TRUE?
I...
GRIP
YOU HATE HUMANS— REMEMBER ?!
WELL, MAYBE I DON'T LIKE MONSTERS, EITHER!
TSU-KUNE!
TMP

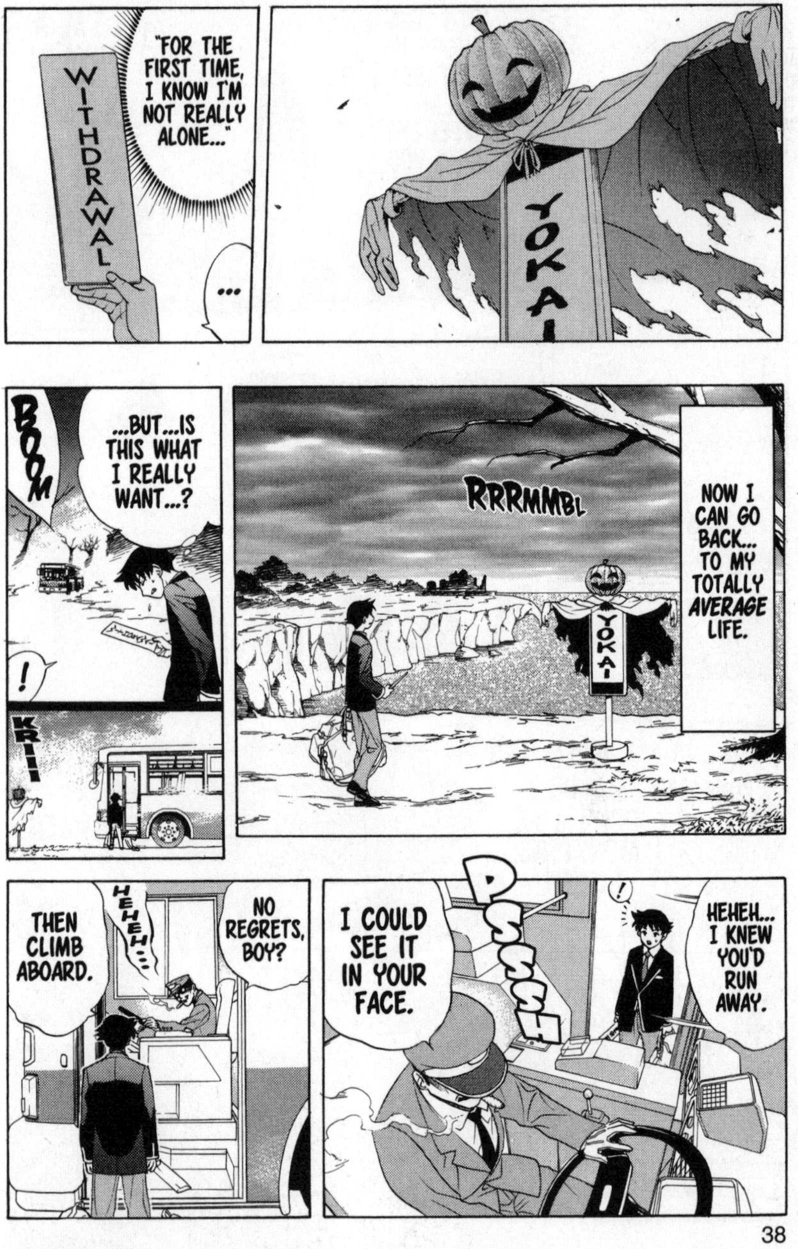
YOKAI
WITHDRAWAL
"FOR THE FIRST TIME, I KNOW I'M NOT REALLY ALONE..."
...
RRRMMBL
NOW I CAN GO BACK... TO MY TOTALLY AVERAGE LIFE.
YOKAI
BOOM
...BUT...IS THIS WHAT I REALLY WANT...?
!
KRIII
PSSSH
!
HEHEH... I KNEW YOU'D RUN AWAY.
I COULD SEE IT IN YOUR FACE.
NO REGRETS, BOY?
HEHEH...
THEN CLIMB ABOARD.

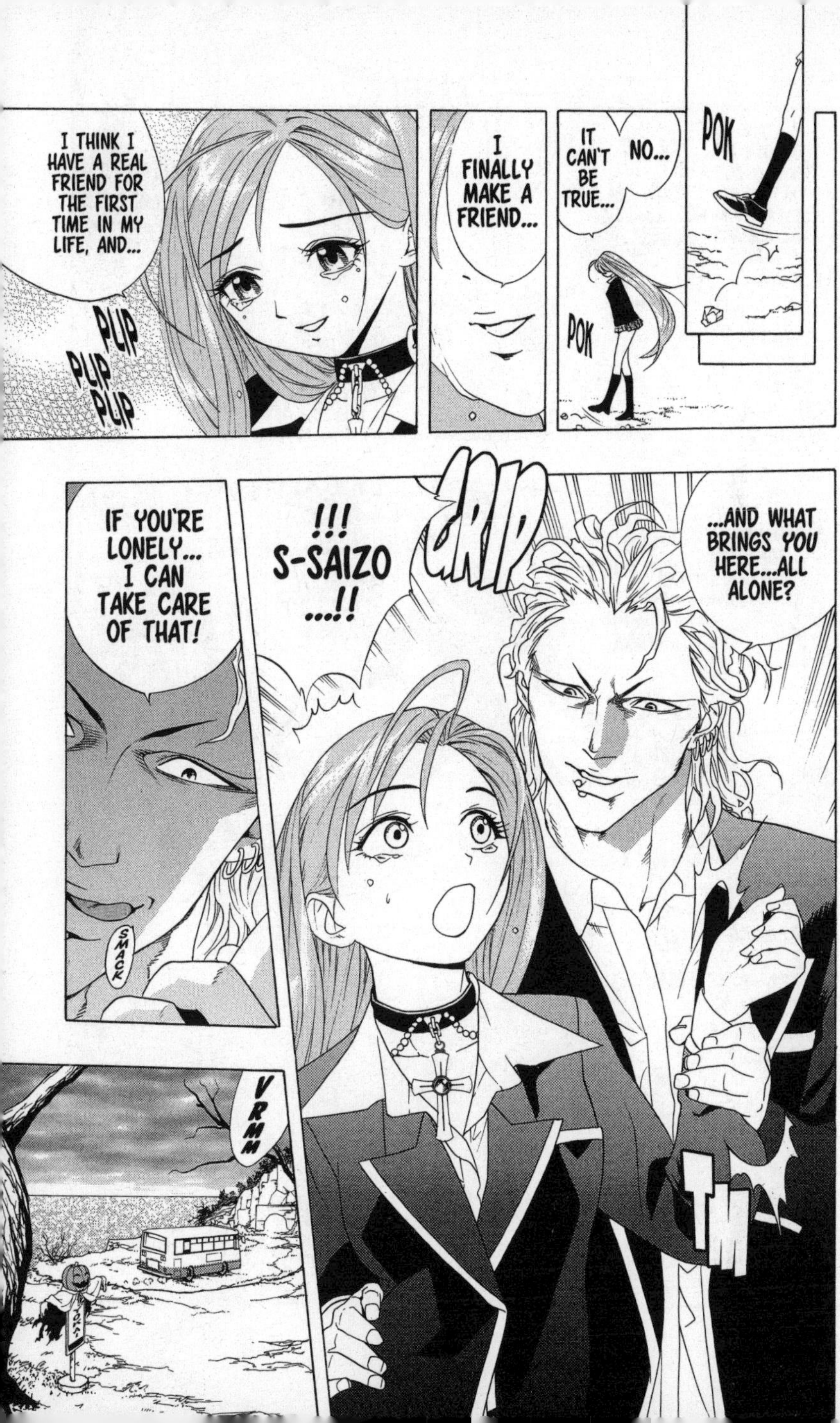
POK
NO...
IT CAN'T BE TRUE...
POK
I FINALLY MAKE A FRIEND...
I THINK I HAVE A REAL FRIEND FOR THE FIRST TIME IN MY LIFE, AND...
PLIP PLIP PLIP
...AND WHAT BRINGS YOU HERE...ALL ALONE?
GRIP
!!! S-SAIZO ...!!
IF YOU'RE LONELY... I CAN TAKE CARE OF THAT!
SMACK
VRMM

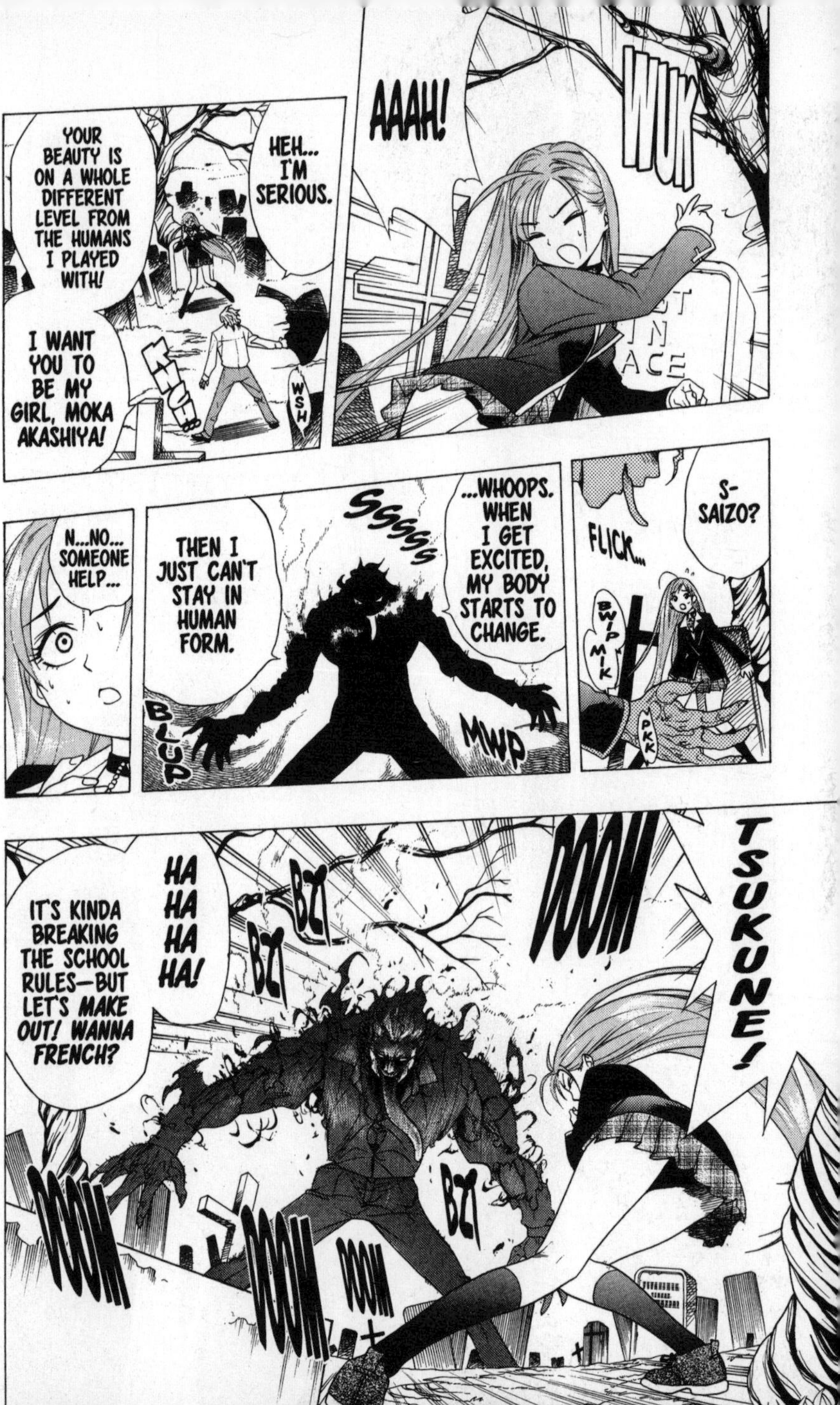
WUK
AAAH!
HEH... I'M SERIOUS.
YOUR BEAUTY IS ON A WHOLE DIFFERENT LEVEL FROM THE HUMANS I PLAYED WITH!
WSH
I WANT YOU TO BE MY GIRL, MOKA AKASHIYA!
S-SAIZO?
FLICK...
BWIP
MIK
PKK
...WHOOPS. WHEN I GET EXCITED, MY BODY STARTS TO CHANGE.
SSSSS
THEN I JUST CAN'T STAY IN HUMAN FORM.
MWP
BLUP
N...NO... SOMEONE HELP...
TSUKUNE!
DOOM
HA HA HA HA HA!
BZT
BZT
IT'S KINDA BREAKING THE SCHOOL RULES—BUT LET'S MAKE OUT! WANNA FRENCH?
BZT
DOOM
DOOM
DOOM

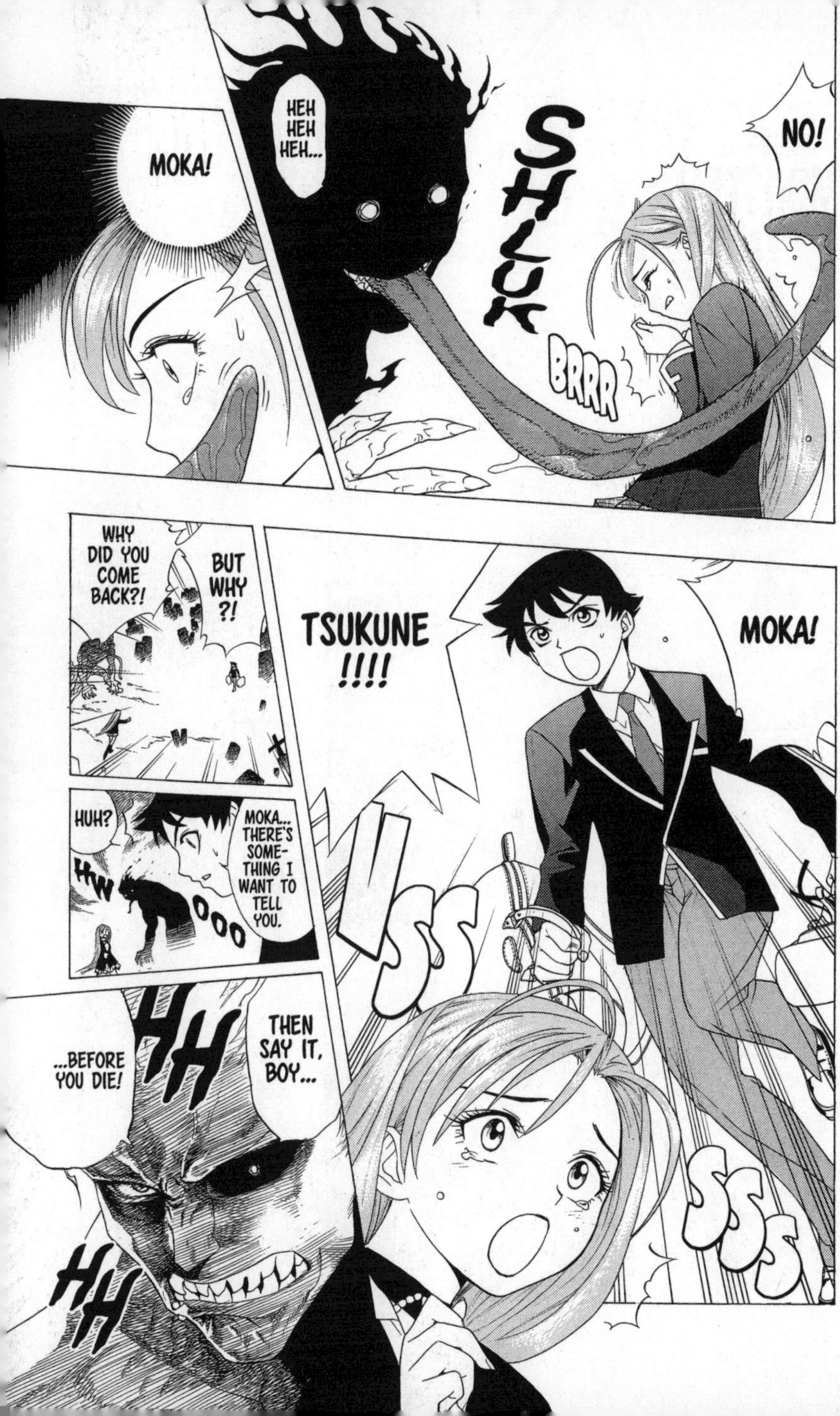
NO!
BRRR
SHLUK
HEH HEH HEH...
MOKA!
MOKA!
TSUKUNE !!!!
SSS
SSSS
BUT WHY ?!
WHY DID YOU COME BACK?!
MOKA... THERE'S SOMETHING I WANT TO TELL YOU.
HUH?
HWOOO
THEN SAY IT, BOY...
...BEFORE YOU DIE!
HH
HH

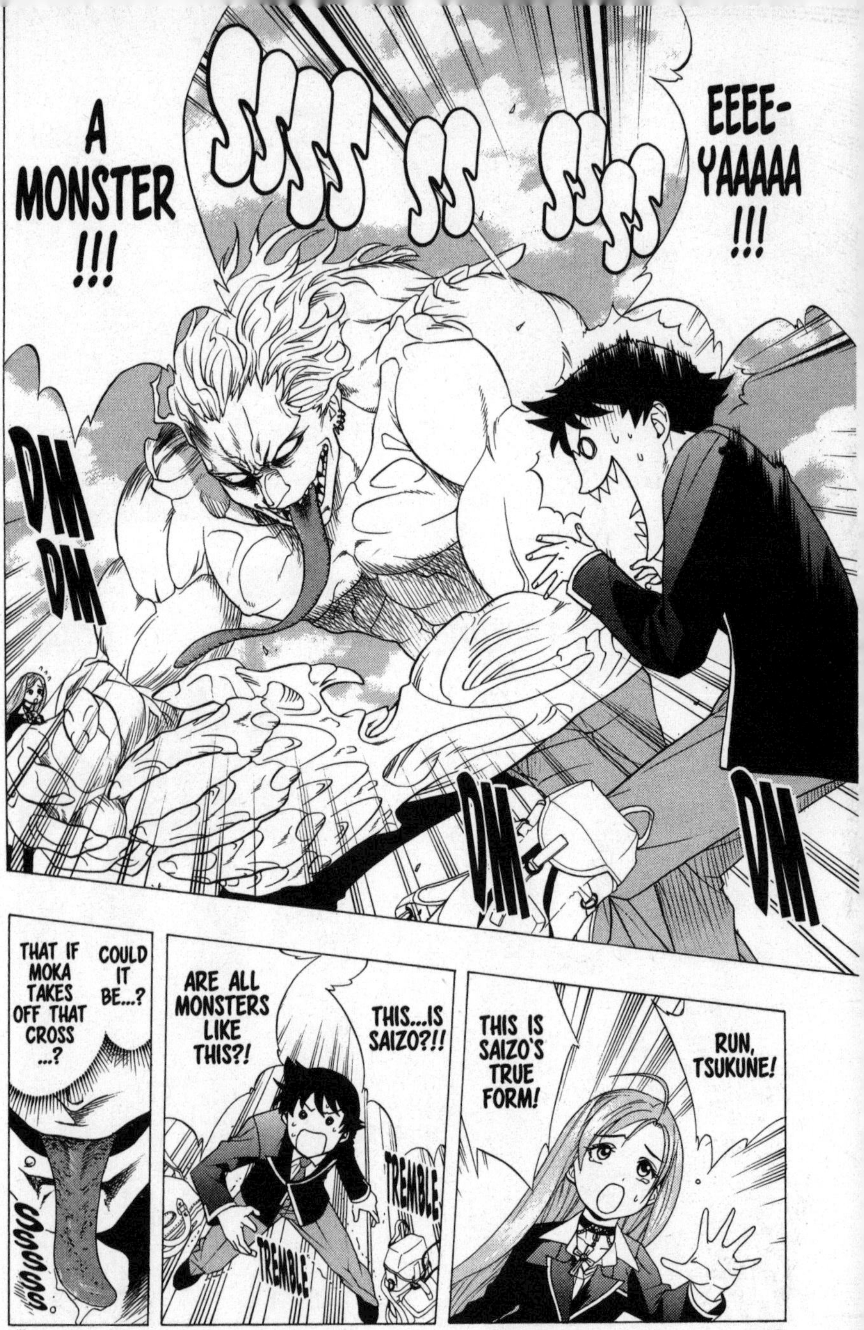
EEEE-YAAAAA!!!
A MONSTER!!!
DM DM
DM
DM
RUN, TSUKUNE!
THIS IS SAIZO'S TRUE FORM!
THIS...IS SAIZO?!!
ARE ALL MONSTERS LIKE THIS?!
TREMBLE
TREMBLE
COULD IT BE...?
THAT IF MOKA TAKES OFF THAT CROSS...?

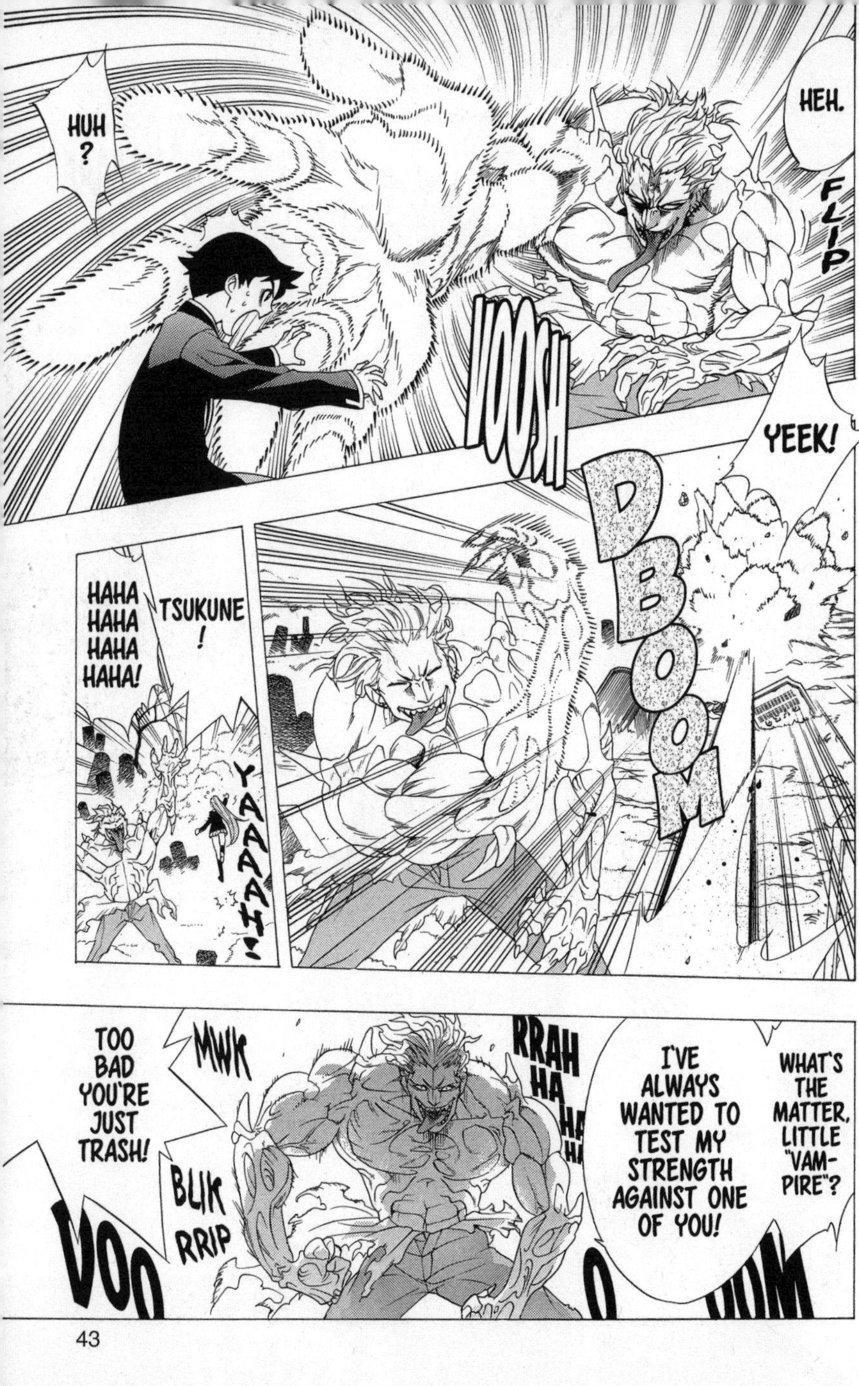
HEH.
FLIP
VOOSH
HUH?
YEEK!
DBOOM
TSUKUNE!
HAHA HAHA HAHA HAHA!
YAAAAH!
WHAT'S THE MATTER, LITTLE "VAMPIRE"?
I'VE ALWAYS WANTED TO TEST MY STRENGTH AGAINST ONE OF YOU!
RRAH HA HA HA
MWK
TOO BAD YOU'RE JUST TRASH!
BLIK
RRIP
VOO O OOM

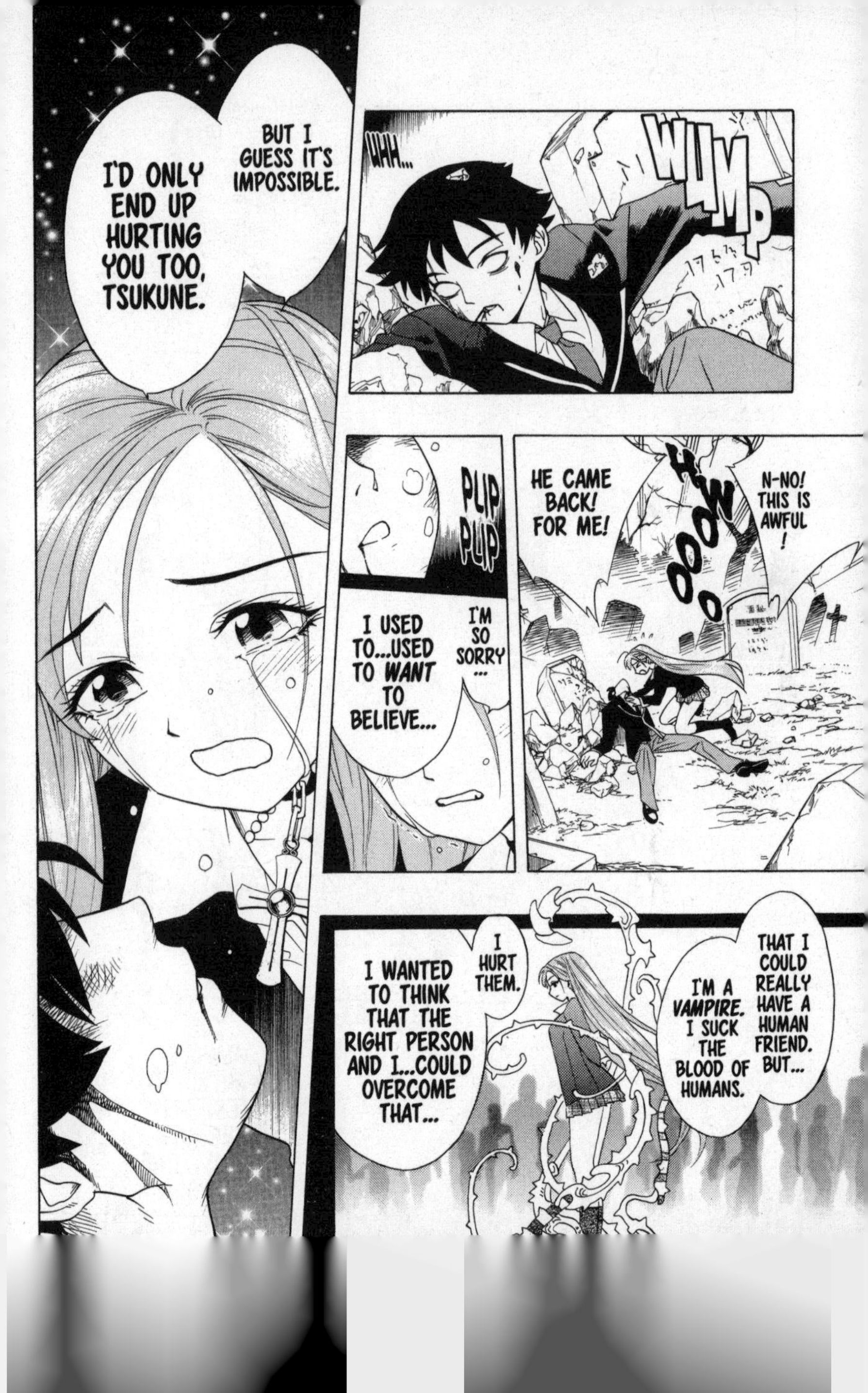
WUMP
WHHH...
N-NO! THIS IS AWFUL!
HOWOOOO
HE CAME BACK! FOR ME!
PLIP PLIP
I'M SO SORRY...
I USED TO...USED TO *WANT* TO BELIEVE...
THAT I COULD REALLY HAVE A HUMAN FRIEND. BUT...
I'M A *VAMPIRE*. I SUCK THE BLOOD OF HUMANS.
I HURT THEM.
I WANTED TO THINK THAT THE RIGHT PERSON AND I...COULD OVERCOME THAT...
BUT I GUESS IT'S IMPOSSIBLE.
I'D ONLY END UP HURTING YOU TOO, TSUKUNE.

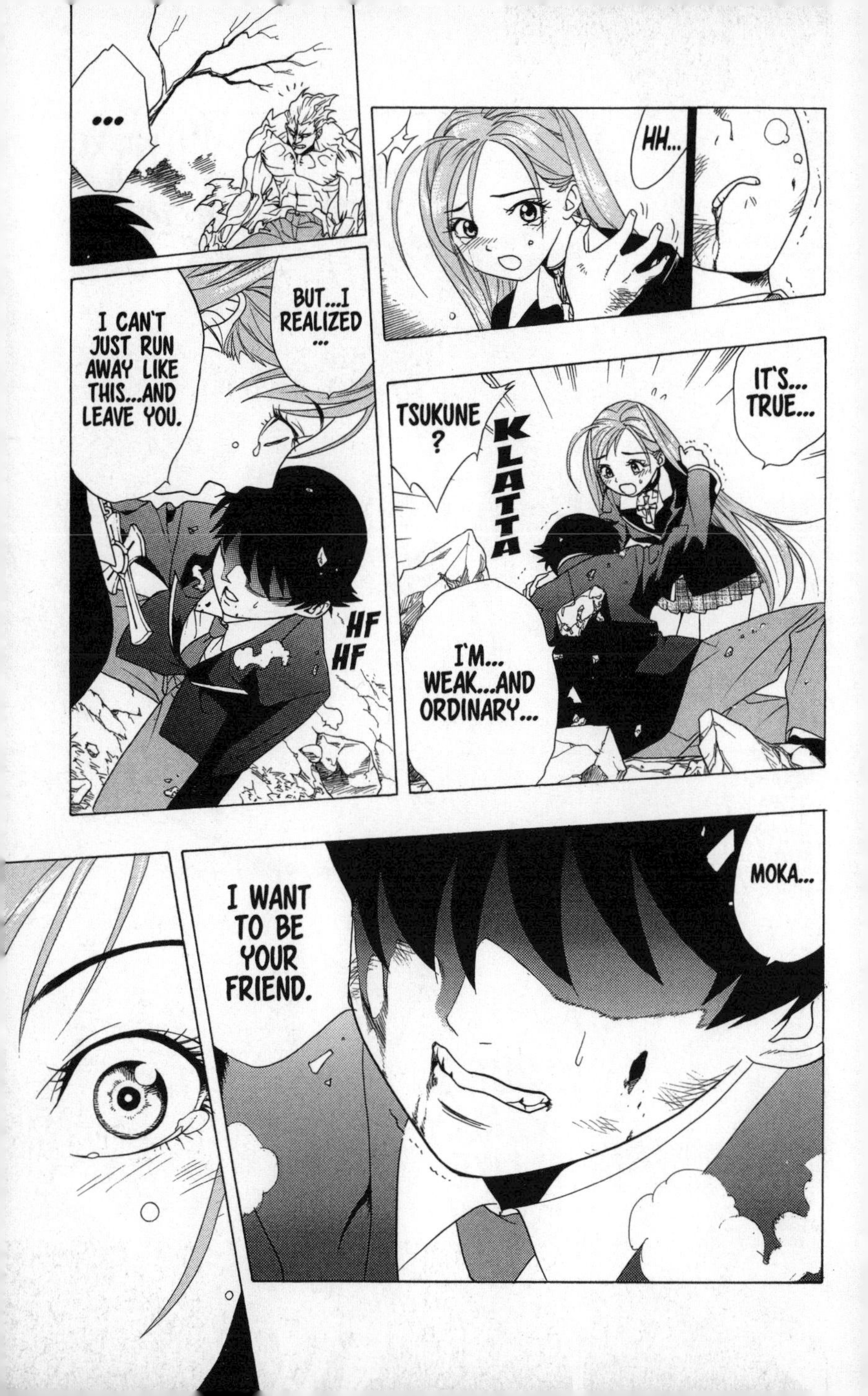
HH...
...
IT'S... TRUE...
TSUKUNE?
KLATTA
I'M... WEAK...AND ORDINARY...
BUT...I REALIZED...
I CAN'T JUST RUN AWAY LIKE THIS...AND LEAVE YOU.
HF HF
MOKA...
I WANT TO BE YOUR FRIEND.

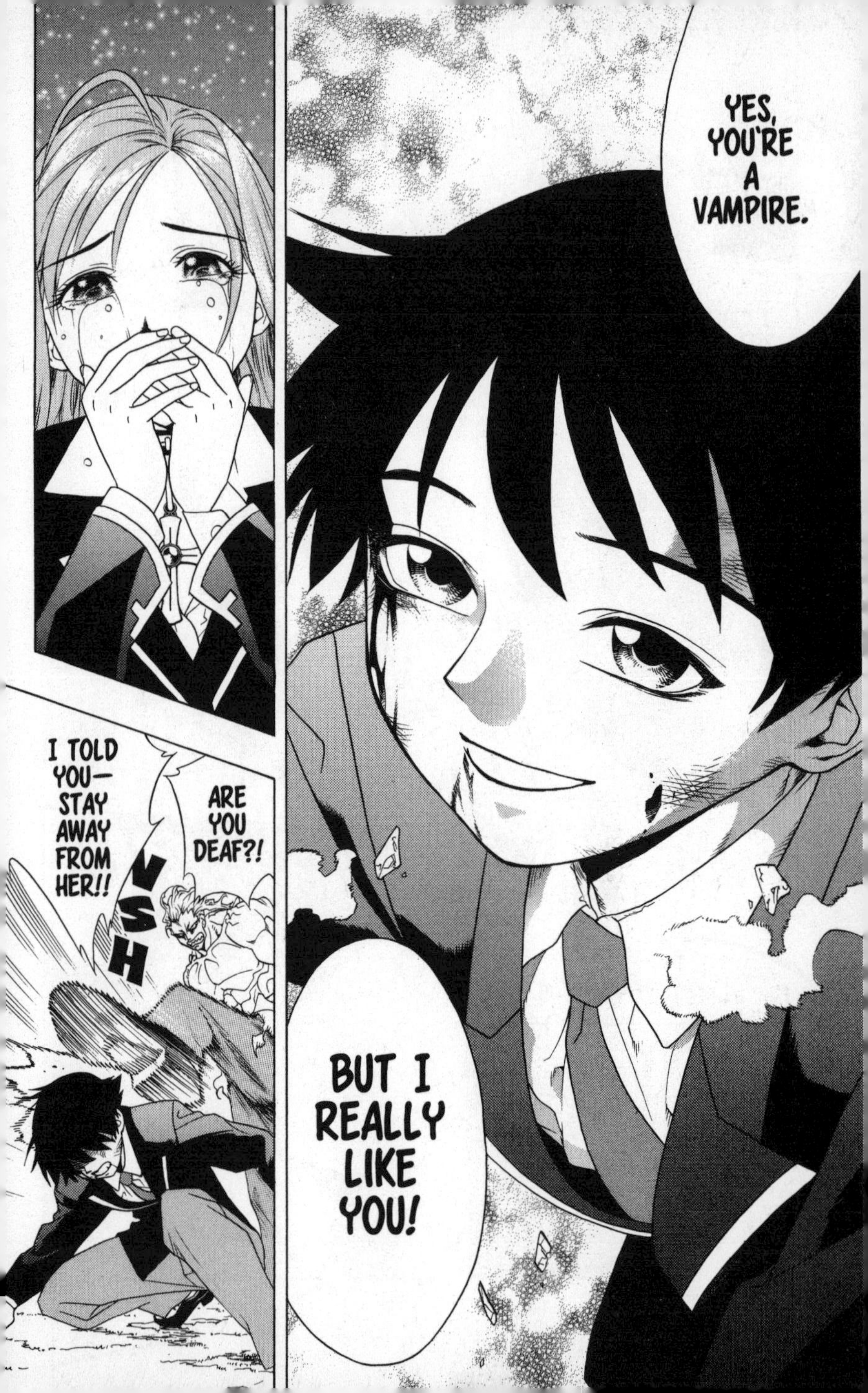
YES, YOU'RE A VAMPIRE.
BUT I REALLY LIKE YOU!
ARE YOU DEAF?!
I TOLD YOU—STAY AWAY FROM HER!!
VSH

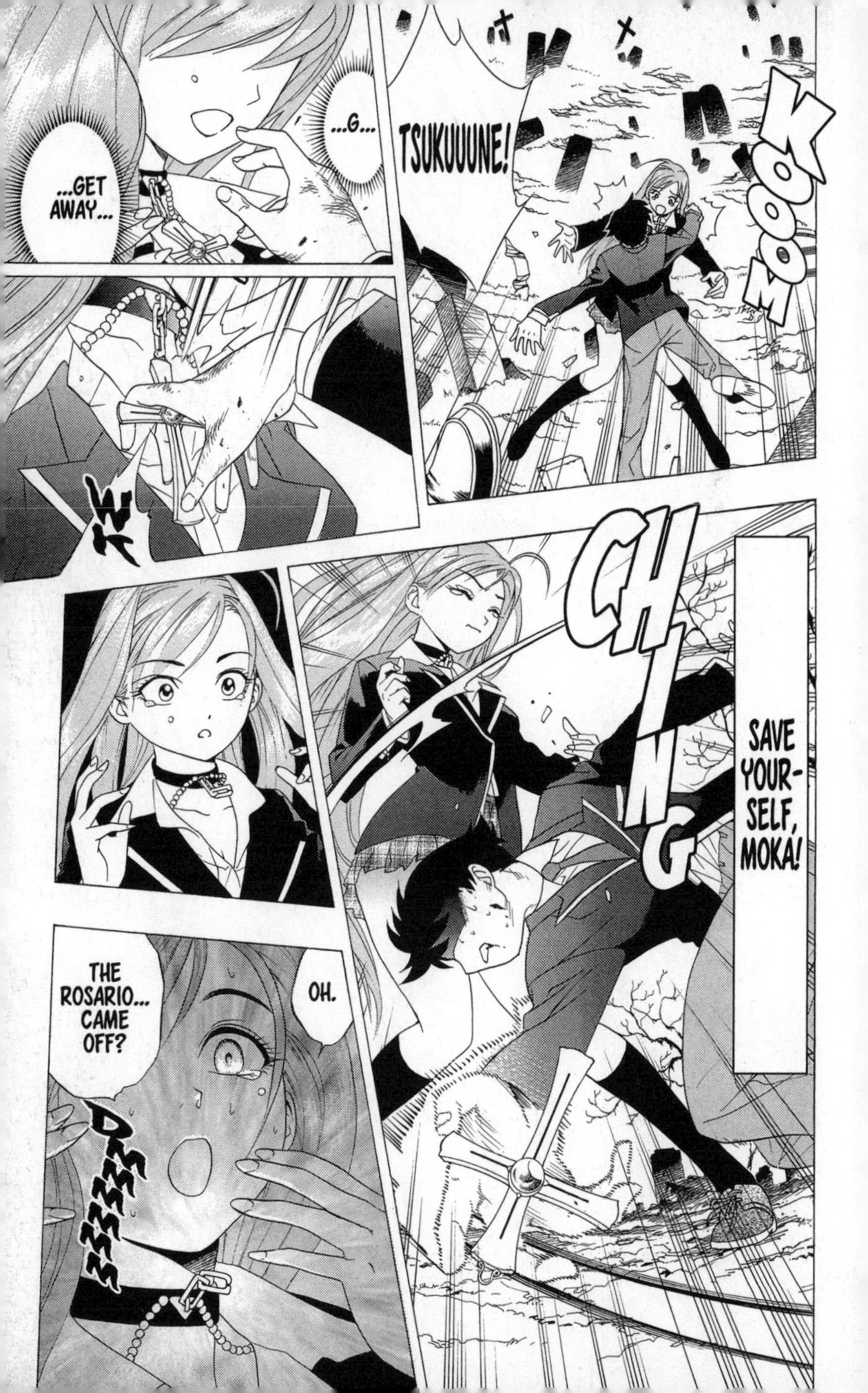
TSUKUUUNE!
KOOOOM
...G...
...GET AWAY...
WT
SAVE YOURSELF, MOKA!
CHING
OH.
THE ROSARIO... CAME OFF?
DMMMMMMM

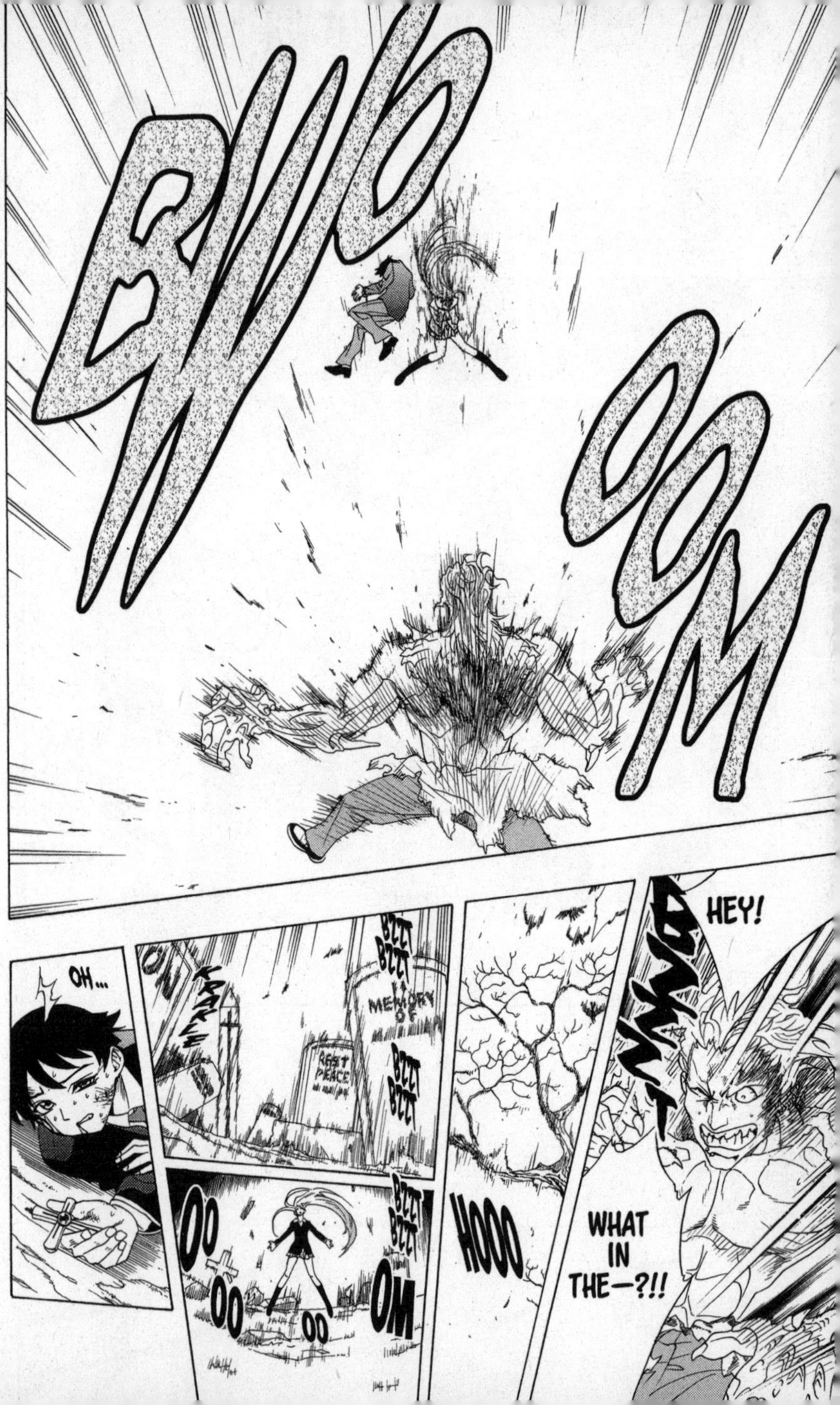
BVOOOM
HEY!
WHAT IN THE—?!!
HOOO
BZZT BZZT
IN MEMORY OF
BZZT BZZT
REST IN PEACE
BZZT BZZT
OOOOOOM
OH...

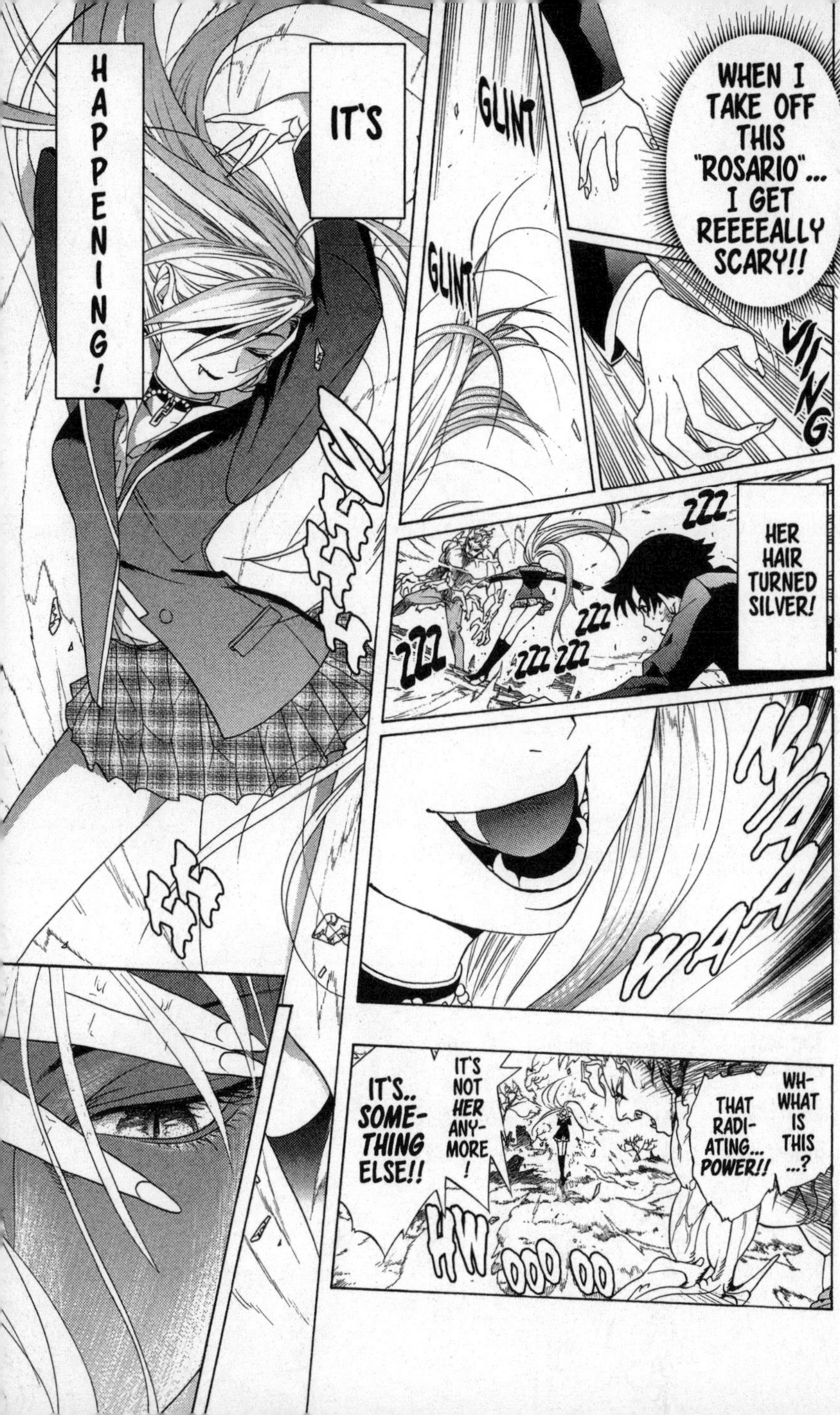
WHEN I TAKE OFF THIS "ROSARIO"... I GET REEEEALLY SCARY!!
VIING
GLINT
GLINT
IT'S
HAPPENING!
HER HAIR TURNED SILVER!
ZZZ
ZZZ
ZZZ ZZZ
ZZZ
WAAAA
WH-WHAT IS THIS ...?
THAT RADIATING... POWER!!
IT'S NOT HER ANYMORE!
IT'S.. SOMETHING ELSE!!
HWOOOOO

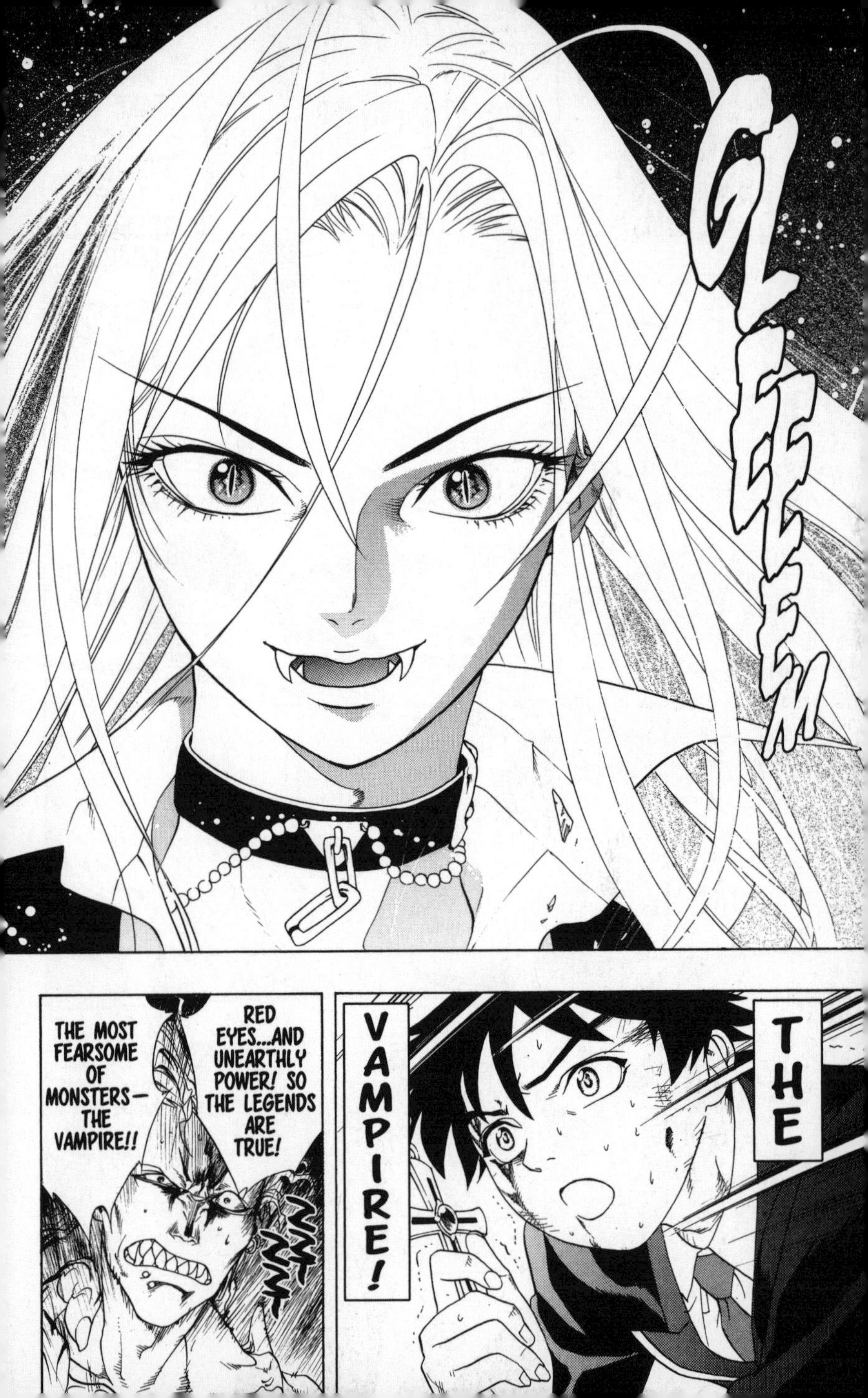
GLEEEM
THE
VAMPIRE!
RED EYES...AND UNEARTHLY POWER! SO THE LEGENDS ARE TRUE!
THE MOST FEARSOME OF MONSTERS— THE VAMPIRE!!

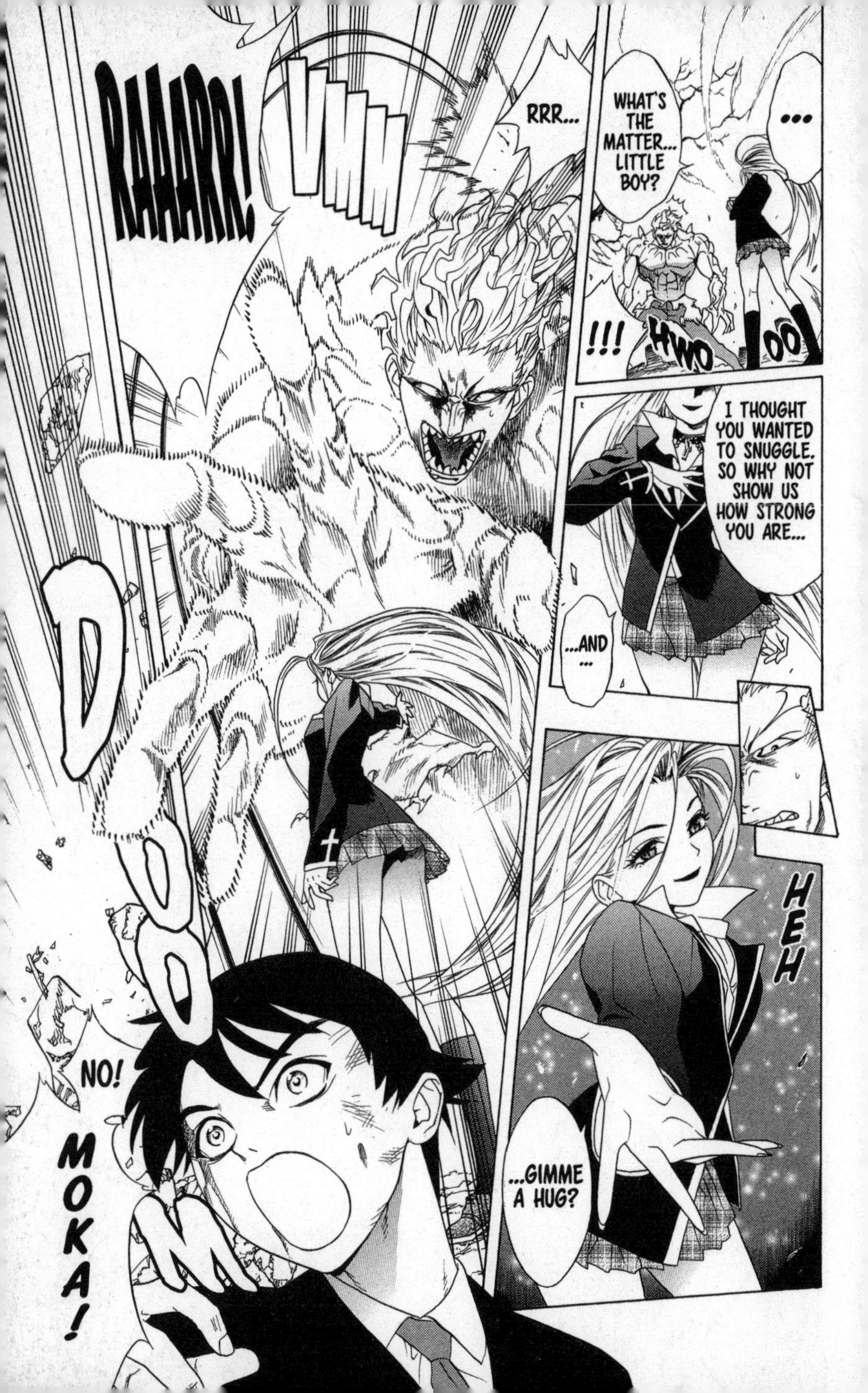
...
WHAT'S THE MATTER... LITTLE BOY?
!!!
HWOOO
I THOUGHT YOU WANTED TO SNUGGLE. SO WHY NOT SHOW US HOW STRONG YOU ARE...
...AND ...
HEH
...GIMME A HUG?
RRR...
RAAARR!
VMMM
DOOO
NO!
MOKA!

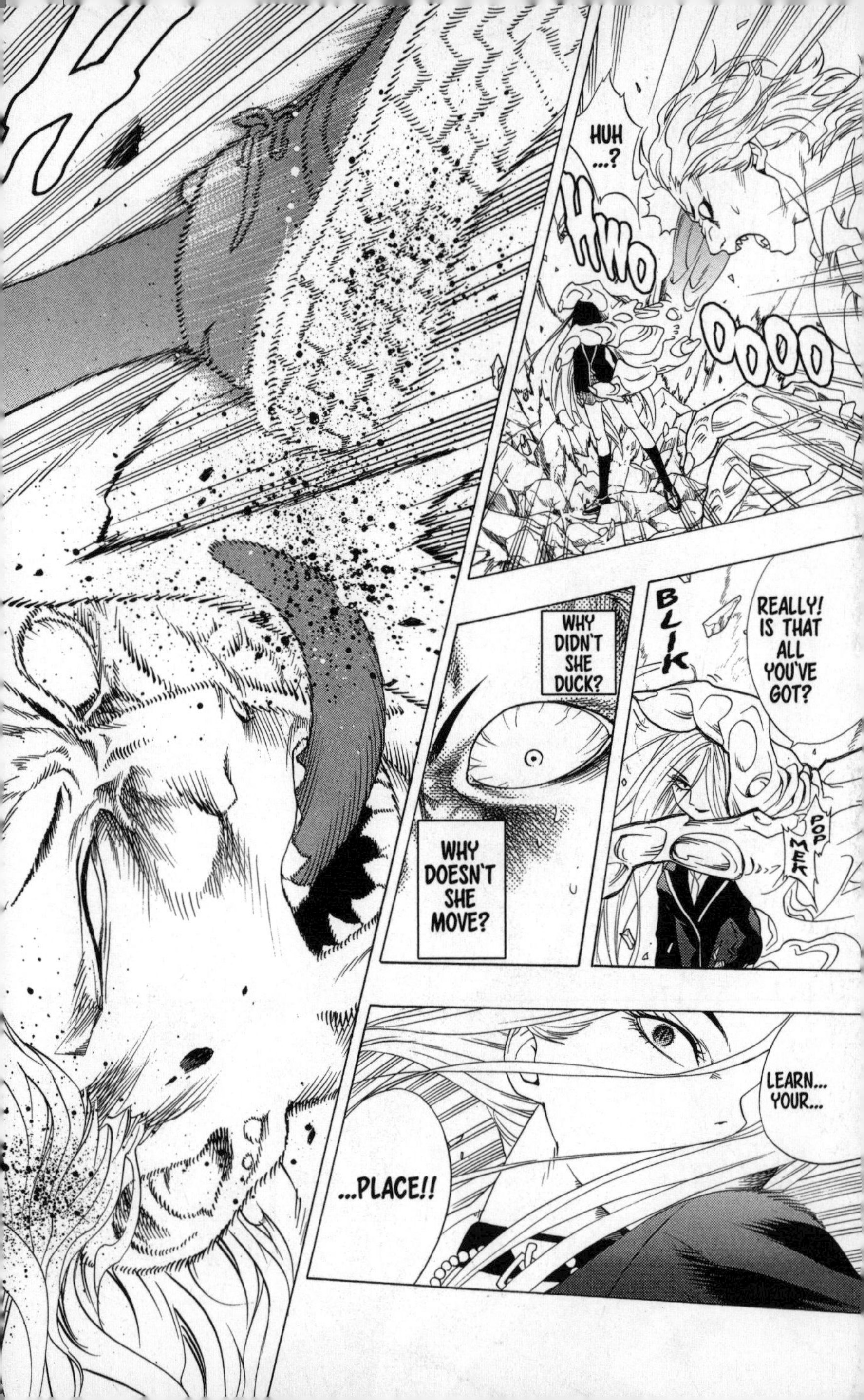
HUH ...?
HWOOOOOO
REALLY! IS THAT ALL YOU'VE GOT?
BLIK
POP
MEK
WHY DIDN'T SHE DUCK?
WHY DOESN'T SHE MOVE?
LEARN... YOUR...
...PLACE!!

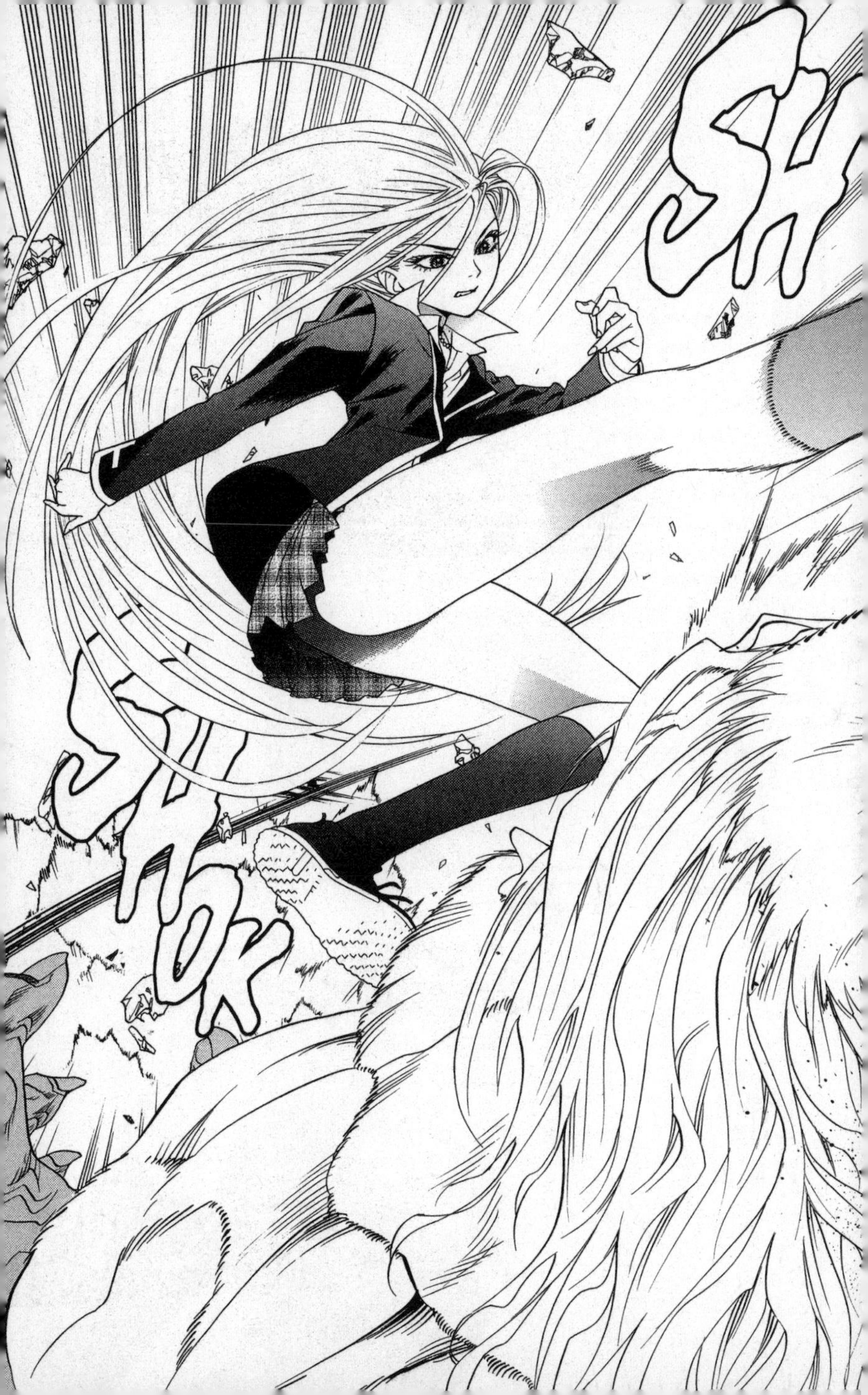
SH
SHOK

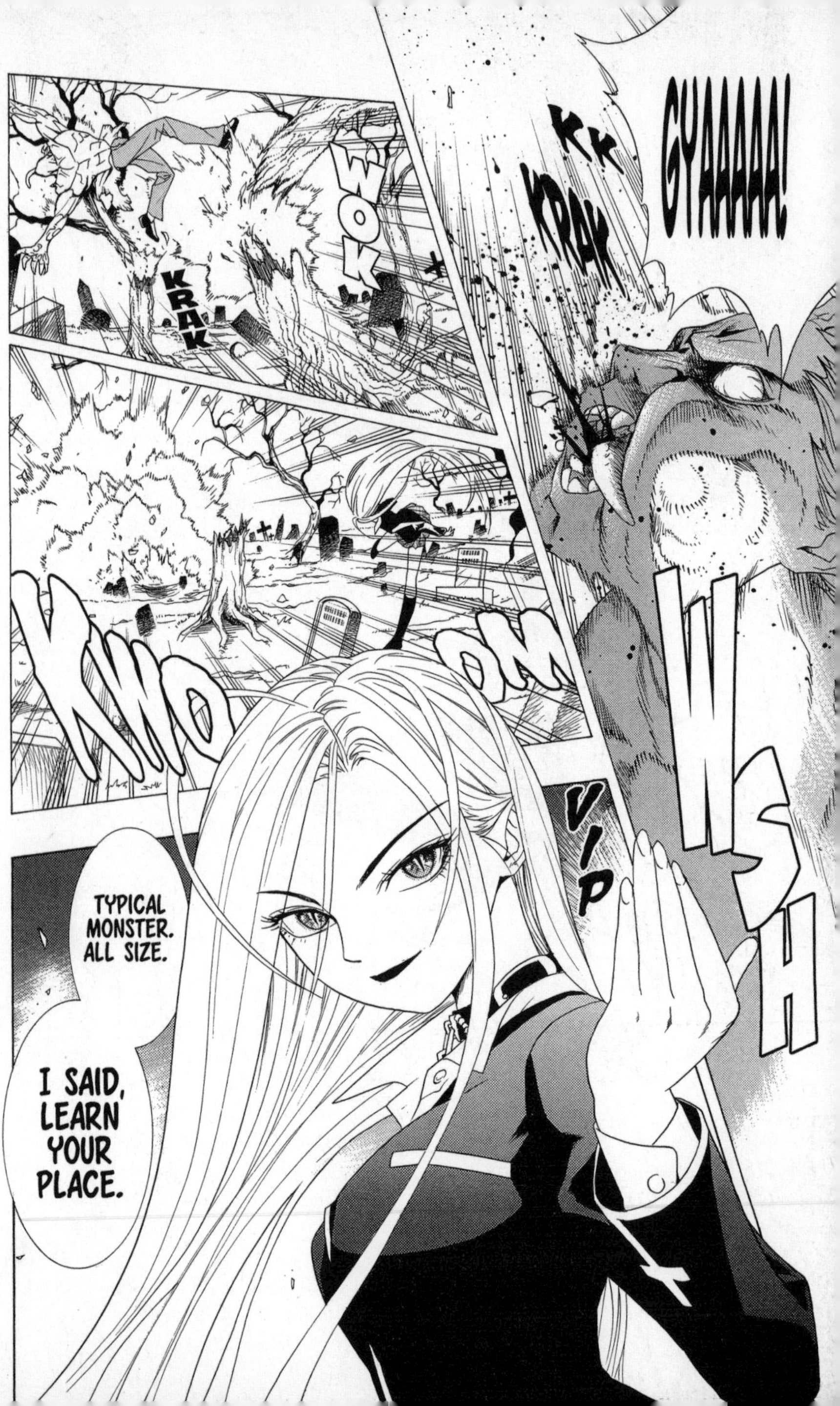
GYAAAAA!
KK KRAK
WOK
KRAK
KWHOOM
WSH
VIP
TYPICAL MONSTER. ALL SIZE.
I SAID, LEARN YOUR PLACE.

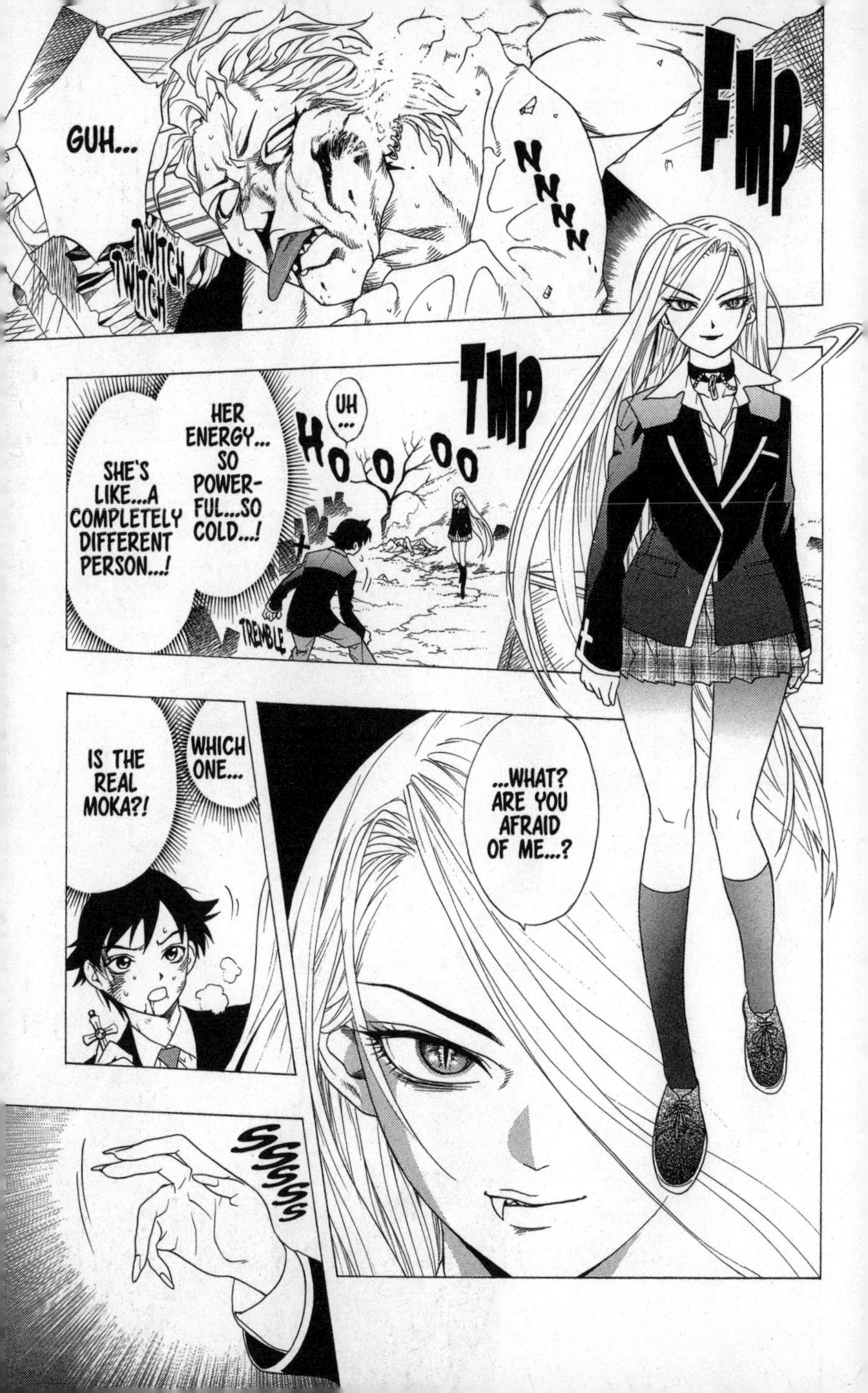
FMP
NNNN...
GUH...
TWITCH TWITCH
TMP
UH...
HOOOO
HER ENERGY... SO POWERFUL... SO COLD...!
SHE'S LIKE...A COMPLETELY DIFFERENT PERSON...!
TREMBLE
...WHAT? ARE YOU AFRAID OF ME...?
WHICH ONE...
IS THE REAL MOKA?!
SSSSS

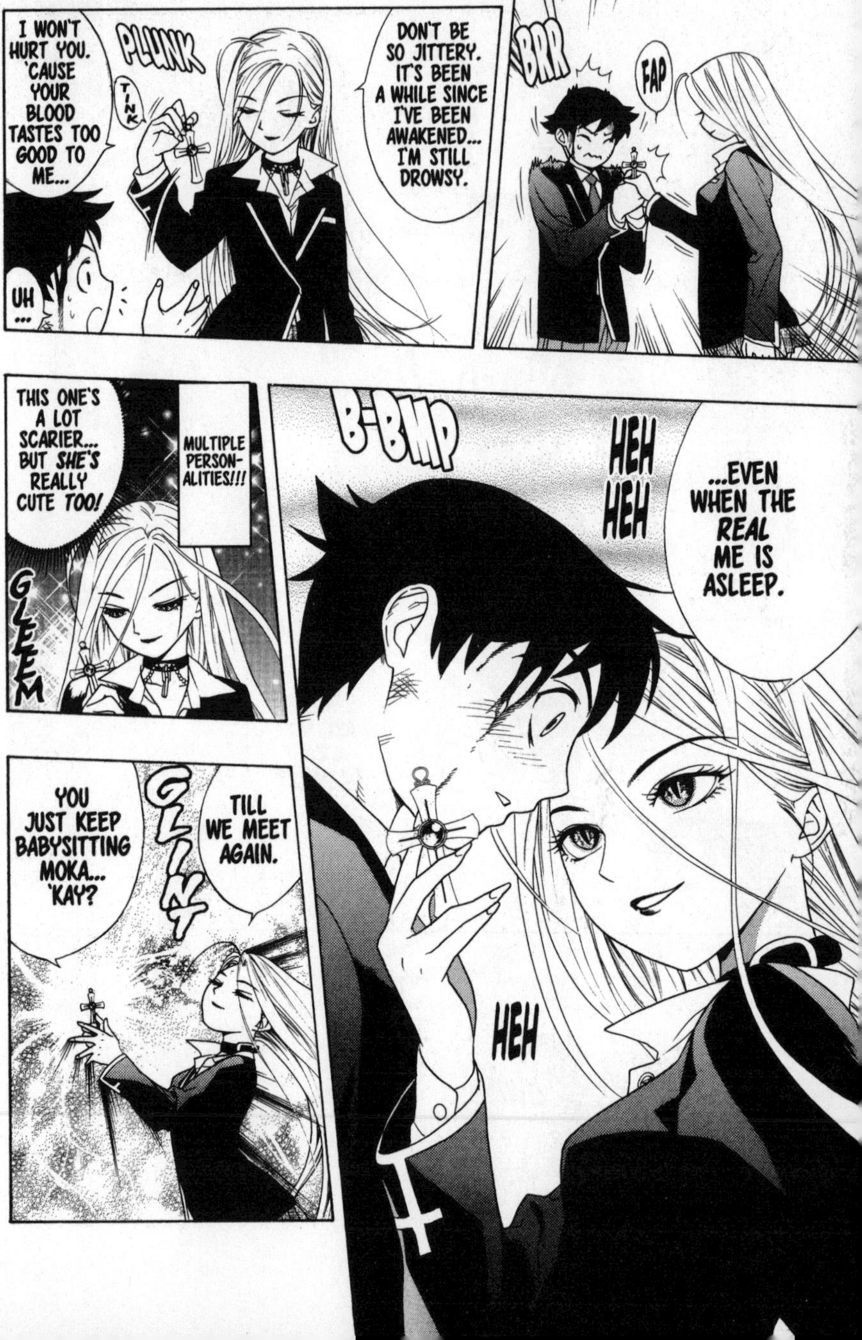
BRR
FAP
DON'T BE SO JITTERY. IT'S BEEN A WHILE SINCE I'VE BEEN AWAKENED... I'M STILL DROWSY.
PLUNK
TINK
I WON'T HURT YOU. 'CAUSE YOUR BLOOD TASTES TOO GOOD TO ME...
UH...
...EVEN WHEN THE REAL ME IS ASLEEP.
HEH HEH
B-BMP
HEH
MULTIPLE PERSONALITIES!!!
THIS ONE'S A LOT SCARIER... BUT SHE'S REALLY CUTE TOO!
GLEEEM
TILL WE MEET AGAIN.
GLINT
YOU JUST KEEP BABYSITTING MOKA... 'KAY?

READ THIS WAY

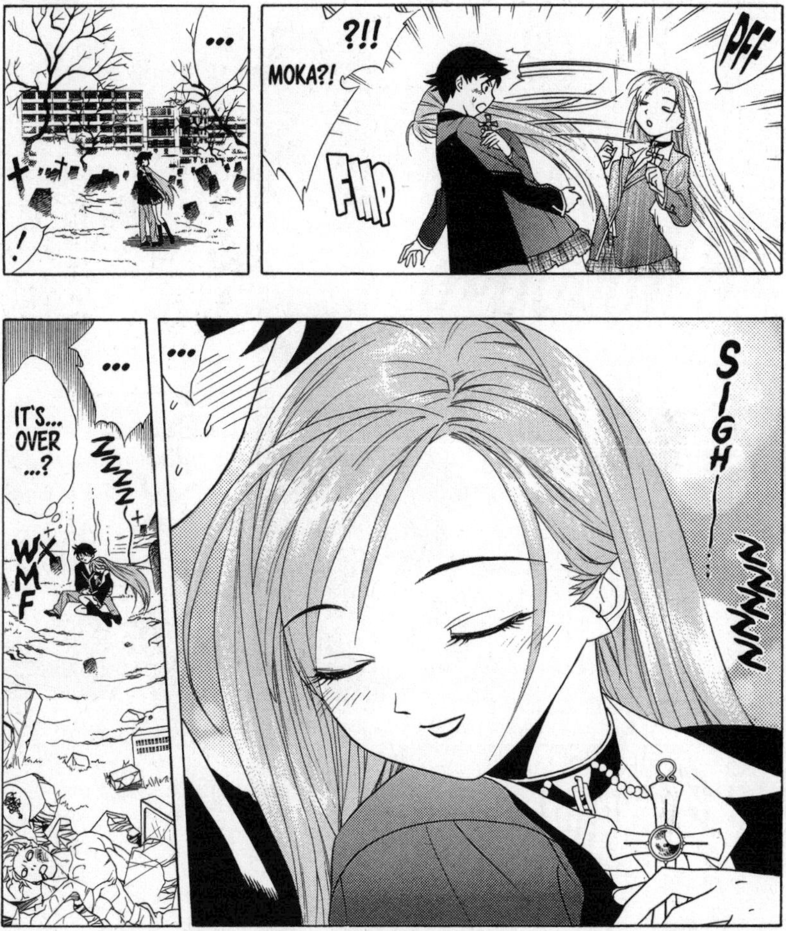
PFF
?!!
MOKA?!
FMP
...
!
SIGH...
NNNNN
...
...
IT'S... OVER ...?
ZZZZ
WMF
RRRRMB
HWOOO
...YOU'RE AWFULLY YOUNG FOR THIS PLACE, SONNY.
HEHEH...
GOOD LUCK TO YOU, NOW...

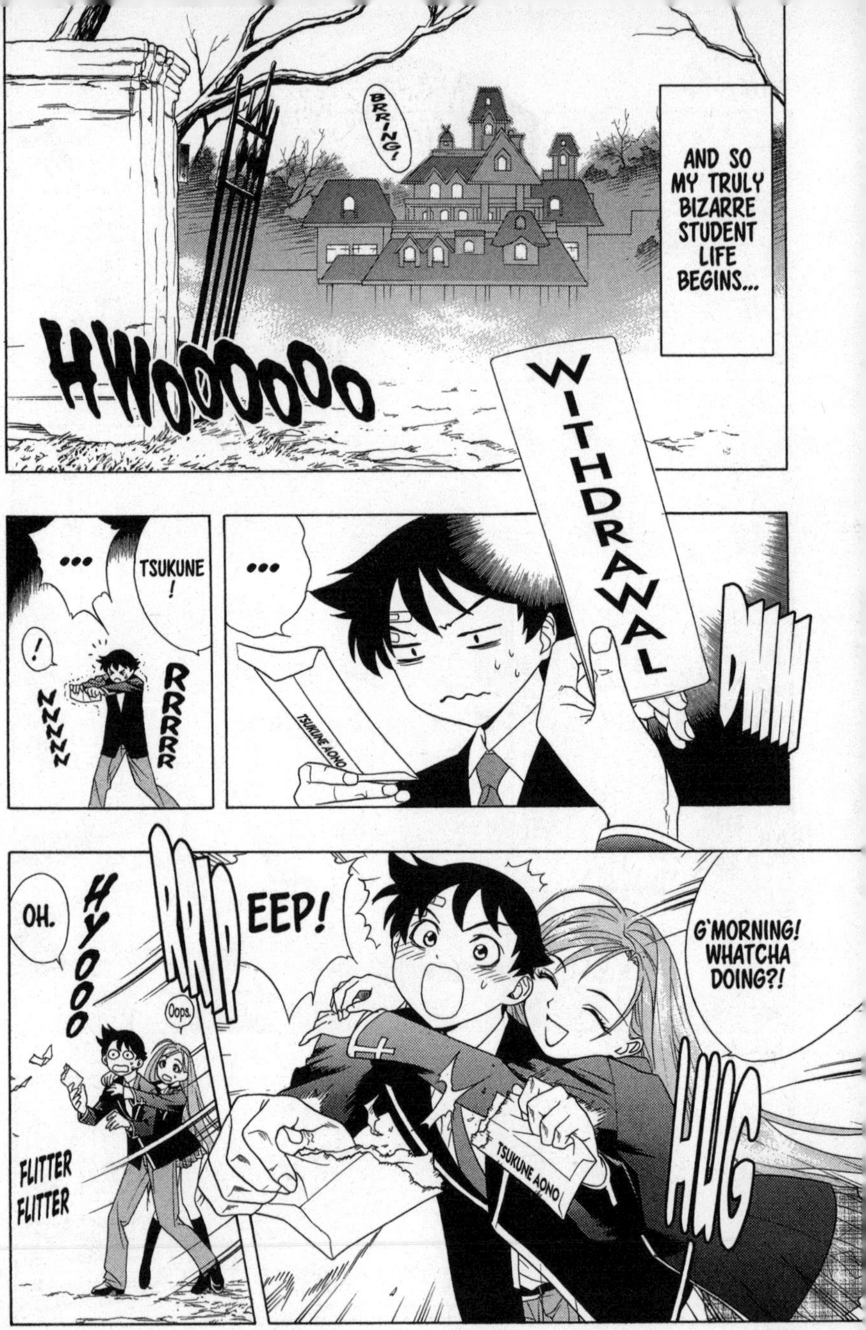
AND SO MY TRULY BIZARRE STUDENT LIFE BEGINS...
BRRING!
HWOOOOOO
WITHDRAWAL
...
TSUKUNE AONO
TSUKUNE!
...
!
RRRRR
NNNNN
G'MORNING! WHATCHA DOING?!
HUG
EEP!
TSUKUNE AONO
HYOOOO
OH.
Oops.
FLITTER FLITTER

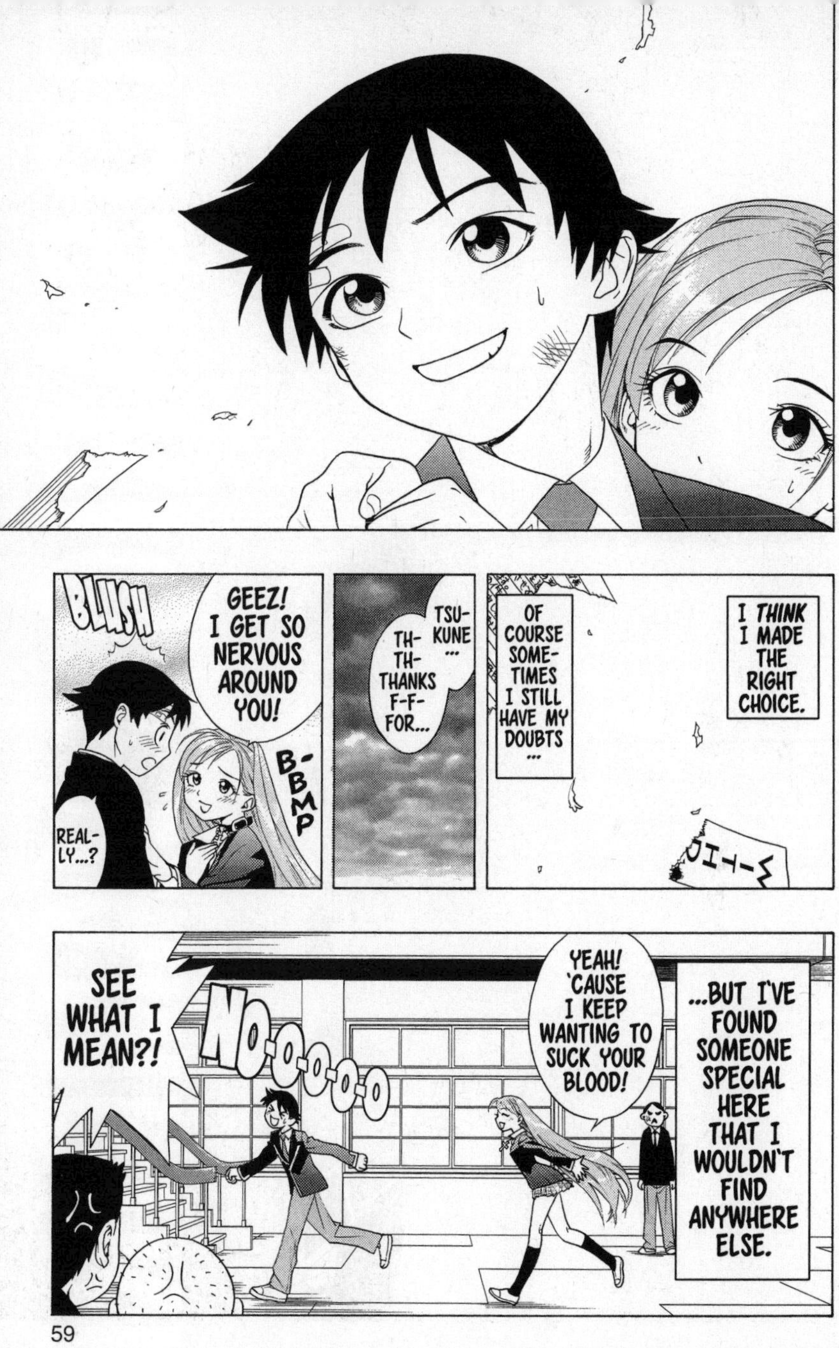
I THINK I MADE THE RIGHT CHOICE.
OF COURSE SOMETIMES I STILL HAVE MY DOUBTS...
TSU-KUNE...
TH-TH-THANKS F-F-FOR...
GEEZ! I GET SO NERVOUS AROUND YOU!
BLUSH
B-BMP
REAL-LY...?
...BUT I'VE FOUND SOMEONE SPECIAL HERE THAT I WOULDN'T FIND ANYWHERE ELSE.
YEAH! 'CAUSE I KEEP WANTING TO SUCK YOUR BLOOD!
NO-O-O-O-O-O
SEE WHAT I MEAN?!

ROSARIO+VAMPIRE

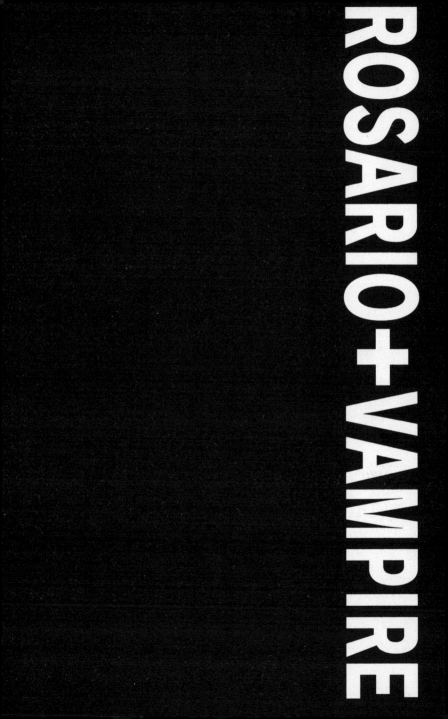

2: Kurumu of Black Dreams

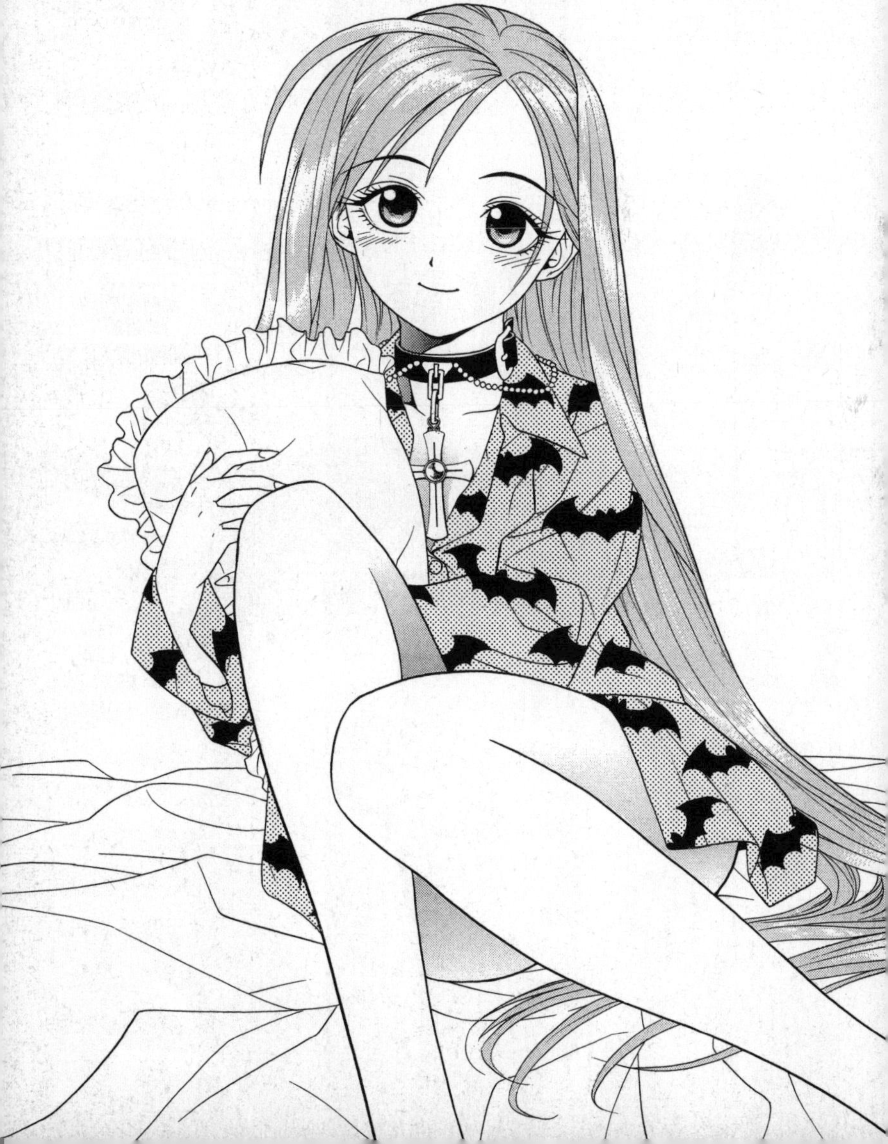

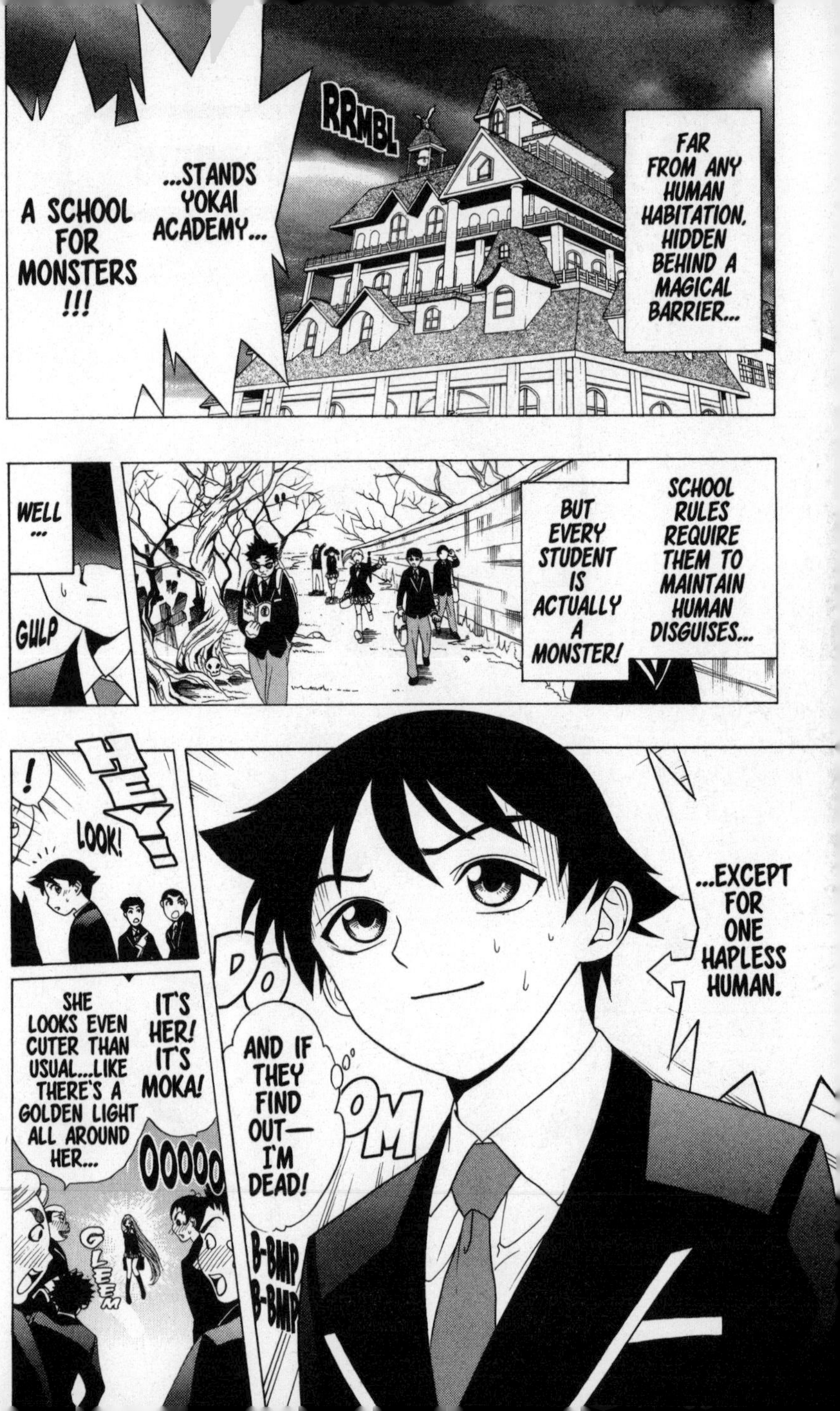
FAR FROM ANY HUMAN HABITATION, HIDDEN BEHIND A MAGICAL BARRIER...
RRMBL
...STANDS YOKAI ACADEMY...
A SCHOOL FOR MONSTERS!!!
SCHOOL RULES REQUIRE THEM TO MAINTAIN HUMAN DISGUISES...
BUT EVERY STUDENT IS ACTUALLY A MONSTER!
WELL...
GULP
...EXCEPT FOR ONE HAPLESS HUMAN.
DOOM
AND IF THEY FIND OUT— I'M DEAD!
B-BMP B-BMP
HEY!
!
LOOK!
IT'S HER! IT'S MOKA!
SHE LOOKS EVEN CUTER THAN USUAL...LIKE THERE'S A GOLDEN LIGHT ALL AROUND HER...
OOOOO
GLEEM

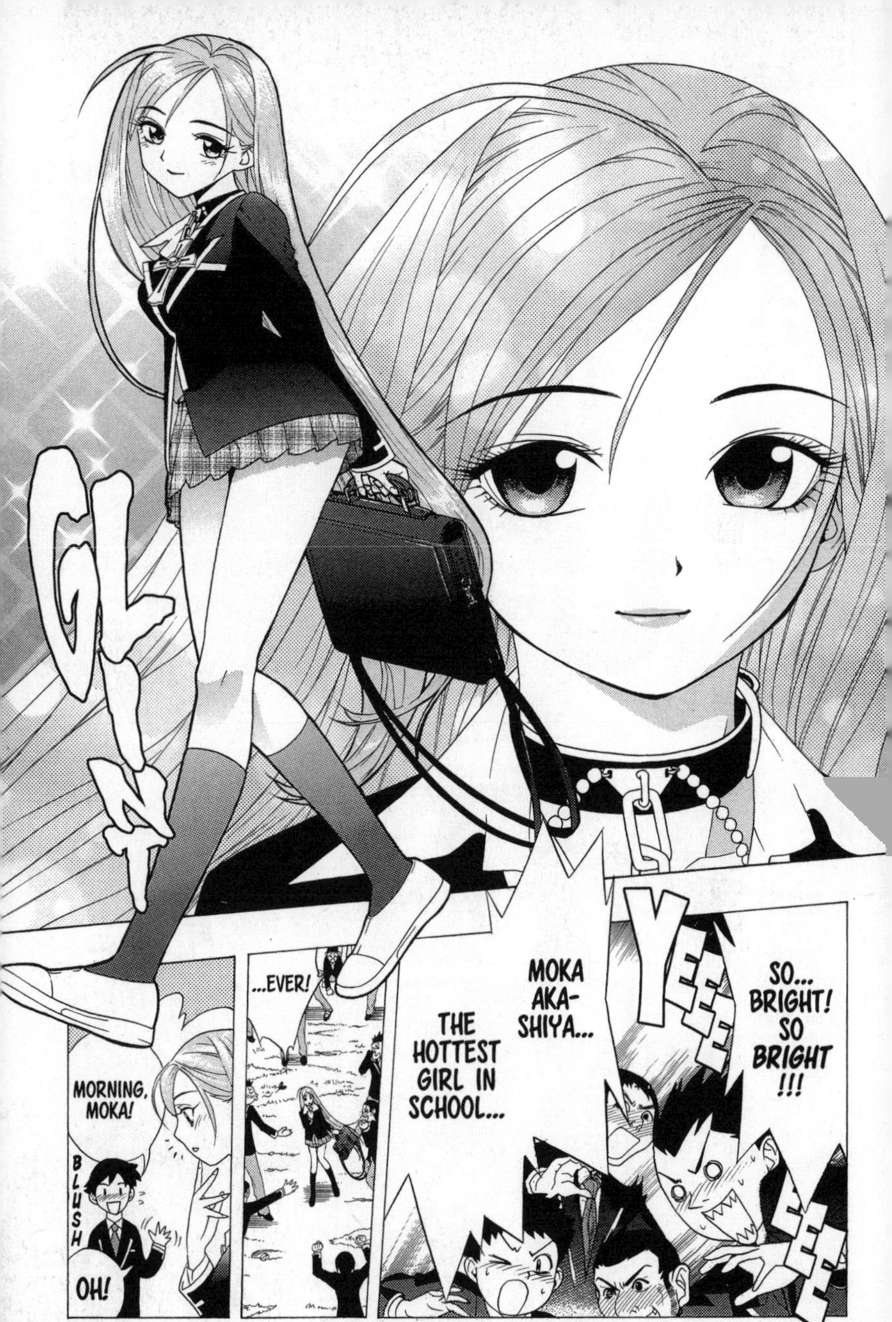
GLINT
YEEEEEEE
SO... BRIGHT! SO BRIGHT!!!
MOKA AKA-SHIYA...
THE HOTTEST GIRL IN SCHOOL...
...EVER!
MORNING, MOKA!
BLUSH
OH!

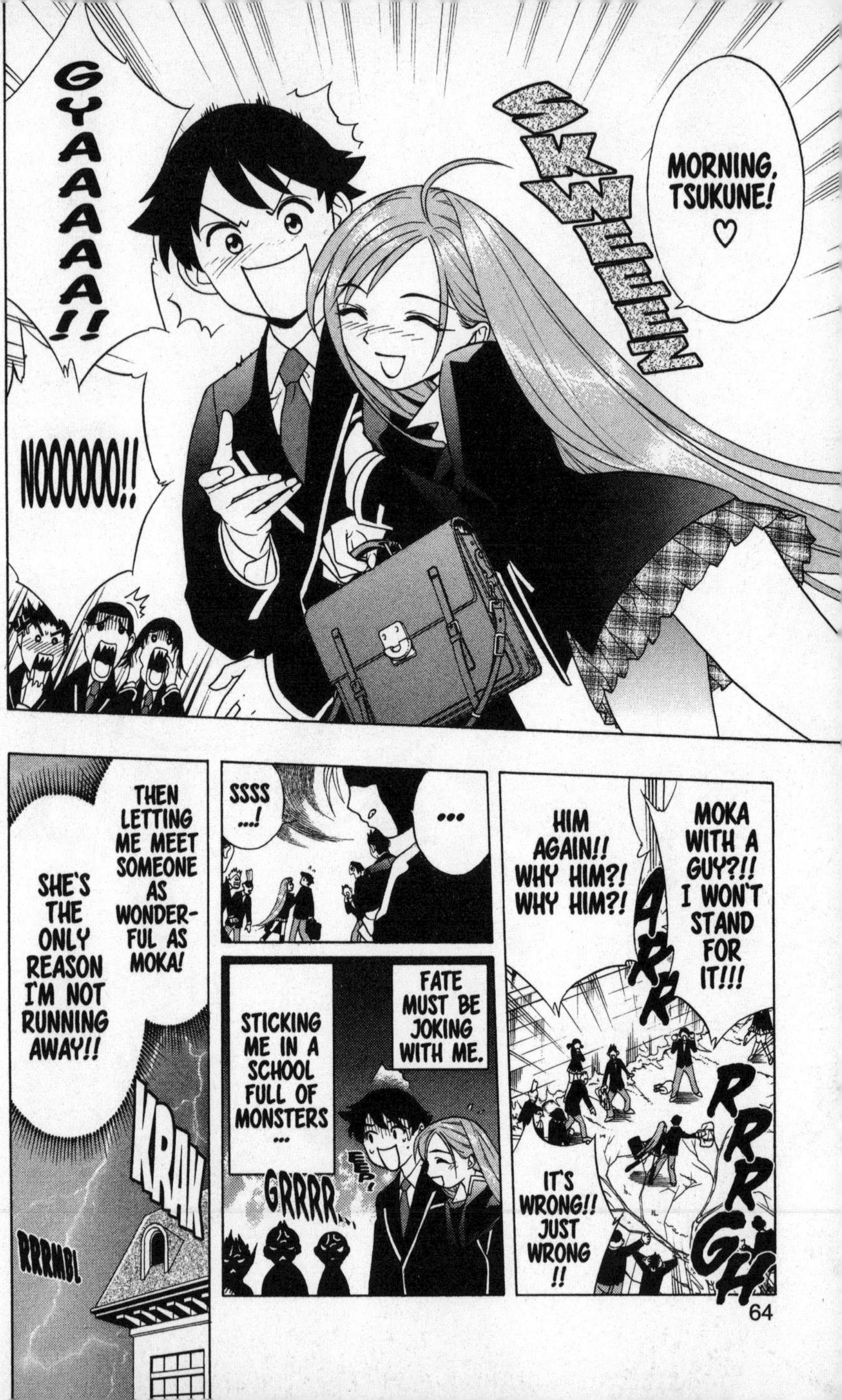
MORNING, TSUKUNE! ♡
SKWEEEEN
GYAAAAAAA!!
NOOOOOO!!
MOKA WITH A GUY?!! I WON'T STAND FOR IT!!!
HIM AGAIN!! WHY HIM?! WHY HIM?!
ARRR
RRRGH
IT'S WRONG!! JUST WRONG!!
...
SSSS ...!
FATE MUST BE JOKING WITH ME.
STICKING ME IN A SCHOOL FULL OF MONSTERS ...
EEEP!
GRRRR
THEN LETTING ME MEET SOMEONE AS WONDERFUL AS MOKA!
SHE'S THE ONLY REASON I'M NOT RUNNING AWAY!!
KRAK
RRRMB!

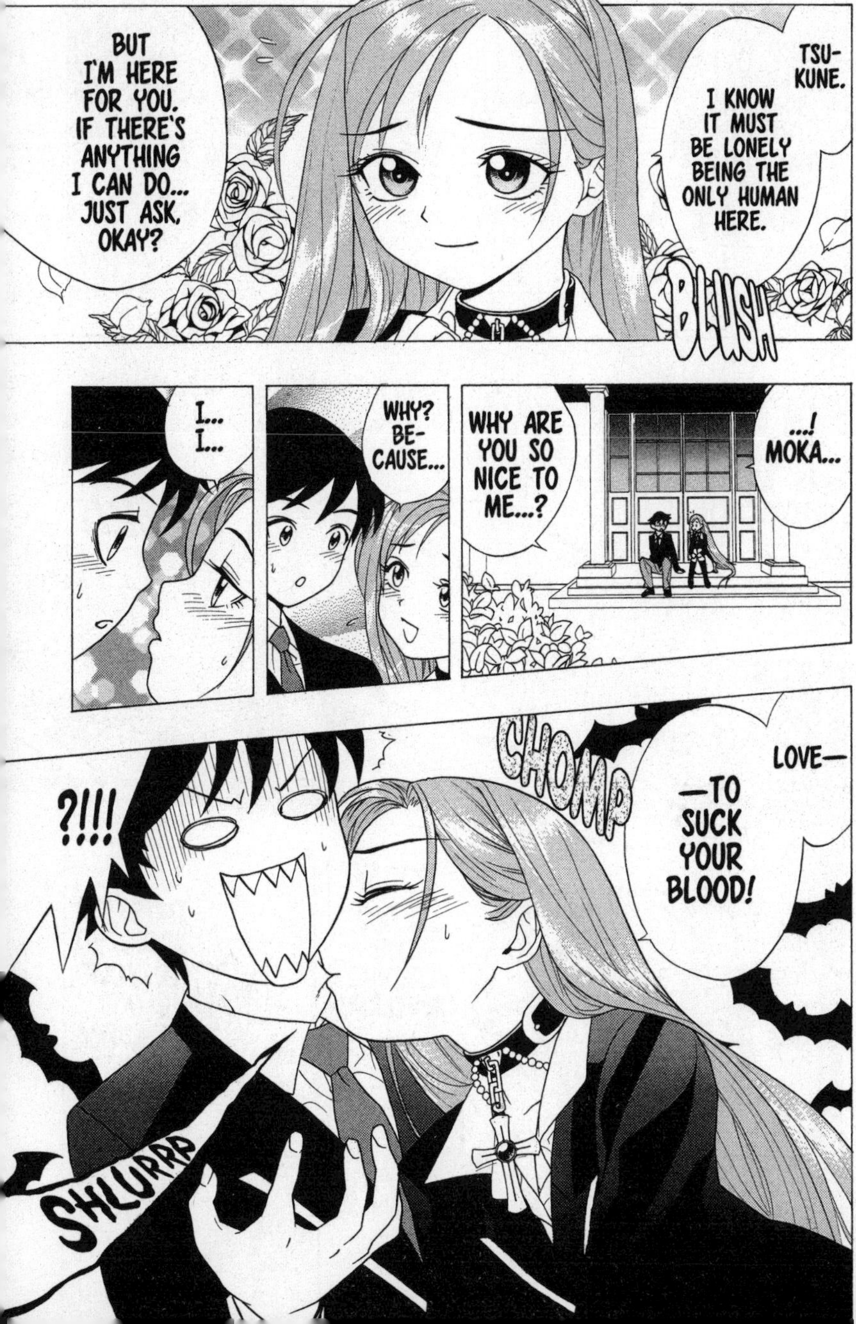
TSU-KUNE.
I KNOW IT MUST BE LONELY BEING THE ONLY HUMAN HERE.
BLUSH
BUT I'M HERE FOR YOU. IF THERE'S ANYTHING I CAN DO... JUST ASK, OKAY?
...! MOKA...
WHY ARE YOU SO NICE TO ME...?
WHY? BE-CAUSE...
I... I...
LOVE—
—TO SUCK YOUR BLOOD!
CHOMP
?!!!
SHLURRP

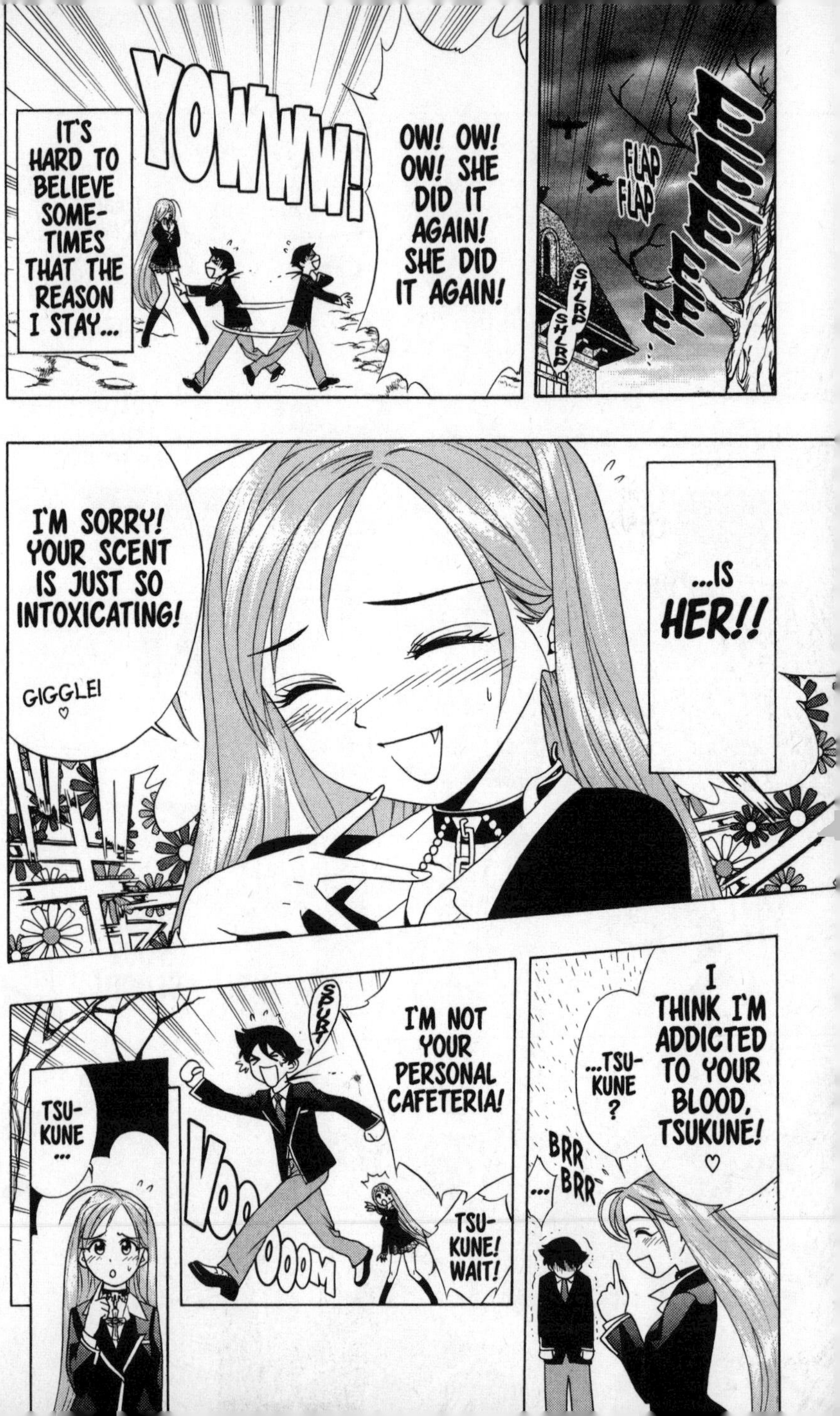

EEEEEEE...
FLAP FLAP
SHLRP SHLRP
OW! OW! OW! SHE DID IT AGAIN! SHE DID IT AGAIN!
YOWWW!
IT'S HARD TO BELIEVE SOMETIMES THAT THE REASON I STAY...
...IS HER!!
I'M SORRY! YOUR SCENT IS JUST SO INTOXICATING!
GIGGLE! ♡
I THINK I'M ADDICTED TO YOUR BLOOD, TSUKUNE! ♡
...TSUKUNE?
BRR BRR
...
I'M NOT YOUR PERSONAL CAFETERIA!
SPURT
VOOOOOM
TSUKUNE! WAIT!
TSUKUNE...

READ THIS WAY

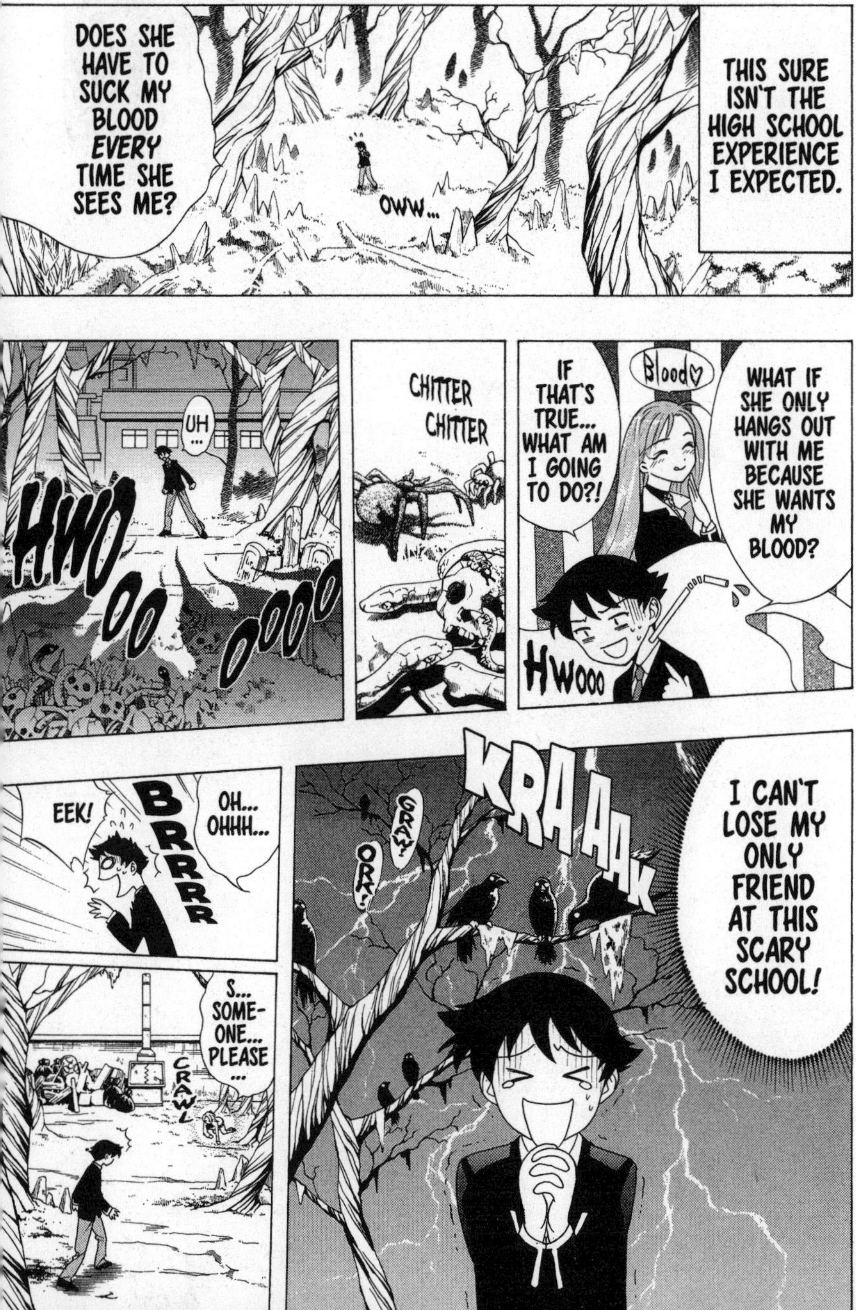
THIS SURE ISN'T THE HIGH SCHOOL EXPERIENCE I EXPECTED.
OWW...
DOES SHE HAVE TO SUCK MY BLOOD *EVERY* TIME SHE SEES ME?
WHAT IF SHE ONLY HANGS OUT WITH ME BECAUSE SHE WANTS MY BLOOD?
Blood♡
IF THAT'S TRUE... WHAT AM I GOING TO DO?!
HWOOO
CHITTER CHITTER
UH...
HWOOOOOOOO
I CAN'T LOSE MY ONLY FRIEND AT THIS SCARY SCHOOL!
KRAAAAK
GRAW!
ORK!
OH... OHHH...
BRRRR
EEK!
S... SOME-ONE... PLEASE...
CRAWL

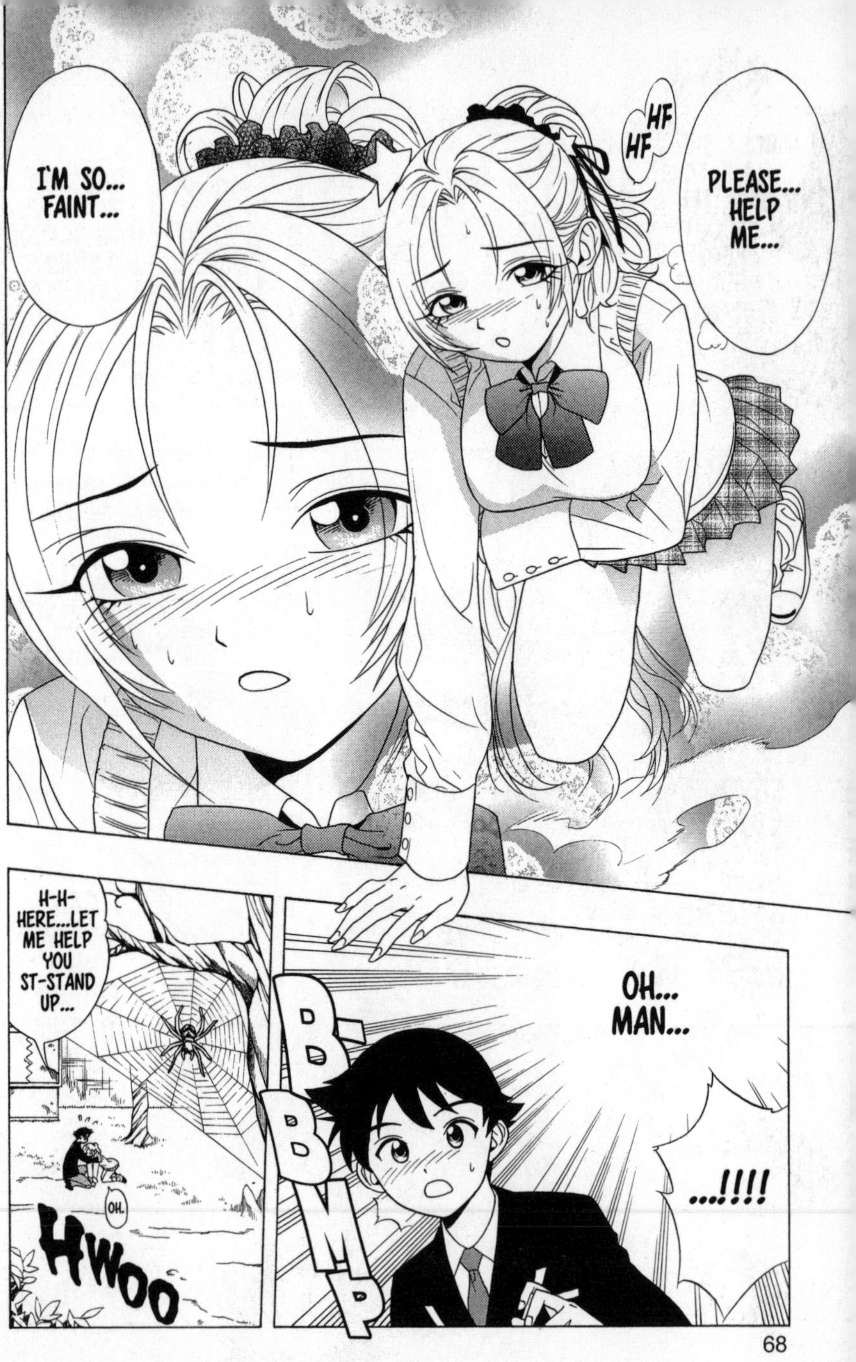
HF HF
PLEASE... HELP ME...
I'M SO... FAINT...
OH... MAN...
...!!!!
B-BMP
H-H-HERE...LET ME HELP YOU ST-STAND UP...
OH.
HWOO

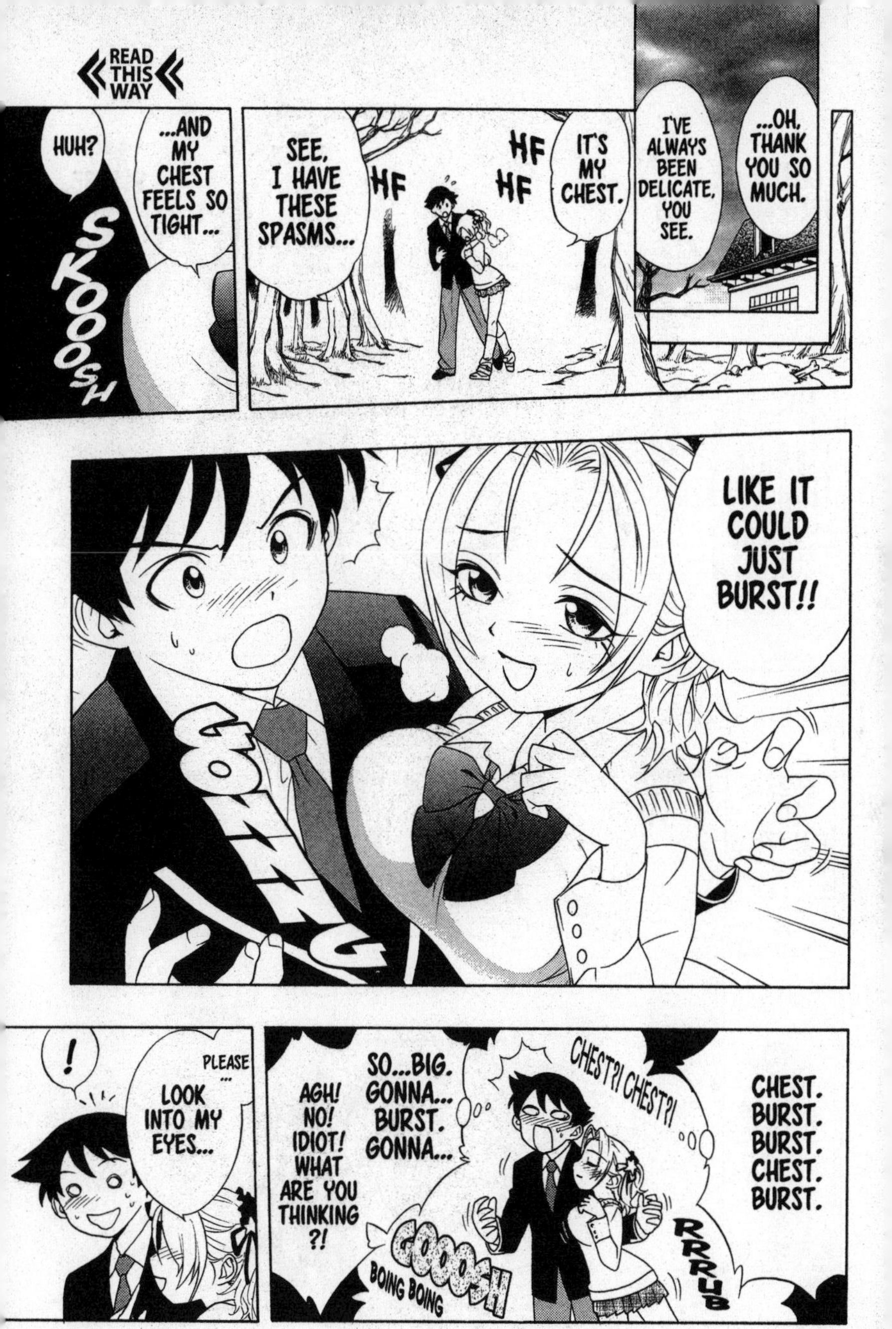
READ THIS WAY
...OH, THANK YOU SO MUCH.
I'VE ALWAYS BEEN DELICATE, YOU SEE.
IT'S MY CHEST.
HF HF
HF
SEE, I HAVE THESE SPASMS...
...AND MY CHEST FEELS SO TIGHT...
HUH?
SKOOOSH
LIKE IT COULD JUST BURST!!
GOING
CHEST. BURST. BURST. CHEST. BURST.
CHEST?! CHEST?!
SO...BIG. GONNA... BURST. GONNA...
AGH! NO! IDIOT! WHAT ARE YOU THINKING?!
RRRUB
GOOOSH
BOING BOING
PLEASE ...
LOOK INTO MY EYES...
!

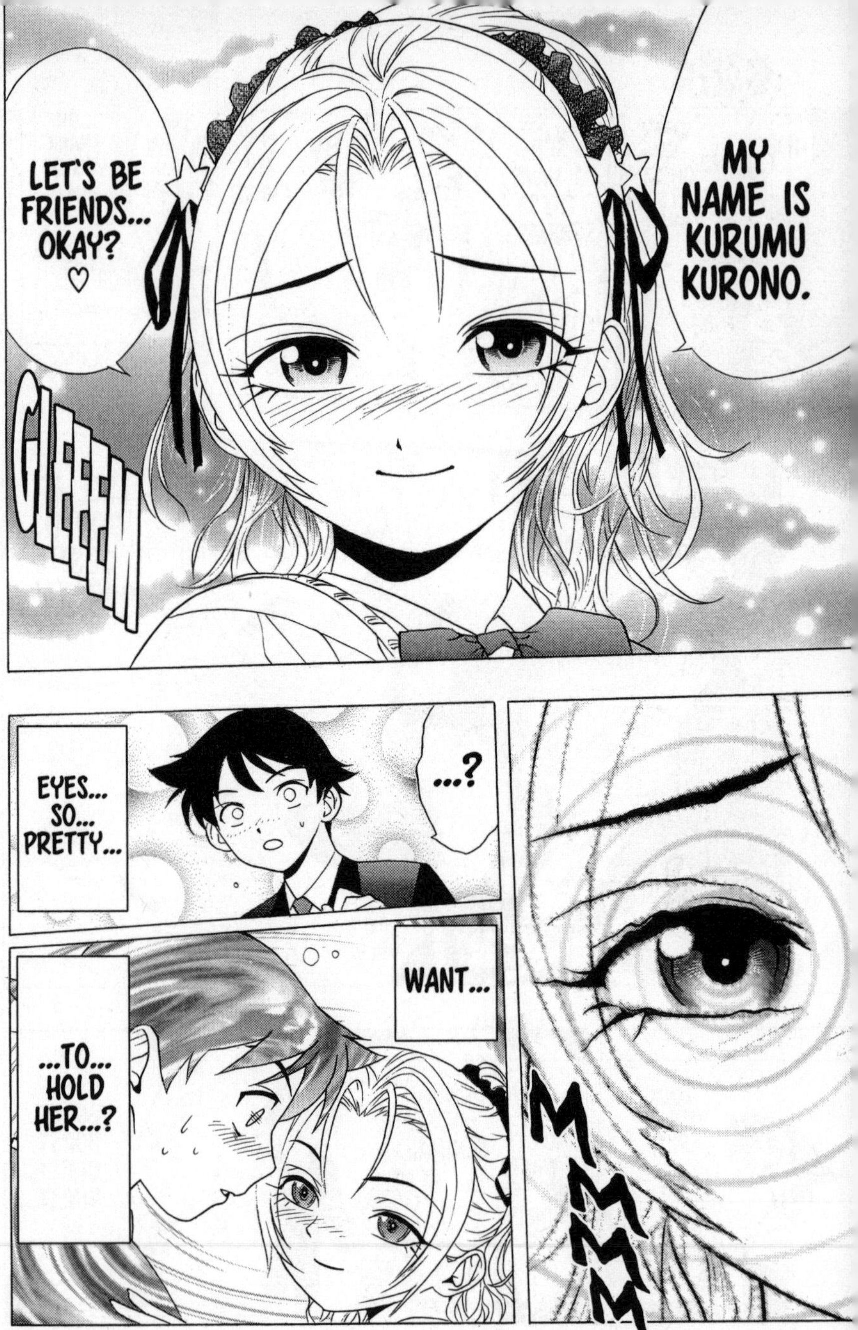
MY NAME IS KURUMU KURONO.
LET'S BE FRIENDS... OKAY? ♡
GLEEEM
MMMM
...?
EYES... SO... PRETTY...
WANT...
...TO... HOLD HER...?

READ THIS WAY

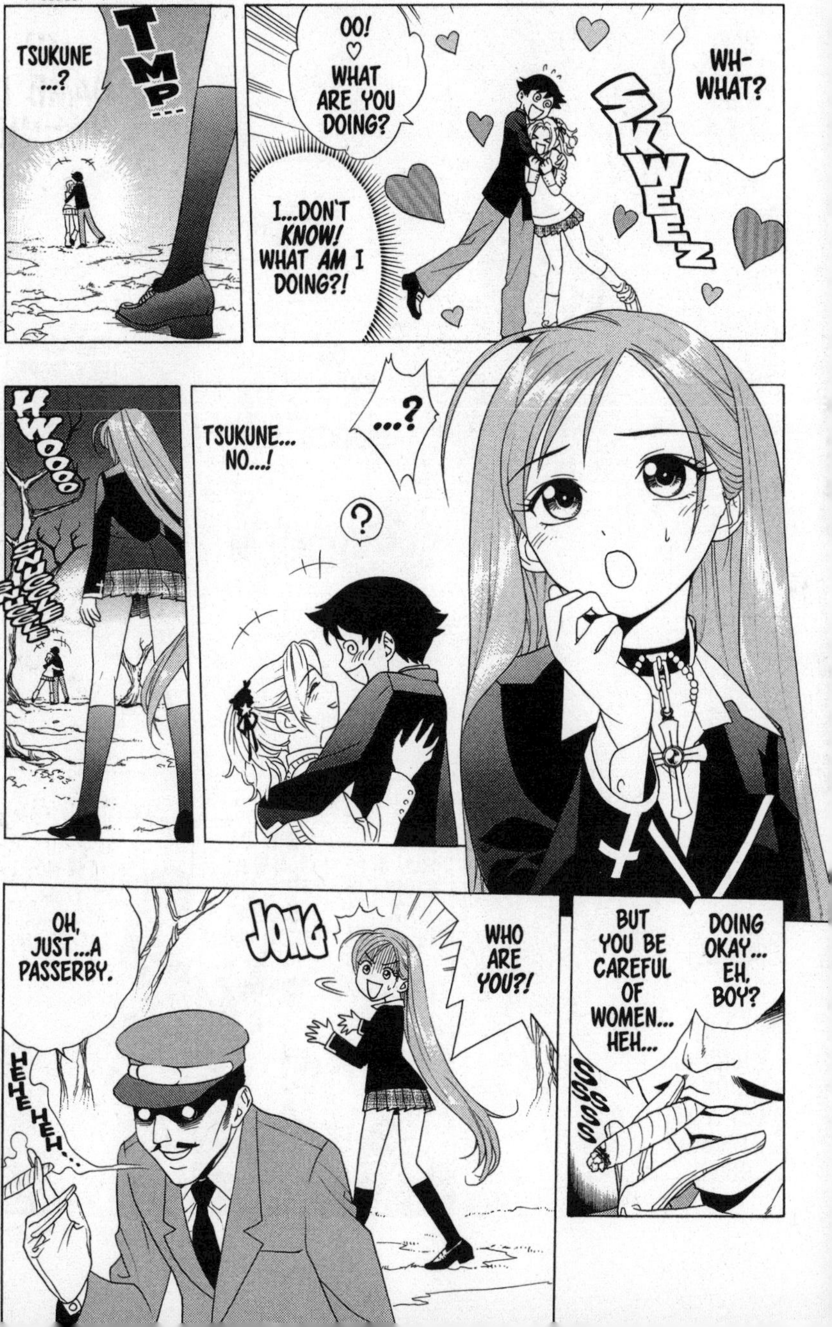
WH-WHAT?
SKWEEZ
OO! ♡ WHAT ARE YOU DOING?
I...DON'T KNOW! WHAT *AM* I DOING?!
TMP...
TSUKUNE...?
...?
TSUKUNE... NO...!
?
HWOOOO
SNUGGLE SNUGGLE
DOING OKAY... EH, BOY?
BUT YOU BE CAREFUL OF WOMEN... HEH...
SSSS
WHO ARE YOU?!
JONG
OH, JUST...A PASSERBY.
HEHEHEH...

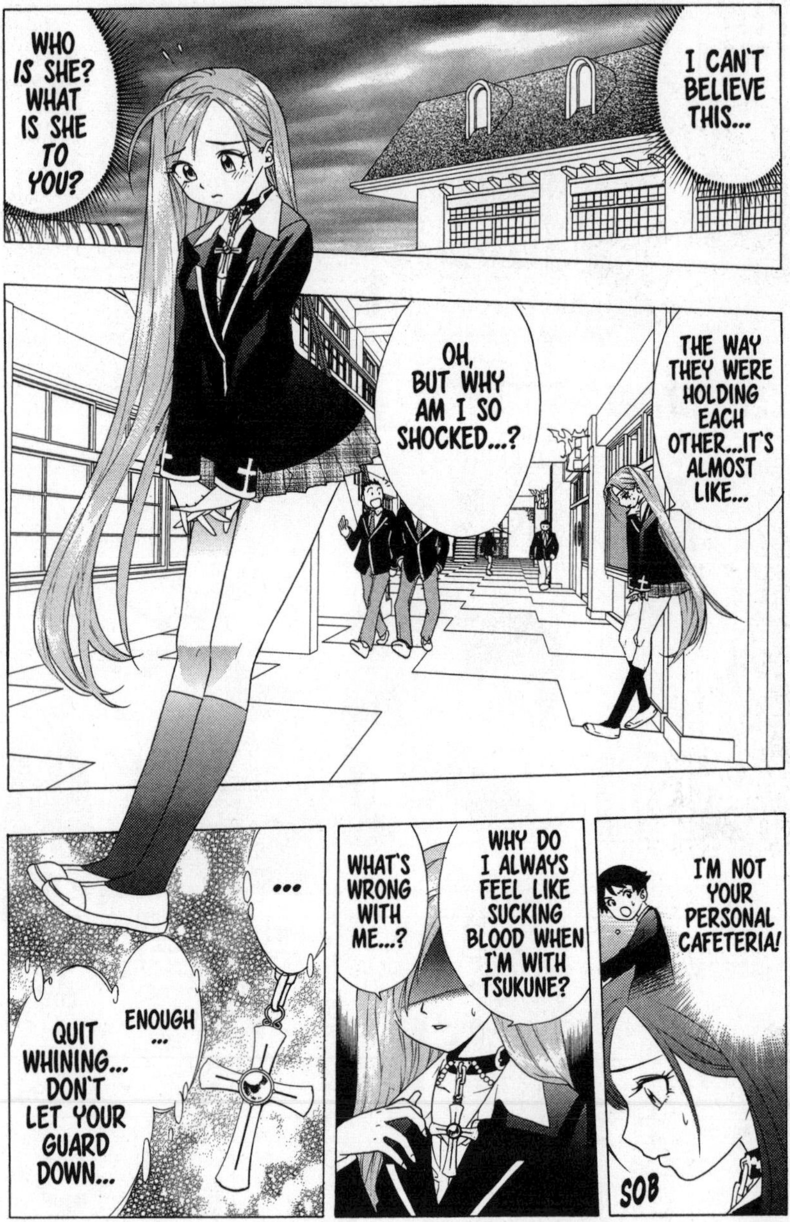
I CAN'T BELIEVE THIS...
WHO IS SHE? WHAT IS SHE TO YOU?
THE WAY THEY WERE HOLDING EACH OTHER...IT'S ALMOST LIKE...
OH, BUT WHY AM I SO SHOCKED...?
I'M NOT YOUR PERSONAL CAFETERIA!
SOB
WHY DO I ALWAYS FEEL LIKE SUCKING BLOOD WHEN I'M WITH TSUKUNE?
WHAT'S WRONG WITH ME...?
...
ENOUGH...
QUIT WHINING... DON'T LET YOUR GUARD DOWN...

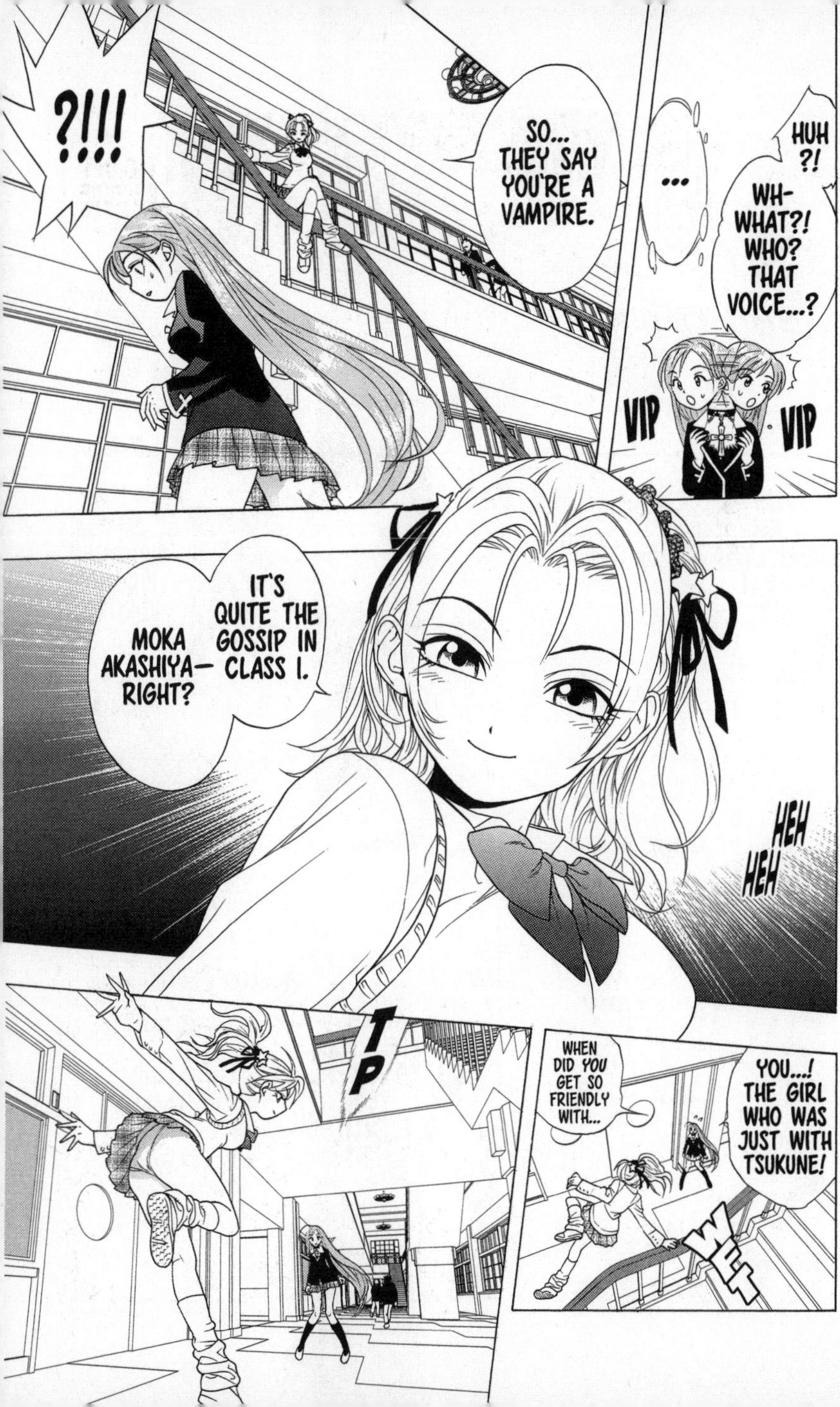
HUH ?!
WH- WHAT?! WHO? THAT VOICE...?
...
VIP
VIP
?!!!
SO... THEY SAY YOU'RE A VAMPIRE.
IT'S QUITE THE GOSSIP IN CLASS 1.
MOKA AKASHIYA— RIGHT?
HEH HEH
YOU...! THE GIRL WHO WAS JUST WITH TSUKUNE!
WHEN DID YOU GET SO FRIENDLY WITH...
WET
TP

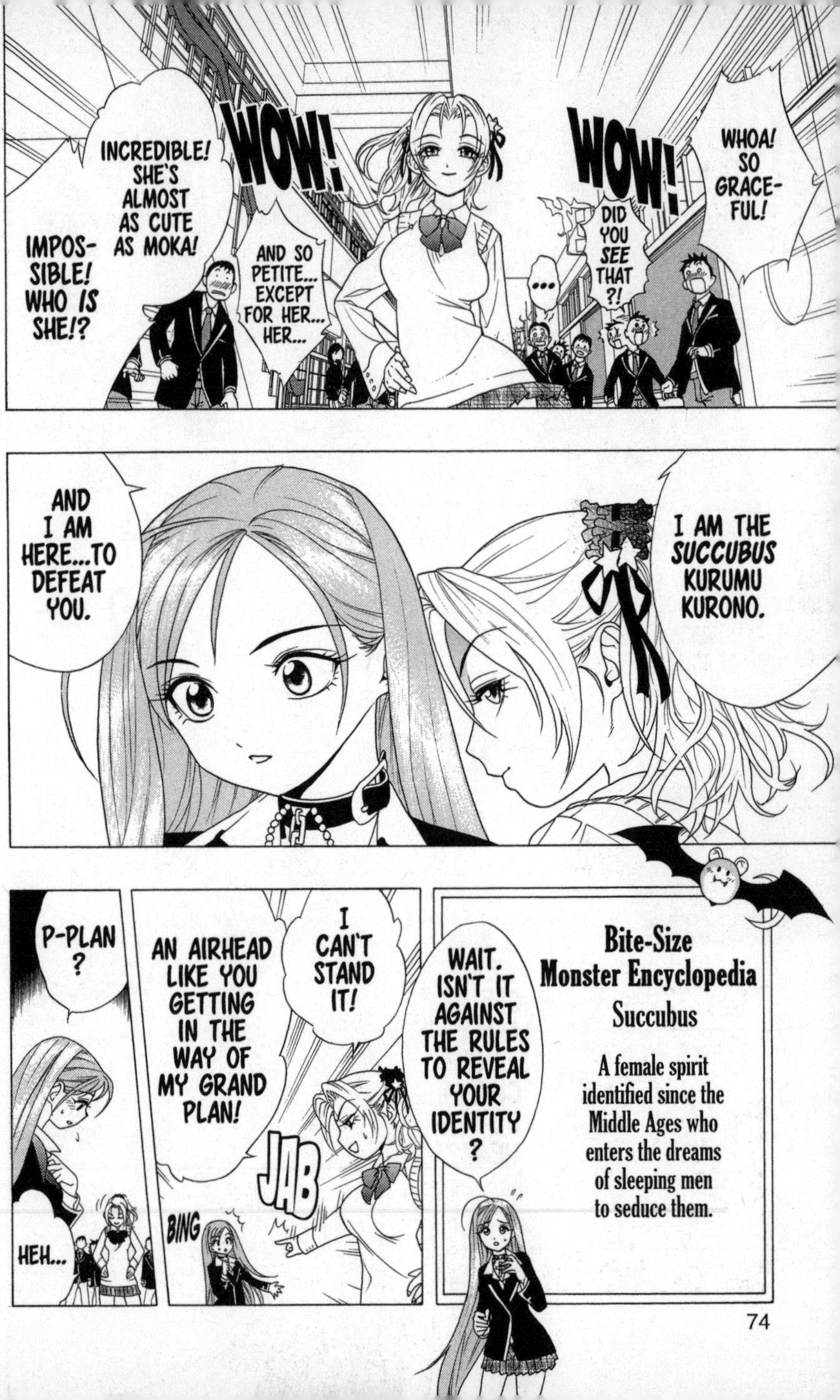
WHOA! SO GRACE-FUL!
WOW!
DID YOU SEE THAT ?!
...
WOW!
AND SO PETITE... EXCEPT FOR HER... HER...
INCREDIBLE! SHE'S ALMOST AS CUTE AS MOKA!
IMPOS-SIBLE! WHO IS SHE!?
I AM THE SUCCUBUS KURUMU KURONO.
AND I AM HERE...TO DEFEAT YOU.
Bite-Size Monster Encyclopedia
Succubus
A female spirit identified since the Middle Ages who enters the dreams of sleeping men to seduce them.
WAIT. ISN'T IT AGAINST THE RULES TO REVEAL YOUR IDENTITY ?
I CAN'T STAND IT!
AN AIRHEAD LIKE YOU GETTING IN THE WAY OF MY GRAND PLAN!
JAB
BING
P-PLAN ?
HEH...

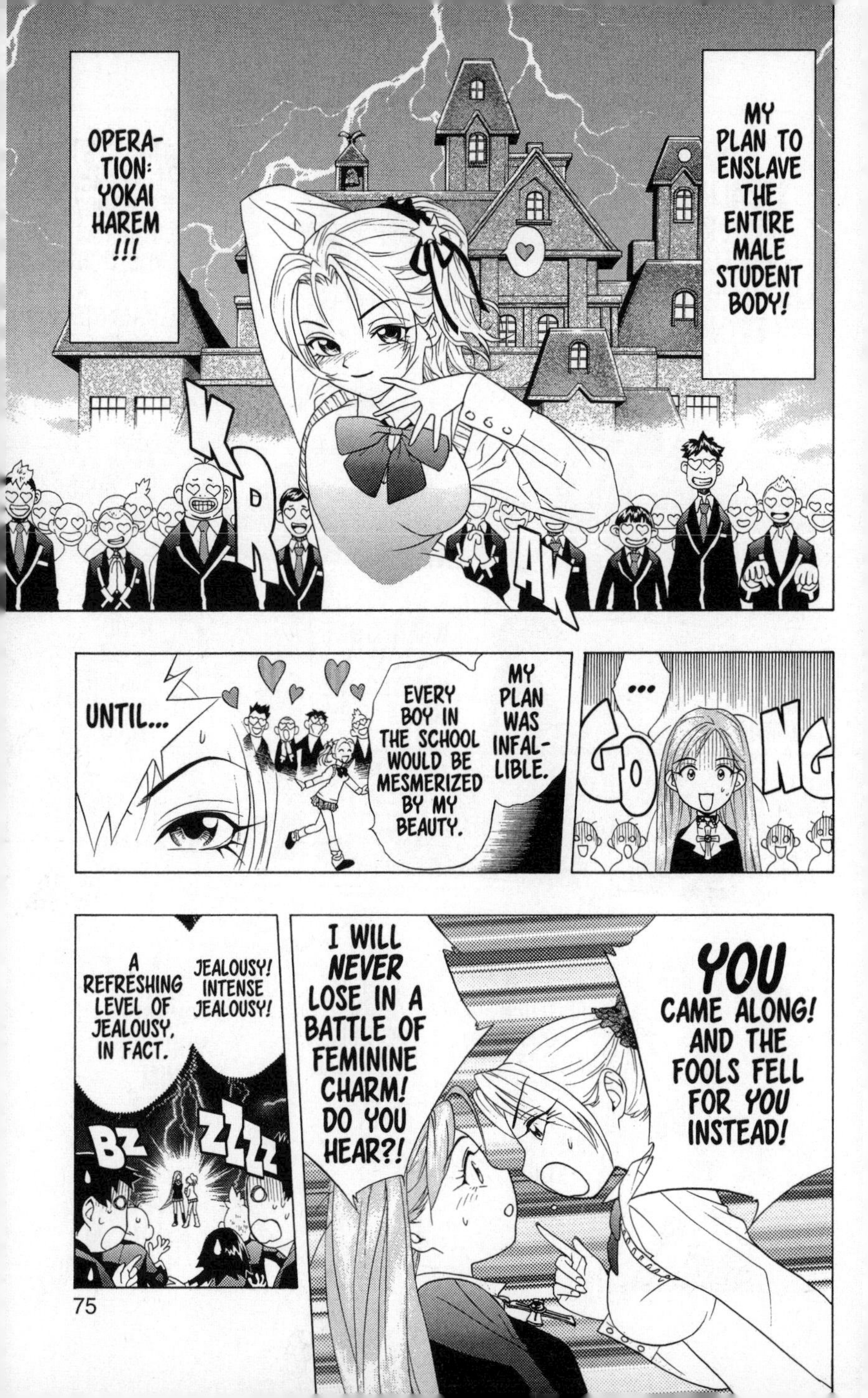
MY PLAN TO ENSLAVE THE ENTIRE MALE STUDENT BODY!
OPERATION: YOKAI HAREM!!!
KRAK
GONG
...
MY PLAN WAS INFALLIBLE.
EVERY BOY IN THE SCHOOL WOULD BE MESMERIZED BY MY BEAUTY.
UNTIL...
YOU CAME ALONG! AND THE FOOLS FELL FOR YOU INSTEAD!
I WILL NEVER LOSE IN A BATTLE OF FEMININE CHARM! DO YOU HEAR?!
JEALOUSY! INTENSE JEALOUSY!
A REFRESHING LEVEL OF JEALOUSY, IN FACT.
Bz
ZZZZ

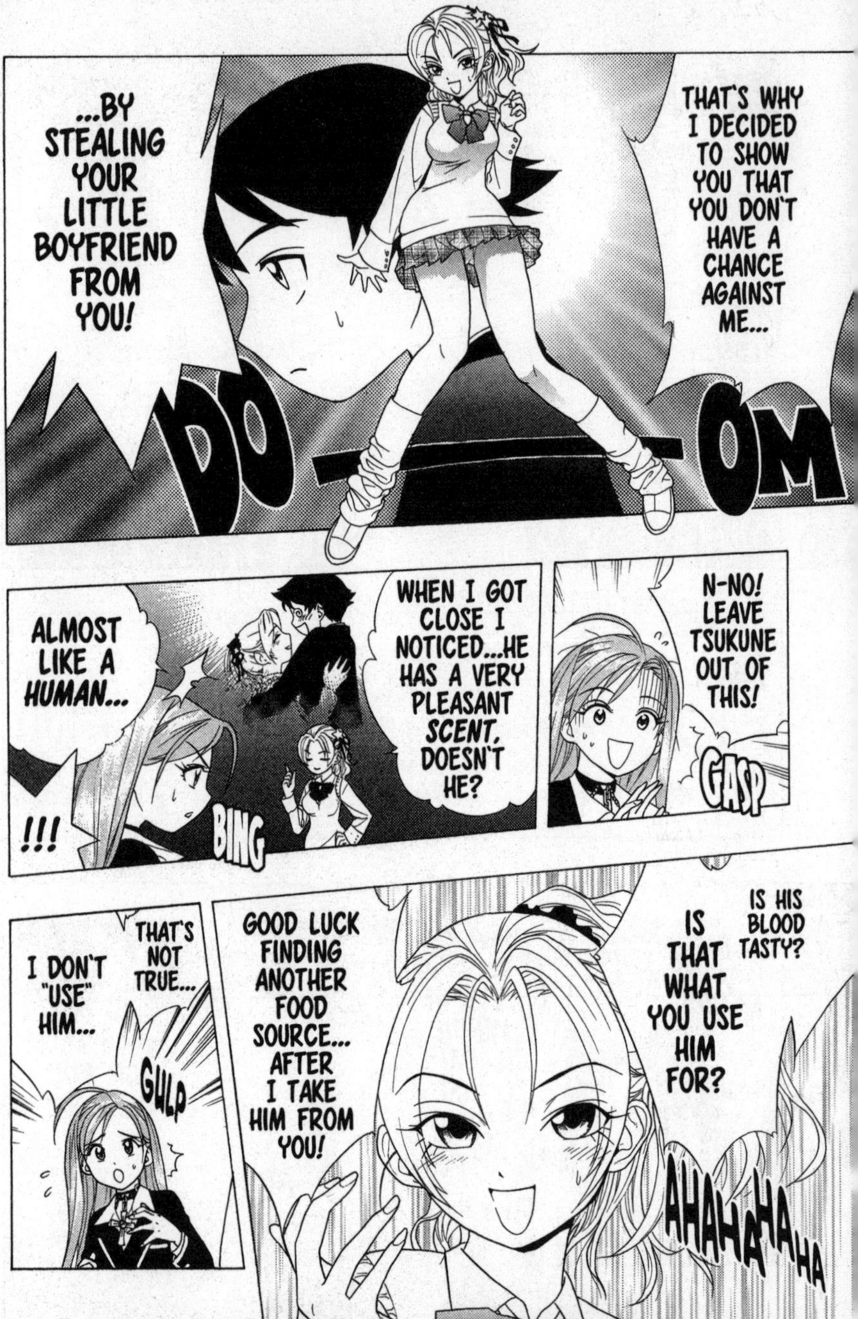
THAT'S WHY I DECIDED TO SHOW YOU THAT YOU DON'T HAVE A CHANCE AGAINST ME...
...BY STEALING YOUR LITTLE BOYFRIEND FROM YOU!
DO—OM
N-NO! LEAVE TSUKUNE OUT OF THIS!
GASP
WHEN I GOT CLOSE I NOTICED...HE HAS A VERY PLEASANT *SCENT,* DOESN'T HE?
ALMOST LIKE A *HUMAN...*
BING
!!!
IS HIS BLOOD TASTY?
IS THAT WHAT YOU USE HIM FOR?
AHAHAHAHAHA
GOOD LUCK FINDING ANOTHER FOOD SOURCE... AFTER I TAKE HIM FROM YOU!
THAT'S NOT TRUE...
I DON'T "USE" HIM...
GULP

READ THIS WAY

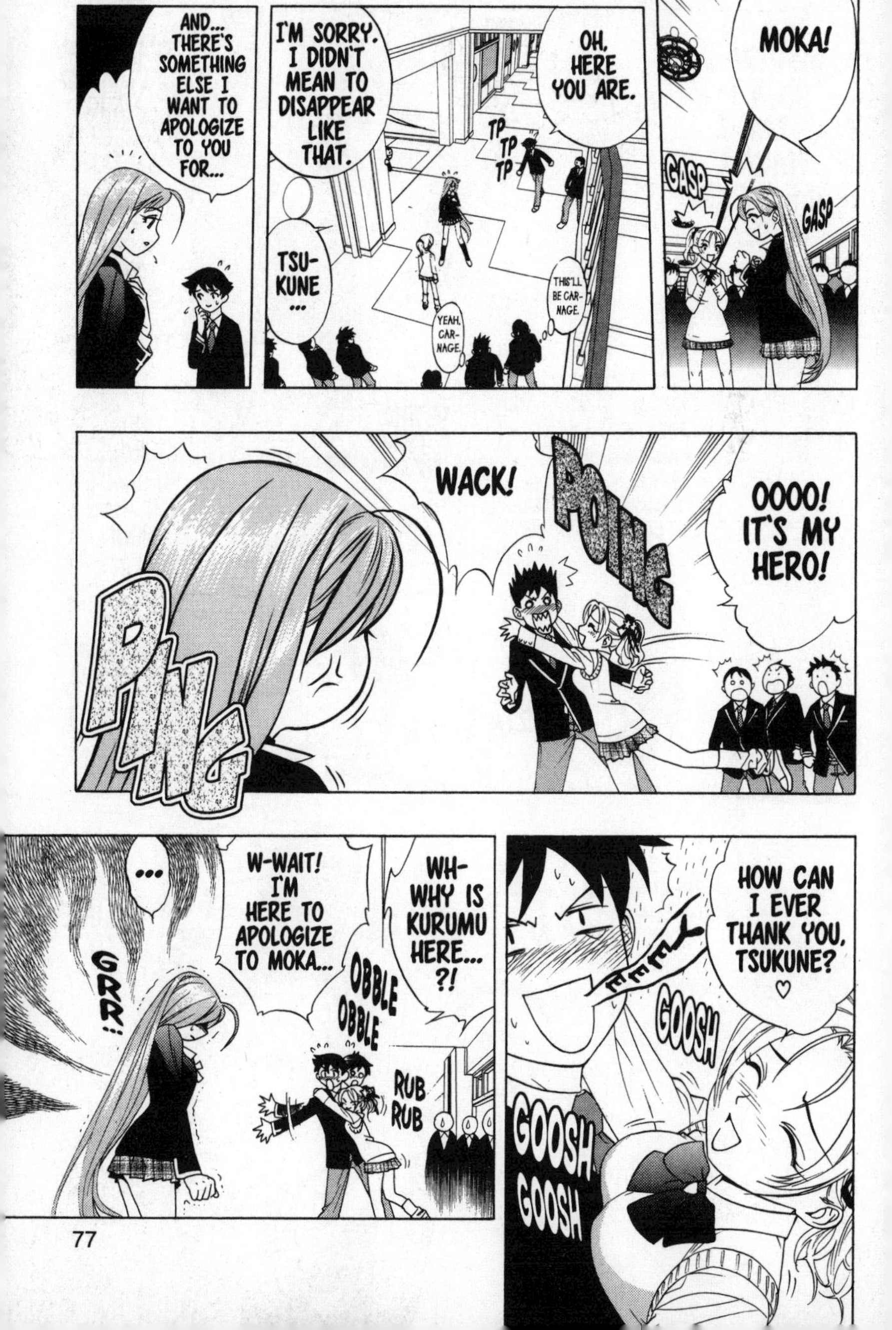
MOKA!
GASP
GASP
OH, HERE YOU ARE.
TP TP TP
THIS'LL BE CARNAGE.
YEAH, CARNAGE.
I'M SORRY. I DIDN'T MEAN TO DISAPPEAR LIKE THAT.
TSUKUNE...
AND... THERE'S SOMETHING ELSE I WANT TO APOLOGIZE TO YOU FOR...
OOOO! IT'S MY HERO!
POING
WACK!
PING
HOW CAN I EVER THANK YOU, TSUKUNE? ♡
GOOSH
GOOSH GOOSH GOOSH
WH-WHY IS KURUMU HERE...?!
W-WAIT! I'M HERE TO APOLOGIZE TO MOKA...
OBBLE OBBLE
RUB RUB
...
GRR...

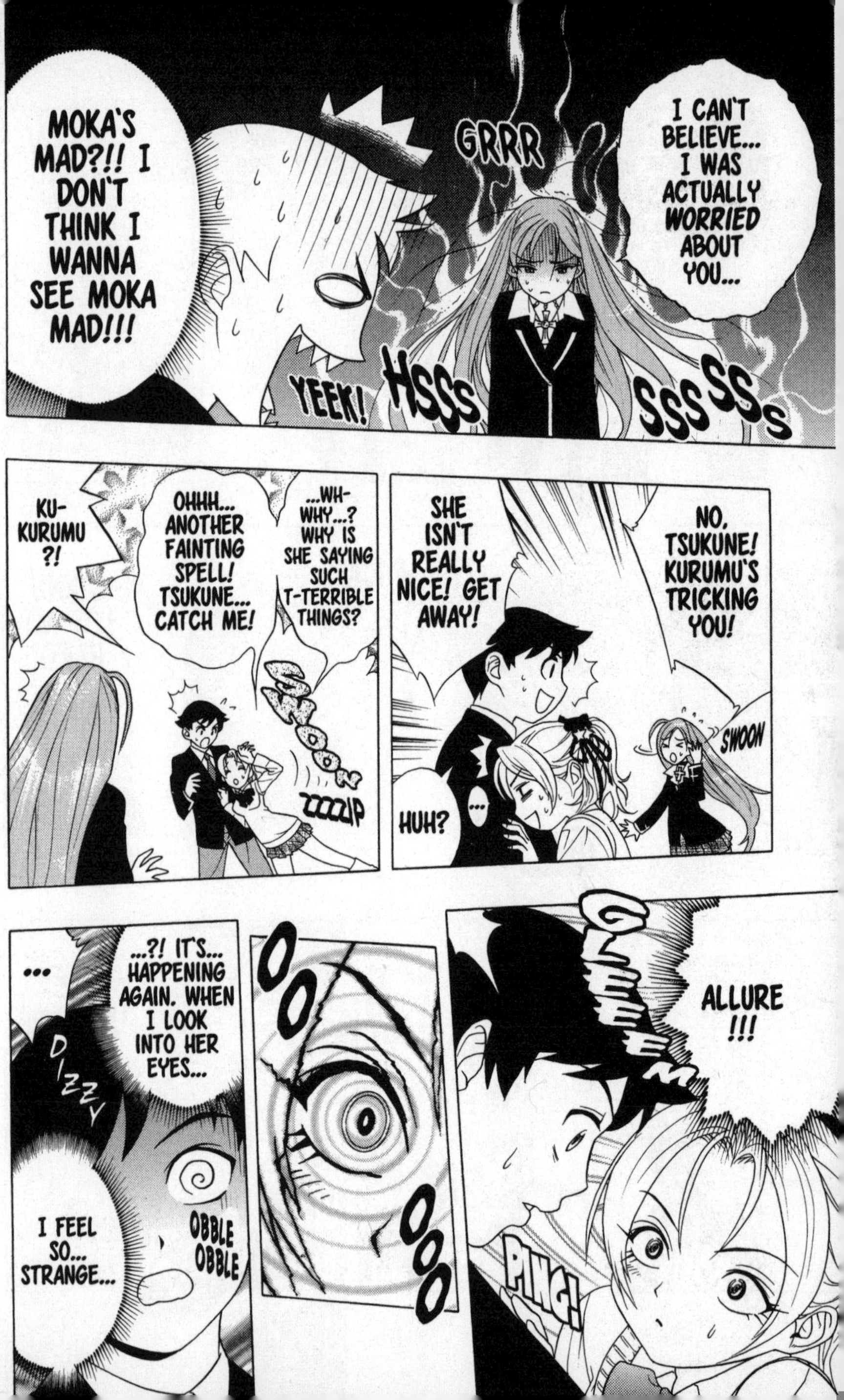
GRRR
I CAN'T BELIEVE... I WAS ACTUALLY WORRIED ABOUT YOU...
MOKA'S MAD?!! I DON'T THINK I WANNA SEE MOKA MAD!!!
YEEK!
HSSS
SSSSSs
NO, TSUKUNE! KURUMU'S TRICKING YOU!
SHE ISN'T REALLY NICE! GET AWAY!
SWOON
...
HUH?
...WH-WHY...? WHY IS SHE SAYING SUCH T-TERRIBLE THINGS?
OHHH... ANOTHER FAINTING SPELL! TSUKUNE... CATCH ME!
KU-KURUMU?!
SWOOON
ZZZZIP
GLEEEM
ALLURE!!!
PING!
OOOOOO
...?! IT'S... HAPPENING AGAIN. WHEN I LOOK INTO HER EYES...
...
DIZZY
I FEEL SO... STRANGE...
OBBLE OBBLE

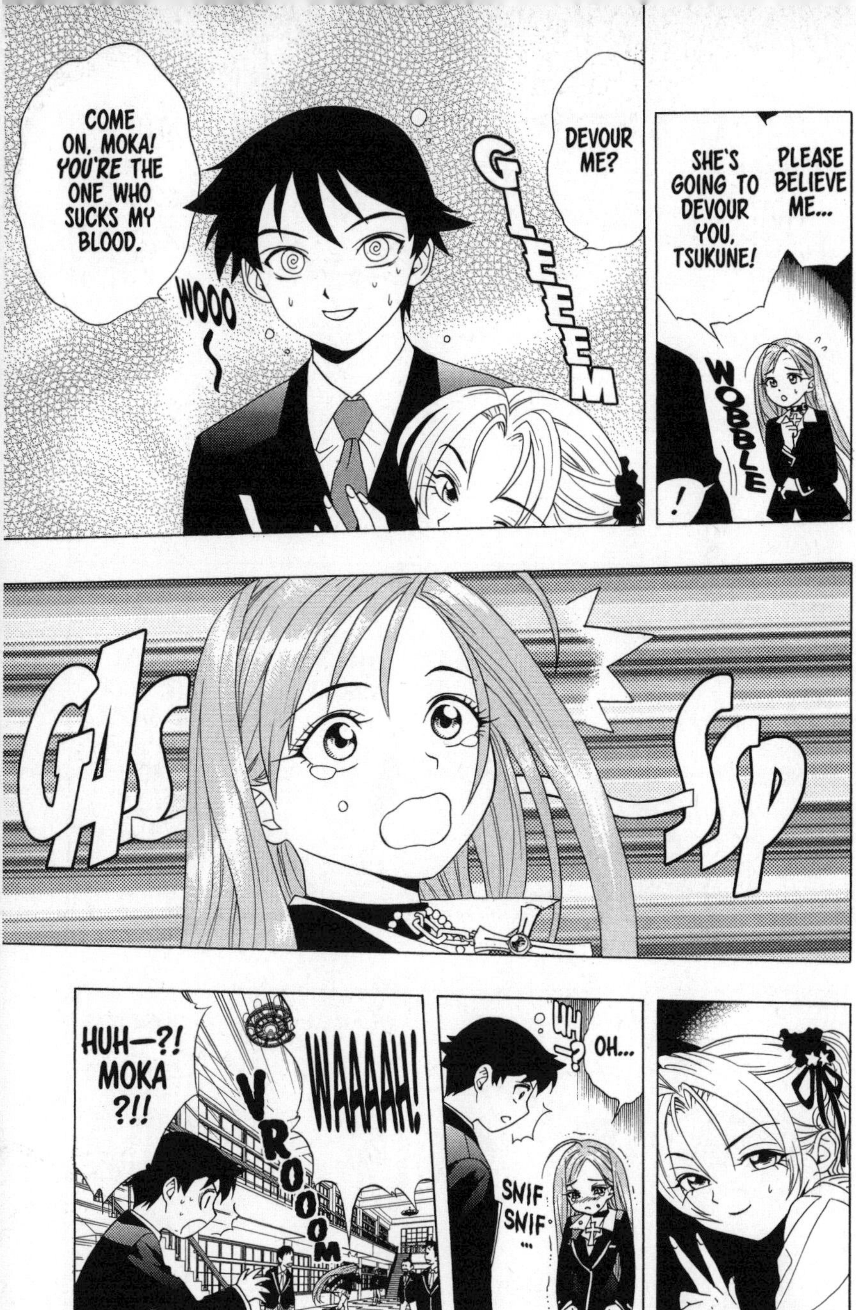
PLEASE BELIEVE ME...
SHE'S GOING TO DEVOUR YOU, TSUKUNE!
WOBBLE
!
DEVOUR ME?
GLEEEM
COME ON, MOKA! YOU'RE THE ONE WHO SUCKS MY BLOOD.
WOOO~
GASSP
OH...
UH—?
SNIF SNIF...
WAAAAH!
HUH—?! MOKA?!!
VROOOM

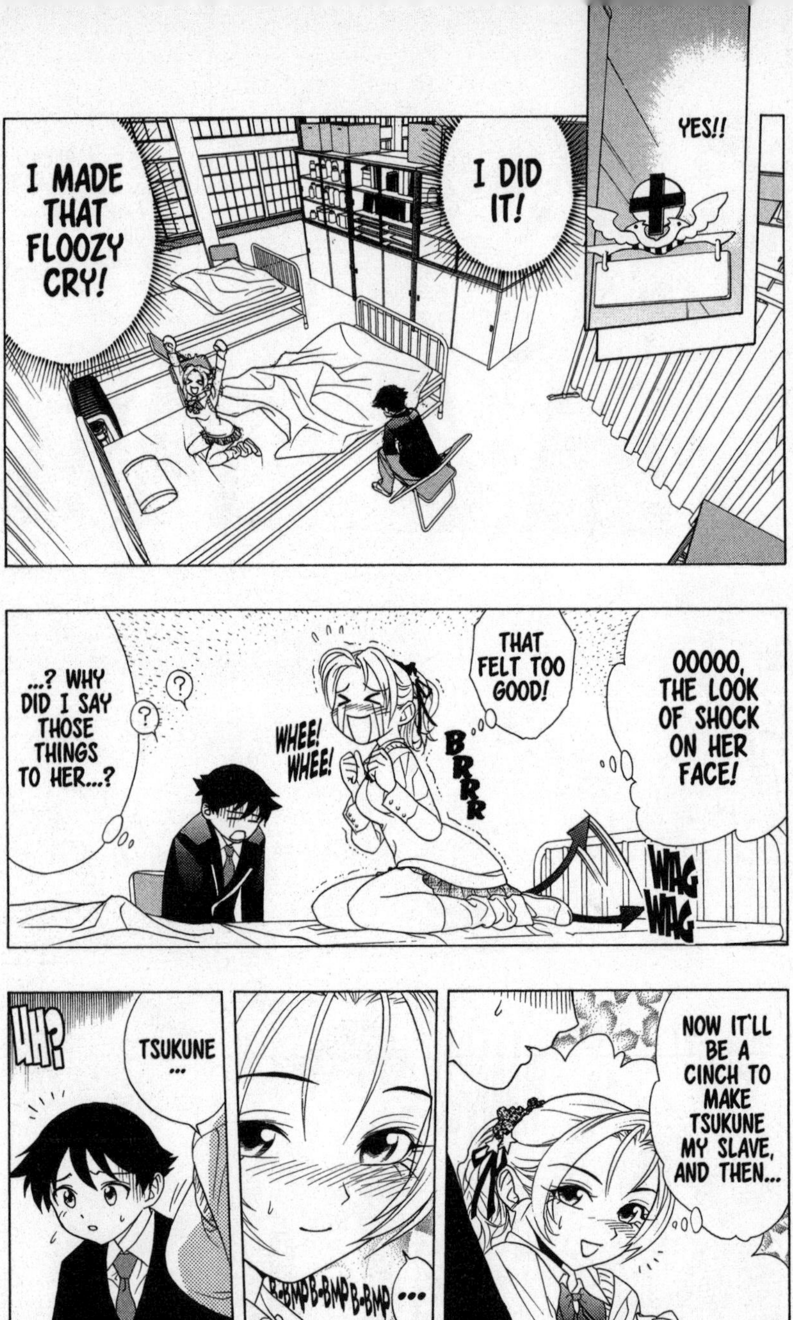
YES!!
I DID IT!
I MADE THAT FLOOZY CRY!
OOOOO, THE LOOK OF SHOCK ON HER FACE!
THAT FELT TOO GOOD!
BRRR
WAG WAG
WHEE! WHEE!
...? WHY DID I SAY THOSE THINGS TO HER...?
NOW IT'LL BE A CINCH TO MAKE TSUKUNE MY SLAVE, AND THEN...
B-BMP B-BMP B-BMP
...
TSUKUNE ...
UH?

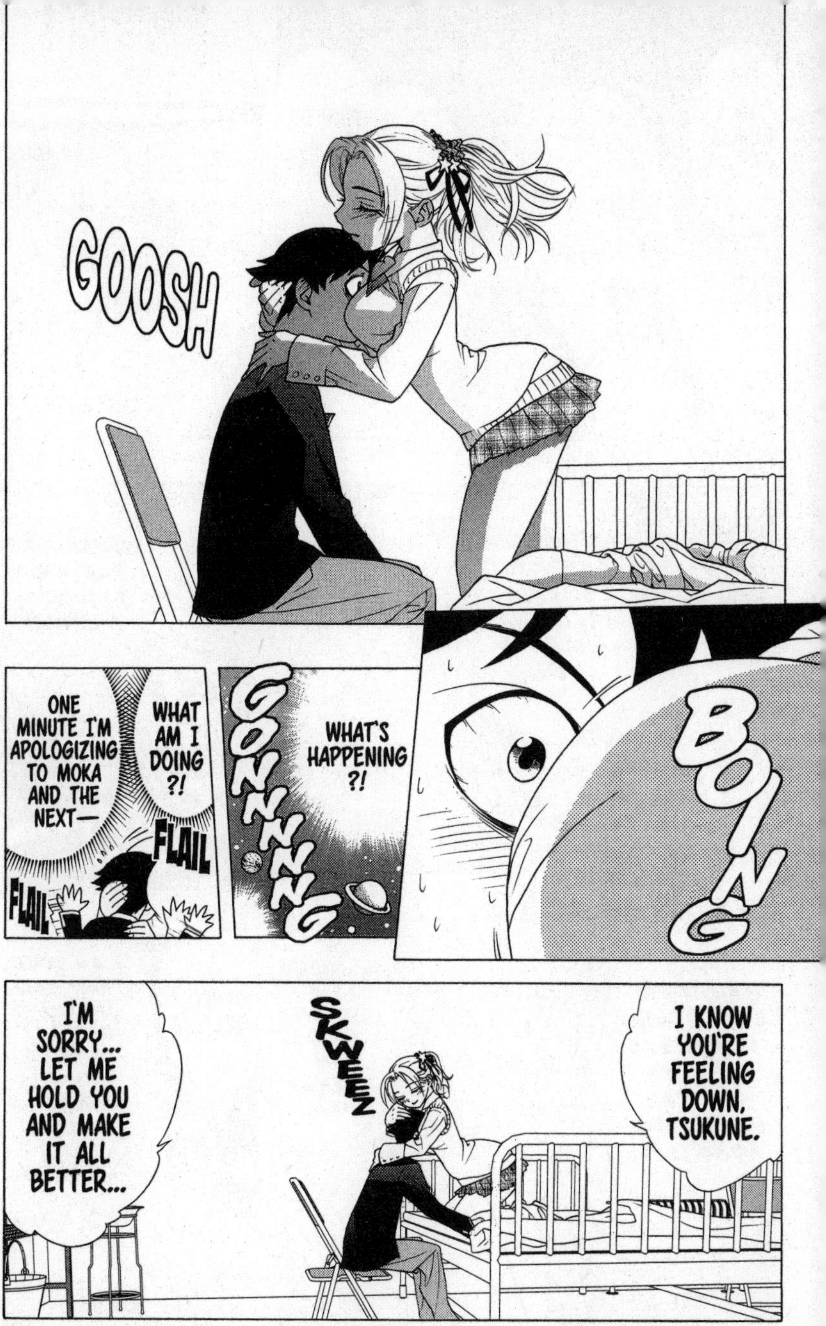
GOOSH
BOING
GONNNNG
WHAT'S HAPPENING ?!
WHAT AM I DOING ?!
ONE MINUTE I'M APOLOGIZING TO MOKA AND THE NEXT—
FLAIL
FLAIL
I KNOW YOU'RE FEELING DOWN, TSUKUNE.
SKWEEZ
I'M SORRY... LET ME HOLD YOU AND MAKE IT ALL BETTER...

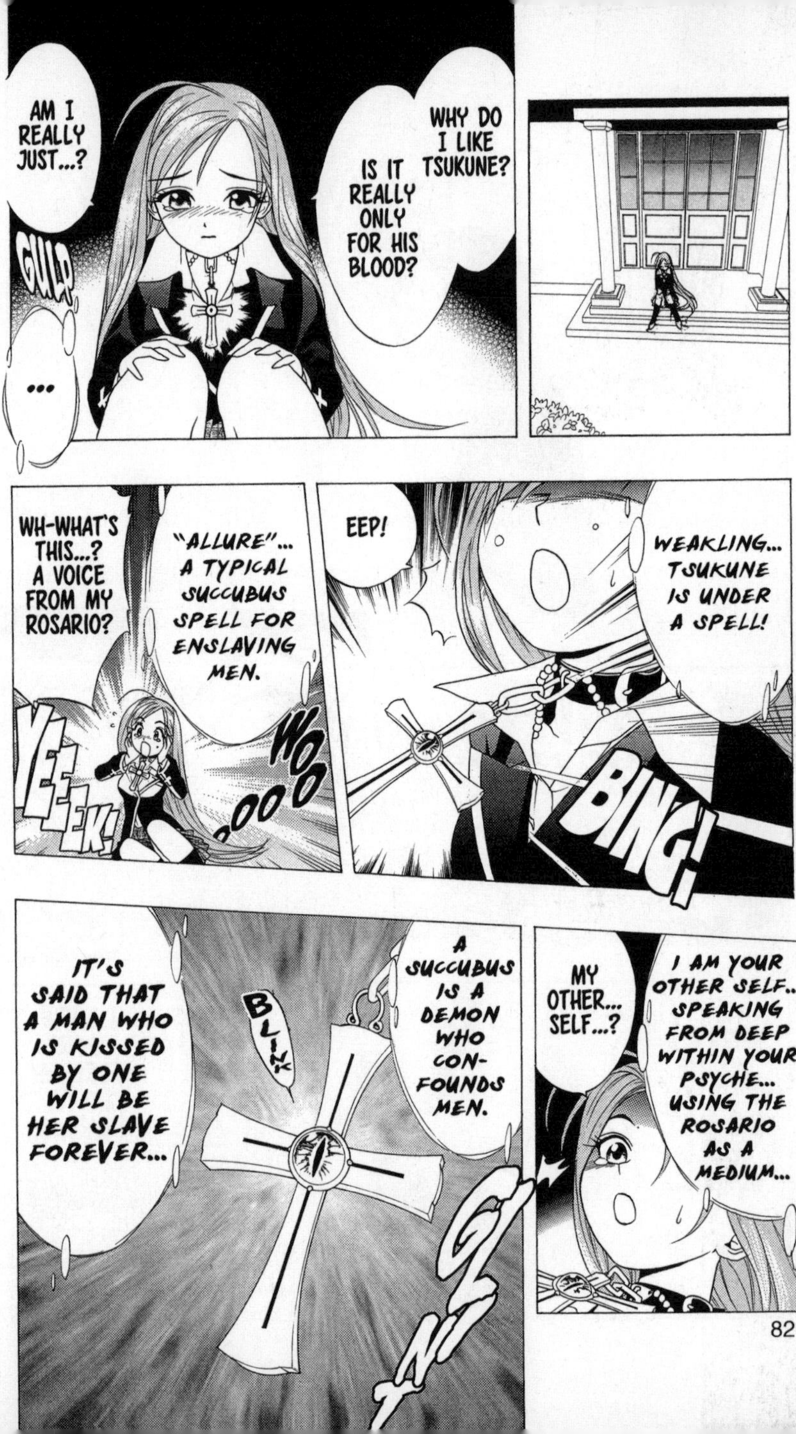
WHY DO I LIKE TSUKUNE?
IS IT REALLY ONLY FOR HIS BLOOD?
AM I REALLY JUST...?
GULP
...
WEAKLING... TSUKUNE IS UNDER A SPELL!
EEP!
BING!
"ALLURE"... A TYPICAL SUCCUBUS SPELL FOR ENSLAVING MEN.
WH-WHAT'S THIS...? A VOICE FROM MY ROSARIO?
YEEEEK!
I AM YOUR OTHER SELF... SPEAKING FROM DEEP WITHIN YOUR PSYCHE... USING THE ROSARIO AS A MEDIUM...
MY OTHER... SELF...?
A SUCCUBUS IS A DEMON WHO CON- FOUNDS MEN.
IT'S SAID THAT A MAN WHO IS KISSED BY ONE WILL BE HER SLAVE FOREVER...
BLINK

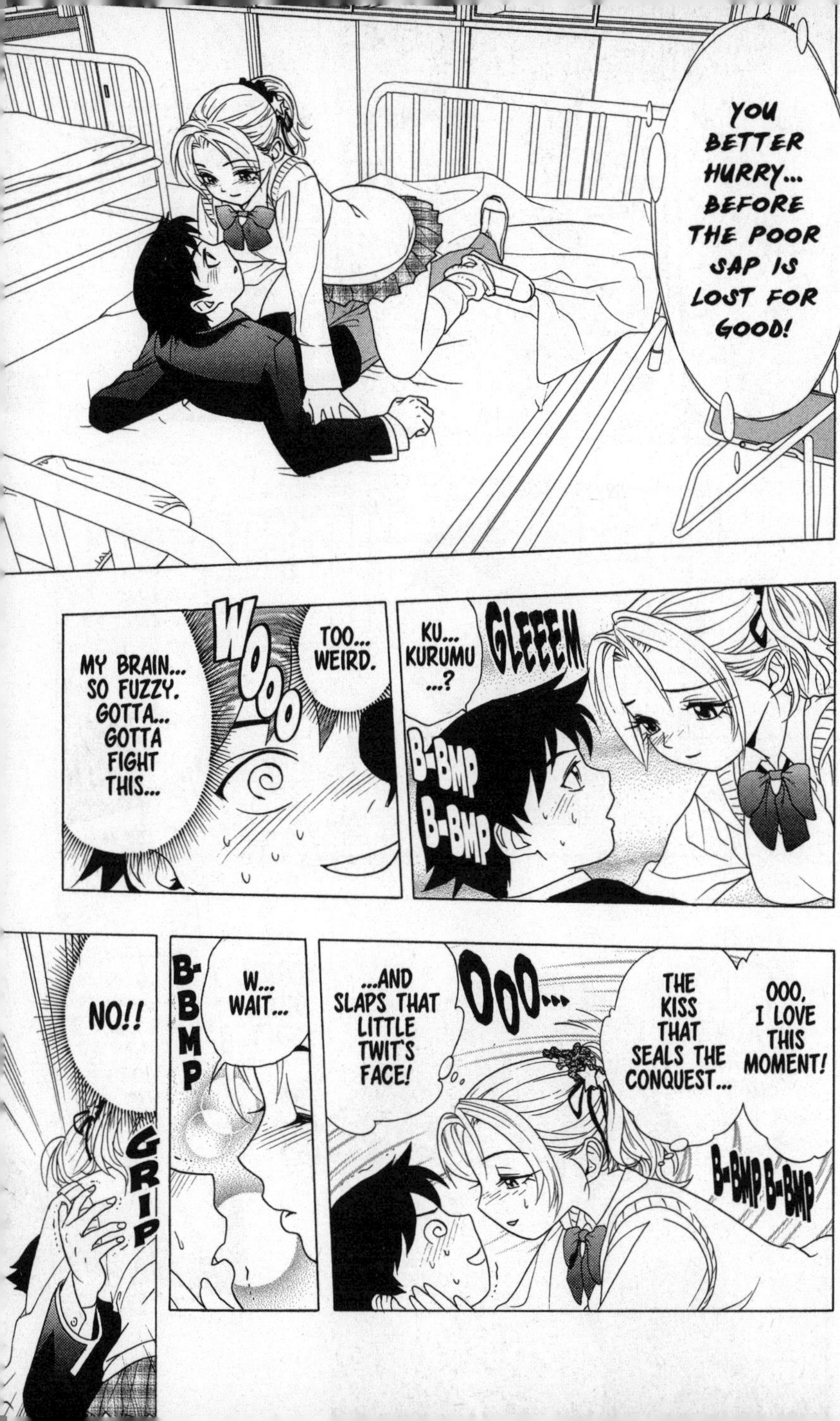
YOU BETTER HURRY... BEFORE THE POOR SAP IS LOST FOR GOOD!
GLEEEM
KU... KURUMU ...?
B-BMP B-BMP
TOO... WEIRD.
WOOOO
MY BRAIN... SO FUZZY. GOTTA... GOTTA FIGHT THIS...
OOO, I LOVE THIS MOMENT!
THE KISS THAT SEALS THE CONQUEST...
OOO...
...AND SLAPS THAT LITTLE TWIT'S FACE!
B-BMP B-BMP
W... WAIT...
B-BMP
NO!!
GRIP

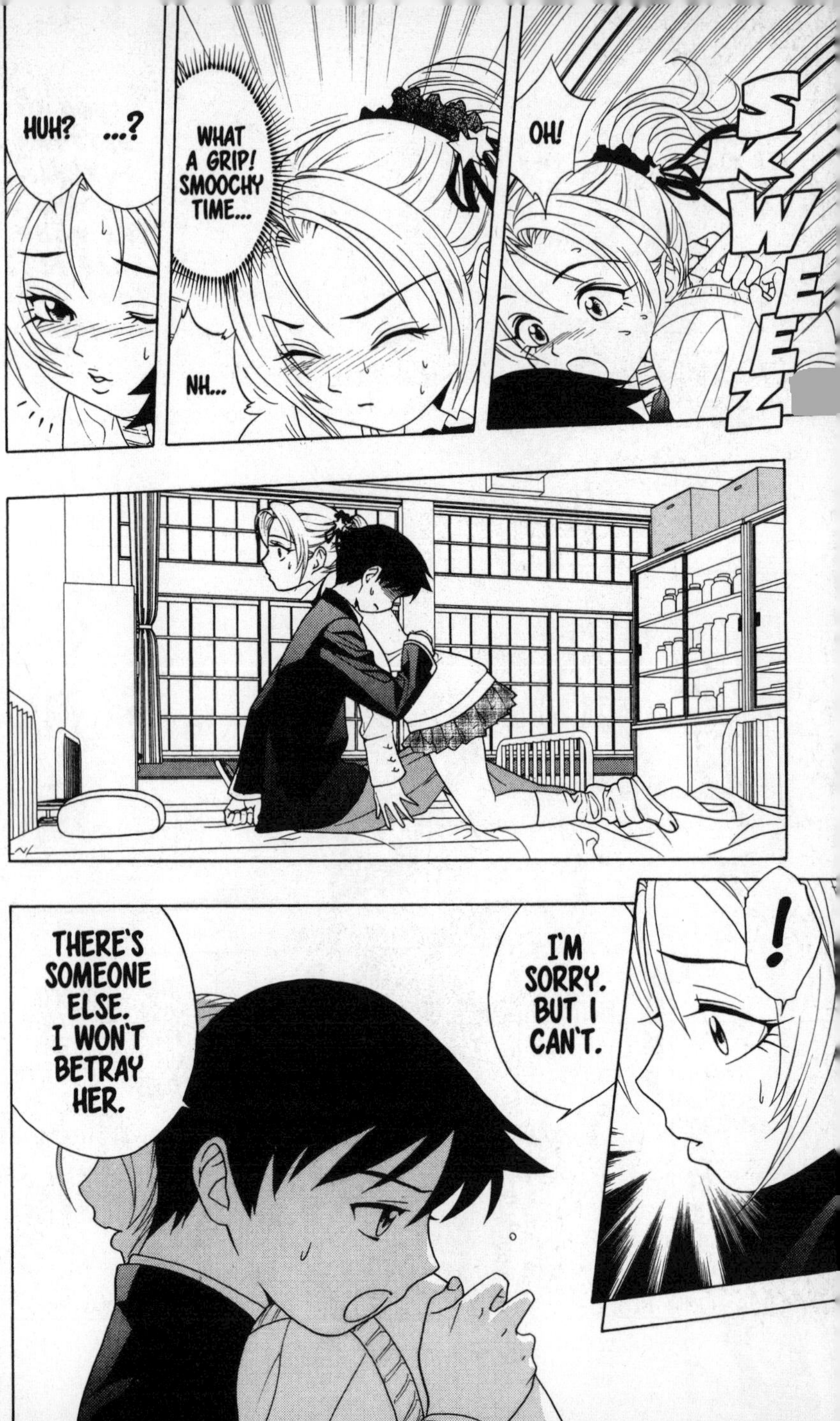
OH!
SKWEEZ
WHAT A GRIP! SMOOCHY TIME...
NH...
HUH? ...?
!
I'M SORRY. BUT I CAN'T.
THERE'S SOMEONE ELSE. I WON'T BETRAY HER.

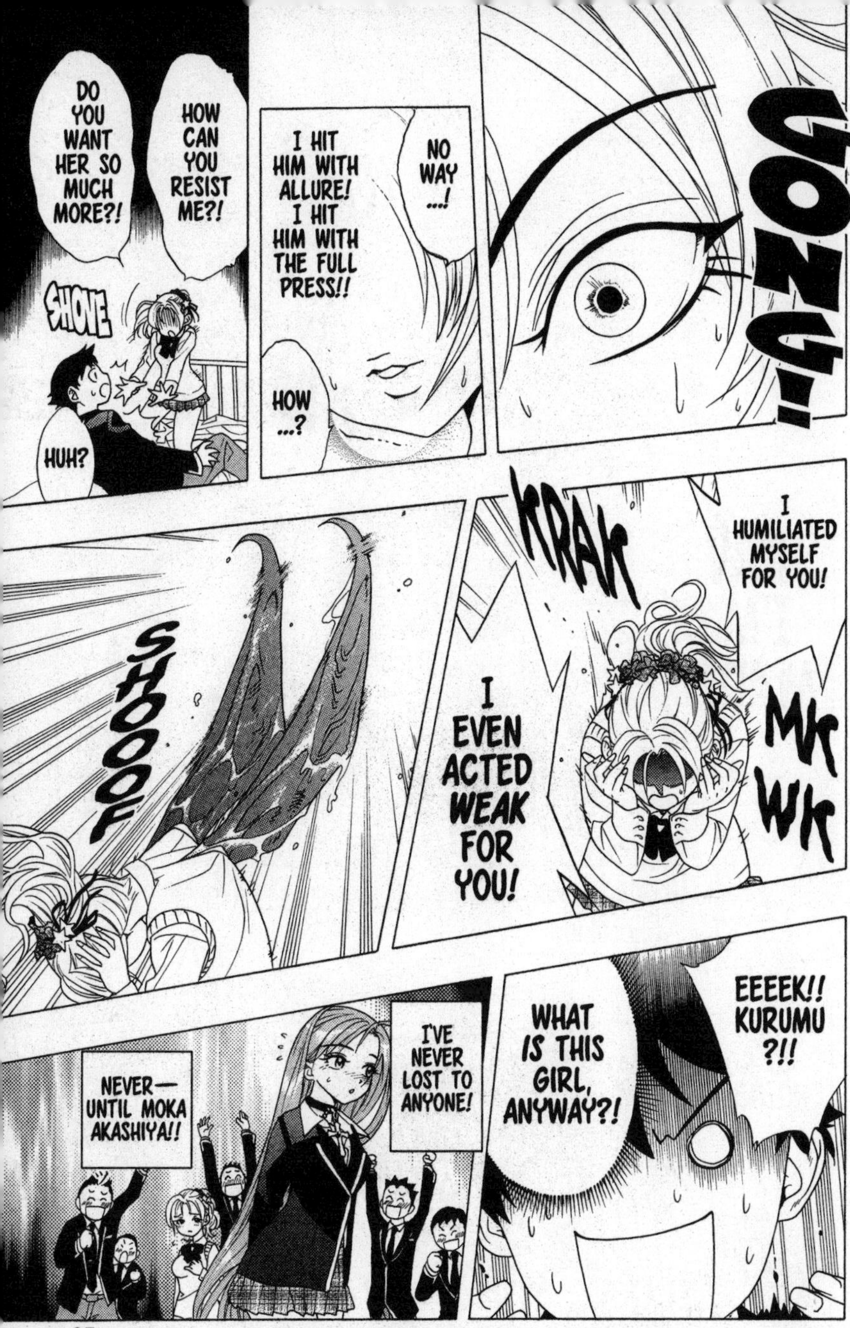
GONG!!
NO WAY ...!
I HIT HIM WITH ALLURE! I HIT HIM WITH THE FULL PRESS!!
HOW ...?
HOW CAN YOU RESIST ME?!
DO YOU WANT HER SO MUCH MORE?!
SHOVE
HUH?
I HUMILIATED MYSELF FOR YOU!
KRAK
MK WK
I EVEN ACTED WEAK FOR YOU!
SHOOOOF
EEEEK!! KURUMU ?!!
WHAT IS THIS GIRL, ANYWAY?!
I'VE NEVER LOST TO ANYONE!
NEVER— UNTIL MOKA AKASHIYA!!

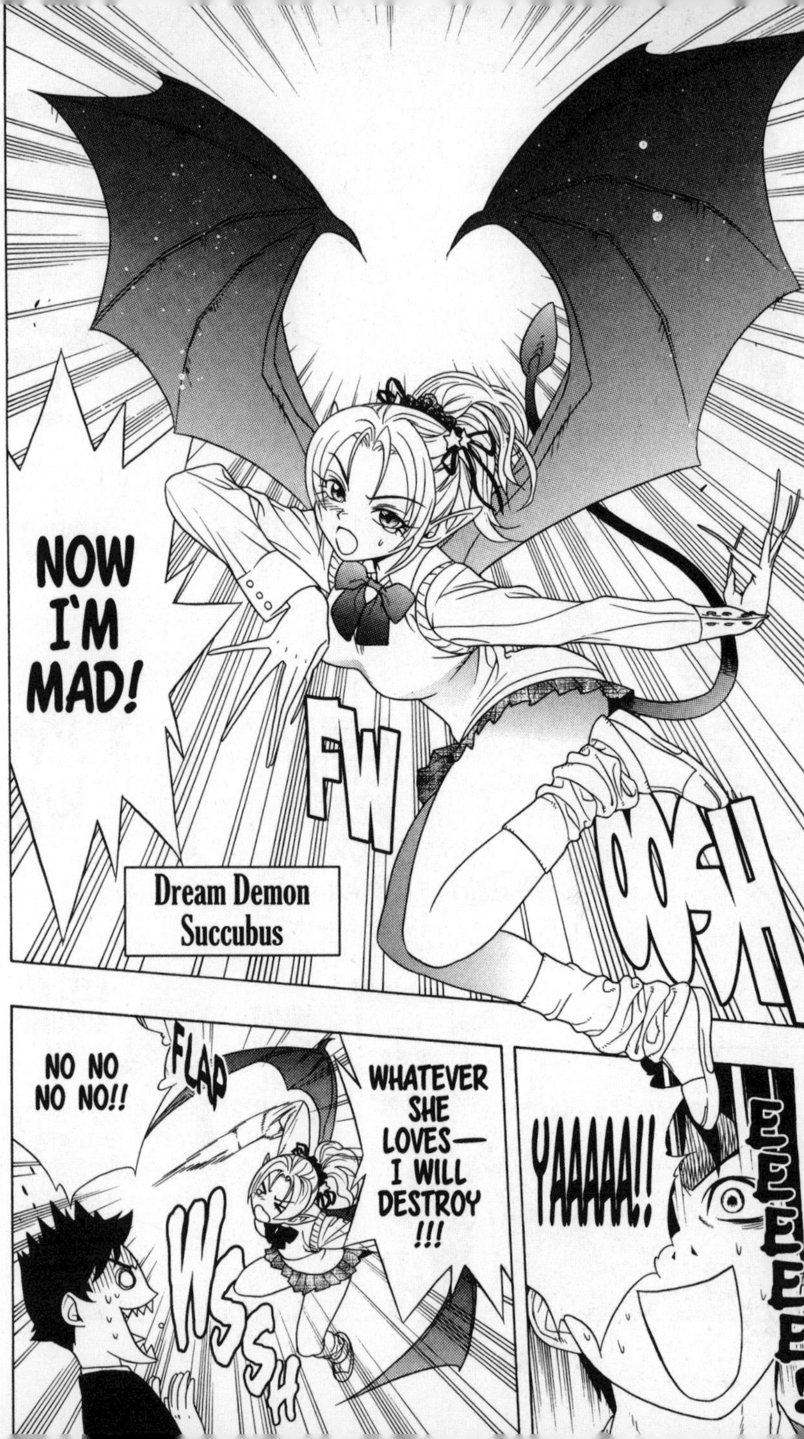
NOW I'M MAD!
FW
OOSH
Dream Demon Succubus
YAAAAA!!
EEEEE...!
WHATEVER SHE LOVES— I WILL DESTROY!!!
FLAP
NO NO NO NO!!
WSSH

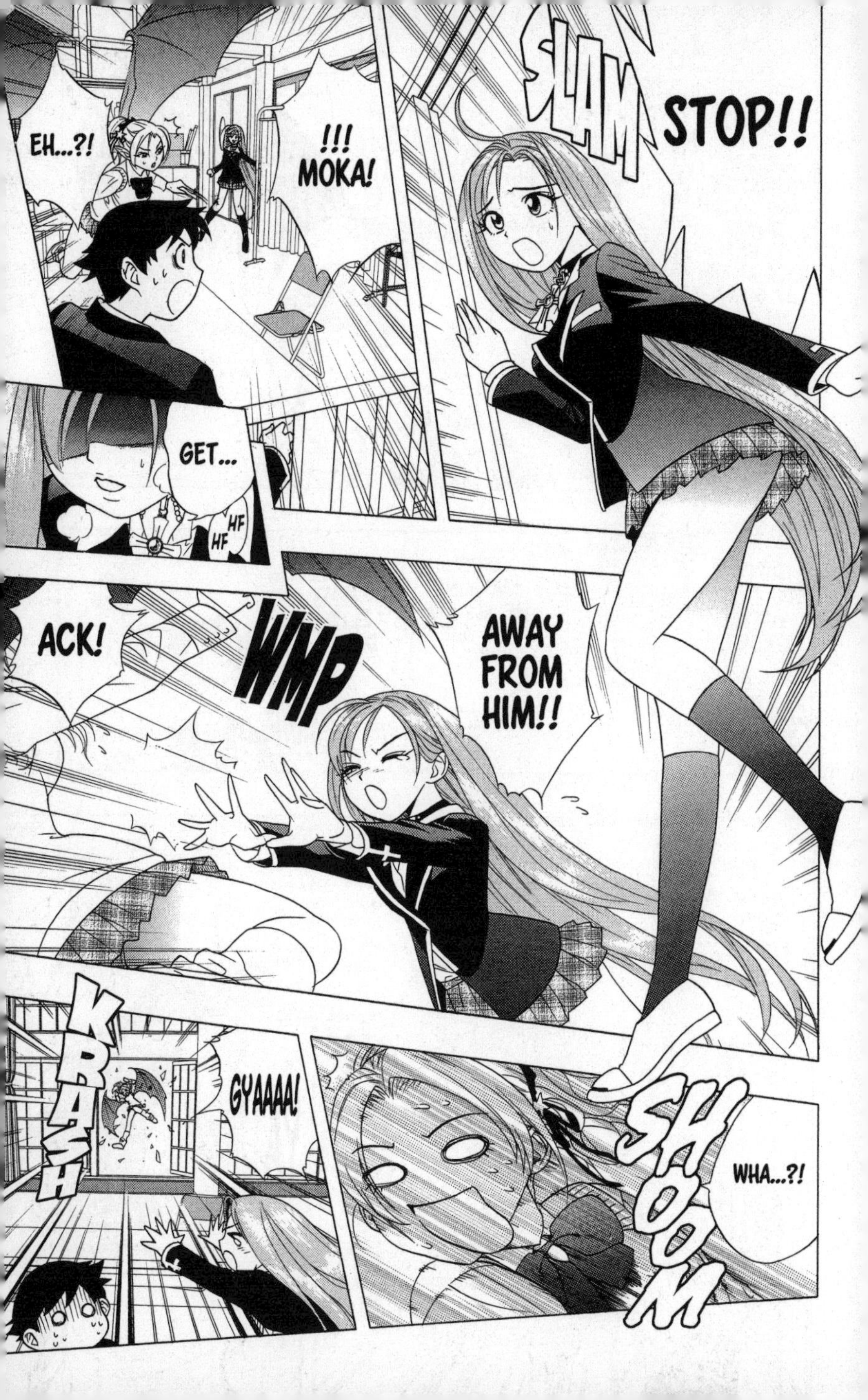
SLAM
STOP!!
!!! MOKA!
EH...?!
GET...
HF HF
AWAY FROM HIM!!
WMP
ACK!
SHOOM
WHA...?!
GYAAAA!
KRASH

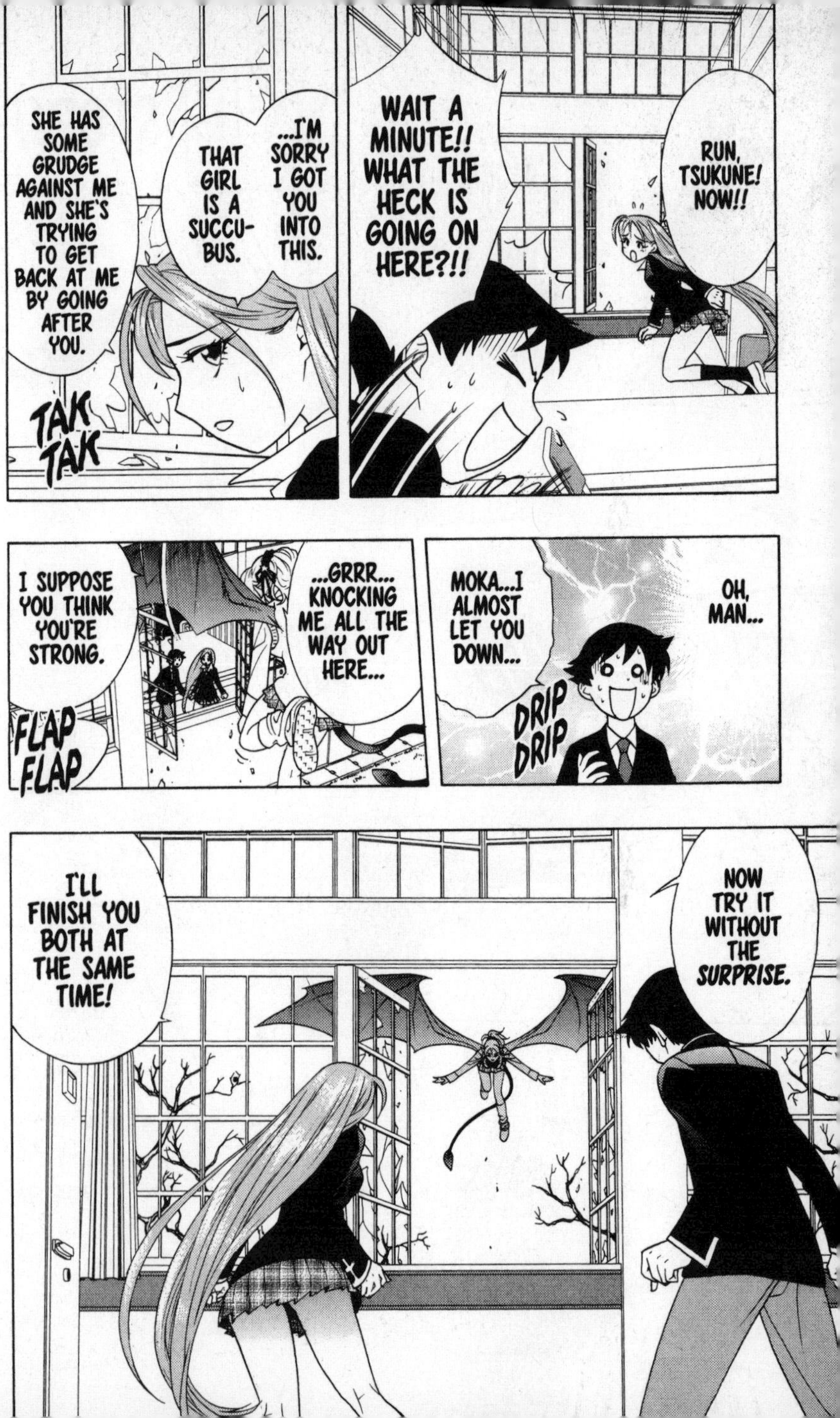
RUN, TSUKUNE! NOW!!
WAIT A MINUTE!! WHAT THE HECK IS GOING ON HERE?!!
...I'M SORRY I GOT YOU INTO THIS.
THAT GIRL IS A SUCCU-BUS.
SHE HAS SOME GRUDGE AGAINST ME AND SHE'S TRYING TO GET BACK AT ME BY GOING AFTER YOU.
TAK TAK
OH, MAN...
MOKA...I ALMOST LET YOU DOWN...
DRIP DRIP
...GRRR... KNOCKING ME ALL THE WAY OUT HERE...
I SUPPOSE YOU THINK YOU'RE STRONG.
FLAP FLAP
NOW TRY IT WITHOUT THE SURPRISE.
I'LL FINISH YOU BOTH AT THE SAME TIME!

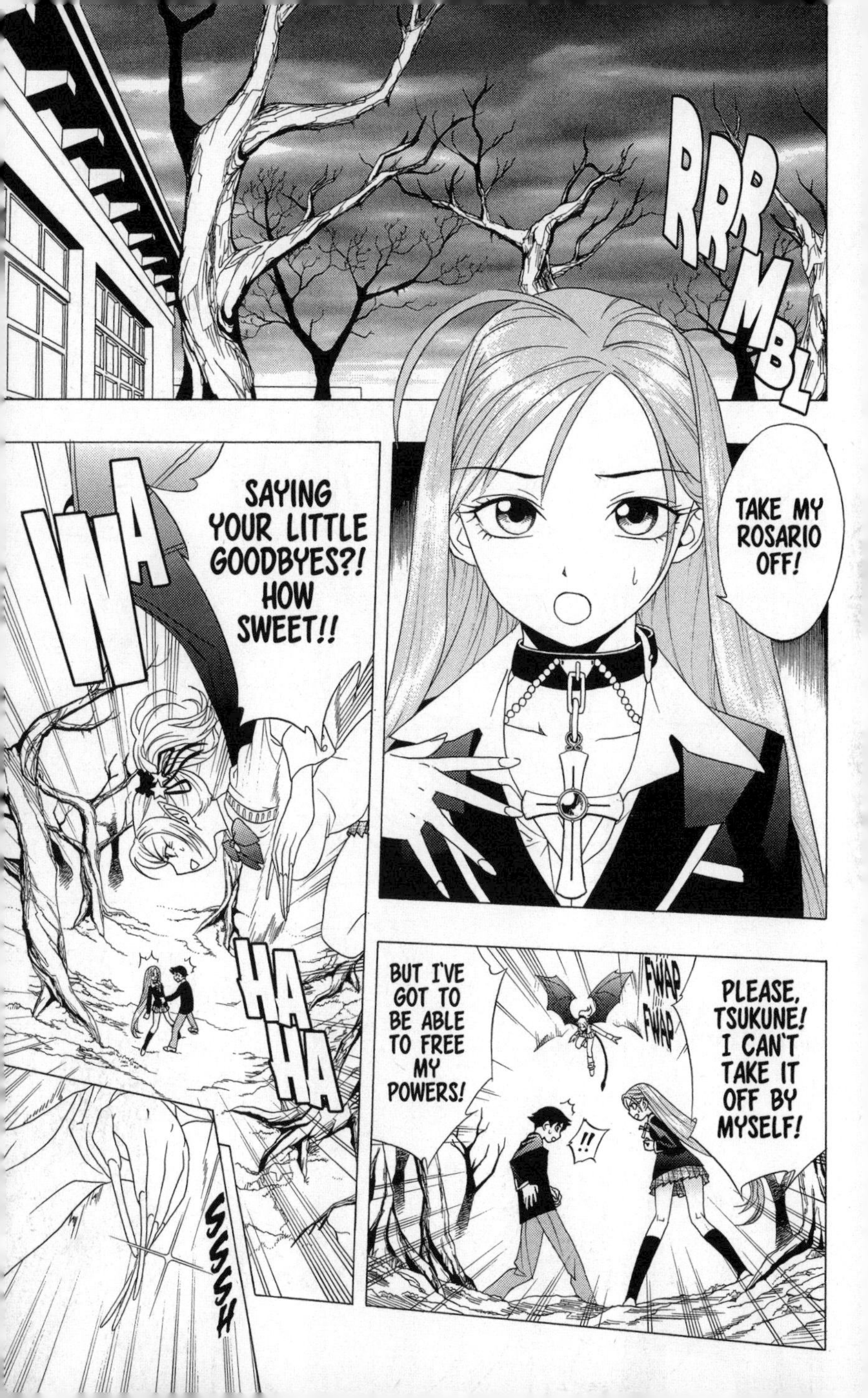
RRRMBL
TAKE MY ROSARIO OFF!
PLEASE, TSUKUNE! I CAN'T TAKE IT OFF BY MYSELF!
FWAP FWAP
BUT I'VE GOT TO BE ABLE TO FREE MY POWERS!
!!
WAA
SAYING YOUR LITTLE GOODBYES?! HOW SWEET!!
HAHAHA
SSSSH

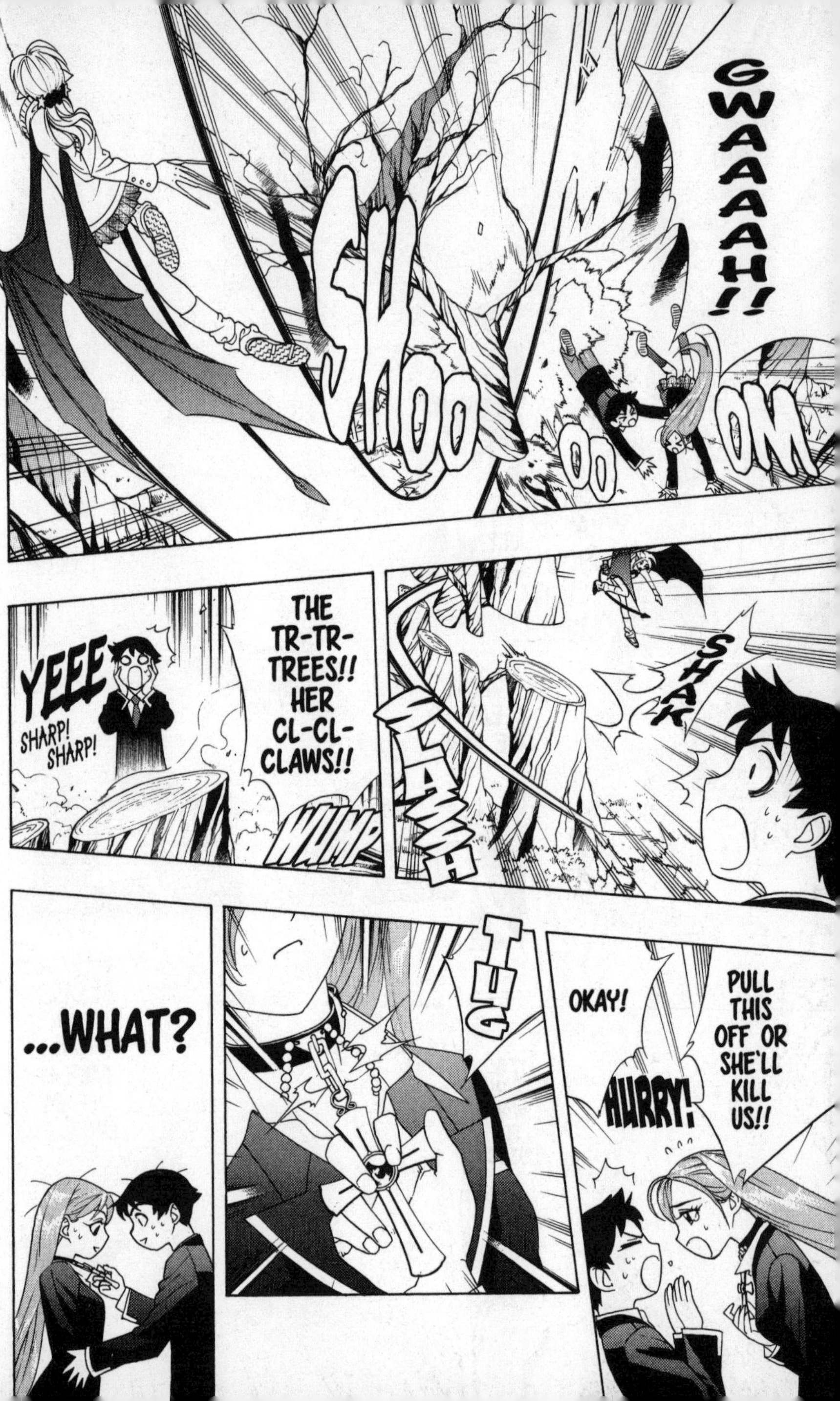
GWAAAAH!!
SHOOOOOM
SHAK
SLAMSH
WUMP
THE TR-TR-TREES!! HER CL-CL-CLAWS!!
YEEE
SHARP! SHARP!
PULL THIS OFF OR SHE'LL KILL US!!
OKAY!
HURRY!
TUG
...WHAT?

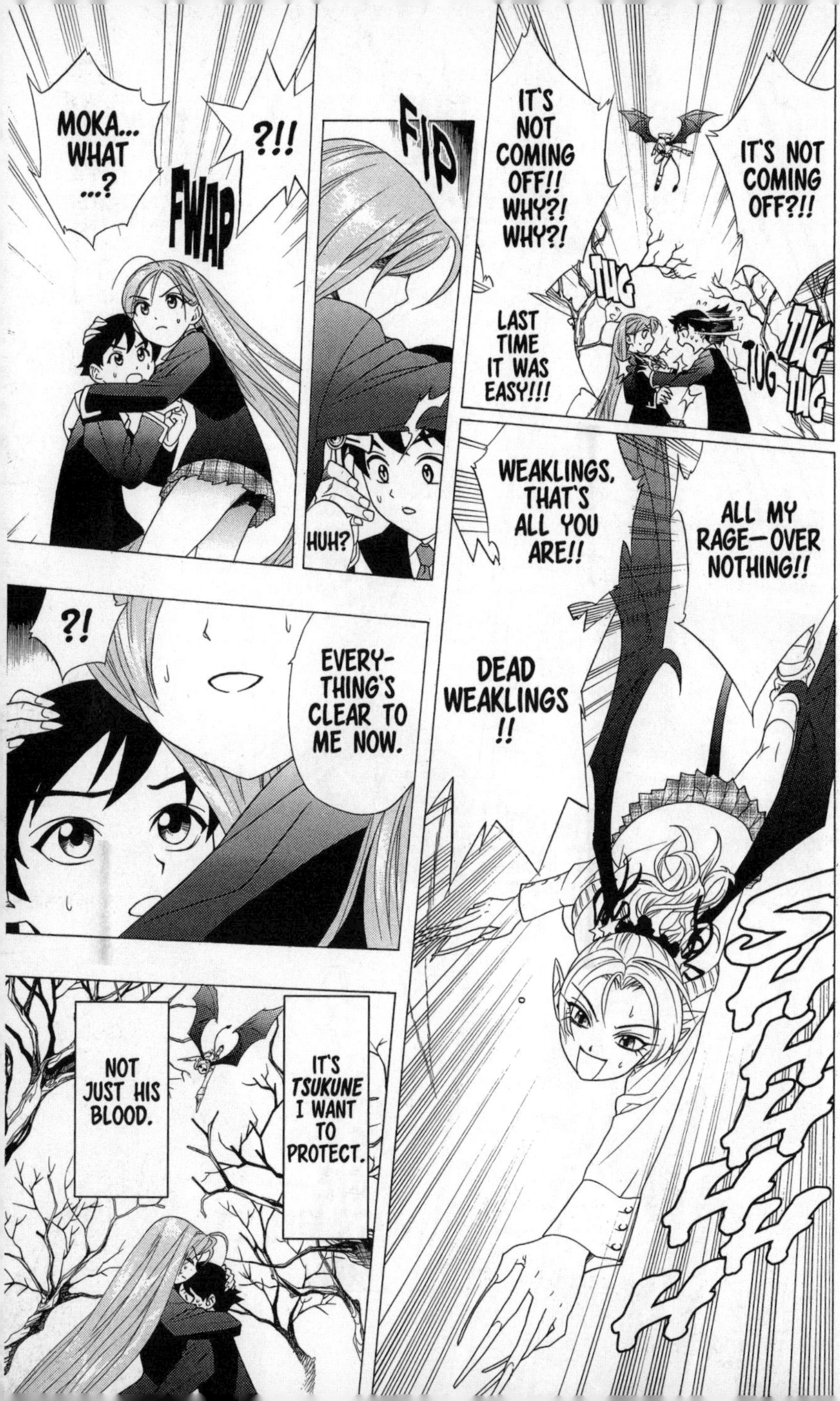

IT'S NOT COMING OFF?!!
IT'S NOT COMING OFF!! WHY?! WHY?!
TUG
TUG TUG
TUG
LAST TIME IT WAS EASY!!!
FIP
HUH?
?!!
MOKA... WHAT ...?
FWAP
ALL MY RAGE—OVER NOTHING!!
WEAKLINGS, THAT'S ALL YOU ARE!!
DEAD WEAKLINGS !!
EVERY-THING'S CLEAR TO ME NOW.
?!
IT'S *TSUKUNE* I WANT TO PROTECT.
NOT JUST HIS BLOOD.

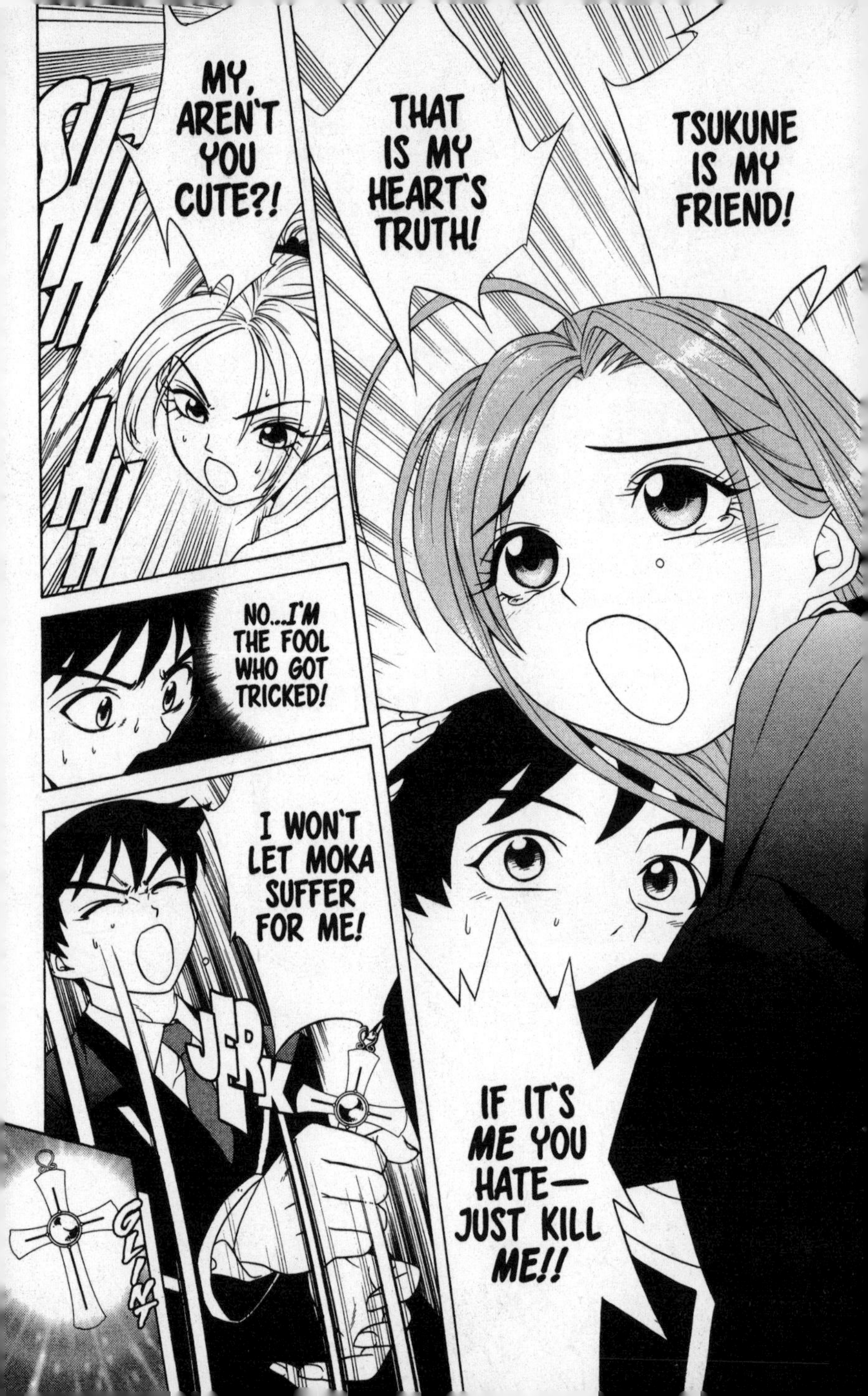
TSUKUNE IS MY FRIEND!
THAT IS MY HEART'S TRUTH!
IF IT'S *ME* YOU HATE— JUST KILL *ME*!!
MY, AREN'T YOU CUTE?!
NO...*I'M* THE FOOL WHO GOT TRICKED!
I WON'T LET MOKA SUFFER FOR ME!
JERK
GLINT

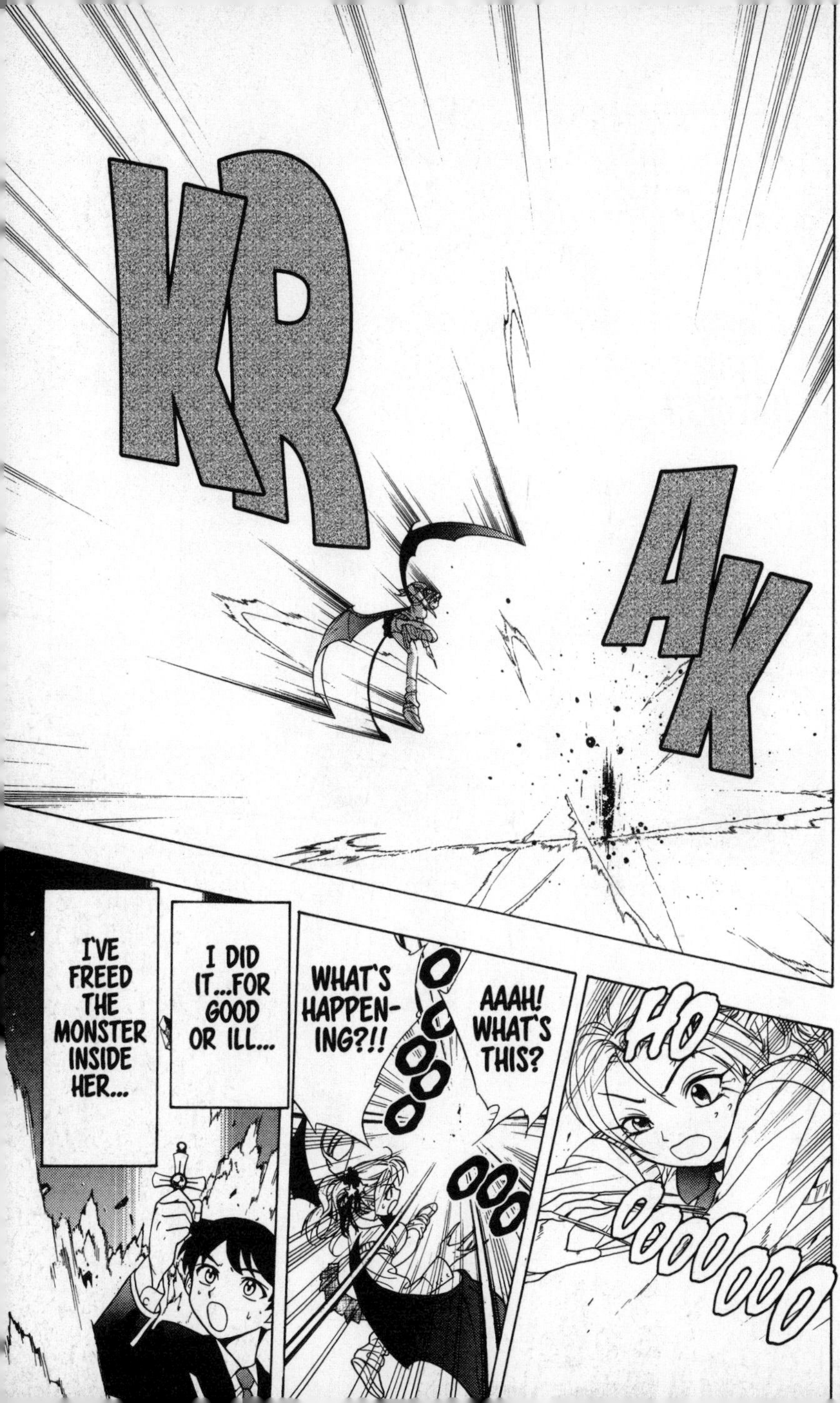
KRAK
HO
AAAH! WHAT'S THIS?
OOOOOOO
WHAT'S HAPPEN-ING?!!
OOOOOO
OOO
I DID IT...FOR GOOD OR ILL...
I'VE FREED THE MONSTER INSIDE HER...

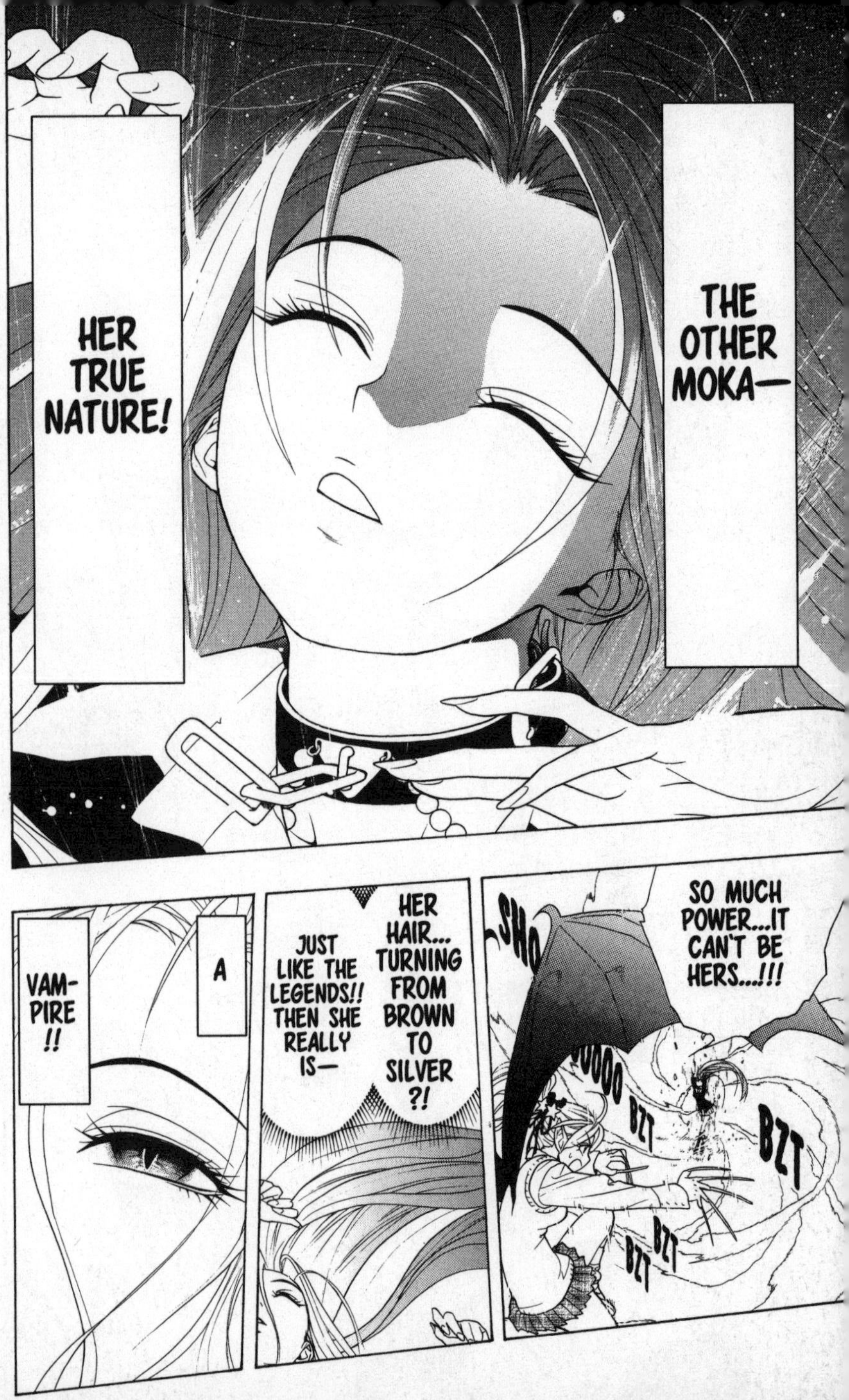
THE OTHER MOKA—
HER TRUE NATURE!
SO MUCH POWER...IT CAN'T BE HERS...!!!
SHOOOOO
BZT
BZT
BZT
BZT
HER HAIR... TURNING FROM BROWN TO SILVER?!
JUST LIKE THE LEGENDS!! THEN SHE REALLY IS—
A
VAM-PIRE!!

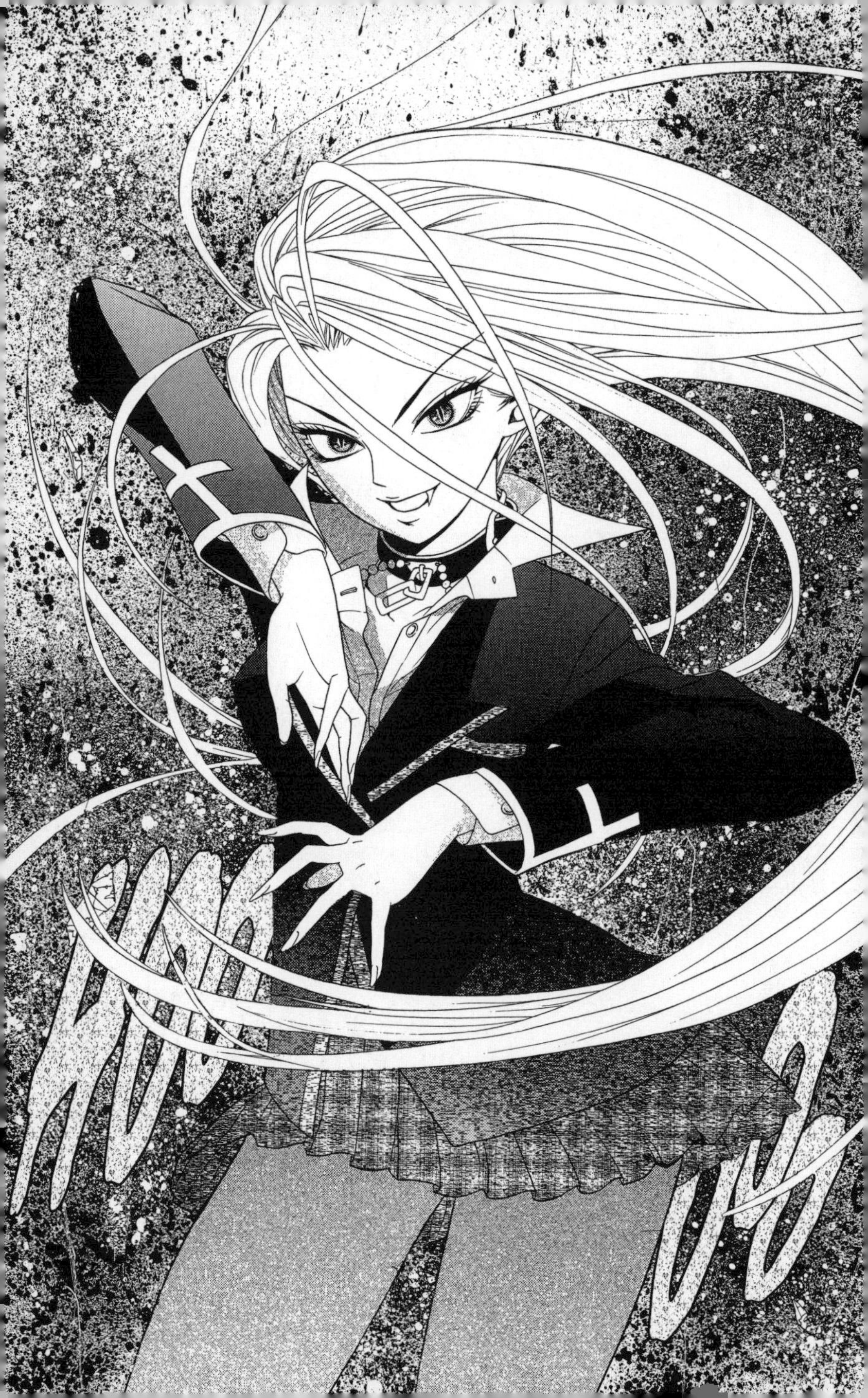

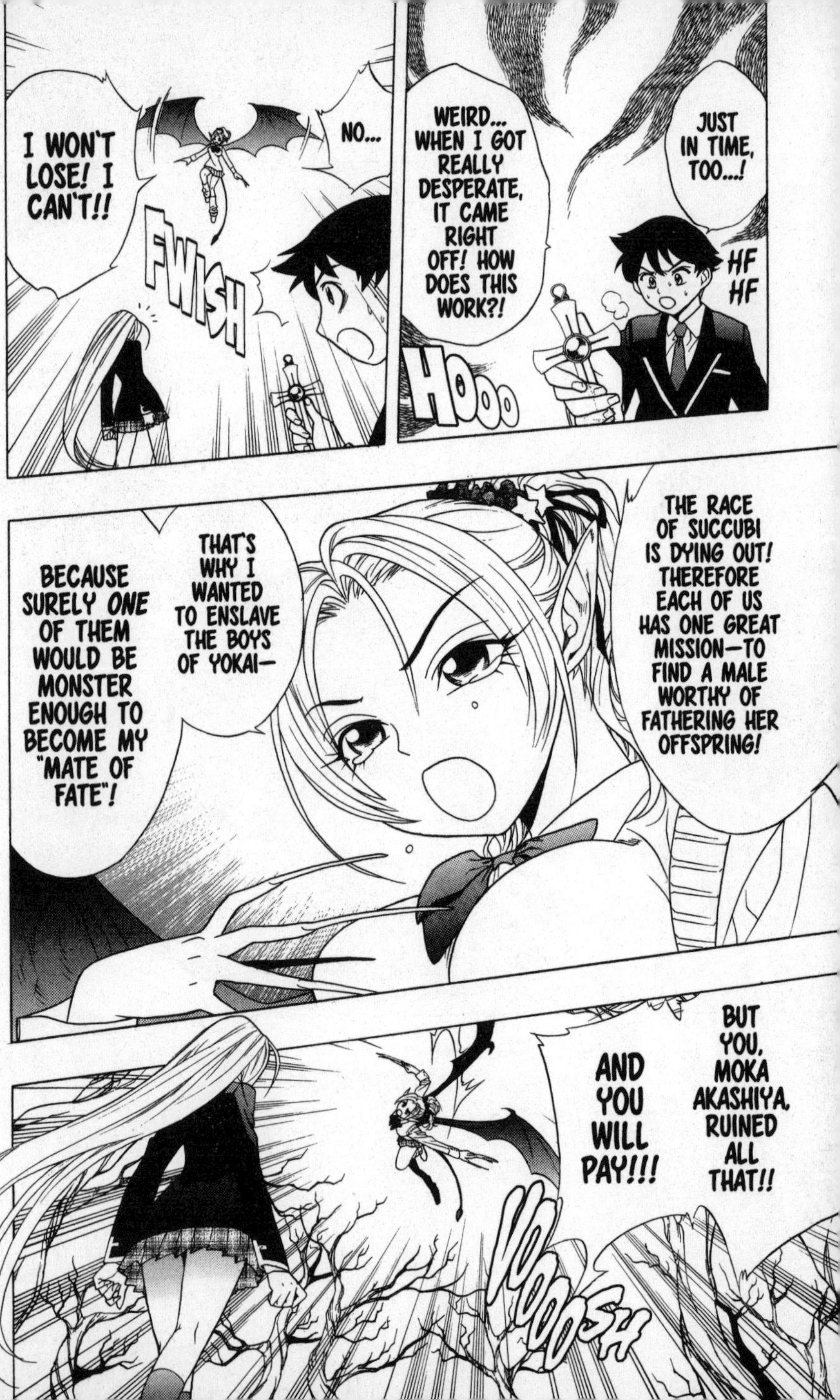
JUST IN TIME, TOO...!
HF HF
HOOO
WEIRD... WHEN I GOT REALLY DESPERATE, IT CAME RIGHT OFF! HOW DOES THIS WORK?!
NO...
FWISH
I WON'T LOSE! I CAN'T!!
THE RACE OF SUCCUBI IS DYING OUT! THEREFORE EACH OF US HAS ONE GREAT MISSION—TO FIND A MALE WORTHY OF FATHERING HER OFFSPRING!
THAT'S WHY I WANTED TO ENSLAVE THE BOYS OF YOKAI—
BECAUSE SURELY *ONE* OF THEM WOULD BE MONSTER ENOUGH TO BECOME MY "MATE OF FATE"!
BUT YOU, MOKA AKASHIYA, RUINED ALL THAT!!
AND YOU WILL PAY!!!
WHOOOSH

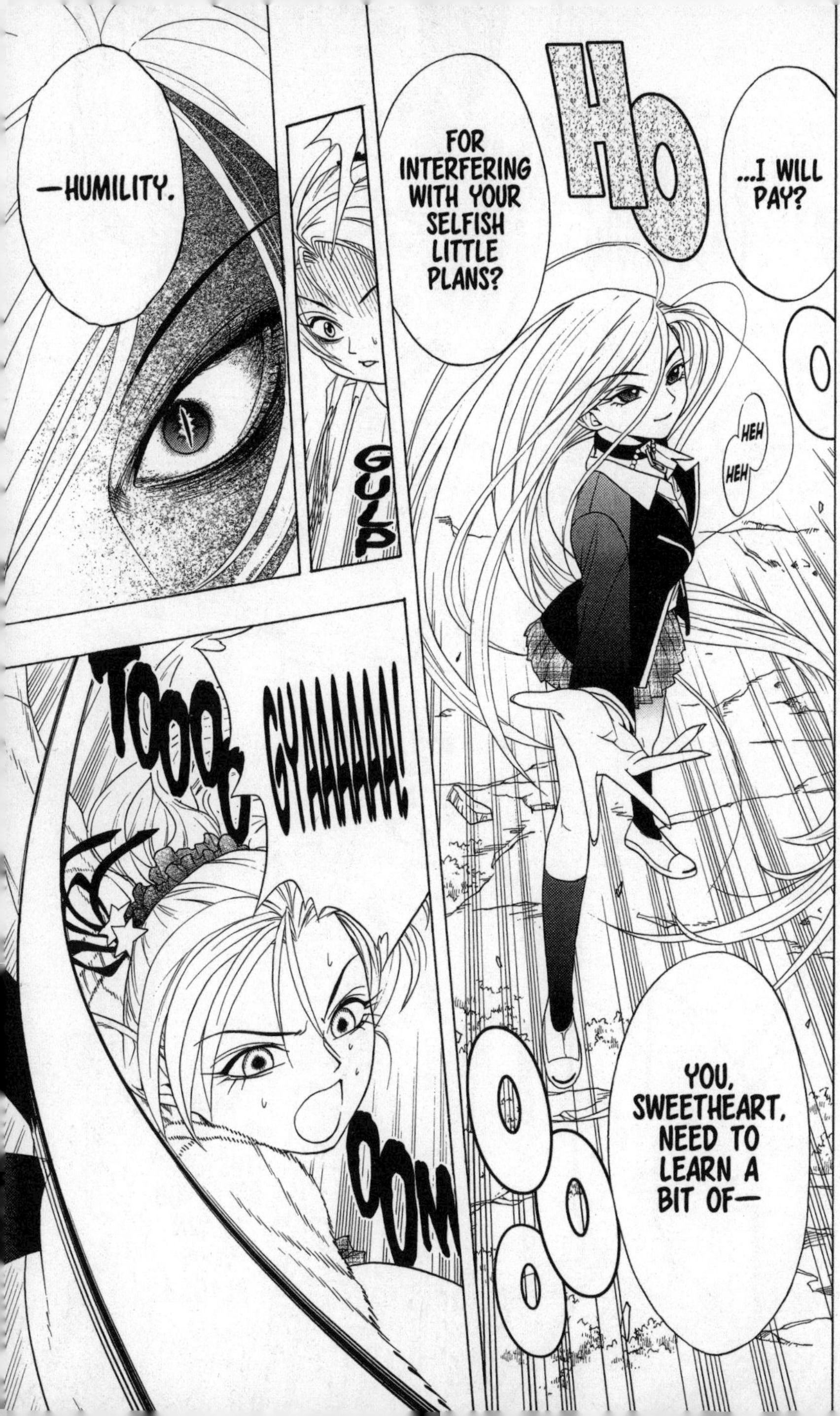
...I WILL PAY?
HO
HEH HEH
FOR INTERFERING WITH YOUR SELFISH LITTLE PLANS?
YOU, SWEETHEART, NEED TO LEARN A BIT OF—
GULP
—HUMILITY.
TOOO
GYAAAAAA!
OOM

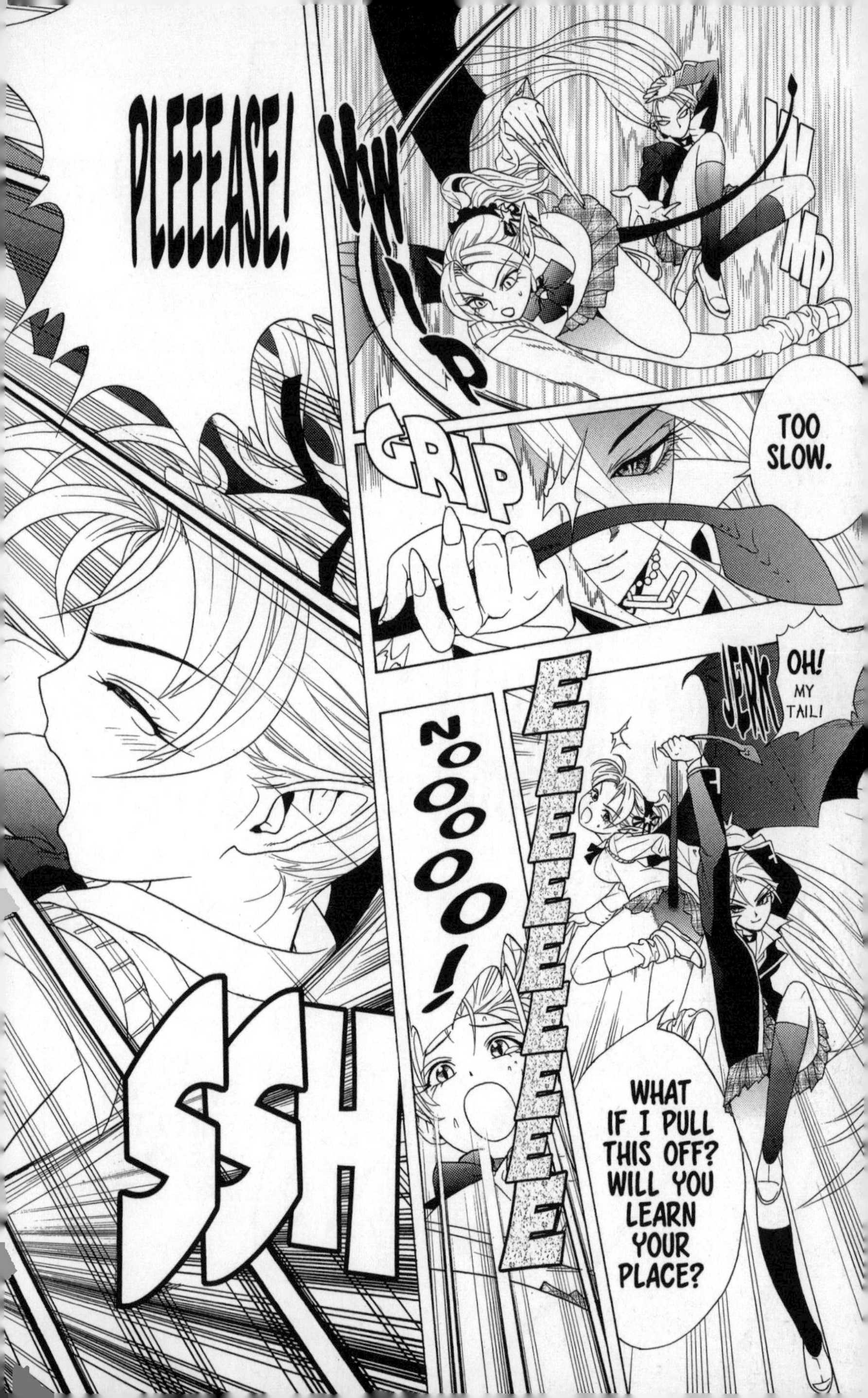
VMP
VWIP
TOO SLOW.
GRIP
OH! MY TAIL!
JERK
WHAT IF I PULL THIS OFF? WILL YOU LEARN YOUR PLACE?
EEEEEEEEEEE
NOOOOO!
PLEEEASE!
SSH

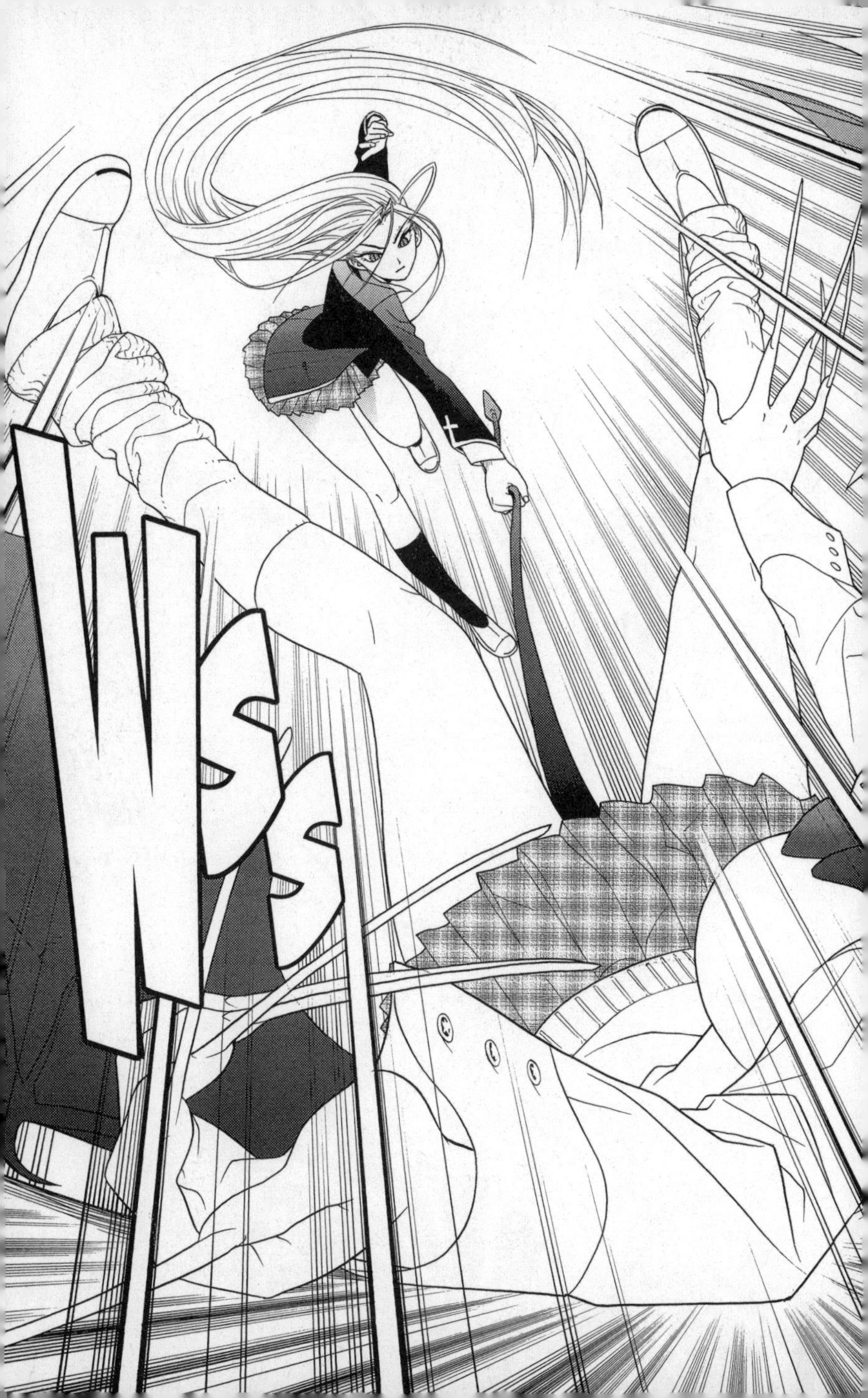
WSS

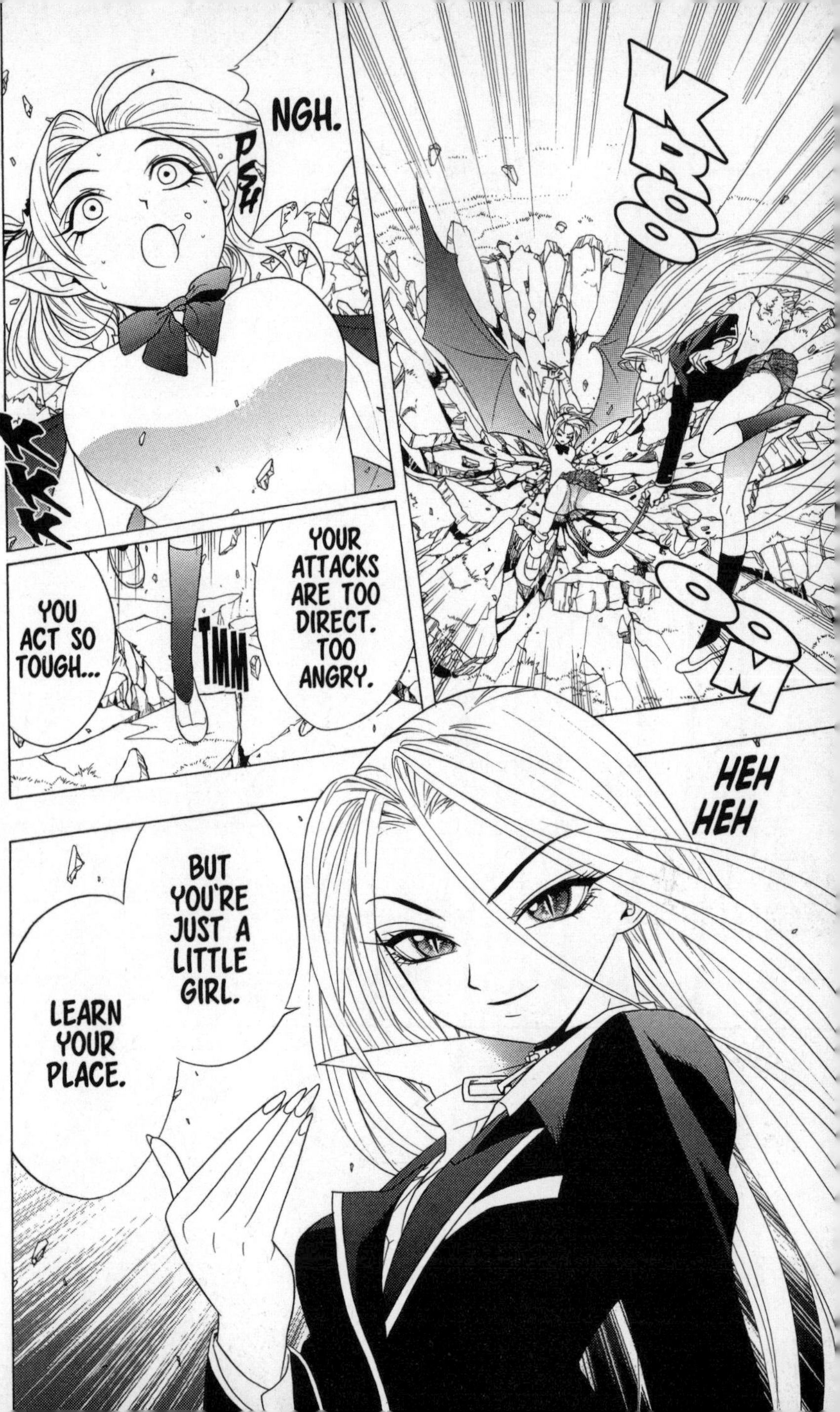
KROOOOOM
NGH.
PSH
KKK
YOUR ATTACKS ARE TOO DIRECT. TOO ANGRY.
TMM
YOU ACT SO TOUGH...
HEH HEH
BUT YOU'RE JUST A LITTLE GIRL.
LEARN YOUR PLACE.

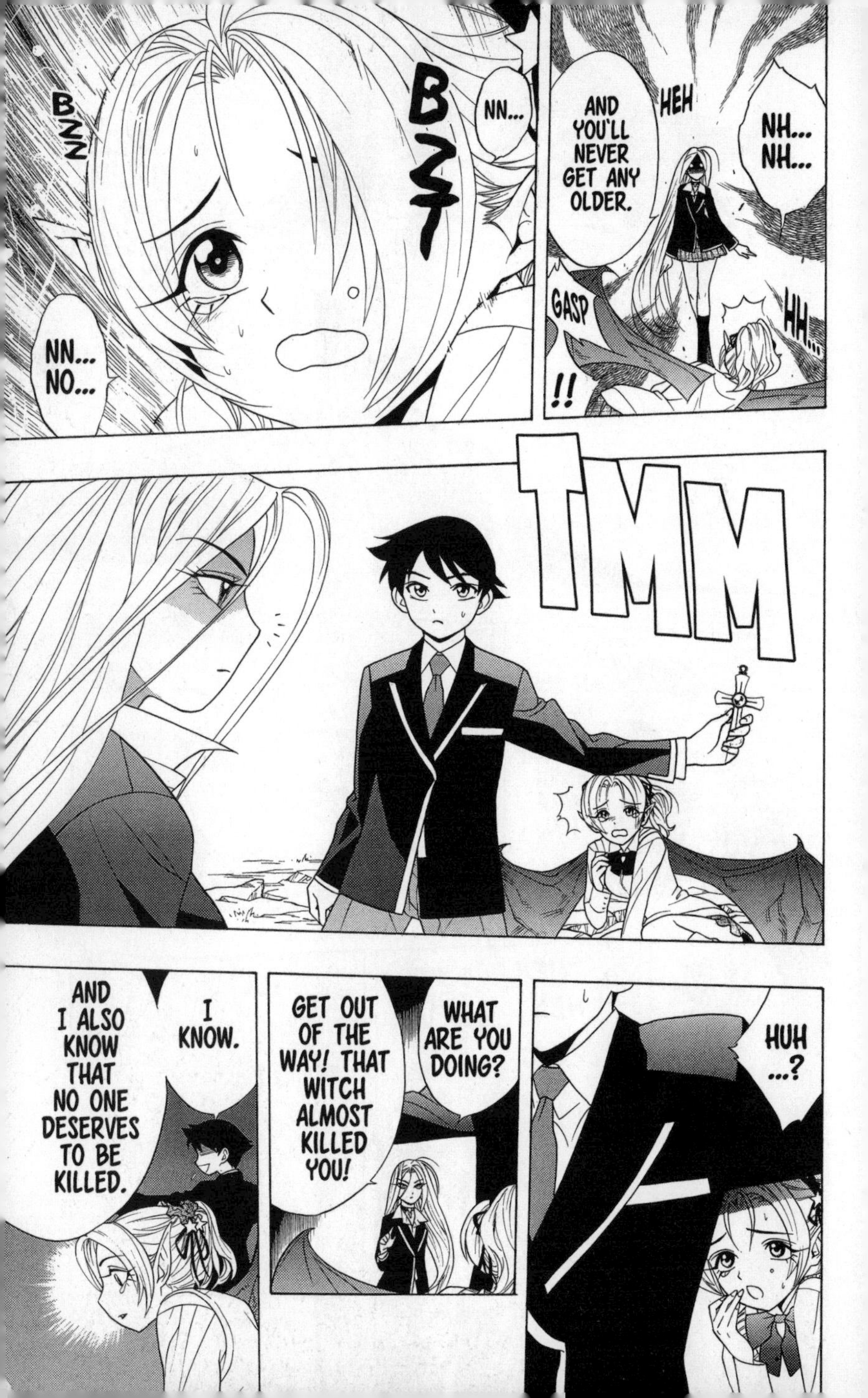
NH... NH...
HEH
AND YOU'LL NEVER GET ANY OLDER.
HH...
GASP
!!
NN...
BZZT
BZZ
NN... NO...
TMM
HUH ...?
WHAT ARE YOU DOING?
GET OUT OF THE WAY! THAT WITCH ALMOST KILLED YOU!
I KNOW.
AND I ALSO KNOW THAT NO ONE DESERVES TO BE KILLED.

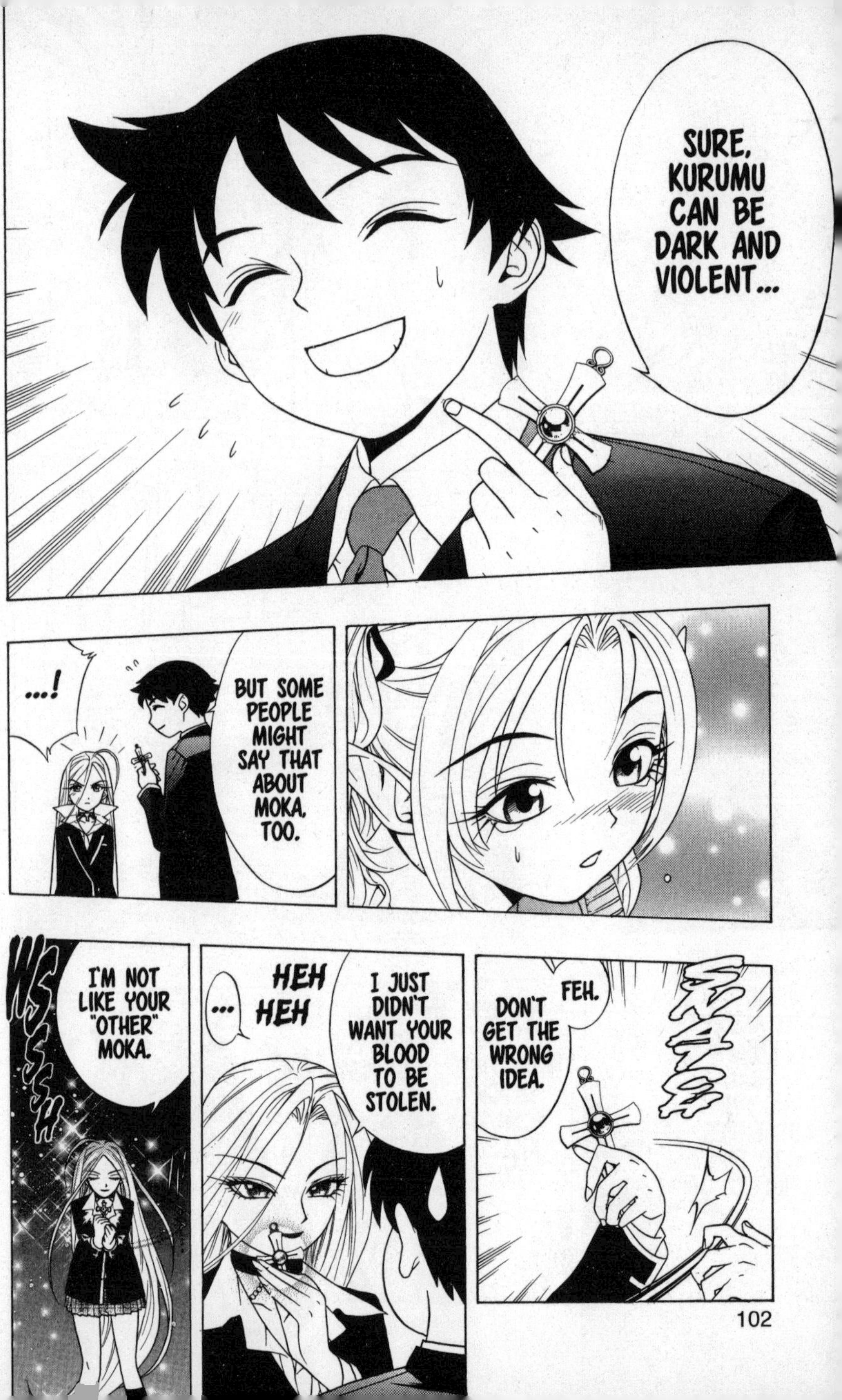
SURE, KURUMU CAN BE DARK AND VIOLENT...
BUT SOME PEOPLE MIGHT SAY THAT ABOUT MOKA, TOO.
...!
FEH.
DON'T GET THE WRONG IDEA.
I JUST DIDN'T WANT YOUR BLOOD TO BE STOLEN.
HEH HEH
...
I'M NOT LIKE YOUR "OTHER" MOKA.

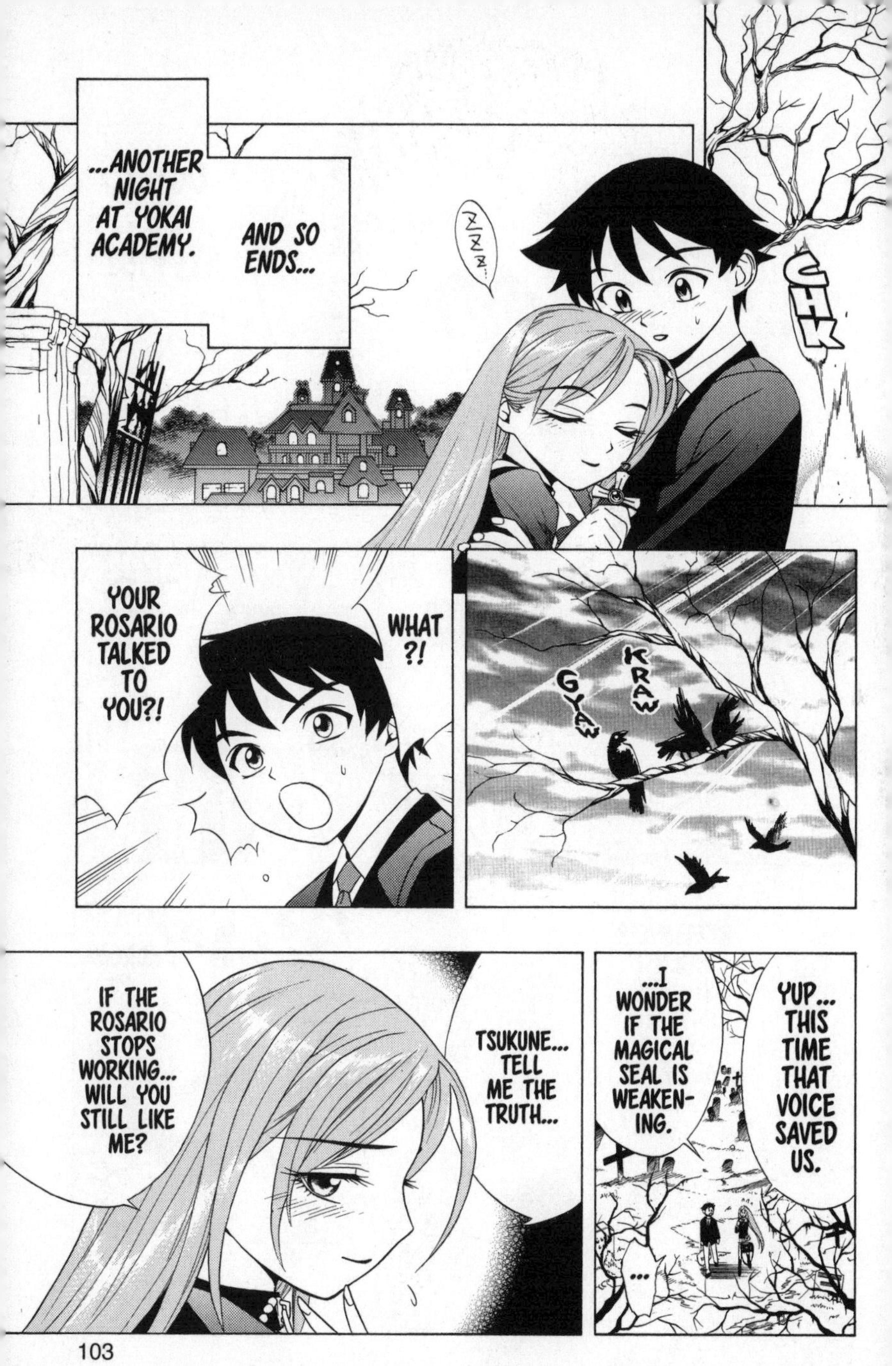
CHK
AND SO ENDS...
...ANOTHER NIGHT AT YOKAI ACADEMY.
Zzz...
KRAW
GYAW
WHAT?!
YOUR ROSARIO TALKED TO YOU?!
YUP... THIS TIME THAT VOICE SAVED US.
...I WONDER IF THE MAGICAL SEAL IS WEAKEN-ING.
...
TSUKUNE... TELL ME THE TRUTH...
IF THE ROSARIO STOPS WORKING... WILL YOU STILL LIKE ME?

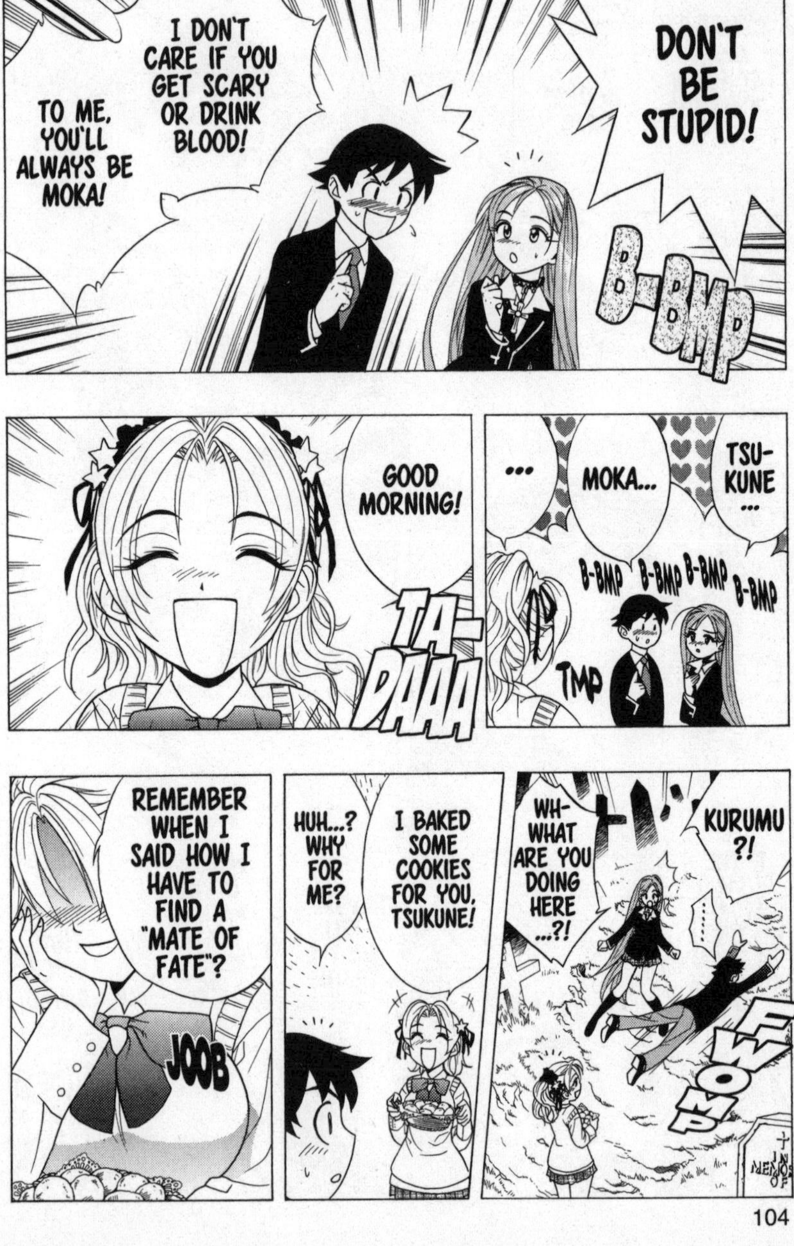
DON'T BE STUPID!
I DON'T CARE IF YOU GET SCARY OR DRINK BLOOD!
TO ME, YOU'LL ALWAYS BE MOKA!
B-BMP
TSU-KUNE...
MOKA...
...
B-BMP B-BMP B-BMP B-BMP
TMP
GOOD MORNING!
TA-DAAA
KURUMU?!
WH-WHAT ARE YOU DOING HERE...?!
FWOMP
I BAKED SOME COOKIES FOR YOU, TSUKUNE!
HUH...? WHY FOR ME?
REMEMBER WHEN I SAID HOW I HAVE TO FIND A "MATE OF FATE"?
JOOB

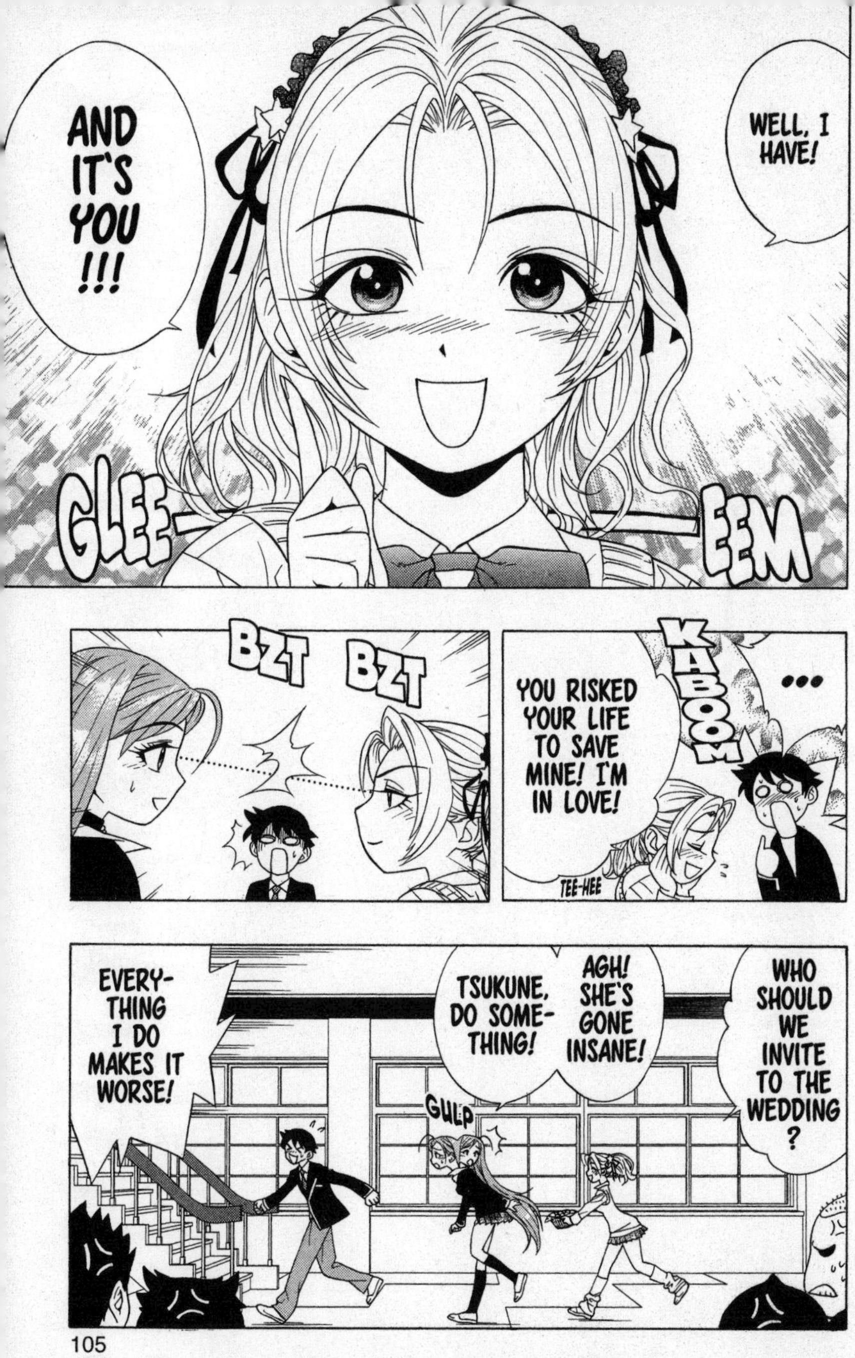
WELL, I HAVE!
AND IT'S YOU!!!
GLEE—
EEM
...
KABOOM
YOU RISKED YOUR LIFE TO SAVE MINE! I'M IN LOVE!
TEE-HEE
BZT
BZT
WHO SHOULD WE INVITE TO THE WEDDING?
AGH! SHE'S GONE INSANE!
TSUKUNE, DO SOME-THING!
GULP
EVERY-THING I DO MAKES IT WORSE!

ROSARIO+VAMPIRE

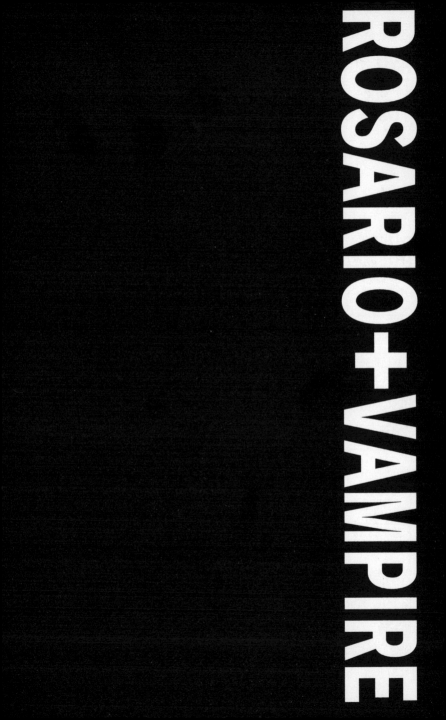

3: Going Clubbing

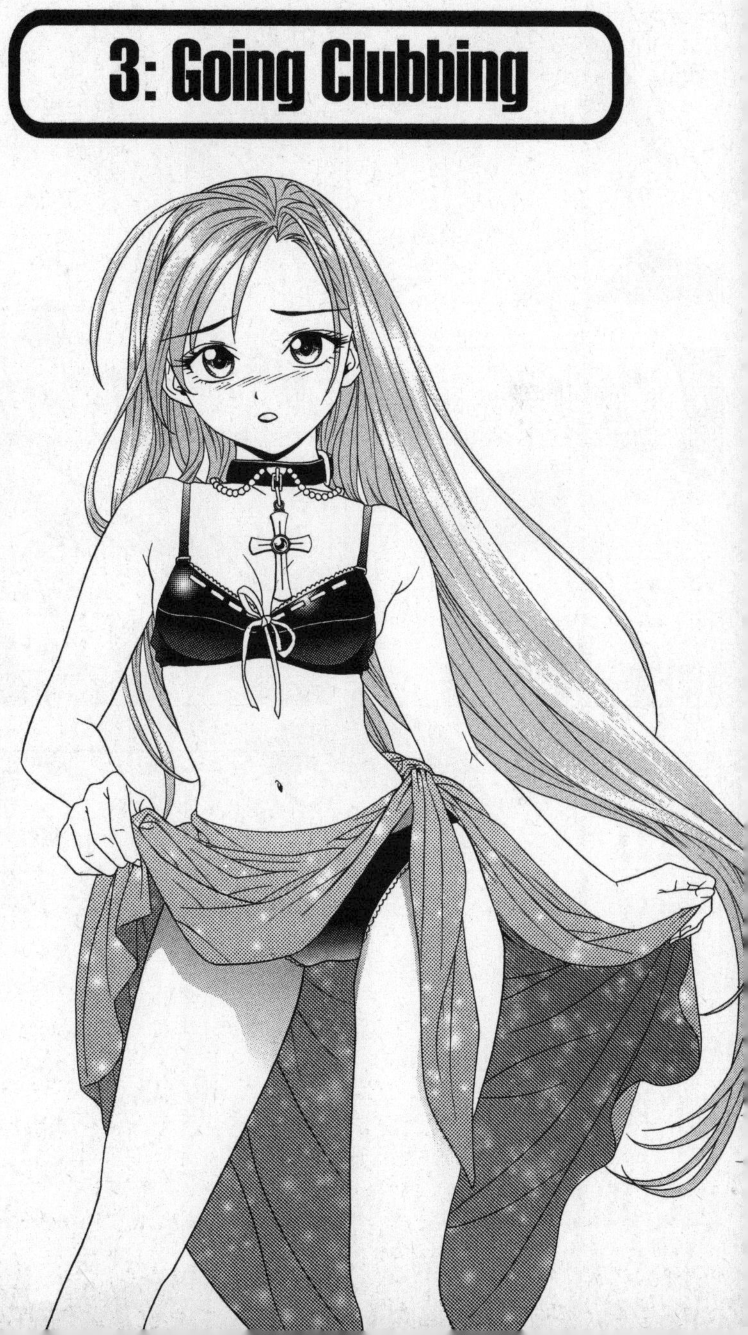

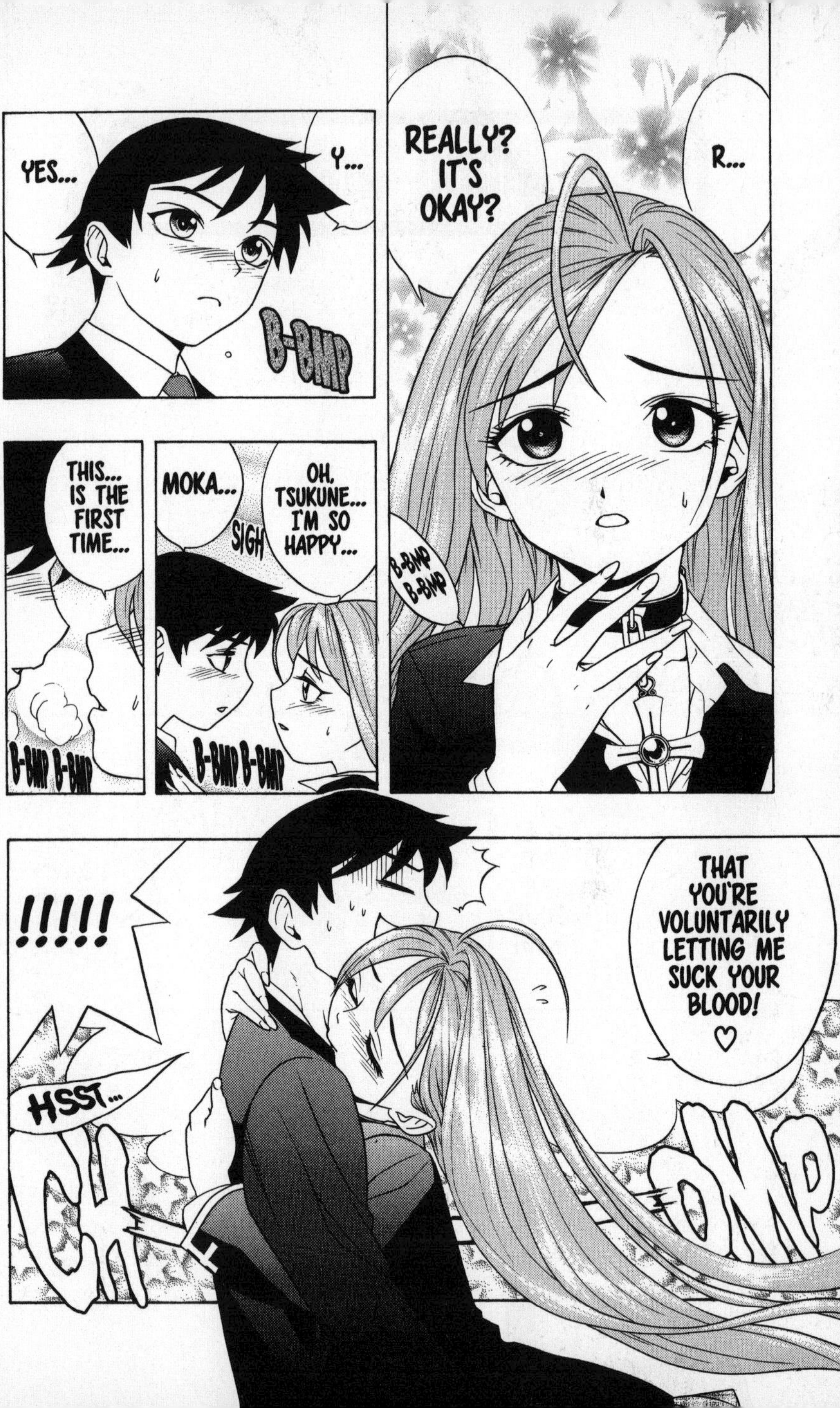

R...
REALLY? IT'S OKAY?
B-BMP B-BMP
Y...
YES...
B-BMP
OH, TSUKUNE... I'M SO HAPPY...
MOKA...
SIGH
B-BMP B-BMP
THIS... IS THE FIRST TIME...
B-BMP B-BMP
THAT YOU'RE VOLUNTARILY LETTING ME SUCK YOUR BLOOD! ♡
!!!!!
HSST...
CH
OMP

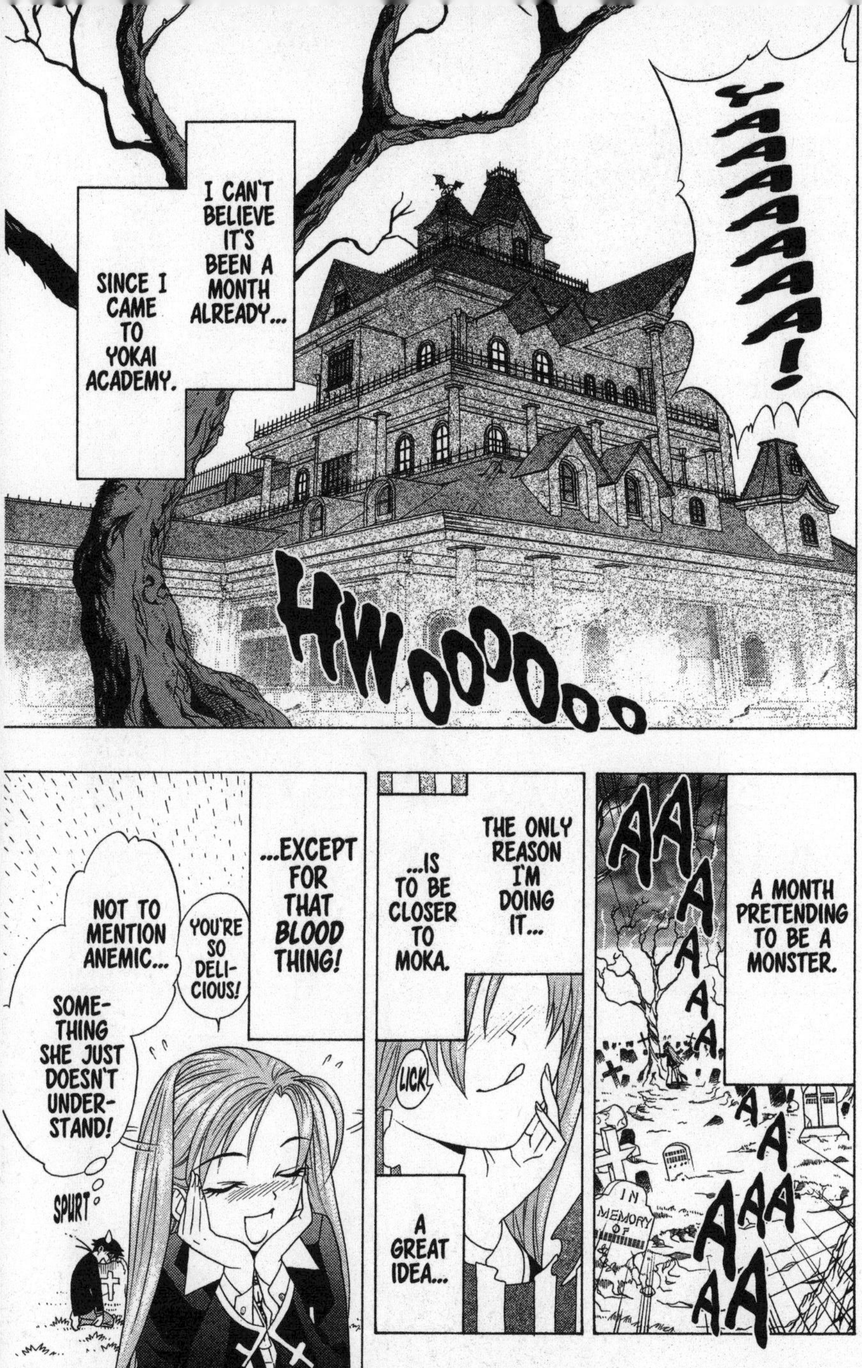

YAAAAAAA!
I CAN'T BELIEVE IT'S BEEN A MONTH ALREADY...
SINCE I CAME TO YOKAI ACADEMY.
HWOOOOOO
A MONTH PRETENDING TO BE A MONSTER.
AAAAAAAAAAAAAAAA
IN MEMORY OF
THE ONLY REASON I'M DOING IT...
...IS TO BE CLOSER TO MOKA.
LICK
A GREAT IDEA...
...EXCEPT FOR THAT BLOOD THING!
YOU'RE SO DELI-CIOUS!
NOT TO MENTION ANEMIC...
SOME-THING SHE JUST DOESN'T UNDER-STAND!
SPURT

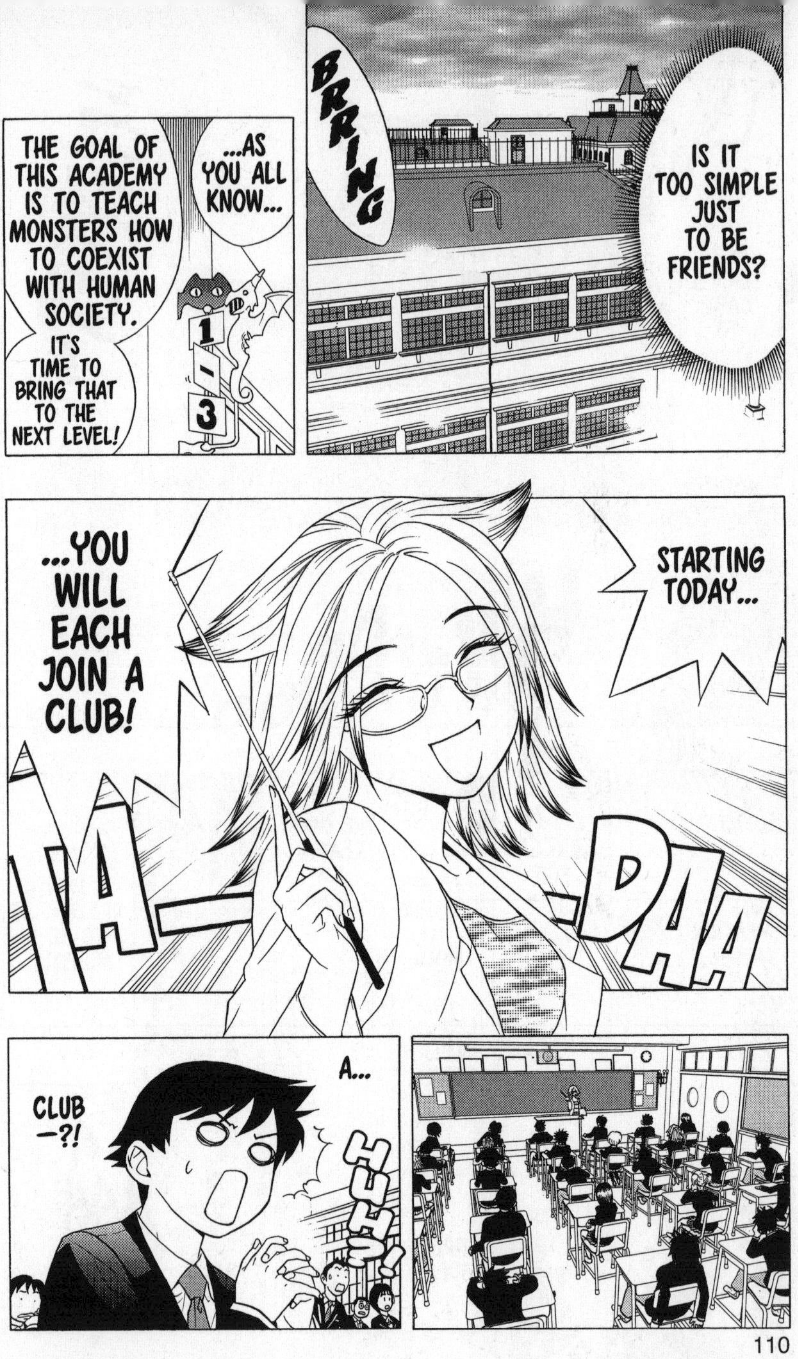
IS IT TOO SIMPLE JUST TO BE FRIENDS?
BRRING
...AS YOU ALL KNOW...
THE GOAL OF THIS ACADEMY IS TO TEACH MONSTERS HOW TO COEXIST WITH HUMAN SOCIETY.
IT'S TIME TO BRING THAT TO THE NEXT LEVEL!
1-3
STARTING TODAY...
...YOU WILL EACH JOIN A CLUB!
A— —DAA
A...
HUH?!
CLUB—?!

READ THIS WAY

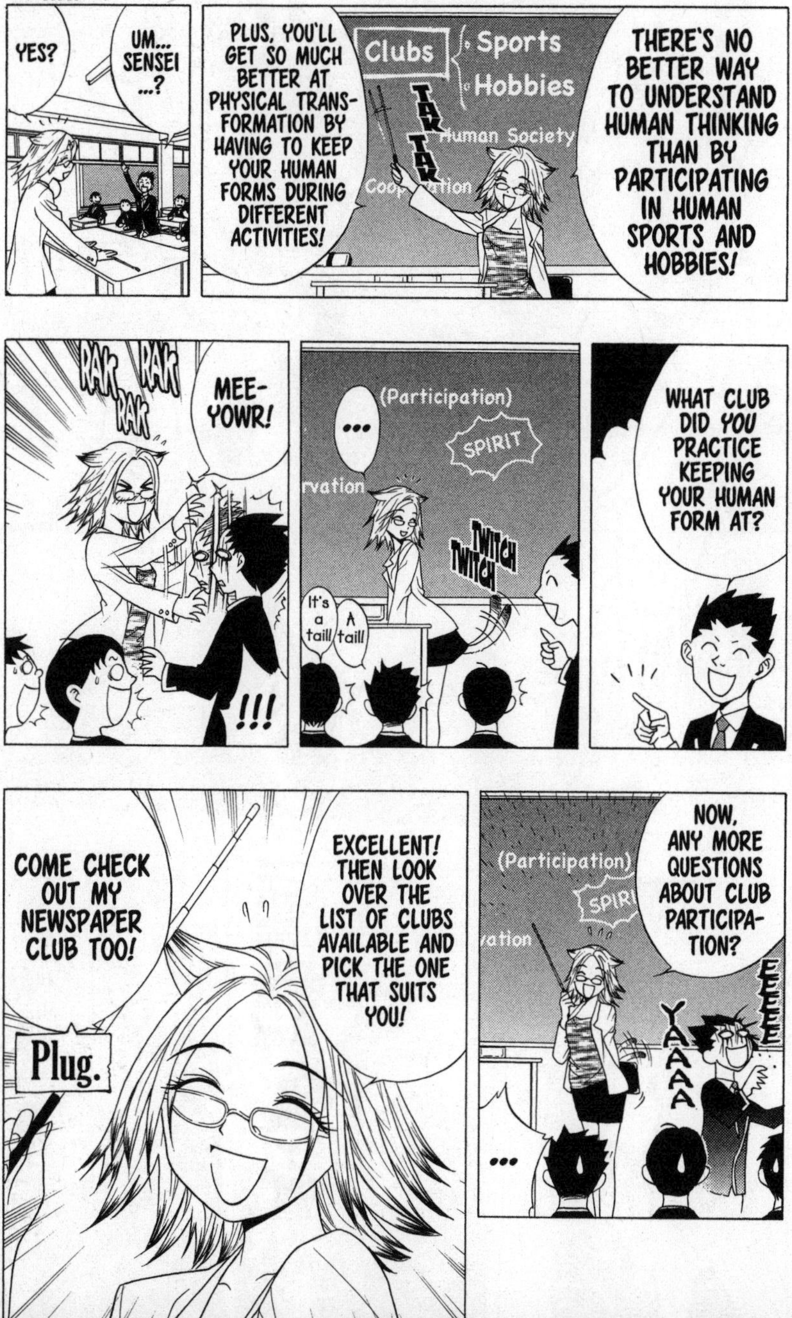
THERE'S NO BETTER WAY TO UNDERSTAND HUMAN THINKING THAN BY PARTICIPATING IN HUMAN SPORTS AND HOBBIES!
Clubs
Sports
Hobbies
Human Society
TAK TAK
PLUS, YOU'LL GET SO MUCH BETTER AT PHYSICAL TRANS-FORMATION BY HAVING TO KEEP YOUR HUMAN FORMS DURING DIFFERENT ACTIVITIES!
UM... SENSEI ...?
YES?
WHAT CLUB DID YOU PRACTICE KEEPING YOUR HUMAN FORM AT?
(Participation)
SPIRIT
...
rvation
TWITCH TWITCH
It's a tail!
A tail!
MEE-YOWR!
RAK RAK RAK
!!!
NOW, ANY MORE QUESTIONS ABOUT CLUB PARTICIPA-TION?
EEEEE
YAAAA
(Participation)
SPIRI
vation
...
EXCELLENT! THEN LOOK OVER THE LIST OF CLUBS AVAILABLE AND PICK THE ONE THAT SUITS YOU!
COME CHECK OUT MY NEWSPAPER CLUB TOO!
Plug.

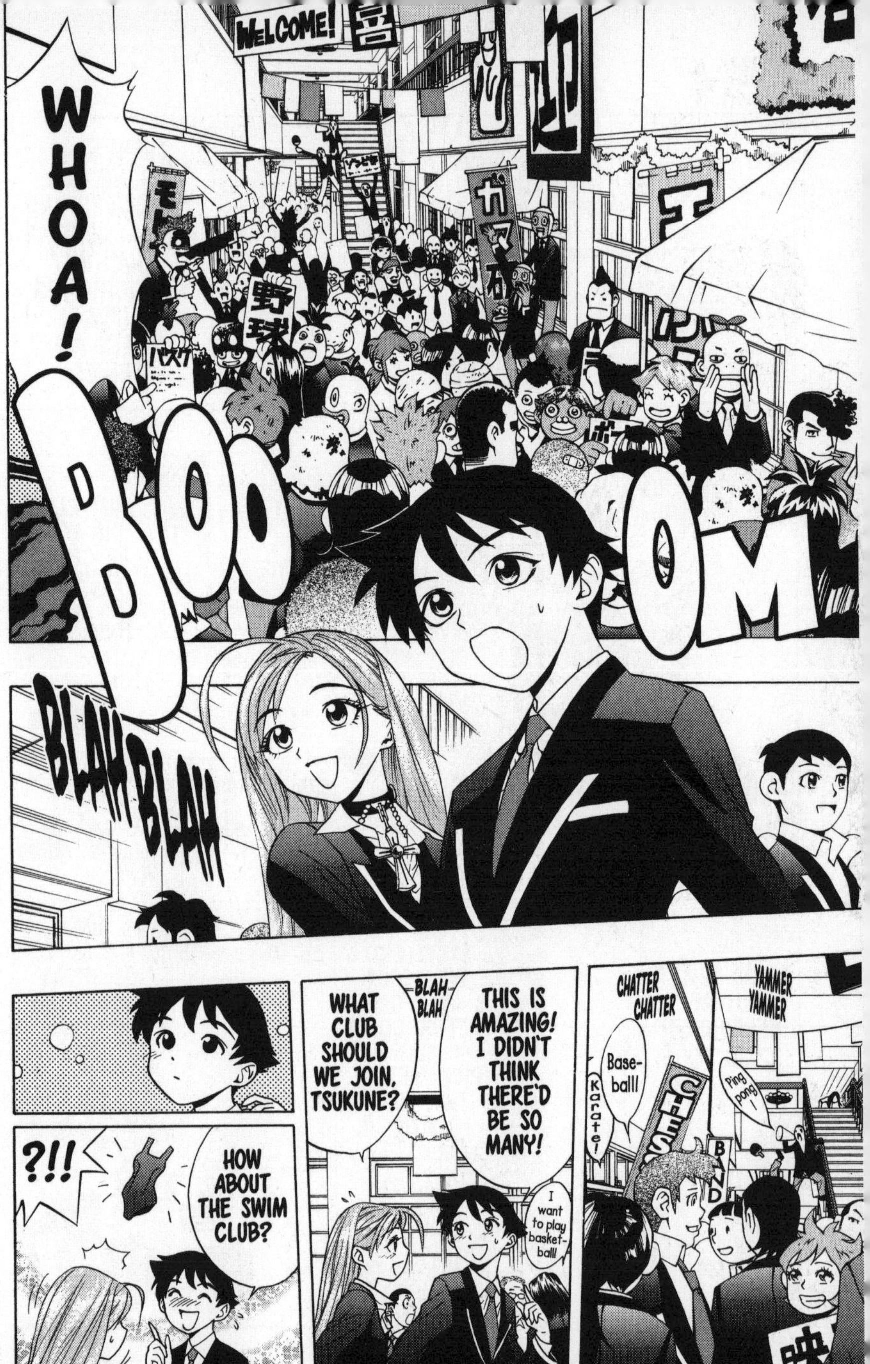

WELCOME!
WHOA!
BOOOM
BLAH BLAH
YAMMER YAMMER
CHATTER CHATTER
Ping pong!
Base-ball!
Karate!
BAND
THIS IS AMAZING! I DIDN'T THINK THERE'D BE SO MANY!
BLAH BLAH
WHAT CLUB SHOULD WE JOIN, TSUKUNE?
I want to play basket-ball!
HOW ABOUT THE SWIM CLUB?
?!!

READ THIS WAY

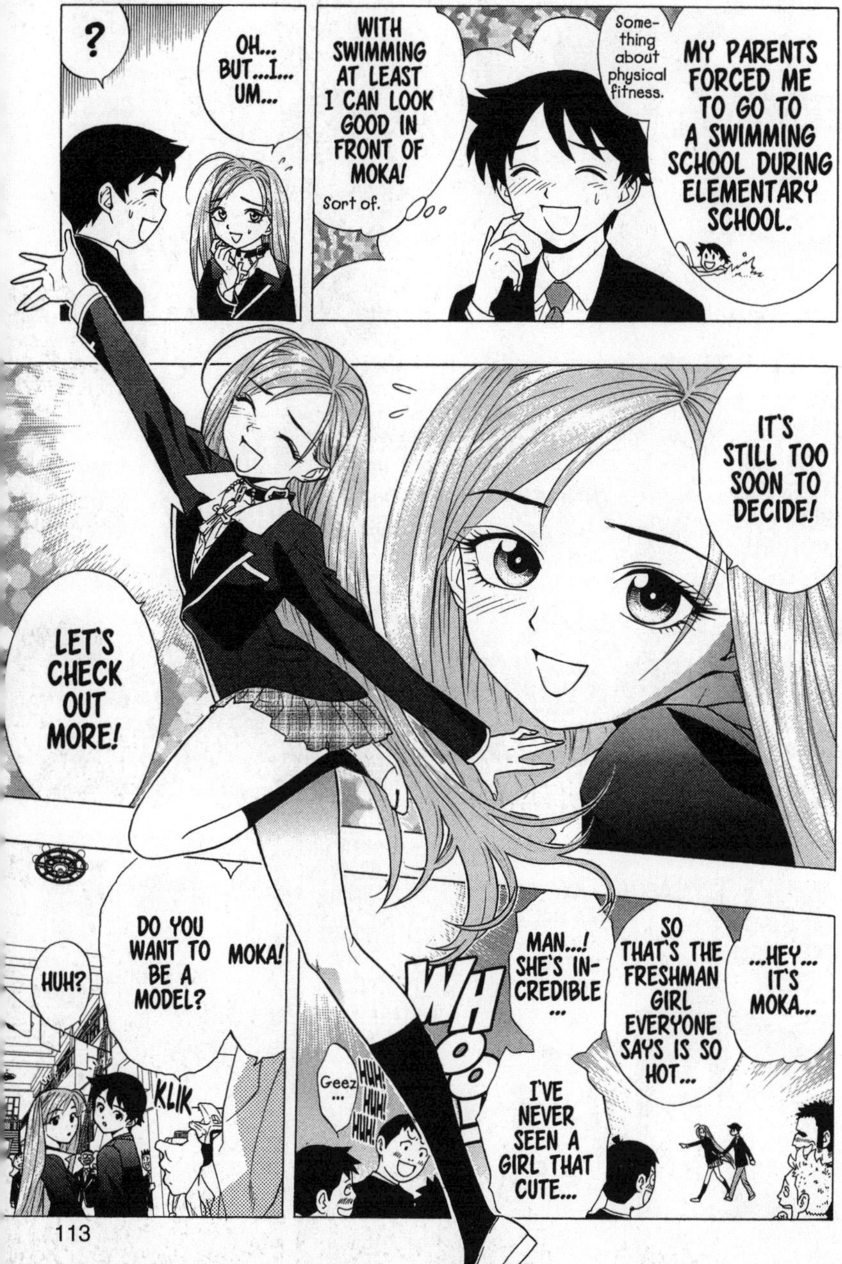
MY PARENTS FORCED ME TO GO TO A SWIMMING SCHOOL DURING ELEMENTARY SCHOOL.
Some-thing about physical fitness.
WITH SWIMMING AT LEAST I CAN LOOK GOOD IN FRONT OF MOKA!
Sort of.
OH... BUT...I... UM...
?
IT'S STILL TOO SOON TO DECIDE!
LET'S CHECK OUT MORE!
...HEY... IT'S MOKA...
SO THAT'S THE FRESHMAN GIRL EVERYONE SAYS IS SO HOT...
MAN...! SHE'S IN-CREDIBLE...
I'VE NEVER SEEN A GIRL THAT CUTE...
WHOOO!
HUH! HUH! HUH!
Geez...
MOKA!
DO YOU WANT TO BE A MODEL?
KLIK
HUH?

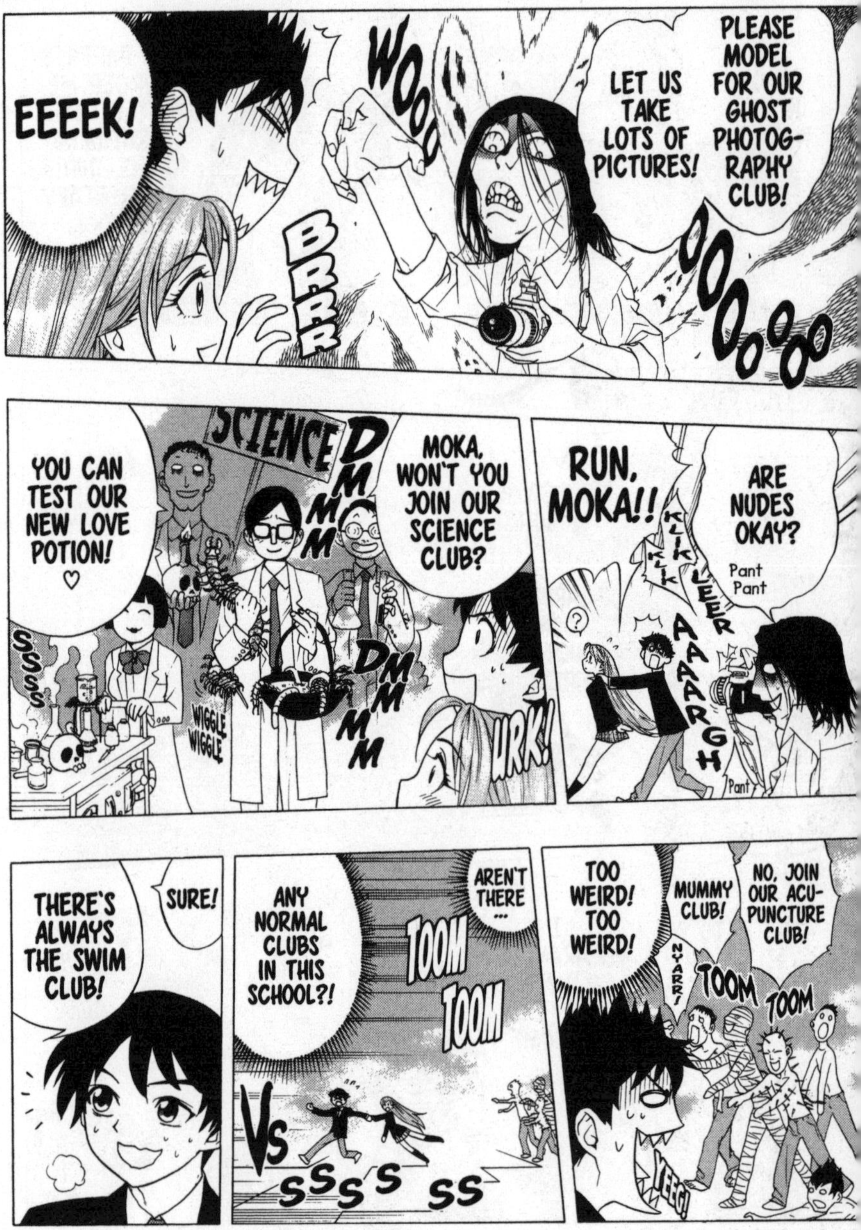
PLEASE MODEL FOR OUR GHOST PHOTOG-RAPHY CLUB!
LET US TAKE LOTS OF PICTURES!
WOOO
OOOOOO
BRRRR
EEEEK!
ARE NUDES OKAY?
Pant Pant
RUN, MOKA!!
KLIK KLIK
LEER
AAAARGH
Pant
MOKA, WON'T YOU JOIN OUR SCIENCE CLUB?
SCIENCE
DMMMM
YOU CAN TEST OUR NEW LOVE POTION! ♡
SSSS
WIGGLE WIGGLE
DMMMM
URK!
NO, JOIN OUR ACU-PUNCTURE CLUB!
MUMMY CLUB!
TOO WEIRD! TOO WEIRD!
NYARR!
TOOM
TOOM
YEEG!
AREN'T THERE...
ANY NORMAL CLUBS IN THIS SCHOOL?!
TOOM TOOM
VS
SSSSS SS
SURE!
THERE'S ALWAYS THE SWIM CLUB!

READ THIS WAY

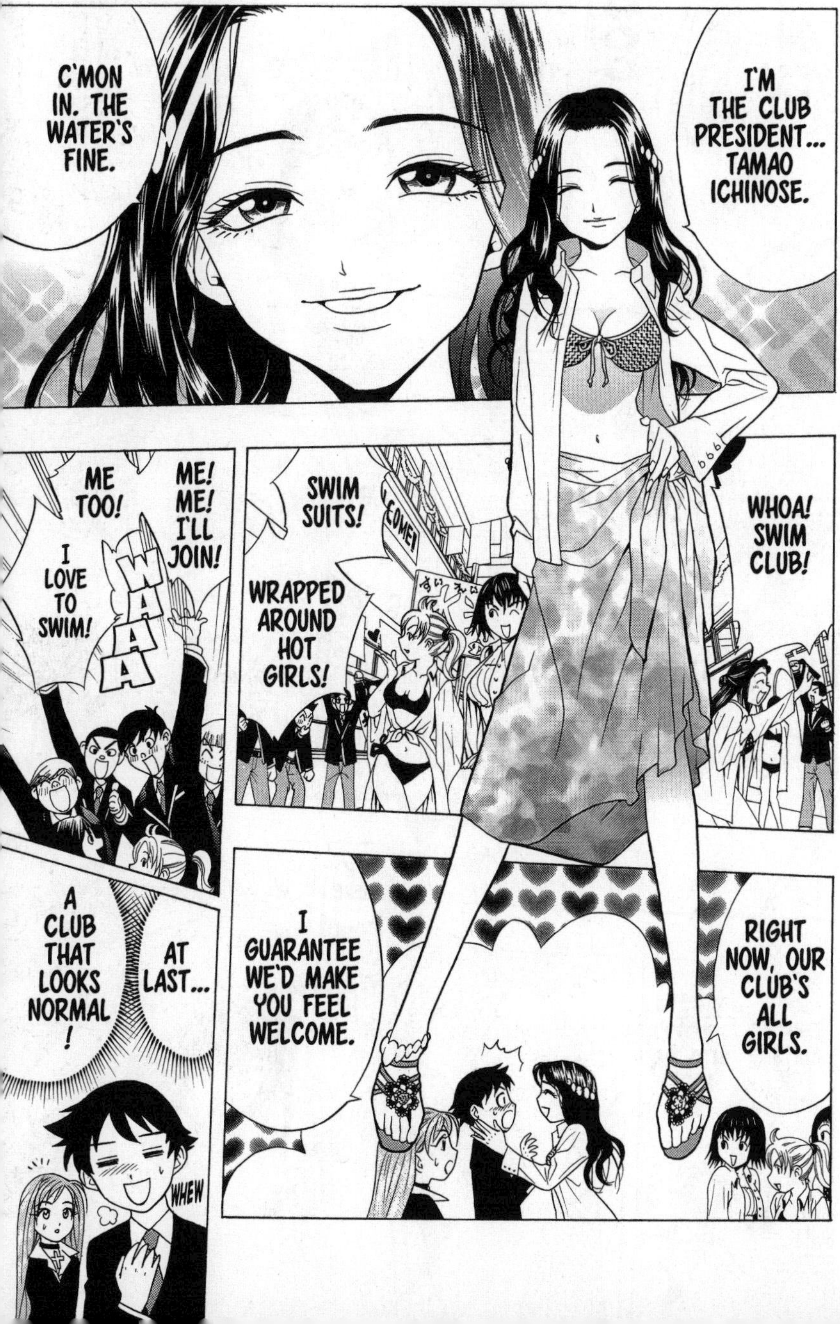

I'M THE CLUB PRESIDENT... TAMAO ICHINOSE.
C'MON IN. THE WATER'S FINE.
WHOA! SWIM CLUB!
SWIM SUITS!
WRAPPED AROUND HOT GIRLS!
ME! ME! I'LL JOIN!
ME TOO!
WAAA
I LOVE TO SWIM!
RIGHT NOW, OUR CLUB'S ALL GIRLS.
I GUARANTEE WE'D MAKE YOU FEEL WELCOME.
AT LAST...
A CLUB THAT LOOKS NORMAL!
WHEW

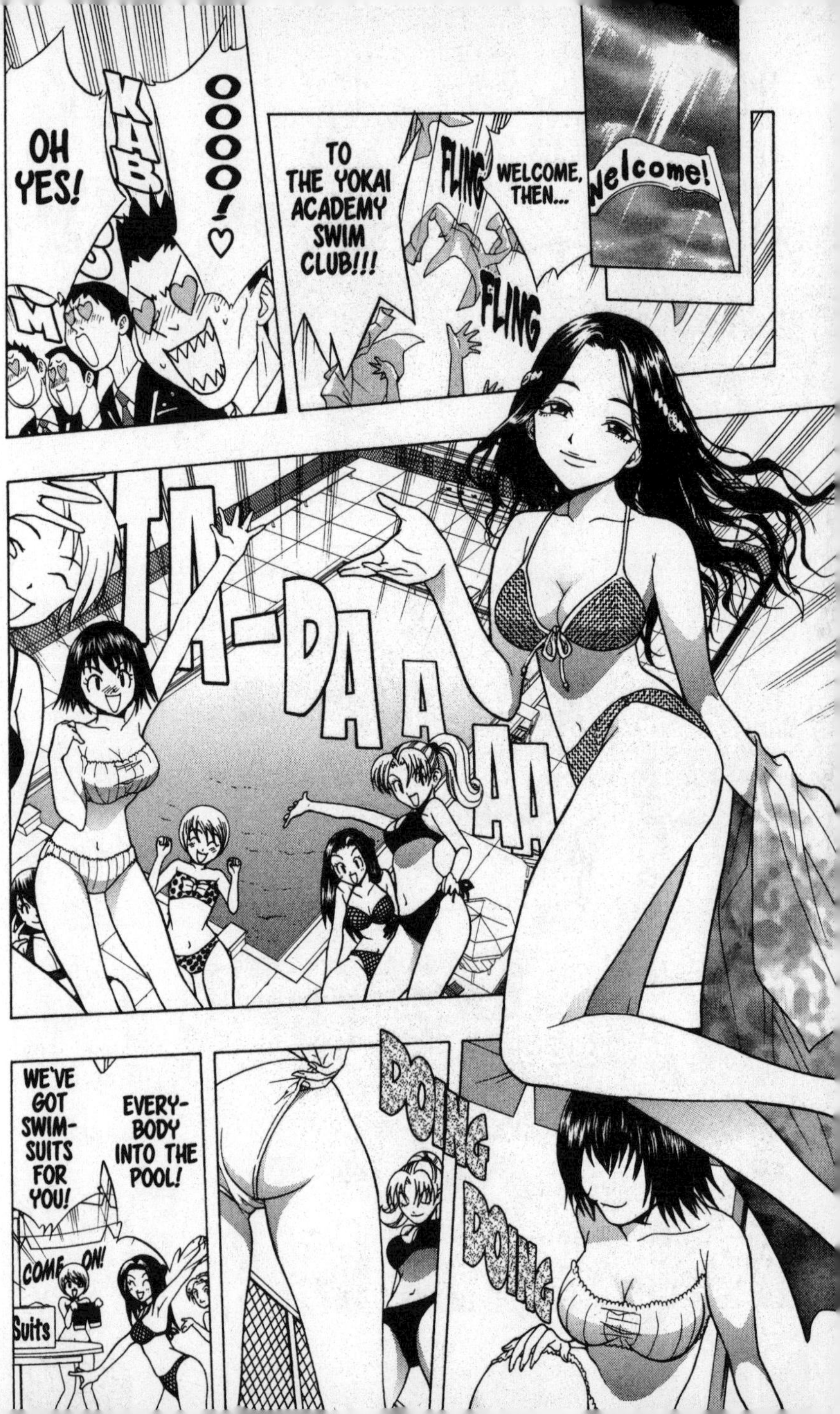
welcome!
WELCOME, THEN...
FLING
FLING
TO THE YOKAI ACADEMY SWIM CLUB!!!
OOOOO!♡
KAB
OH YES!
TA-DAAAA
DOING
DOING
EVERY-BODY INTO THE POOL!
WE'VE GOT SWIM-SUITS FOR YOU!
COME ON!
Suits

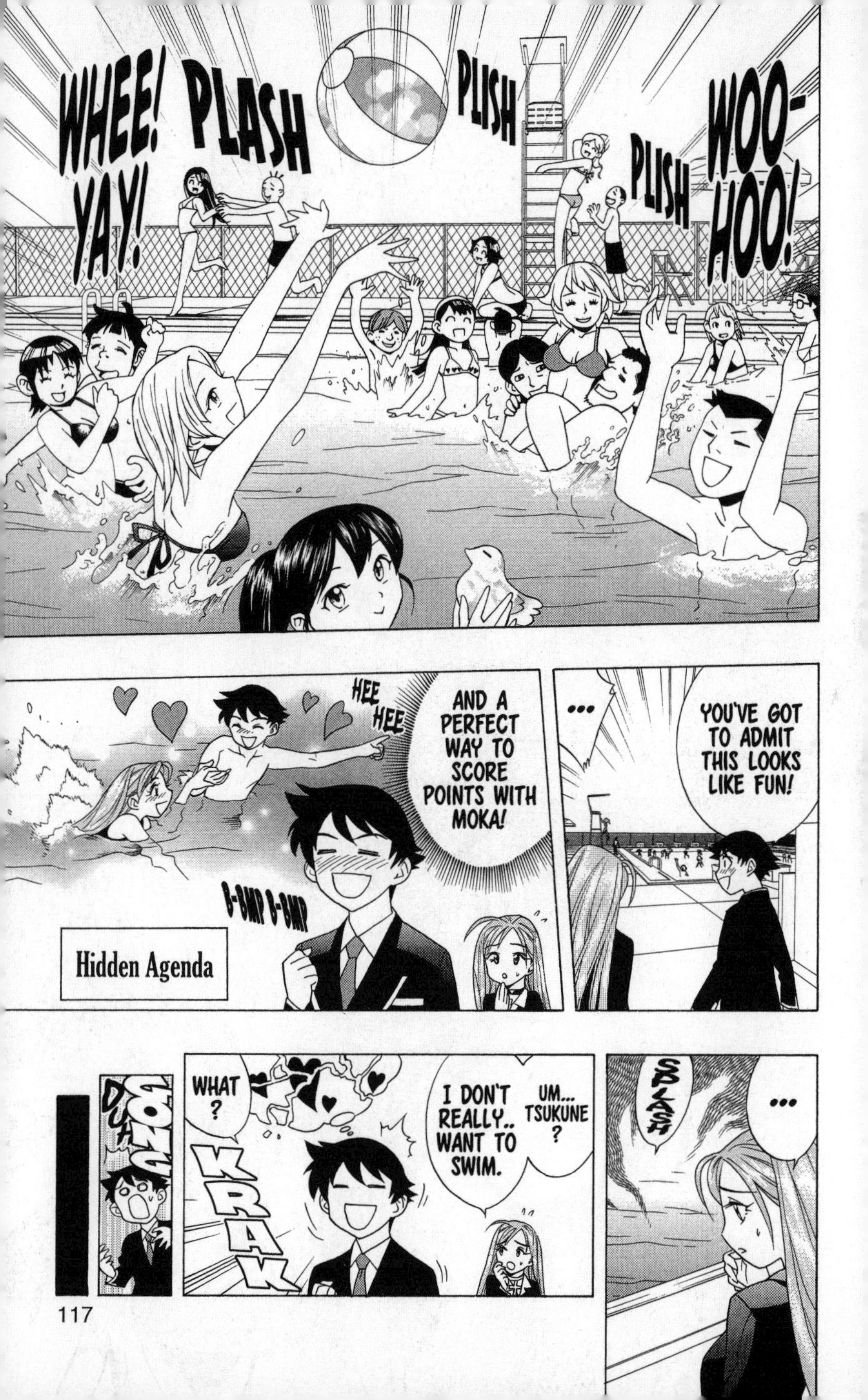
WOO-HOO!
PLISH
PLISH
PLASH
WHEE! YAY!
...
YOU'VE GOT TO ADMIT THIS LOOKS LIKE FUN!
HEE HEE
AND A PERFECT WAY TO SCORE POINTS WITH MOKA!
B-BMP B-BMP
Hidden Agenda
SPLASH
...
UM... TSUKUNE?
I DON'T REALLY.. WANT TO SWIM.
WHAT?
KRAK
DONG

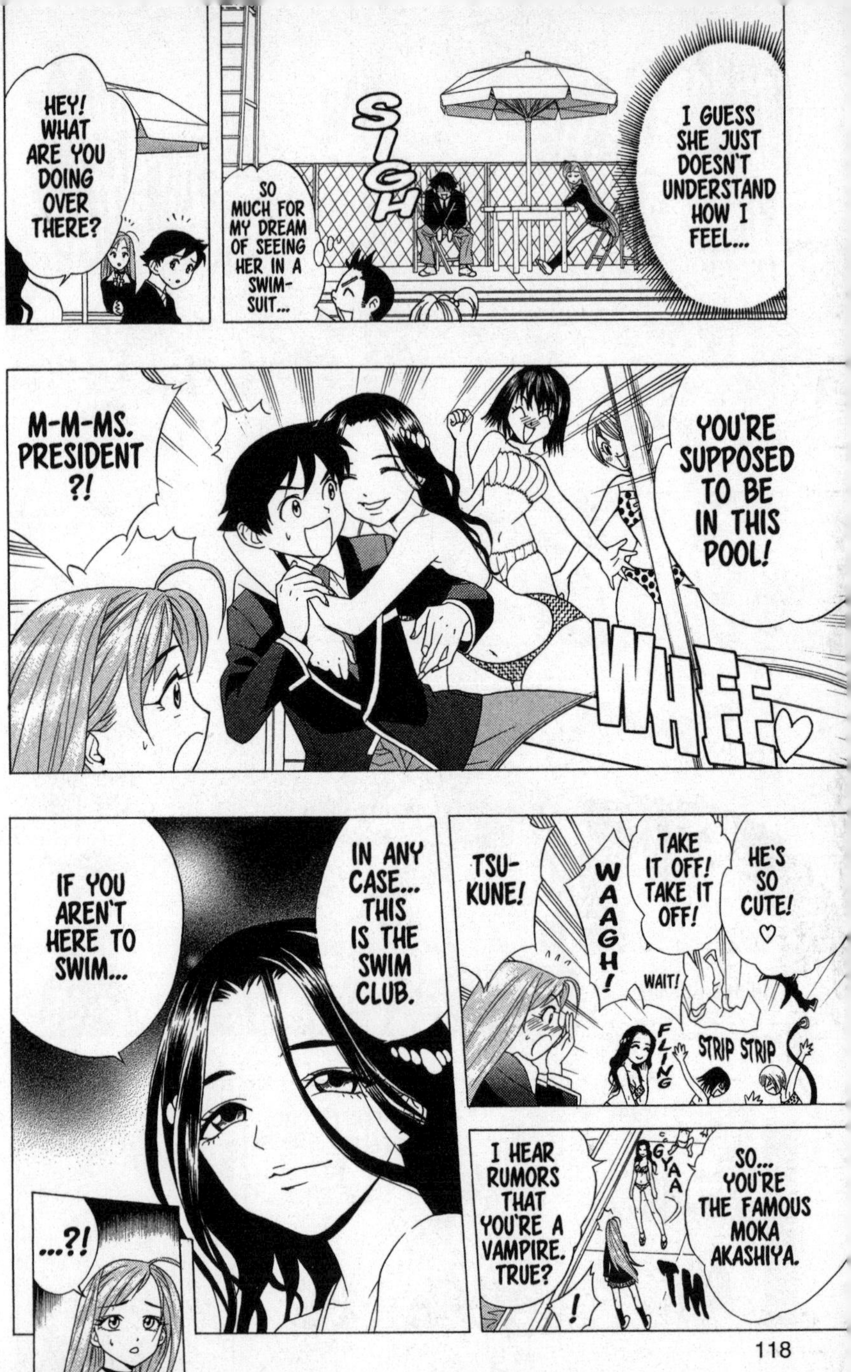
I GUESS SHE JUST DOESN'T UNDERSTAND HOW I FEEL...
SIGH
SO MUCH FOR MY DREAM OF SEEING HER IN A SWIM-SUIT...
HEY! WHAT ARE YOU DOING OVER THERE?
YOU'RE SUPPOSED TO BE IN THIS POOL!
WHEE♥
M-M-MS. PRESIDENT ?!
HE'S SO CUTE! ♡
TAKE IT OFF! TAKE IT OFF!
WAAGH!
WAIT!
TSU-KUNE!
STRIP STRIP
FLING
SO... YOU'RE THE FAMOUS MOKA AKASHIYA.
TM
GYAA
I HEAR RUMORS THAT YOU'RE A VAMPIRE. TRUE?
!
IN ANY CASE... THIS IS THE SWIM CLUB.
IF YOU AREN'T HERE TO SWIM...
...?!

READ THIS WAY

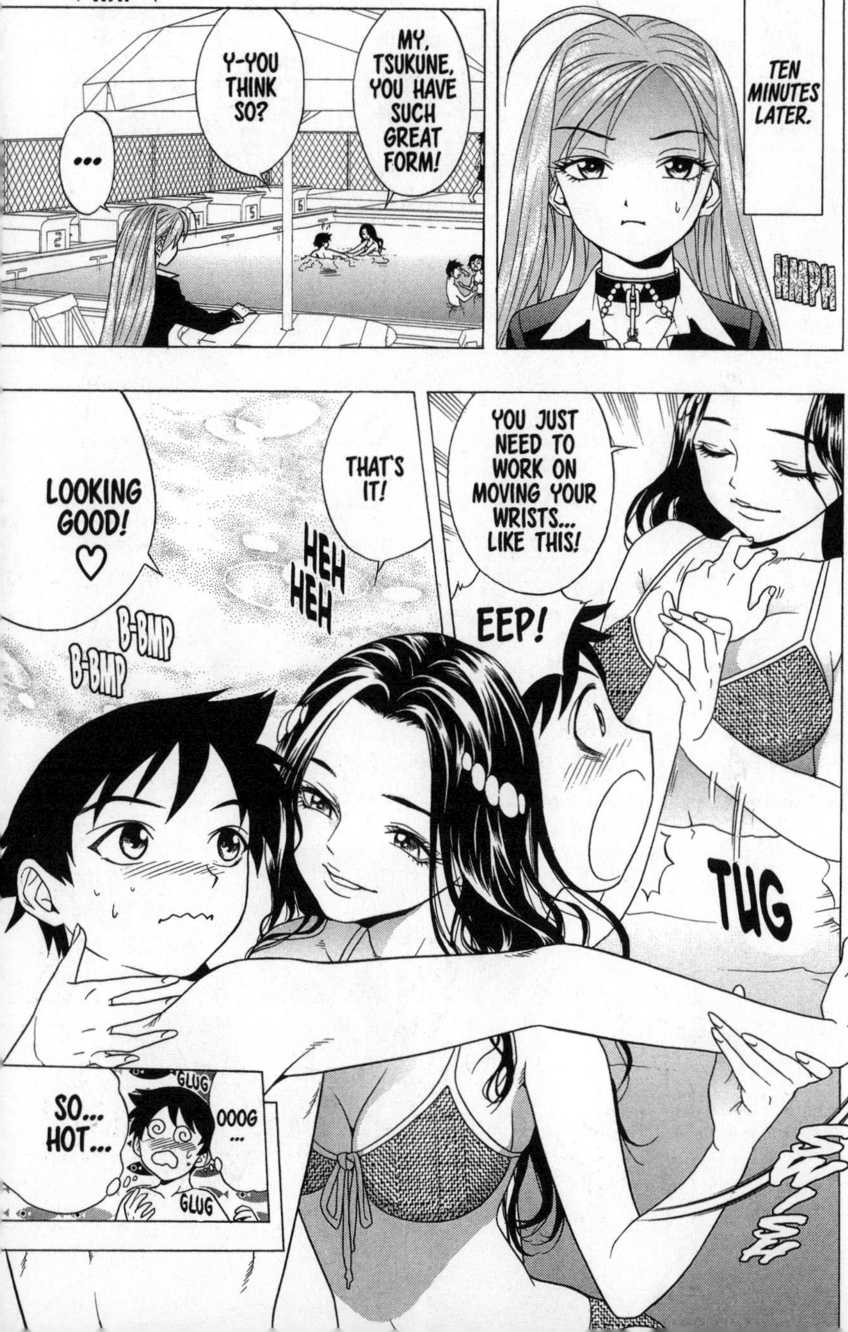
TEN MINUTES LATER.
HMPH
MY, TSUKUNE, YOU HAVE SUCH GREAT FORM!
Y-YOU THINK SO?
...
YOU JUST NEED TO WORK ON MOVING YOUR WRISTS... LIKE THIS!
EEP!
TUG
THAT'S IT!
HEH HEH
LOOKING GOOD! ♡
B-BMP
B-BMP
GLUG
OOOG...
SO... HOT...
GLUG

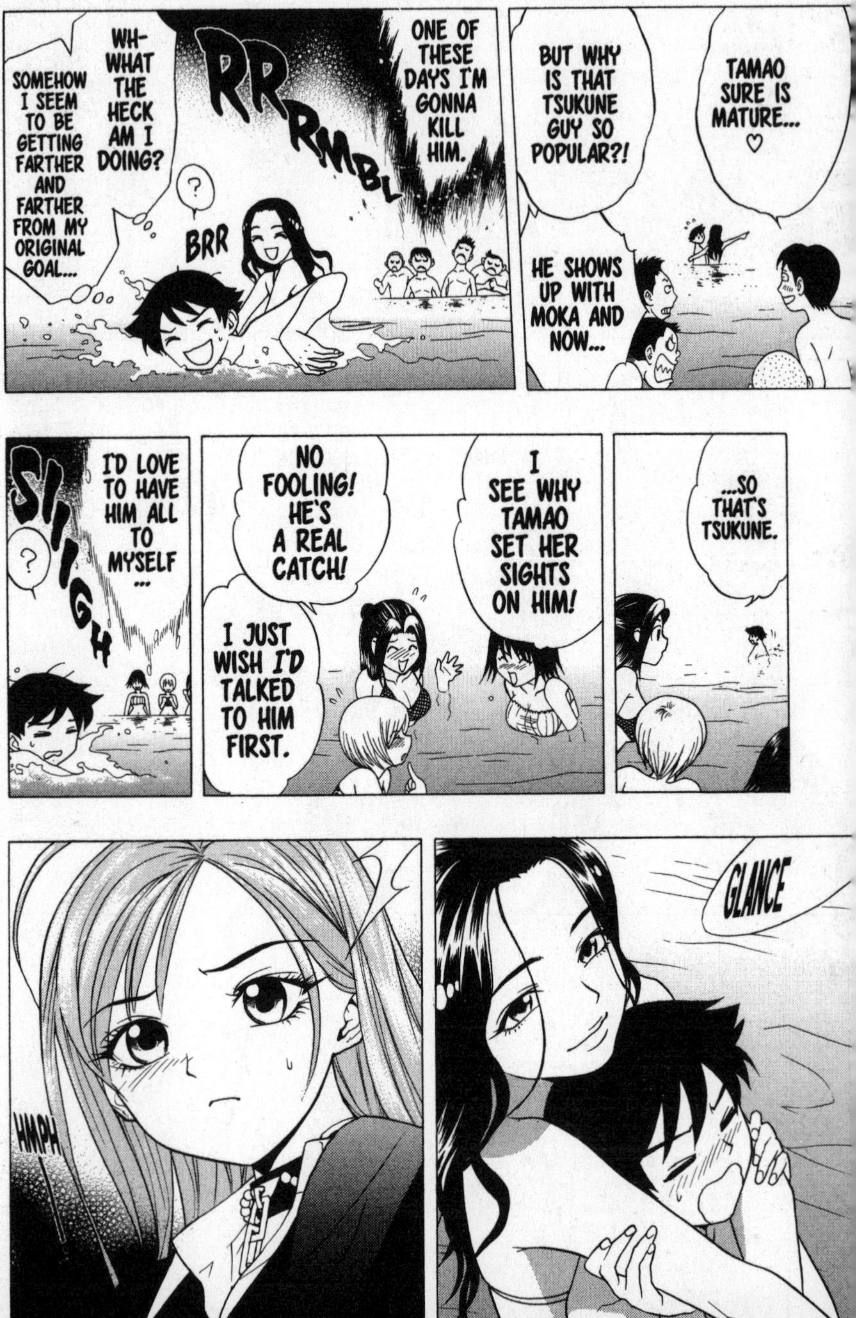
TAMAO SURE IS MATURE... ♡
BUT WHY IS THAT TSUKUNE GUY SO POPULAR?!
HE SHOWS UP WITH MOKA AND NOW...
ONE OF THESE DAYS I'M GONNA KILL HIM.
RRRRMBL
WH-WHAT THE HECK AM I DOING?
SOMEHOW I SEEM TO BE GETTING FARTHER AND FARTHER FROM MY ORIGINAL GOAL...
?
BRR
...SO THAT'S TSUKUNE.
I SEE WHY TAMAO SET HER SIGHTS ON HIM!
NO FOOLING! HE'S A REAL CATCH!
I JUST WISH I'D TALKED TO HIM FIRST.
I'D LOVE TO HAVE HIM ALL TO MYSELF...
SIIIGH
?
GLANCE
HMPH

READ THIS WAY

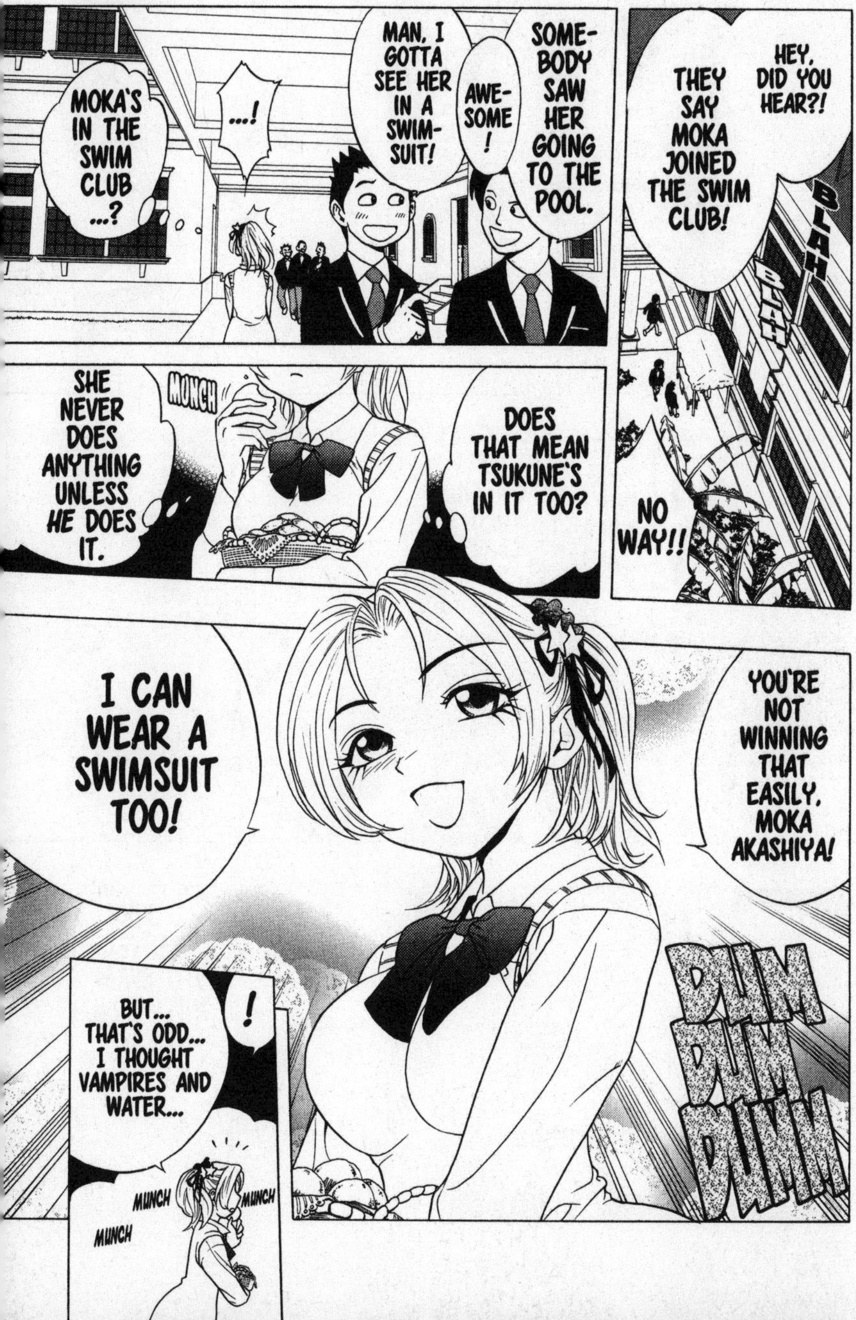

HEY, DID YOU HEAR?!
THEY SAY MOKA JOINED THE SWIM CLUB!
BLAH
BLAH
NO WAY!!
SOME-BODY SAW HER GOING TO THE POOL.
AWE-SOME!
MAN, I GOTTA SEE HER IN A SWIM-SUIT!
...!
MOKA'S IN THE SWIM CLUB ...?
DOES THAT MEAN TSUKUNE'S IN IT TOO?
MUNCH
SHE NEVER DOES ANYTHING UNLESS HE DOES IT.
YOU'RE NOT WINNING THAT EASILY, MOKA AKASHIYA!
I CAN WEAR A SWIMSUIT TOO!
DUM DUM DUMM
!
BUT... THAT'S ODD... I THOUGHT VAMPIRES AND WATER...
MUNCH
MUNCH
MUNCH

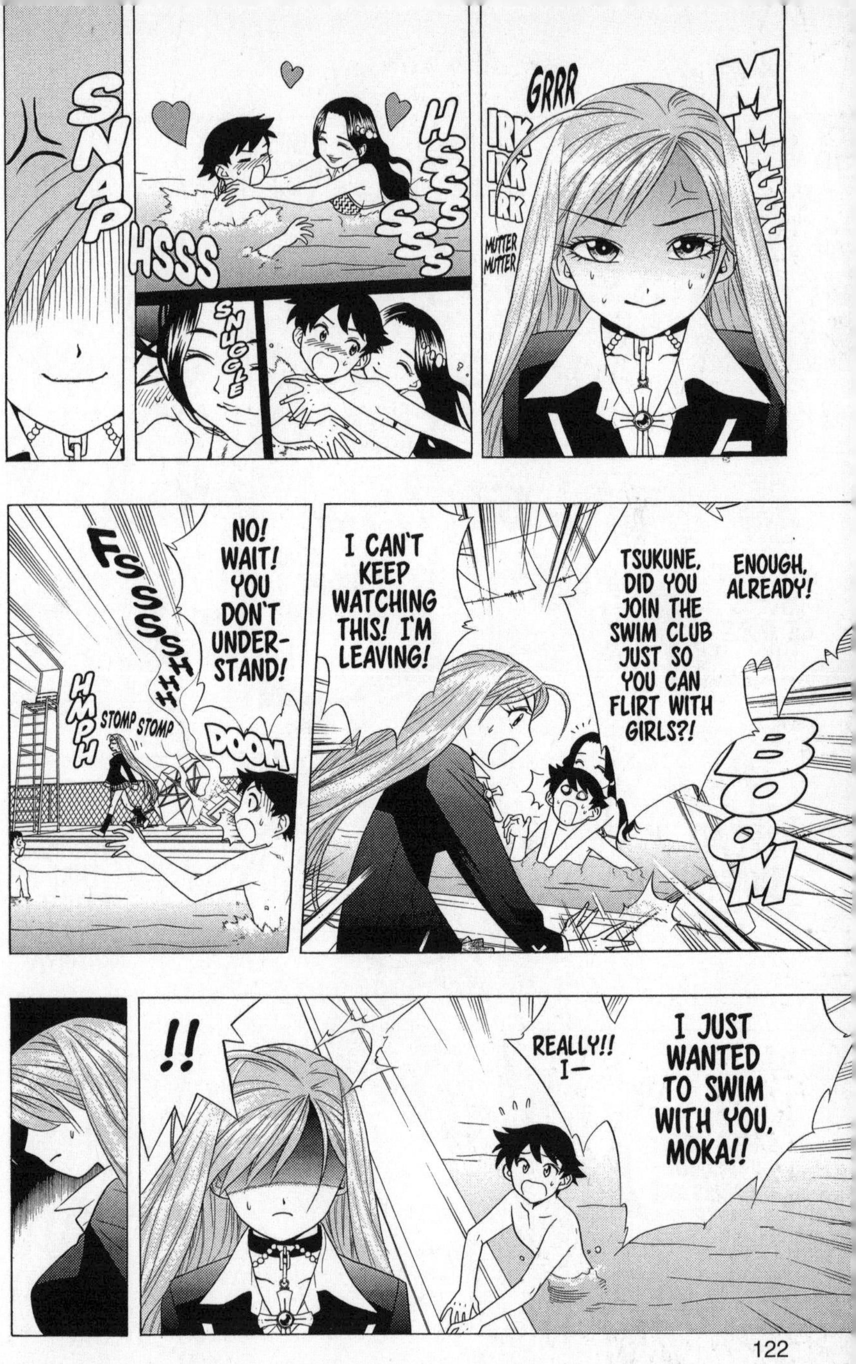
GRRR
MMMGGG
IRK IRK IRK
MUTTER MUTTER
HSSSSSS
HSSS
SNUGGLE
SNAP
ENOUGH, ALREADY!
TSUKUNE, DID YOU JOIN THE SWIM CLUB JUST SO YOU CAN FLIRT WITH GIRLS?!
BOOM
I CAN'T KEEP WATCHING THIS! I'M LEAVING!
NO! WAIT! YOU DON'T UNDER-STAND!
FSSSSHHH
HMPH
STOMP STOMP
DOOM
I JUST WANTED TO SWIM WITH YOU, MOKA!!
REALLY!! I—
!!

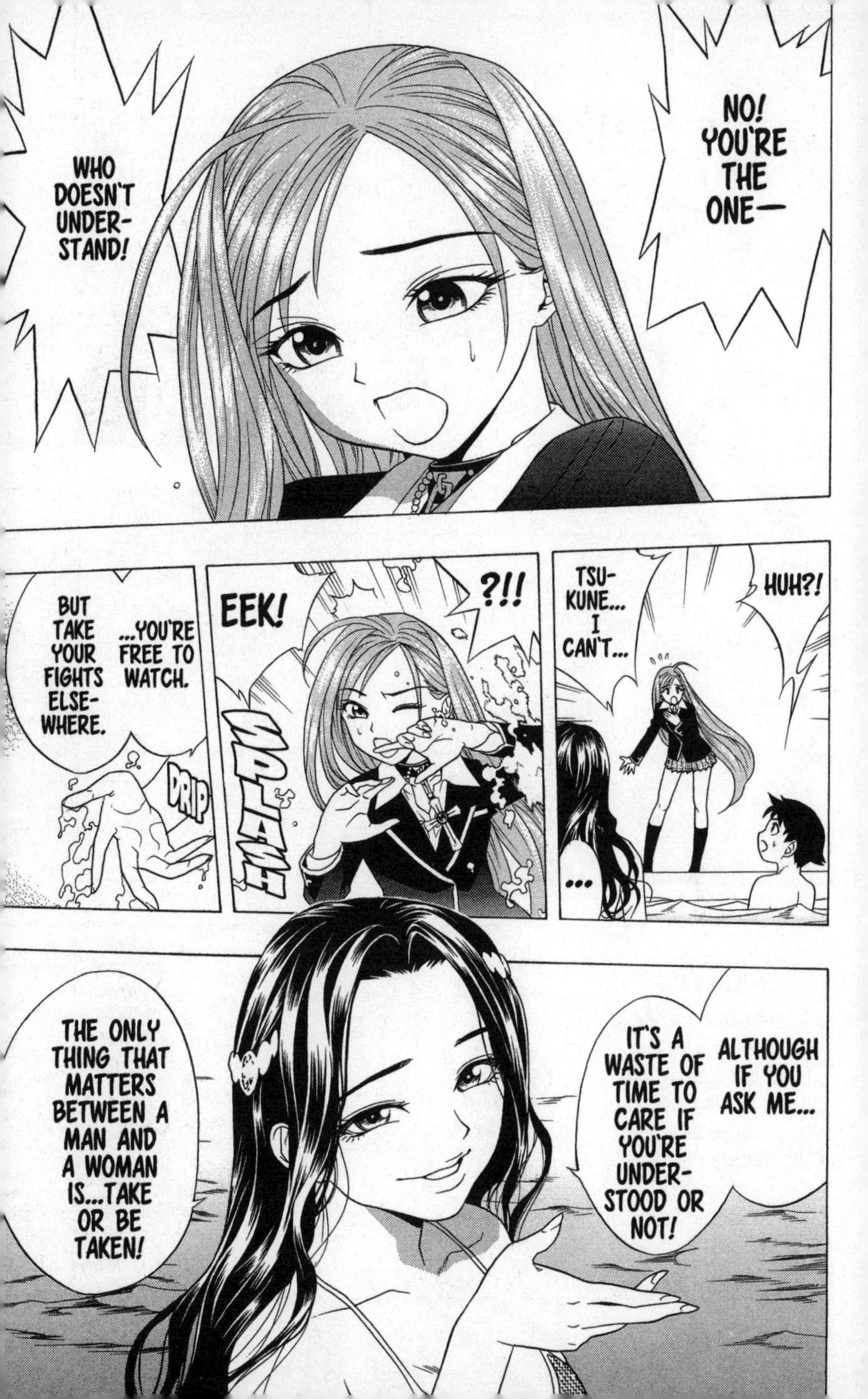
NO! YOU'RE THE ONE—
WHO DOESN'T UNDER-STAND!
HUH?!
TSU-KUNE... I CAN'T...
...
?!!
EEK!
SPLASH
...YOU'RE FREE TO WATCH.
BUT TAKE YOUR FIGHTS ELSE-WHERE.
DRIP
ALTHOUGH IF YOU ASK ME...
IT'S A WASTE OF TIME TO CARE IF YOU'RE UNDER-STOOD OR NOT!
THE ONLY THING THAT MATTERS BETWEEN A MAN AND A WOMAN IS...TAKE OR BE TAKEN!

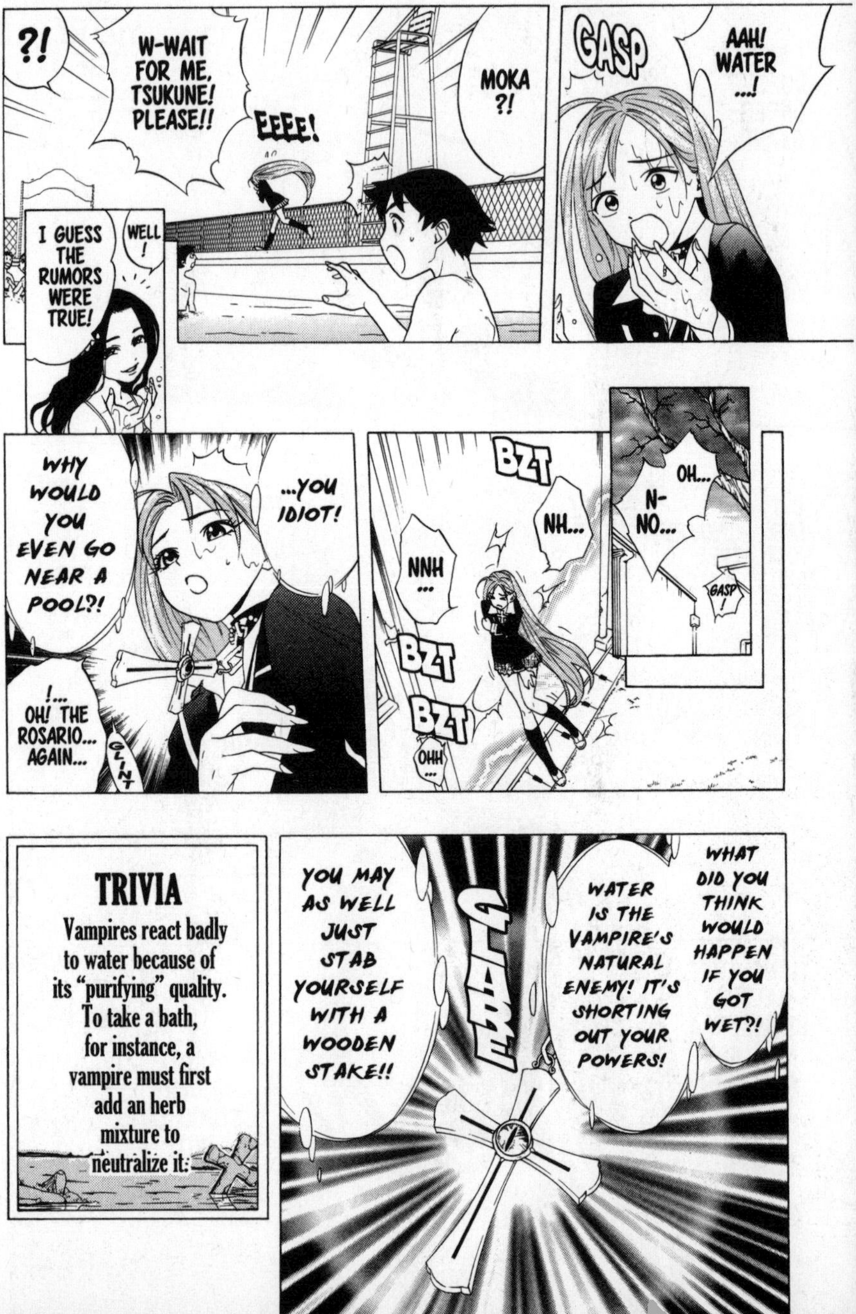
GASP
AAH! WATER ...!
MOKA ?!
W-WAIT FOR ME, TSUKUNE! PLEASE!!
?!
EEEE!
WELL !
I GUESS THE RUMORS WERE TRUE!
OH...
N- NO...
GASP !
BZT
NH...
NNH ...
BZT
BZT
OHH ...
...YOU IDIOT!
WHY WOULD YOU EVEN GO NEAR A POOL?!
!... OH! THE ROSARIO... AGAIN...
GLINT
WHAT DID YOU THINK WOULD HAPPEN IF YOU GOT WET?!
WATER IS THE VAMPIRE'S NATURAL ENEMY! IT'S SHORTING OUT YOUR POWERS!
GLARE
YOU MAY AS WELL JUST STAB YOURSELF WITH A WOODEN STAKE!!
TRIVIA
Vampires react badly to water because of its "purifying" quality. To take a bath, for instance, a vampire must first add an herb mixture to neutralize it.

READ THIS WAY

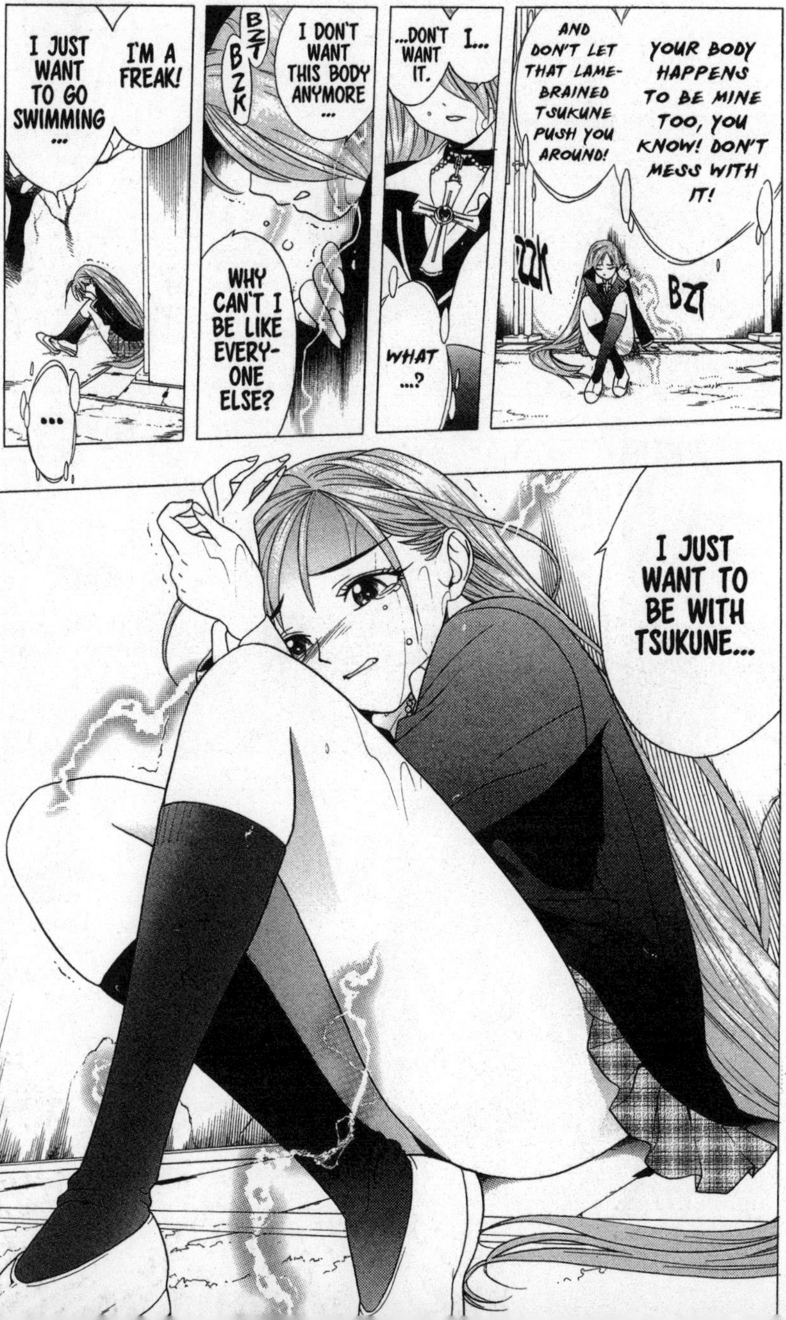
YOUR BODY HAPPENS TO BE MINE TOO, YOU KNOW! DON'T MESS WITH IT!
AND DON'T LET THAT LAME-BRAINED TSUKUNE PUSH YOU AROUND!
ZZK
BZT
I...
...DON'T WANT IT.
WHAT ...?
BZT
BZK
I DON'T WANT THIS BODY ANYMORE ...
WHY CAN'T I BE LIKE EVERYONE ELSE?
I'M A FREAK!
I JUST WANT TO GO SWIMMING ...
...
I JUST WANT TO BE WITH TSUKUNE...

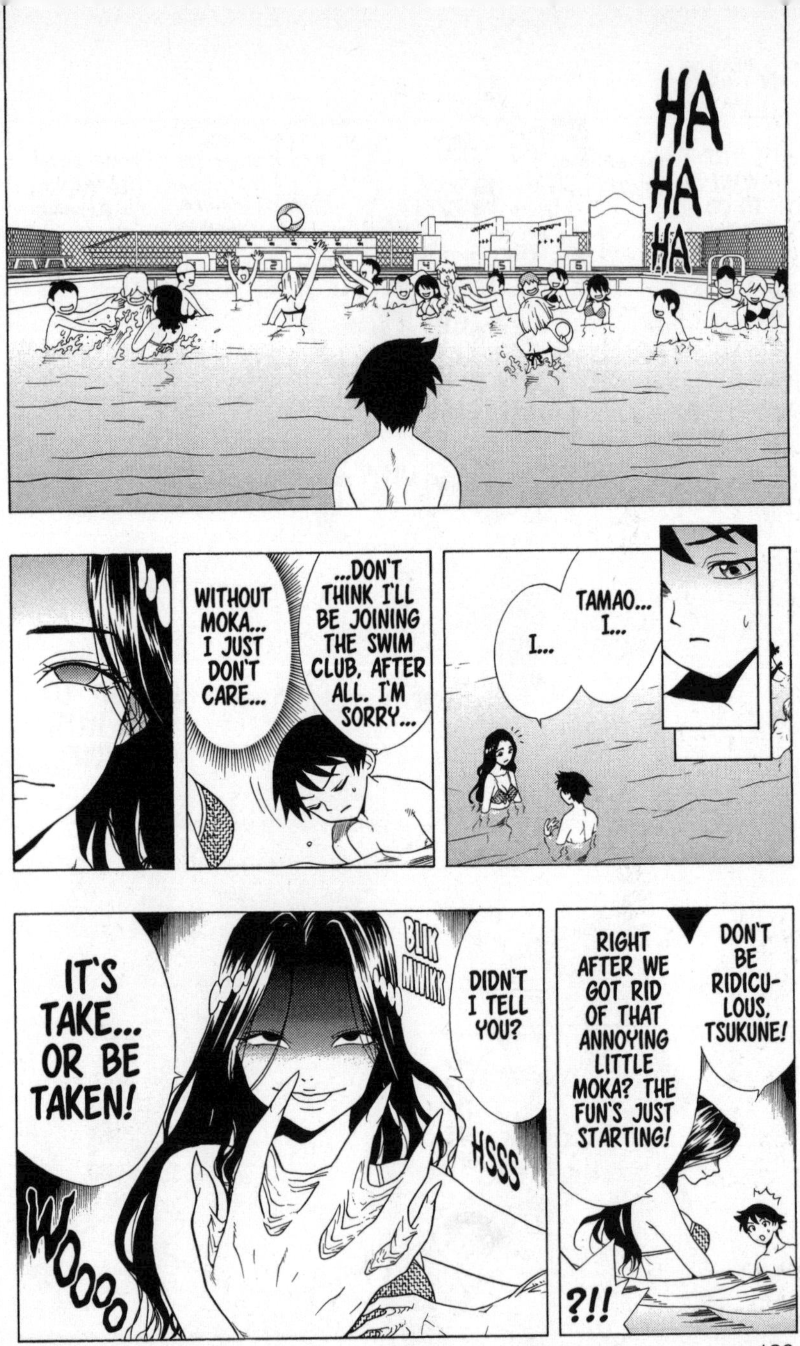
HA HA HA
TAMAO... I...
I...
...DON'T THINK I'LL BE JOINING THE SWIM CLUB, AFTER ALL. I'M SORRY...
WITHOUT MOKA... I JUST DON'T CARE...
DON'T BE RIDICULOUS, TSUKUNE!
RIGHT AFTER WE GOT RID OF THAT ANNOYING LITTLE MOKA? THE FUN'S JUST STARTING!
?!!
BLIK MWIKK
DIDN'T I TELL YOU?
IT'S TAKE... OR BE TAKEN!
HSSS
WOOOO

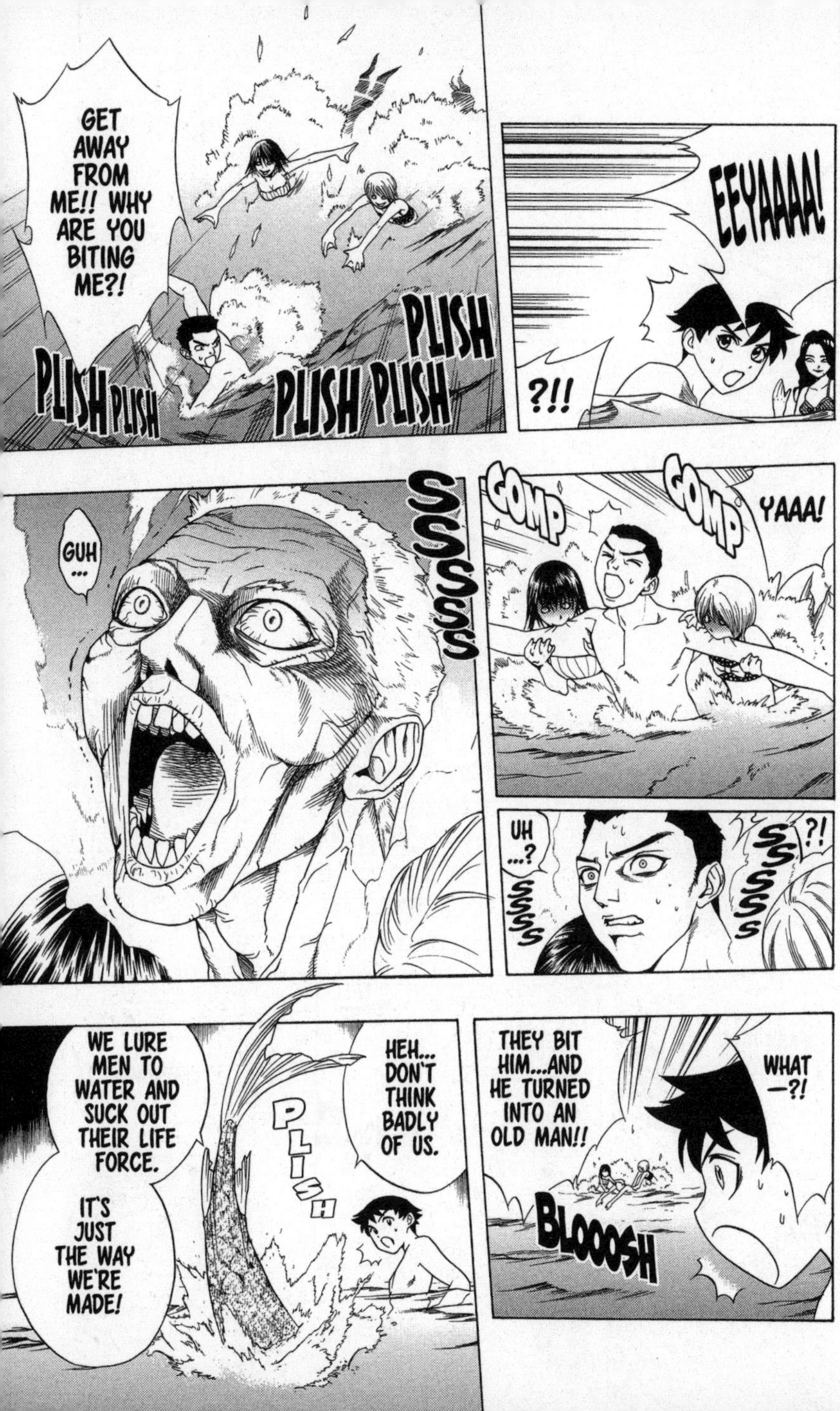
EEYAAAA!
?!!
GET AWAY FROM ME!! WHY ARE YOU BITING ME?!
PLISH
PLISH PLISH
PLISH PLISH
GOMP
GOMP
YAAA!
?!
SSSSS
UH ...?
SSSS
SSSSSS
GUH ...
WHAT—?!
THEY BIT HIM...AND HE TURNED INTO AN OLD MAN!!
BLOOOSH
HEH... DON'T THINK BADLY OF US.
PLISH
WE LURE MEN TO WATER AND SUCK OUT THEIR LIFE FORCE.
IT'S JUST THE WAY WE'RE MADE!

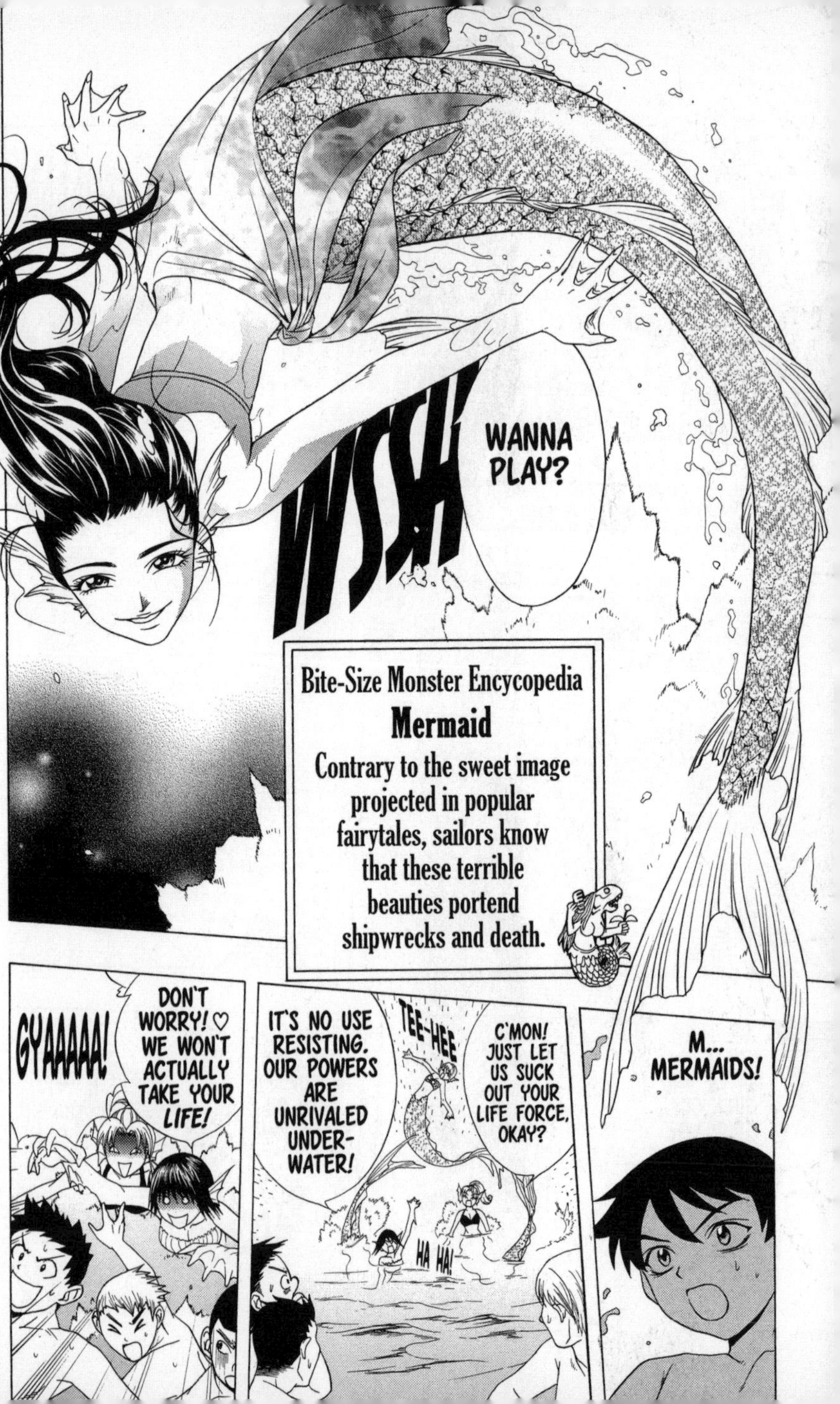
WANNA PLAY?
WSSH
Bite-Size Monster Encyclopedia
Mermaid
Contrary to the sweet image projected in popular fairytales, sailors know that these terrible beauties portend shipwrecks and death.
M... MERMAIDS!
C'MON! JUST LET US SUCK OUT YOUR LIFE FORCE, OKAY?
TEE-HEE
IT'S NO USE RESISTING. OUR POWERS ARE UNRIVALED UNDER-WATER!
HA HA!
DON'T WORRY! ♡ WE WON'T ACTUALLY TAKE YOUR LIFE!
GYAAAAA!

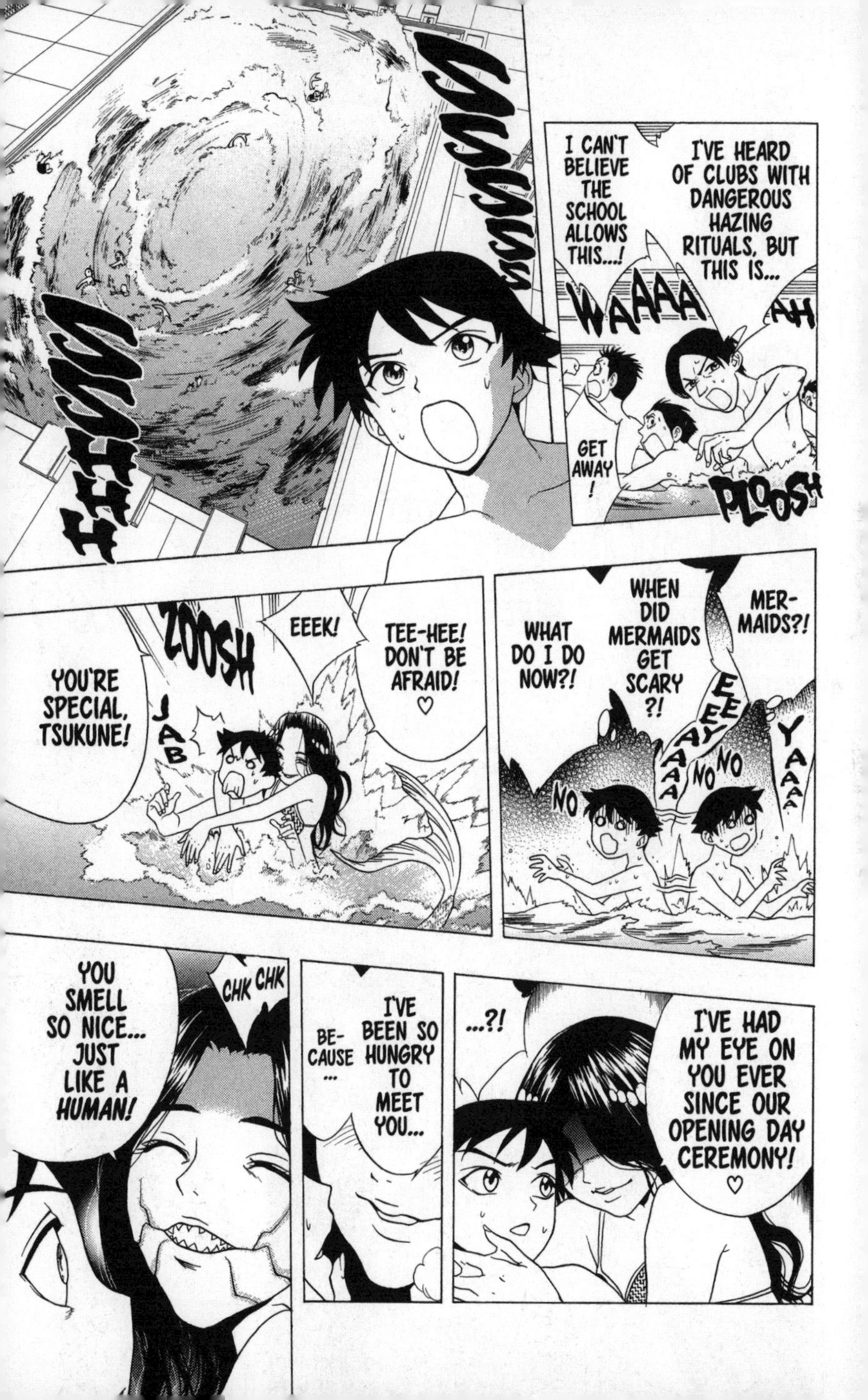
I'VE HEARD OF CLUBS WITH DANGEROUS HAZING RITUALS, BUT THIS IS...
I CAN'T BELIEVE THE SCHOOL ALLOWS THIS...!
AH
WAAAA
GET AWAY!
PLOOSH
MER-MAIDS?!
WHEN DID MERMAIDS GET SCARY?!
WHAT DO I DO NOW?!
YAAAA
EEEYAAAA
NO NO
NO
TEE-HEE! DON'T BE AFRAID! ♡
EEEK!
ZOOSH
JAB
YOU'RE SPECIAL, TSUKUNE!
I'VE HAD MY EYE ON YOU EVER SINCE OUR OPENING DAY CEREMONY! ♡
...?!
I'VE BEEN SO HUNGRY TO MEET YOU...
BE-CAUSE...
CHK CHK
YOU SMELL SO NICE... JUST LIKE A HUMAN!

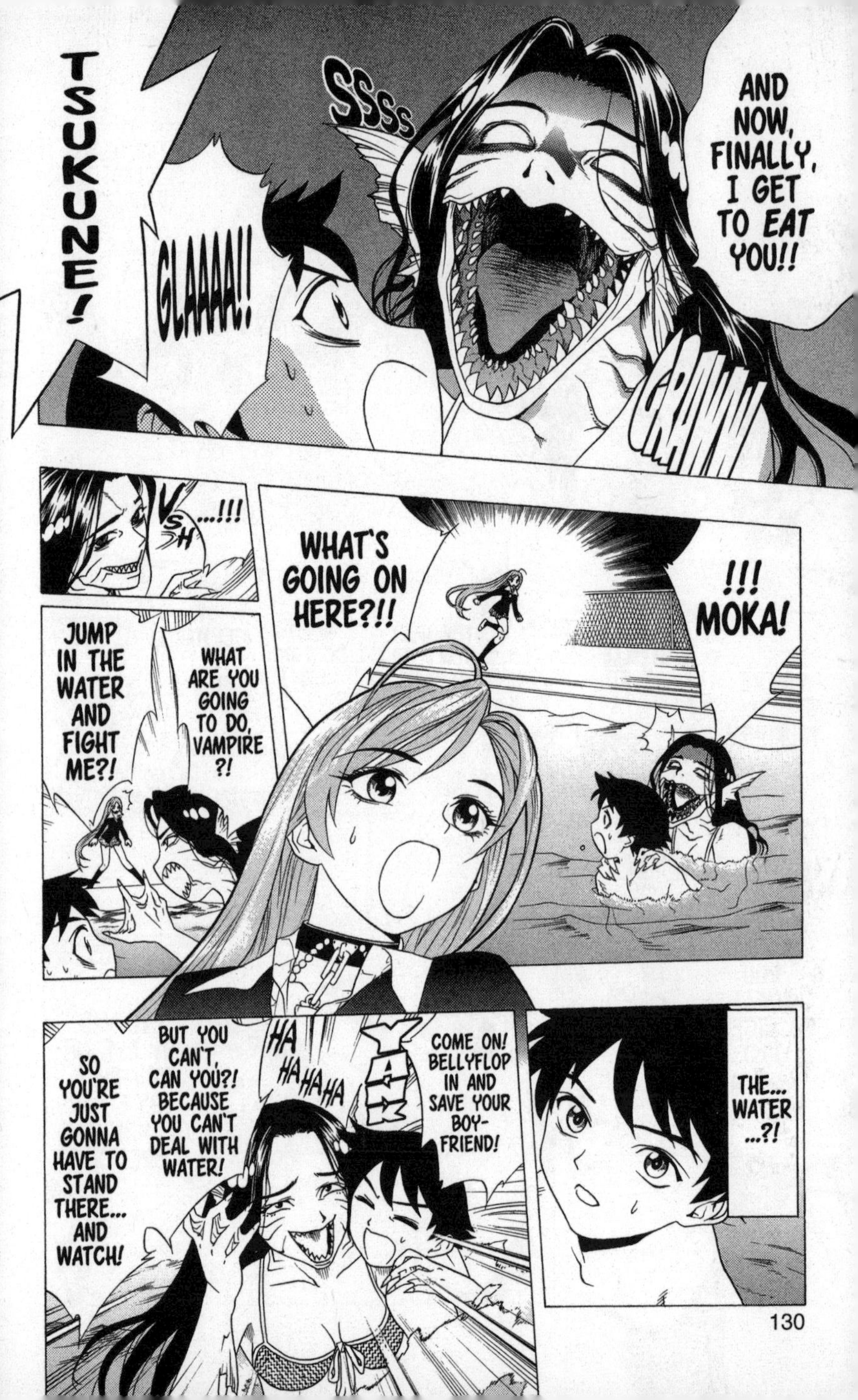
AND NOW, FINALLY, I GET TO EAT YOU!!
SSSS
GLAAAA!!
TSUKUNE!
!!! MOKA!
WHAT'S GOING ON HERE?!!
VSH
...!!!
WHAT ARE YOU GOING TO DO, VAMPIRE ?!
JUMP IN THE WATER AND FIGHT ME?!
THE... WATER ...?!
COME ON! BELLYFLOP IN AND SAVE YOUR BOY-FRIEND!
YANK
HA HA HA HA HA
BUT YOU CAN'T, CAN YOU?! BECAUSE YOU CAN'T DEAL WITH WATER!
SO YOU'RE JUST GONNA HAVE TO STAND THERE... AND WATCH!

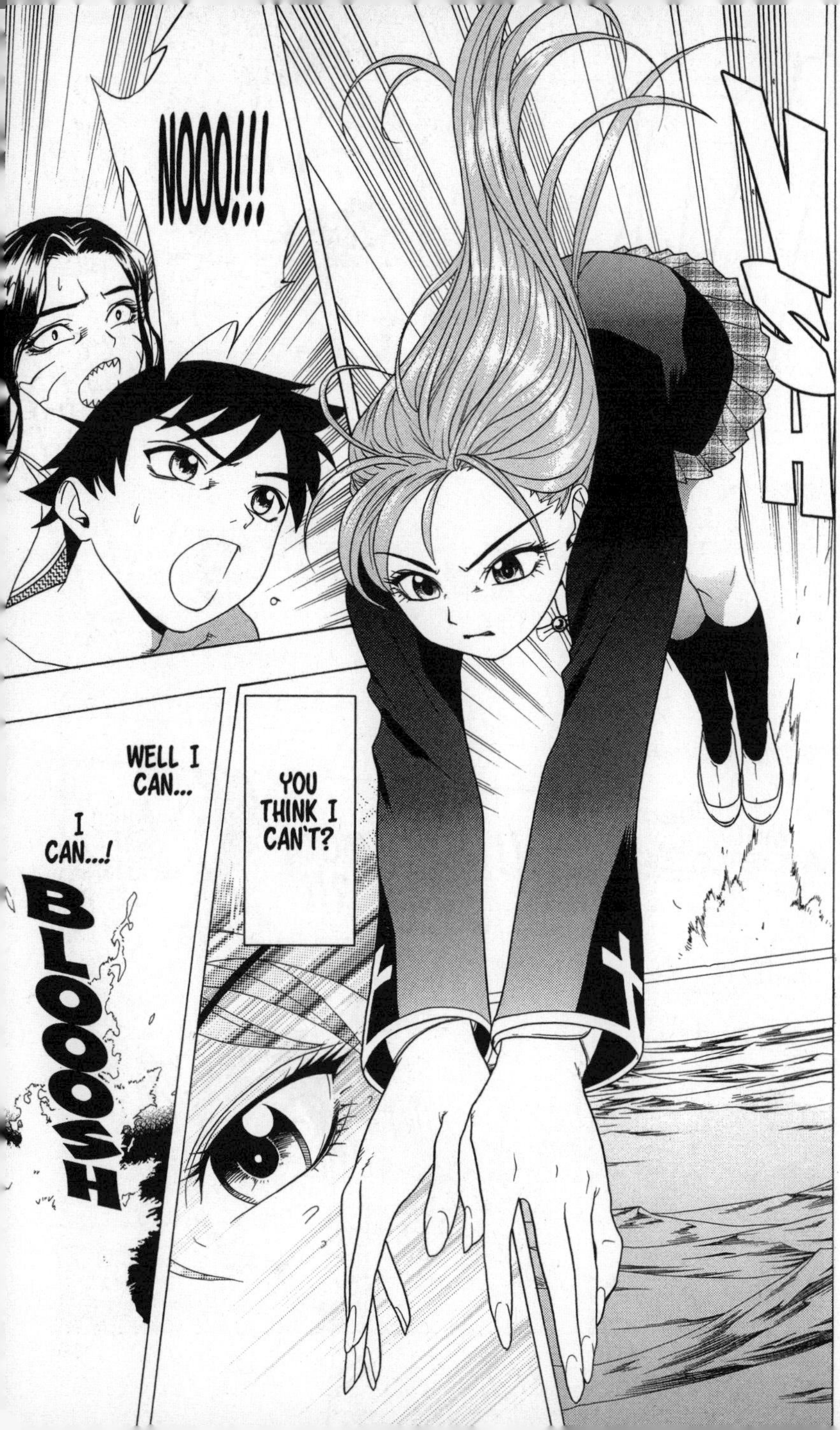
VSH
NOOO!!!
YOU THINK I CAN'T?
WELL I CAN...
I CAN...!
BLOOOSH

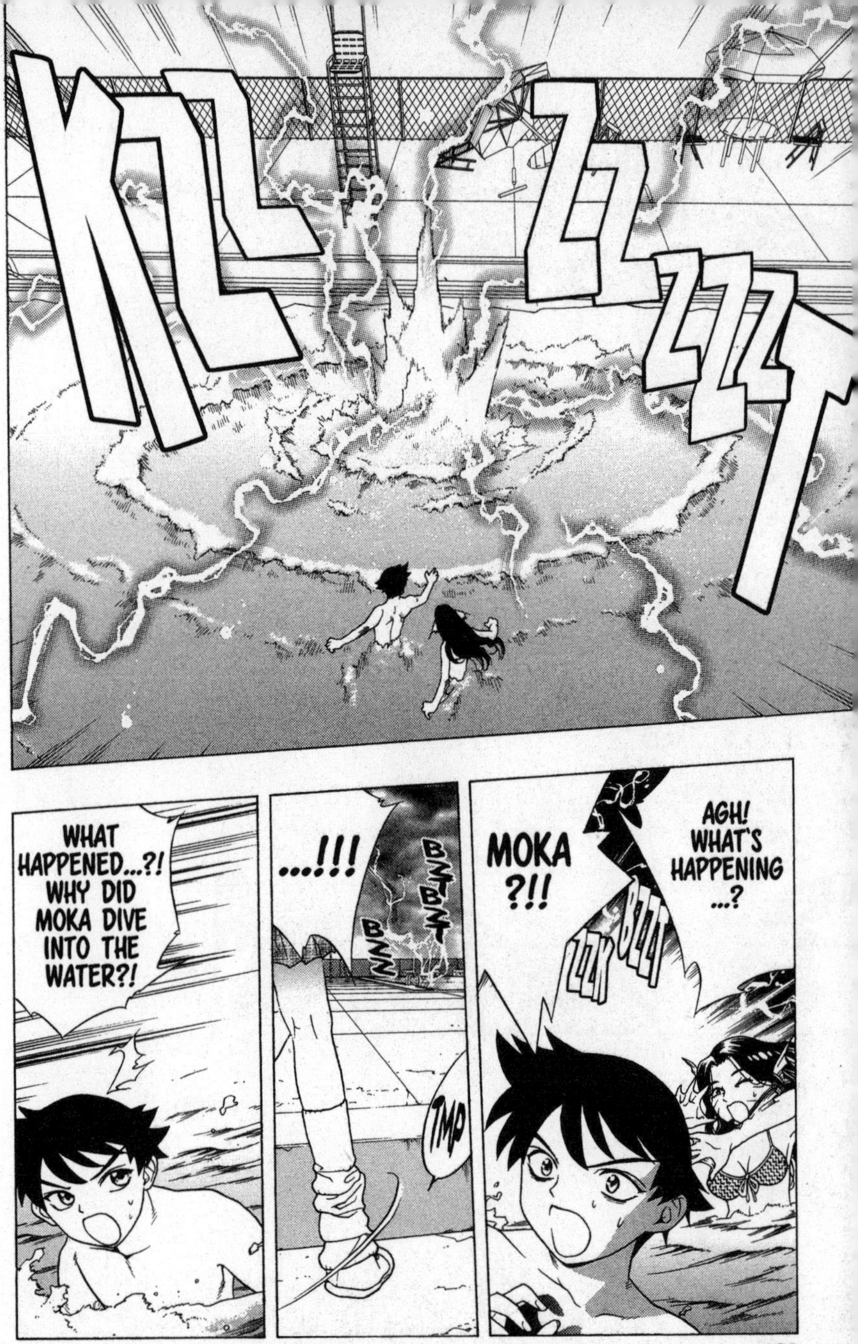
KZZ
ZZZZT
AGH! WHAT'S HAPPENING ...?
MOKA ?!!
...!!!
BZZT BZZT
BZZ
TMP
WHAT HAPPENED...?! WHY DID MOKA DIVE INTO THE WATER?!

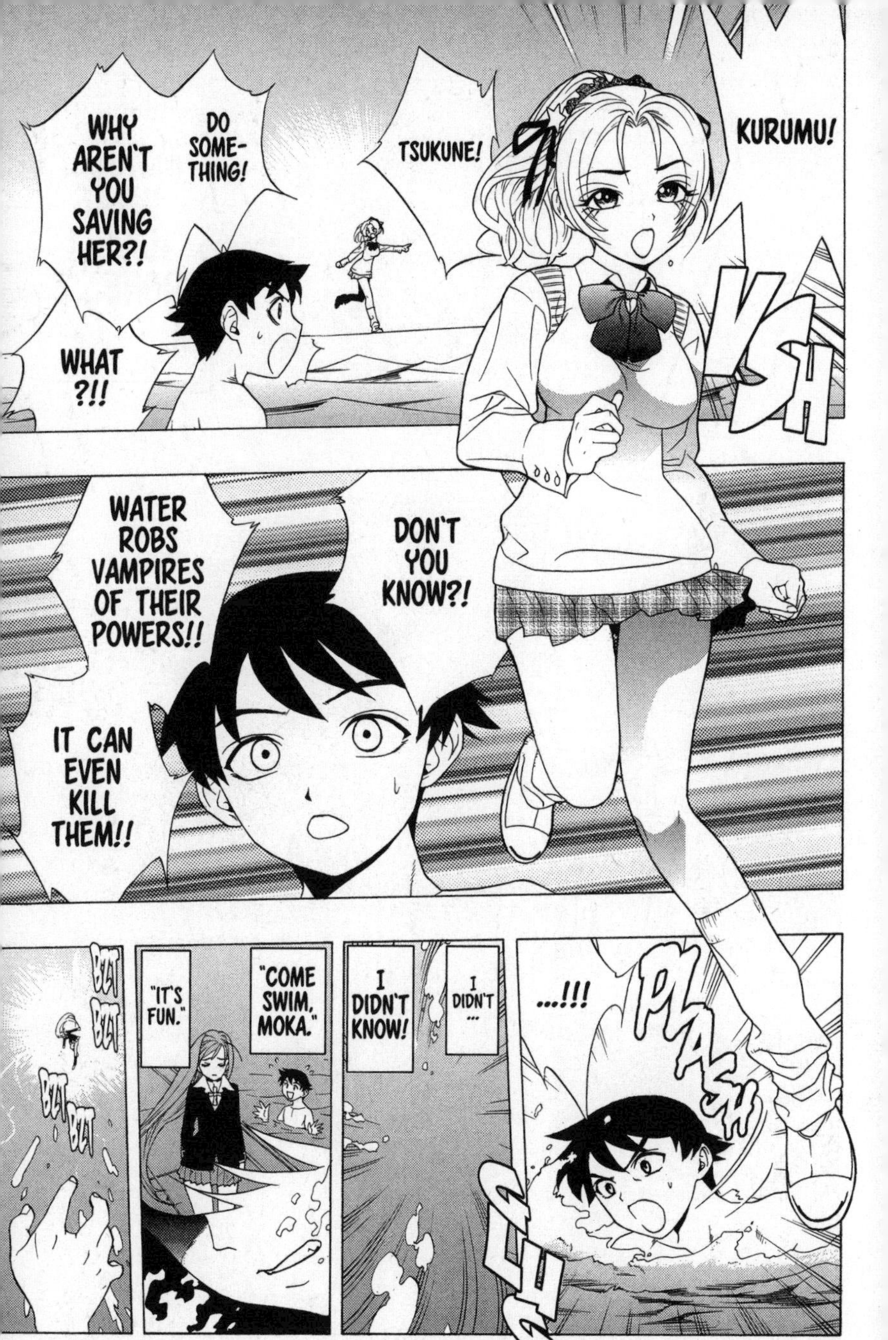
KURUMU!
TSUKUNE!
DO SOME-THING!
WHY AREN'T YOU SAVING HER?!
WHAT?!!
VSH
DON'T YOU KNOW?!
WATER ROBS VAMPIRES OF THEIR POWERS!!
IT CAN EVEN KILL THEM!!
...!!!
PLASH
I DIDN'T ...
I DIDN'T KNOW!
"COME SWIM, MOKA."
"IT'S FUN."

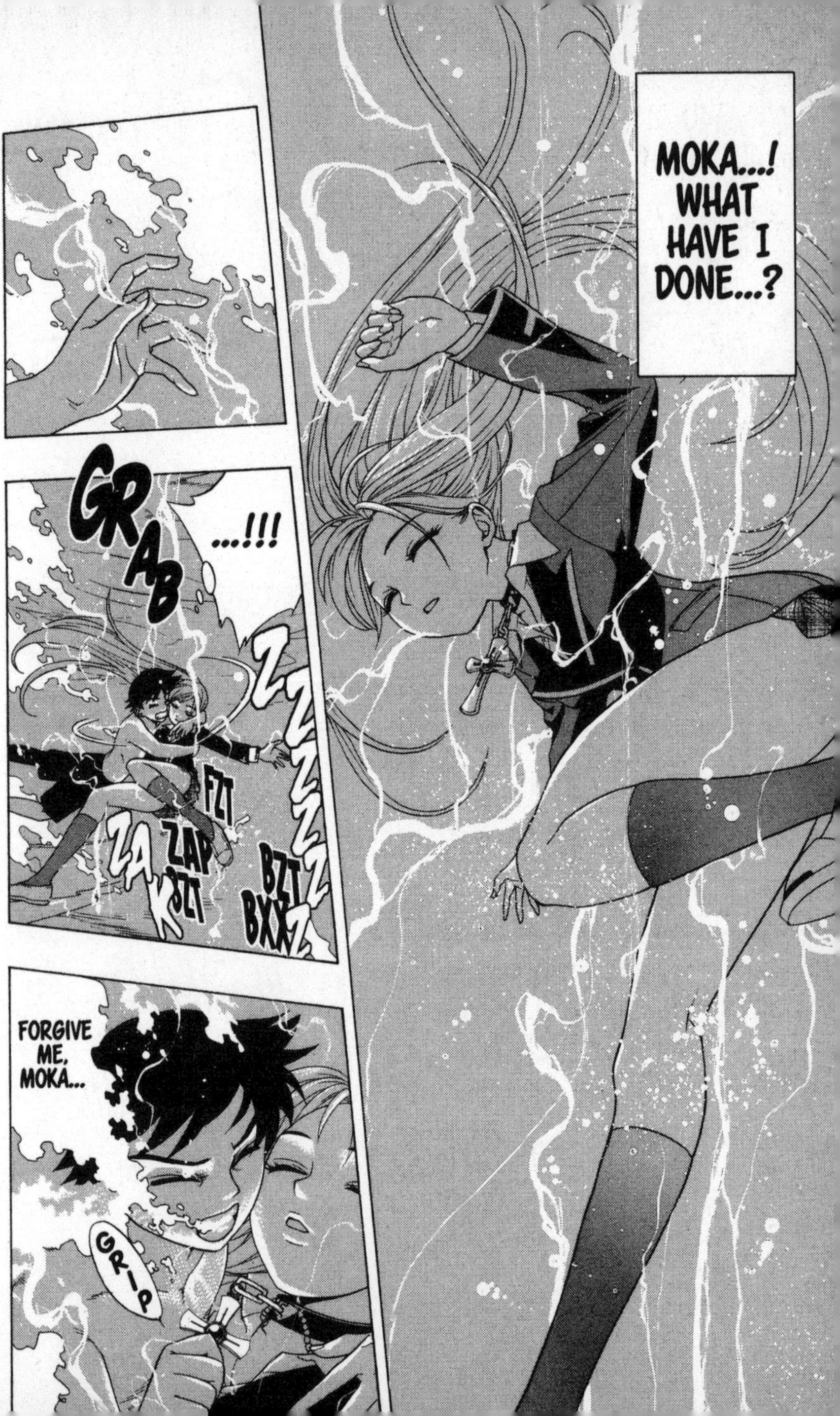
MOKA...! WHAT HAVE I DONE...?
GRAB
...!!!
ZZZZZZ
FZT
ZAP
ZAK
SZT
BZT
BXXZ
FORGIVE ME, MOKA...
GRIP

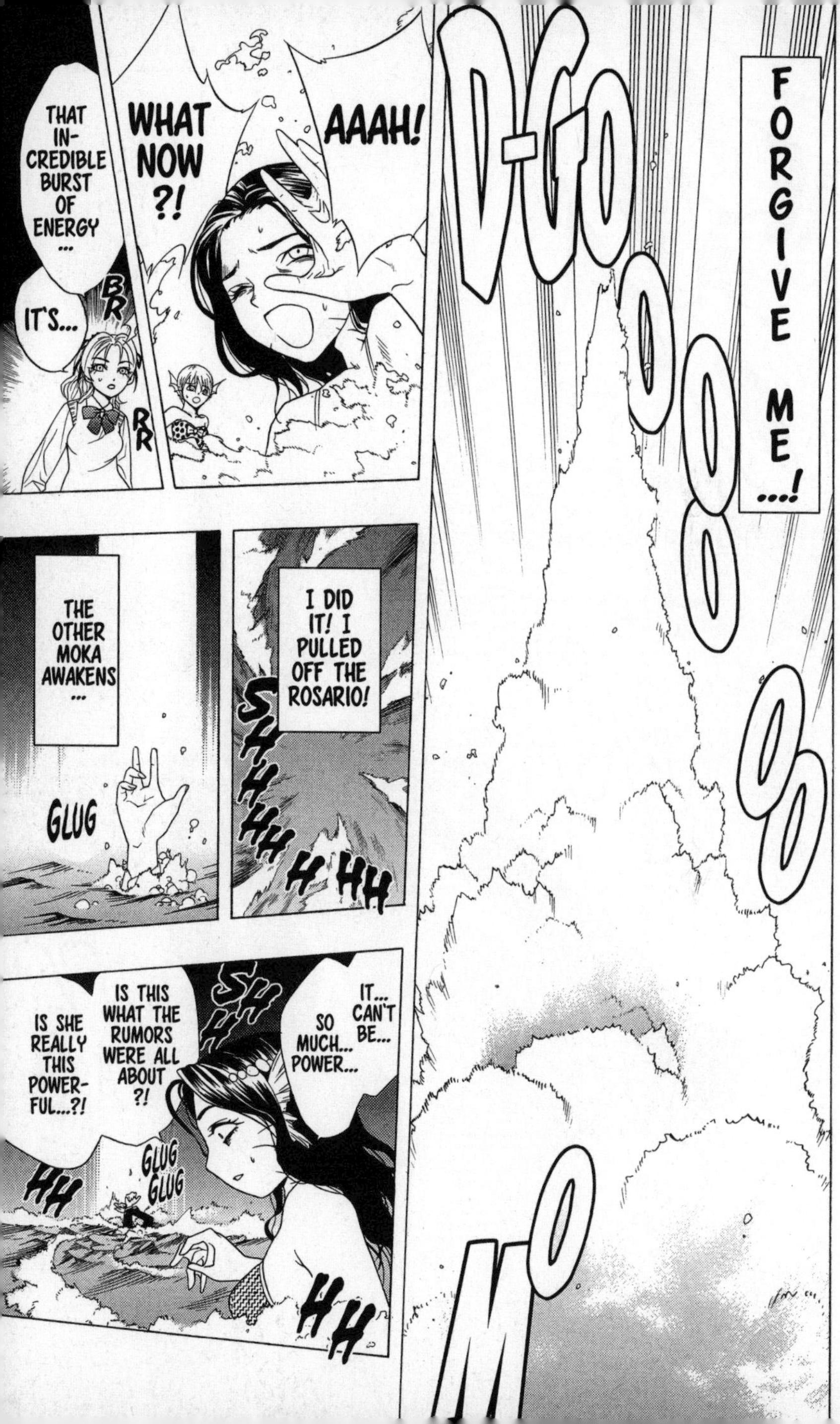
FORGIVE ME...!
D-GOOOOOOOM
AAAH!
WHAT NOW?!
THAT INCREDIBLE BURST OF ENERGY...
IT'S...
BRRR
I DID IT! I PULLED OFF THE ROSARIO!
SHHHHHHHHH
THE OTHER MOKA AWAKENS...
GLUG
IT... CAN'T BE...
SO MUCH... POWER...
SHH
IS THIS WHAT THE RUMORS WERE ALL ABOUT?!
IS SHE REALLY THIS POWERFUL...?!
GLUG GLUG
HH
HH

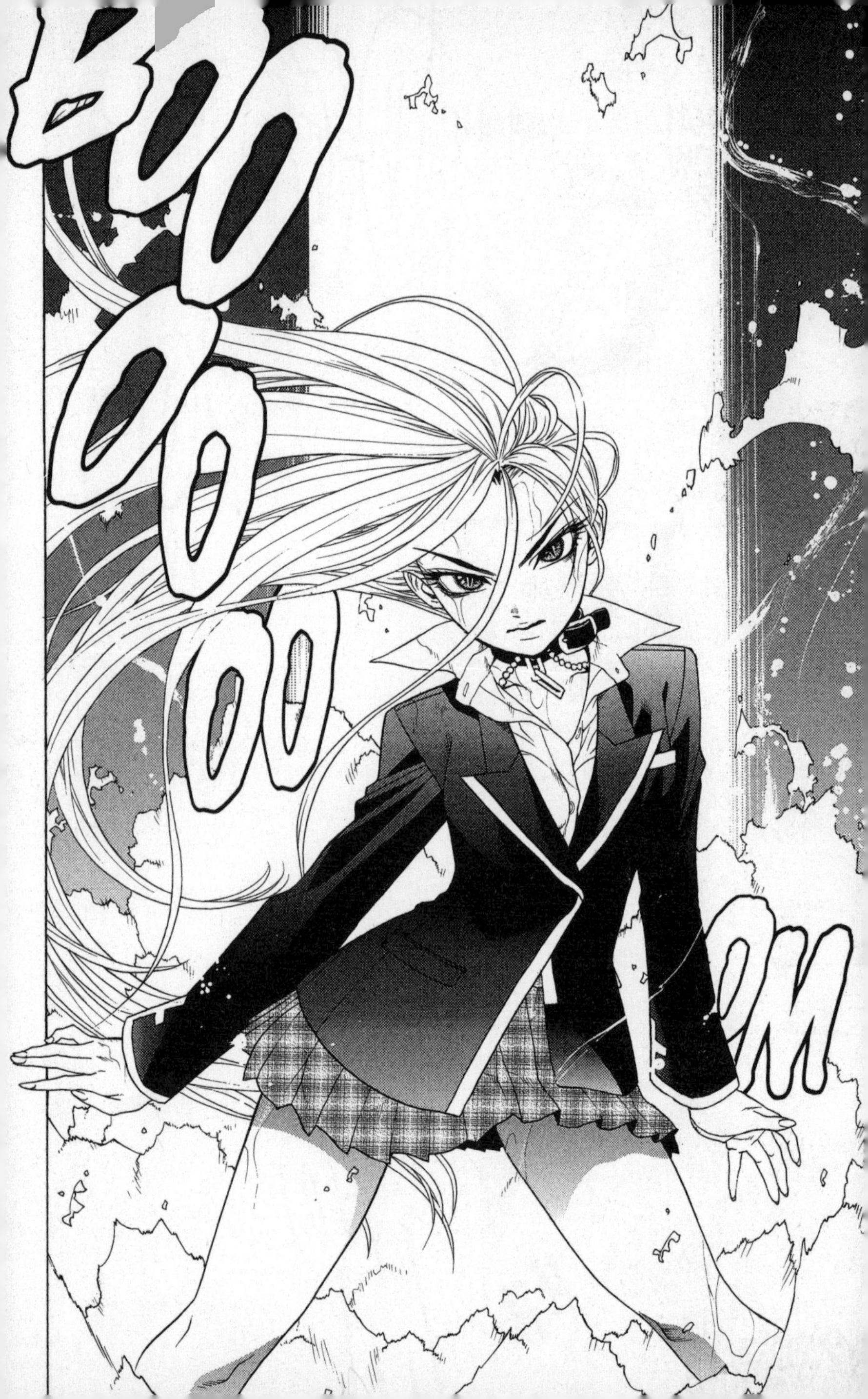
BOOOOOO
OM

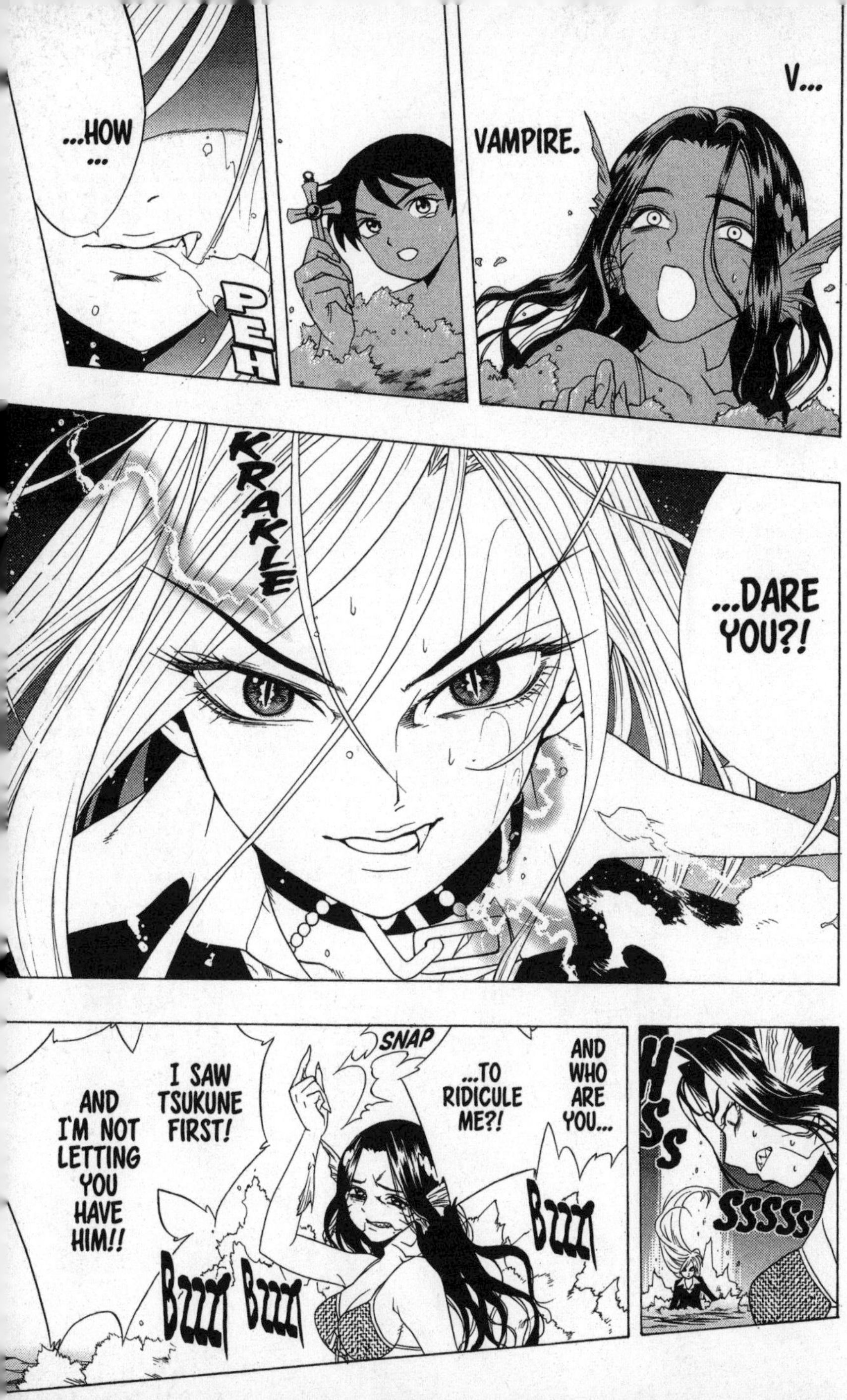
V...
VAMPIRE.
...HOW ...
PEH
...DARE YOU?!
KRAKLE
HSS
SSSSS
AND WHO ARE YOU...
SNAP
...TO RIDICULE ME?!
I SAW TSUKUNE FIRST!
AND I'M NOT LETTING YOU HAVE HIM!!
Bzzzt
Bzzzt Bzzzt

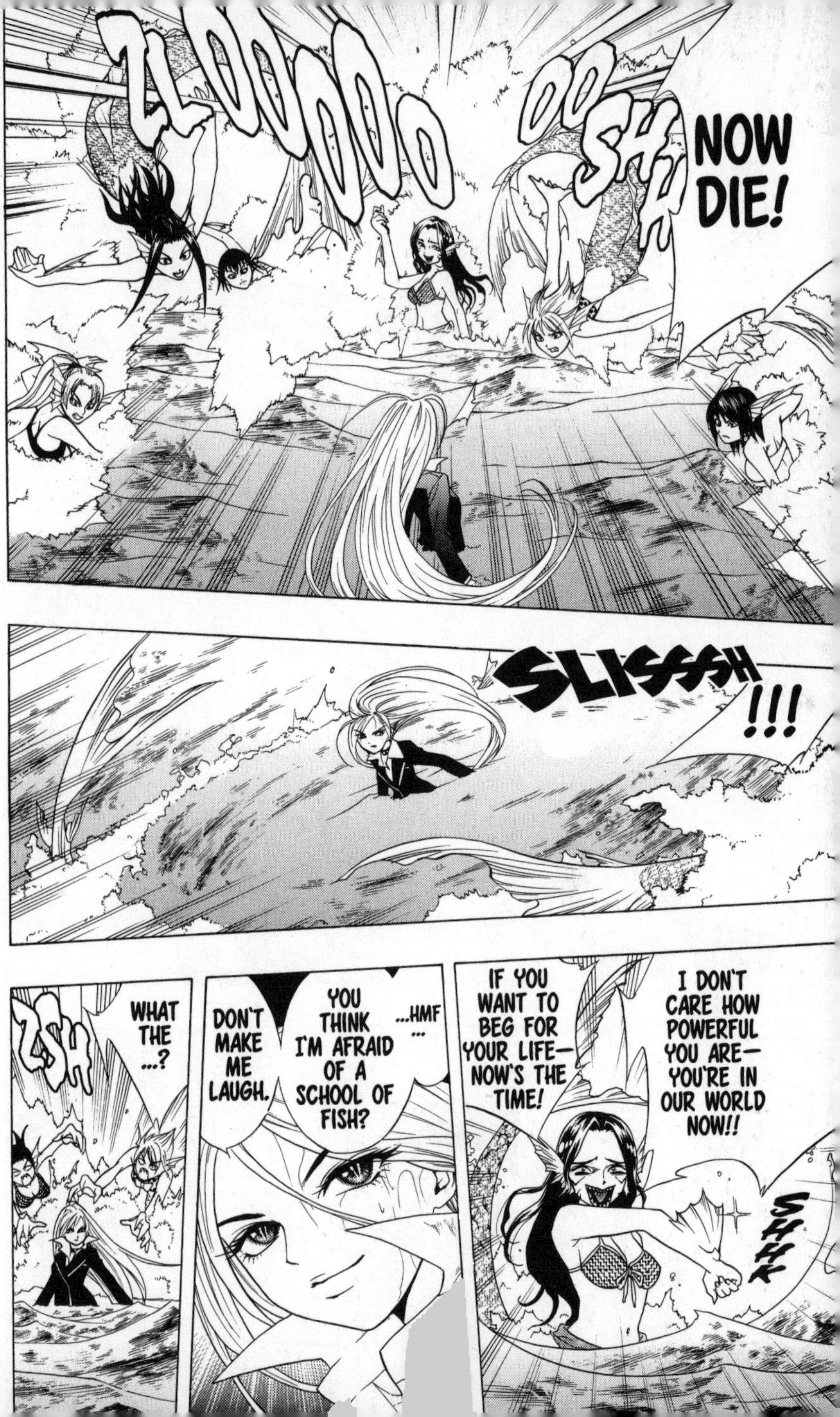
NOW DIE!
OOSH
ZLOOOOOO
SLISSSH!!!
I DON'T CARE HOW POWERFUL YOU ARE— YOU'RE IN OUR WORLD NOW!!
IF YOU WANT TO BEG FOR YOUR LIFE— NOW'S THE TIME!
SHHK
...HMF...
YOU THINK I'M AFRAID OF A SCHOOL OF FISH?
DON'T MAKE ME LAUGH.
WHAT THE ...?
ZSH

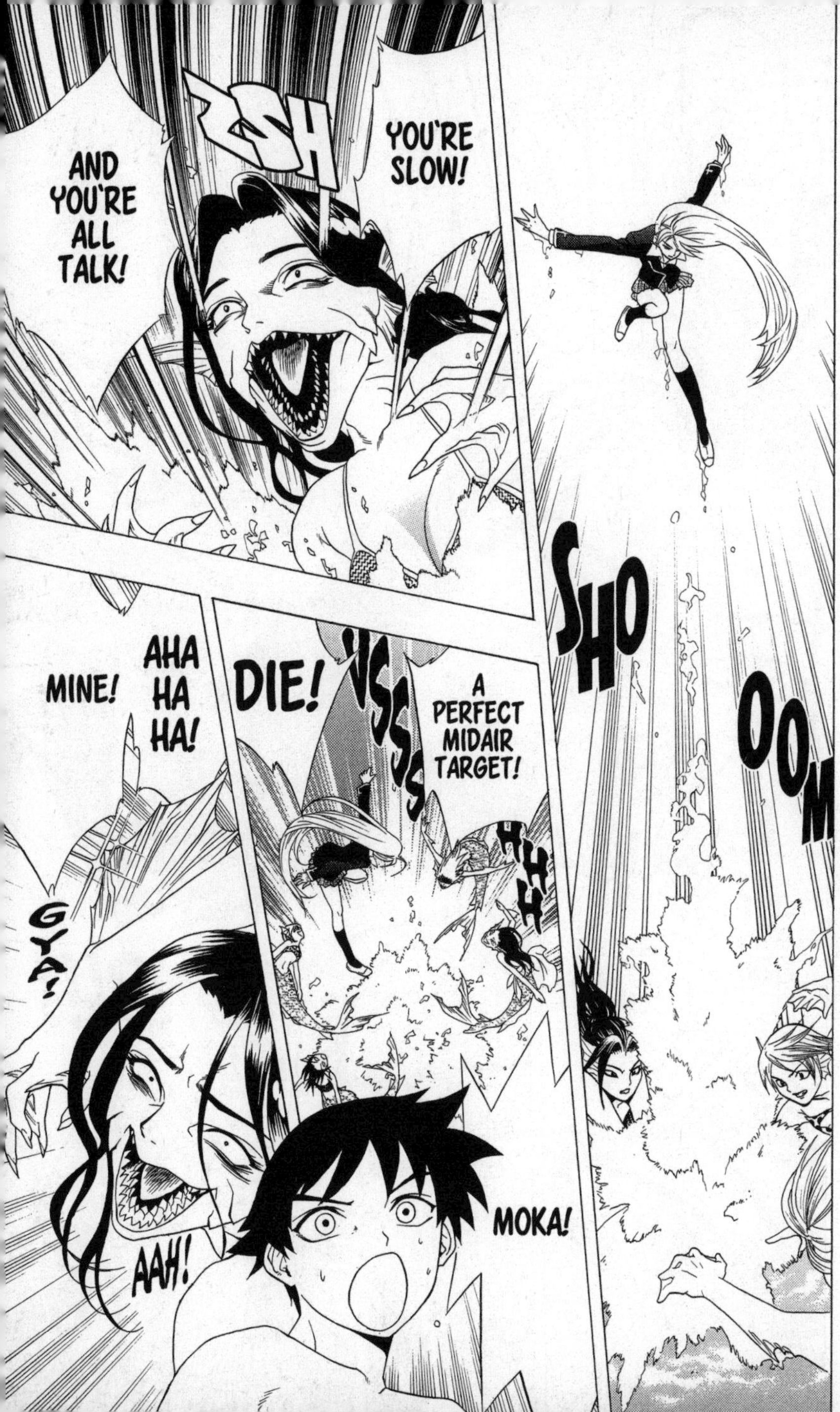
SHOOOM
YOU'RE SLOW!
ZSH
AND YOU'RE ALL TALK!
A PERFECT MIDAIR TARGET!
HHHH
VSSSS
DIE!
MOKA!
AHA HA HA!
MINE!
GYA!
AAH!

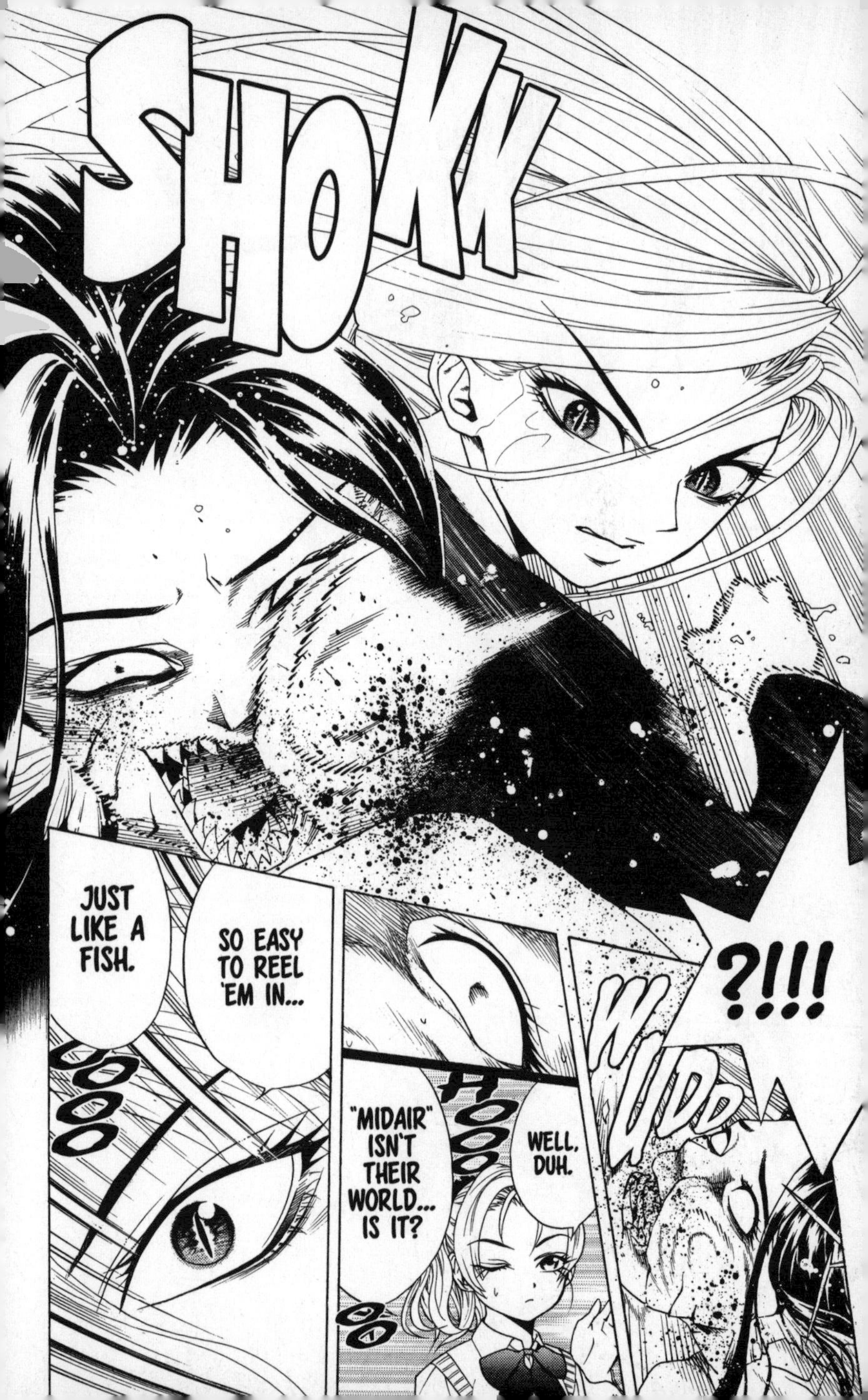
SHOKK
?!!!
WUDD
WELL, DUH.
"MIDAIR" ISN'T THEIR WORLD... IS IT?
FOOO
SO EASY TO REEL 'EM IN...
JUST LIKE A FISH.
OOOO

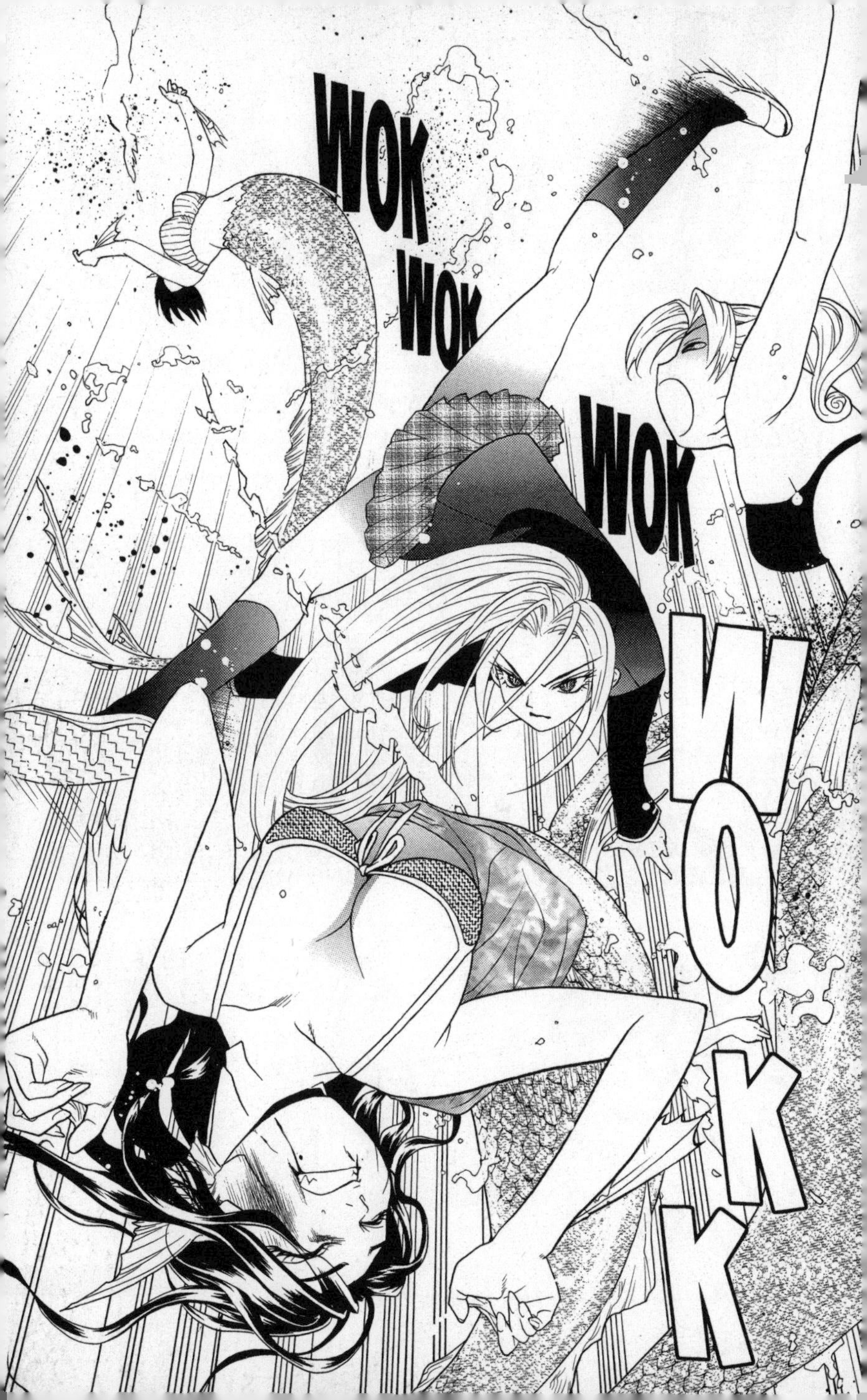
WOK
WOK
WOK
WOK

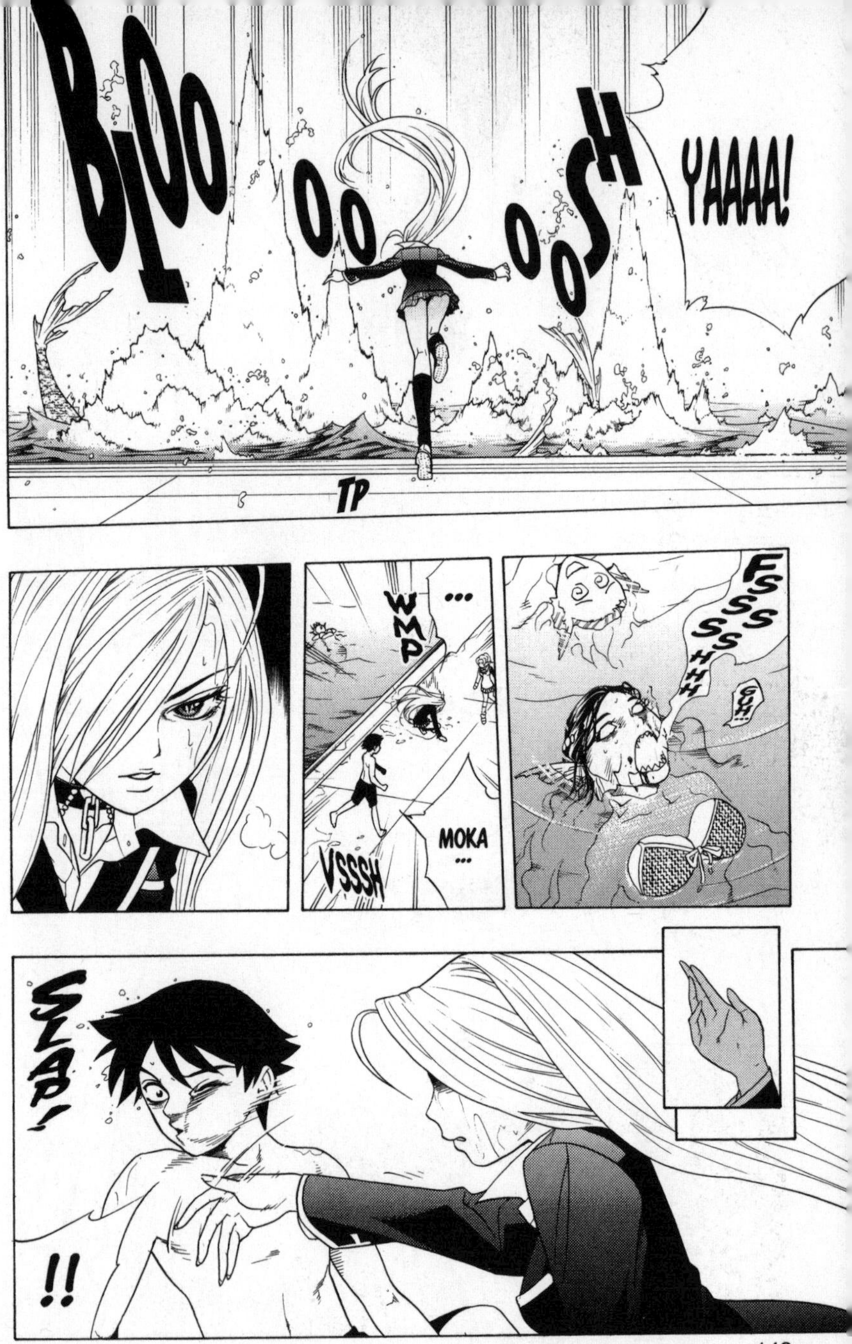

YAAAA!
BLOOOOOOSH
TP
FSSSSSHHH
GUH...
...
WMP
MOKA...
VSSSH
SLAP!
!!

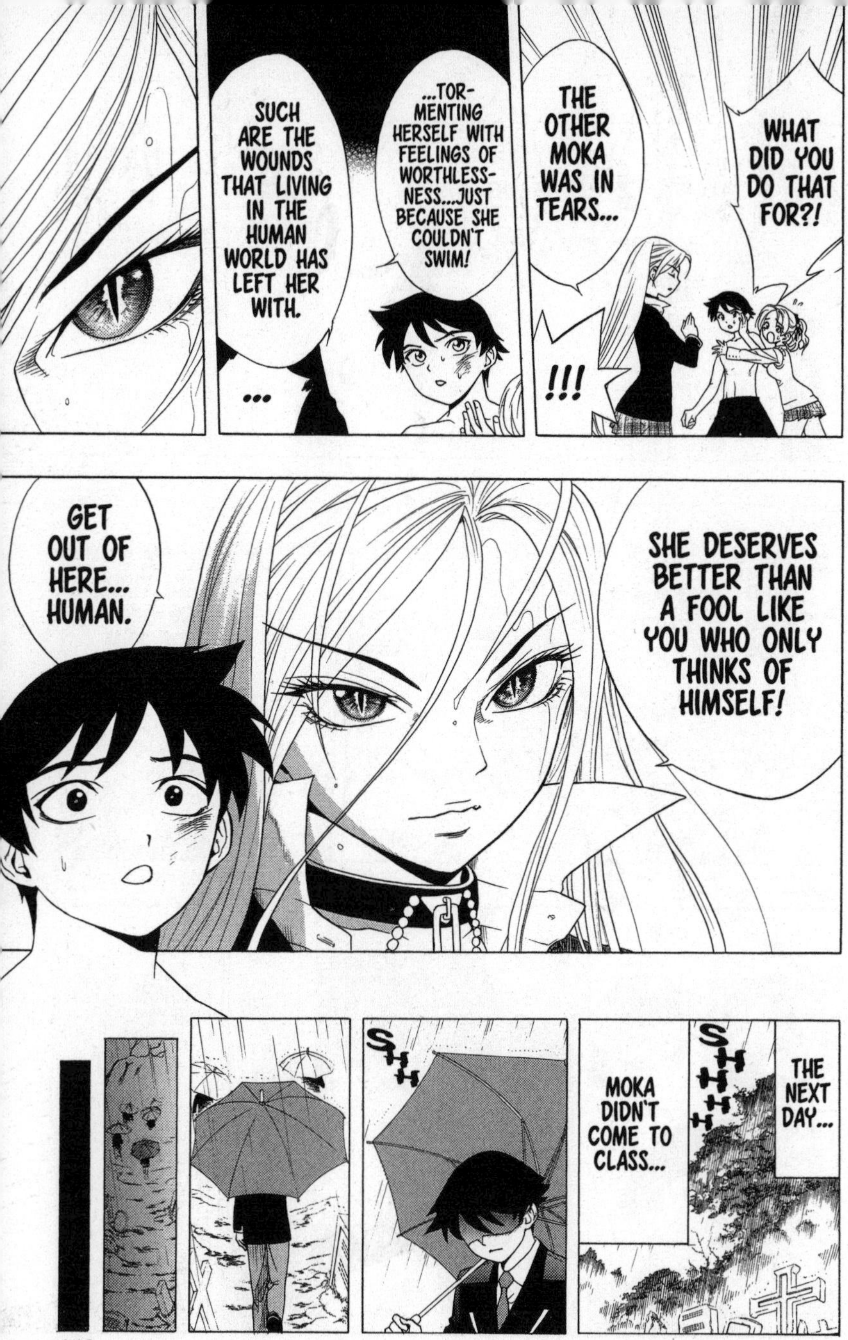
WHAT DID YOU DO THAT FOR?!
THE OTHER MOKA WAS IN TEARS...
!!!
...TORMENTING HERSELF WITH FEELINGS OF WORTHLESSNESS...JUST BECAUSE SHE COULDN'T SWIM!
SUCH ARE THE WOUNDS THAT LIVING IN THE HUMAN WORLD HAS LEFT HER WITH.
...
SHE DESERVES BETTER THAN A FOOL LIKE YOU WHO ONLY THINKS OF HIMSELF!
GET OUT OF HERE... HUMAN.
THE NEXT DAY...
SHHHHH
MOKA DIDN'T COME TO CLASS...
SHH

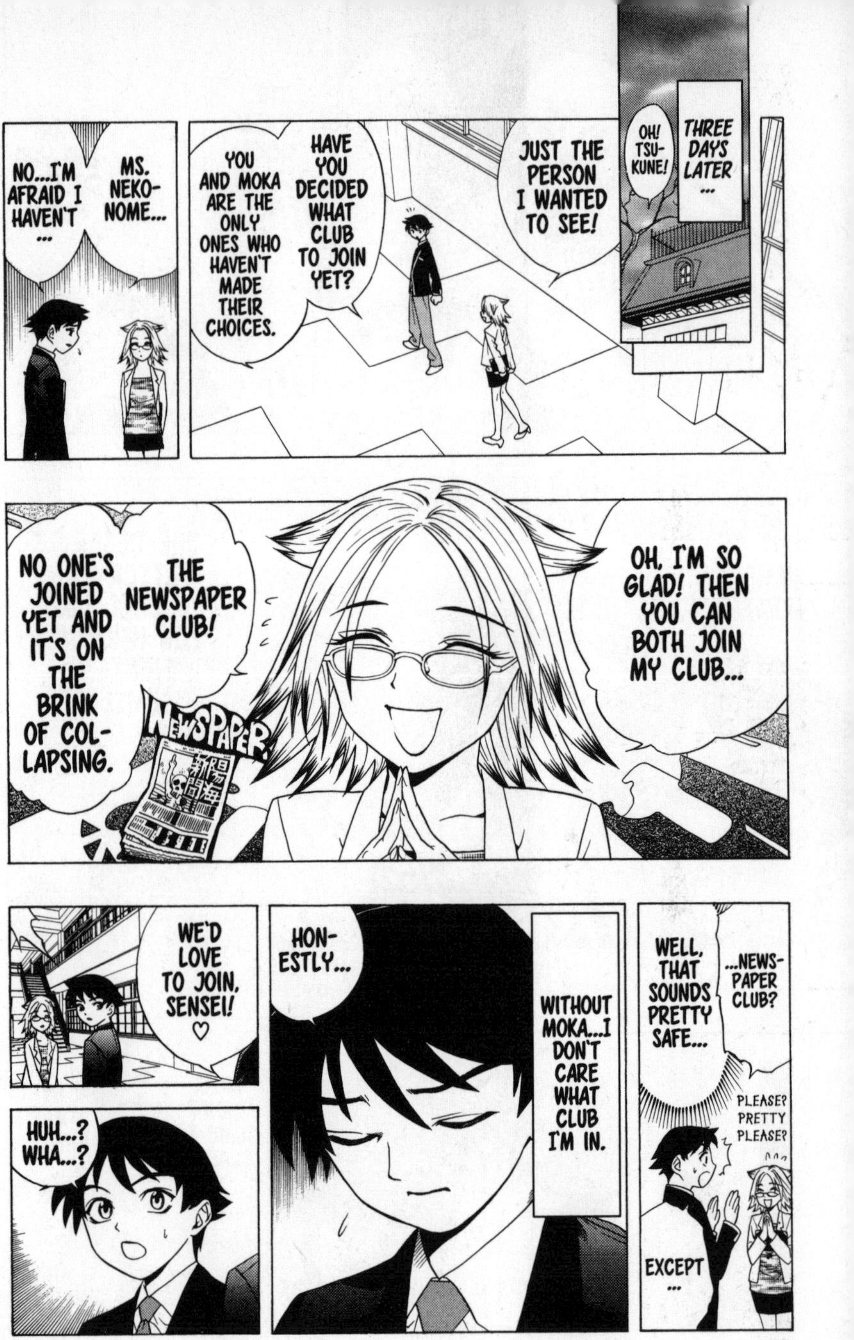
THREE DAYS LATER ...
OH! TSU-KUNE!
JUST THE PERSON I WANTED TO SEE!
HAVE YOU DECIDED WHAT CLUB TO JOIN YET?
YOU AND MOKA ARE THE ONLY ONES WHO HAVEN'T MADE THEIR CHOICES.
MS. NEKO-NOME...
NO...I'M AFRAID I HAVEN'T ...
OH, I'M SO GLAD! THEN YOU CAN BOTH JOIN MY CLUB...
THE NEWSPAPER CLUB!
NO ONE'S JOINED YET AND IT'S ON THE BRINK OF COL-LAPSING.
NEWSPAPER
...NEWS-PAPER CLUB?
WELL, THAT SOUNDS PRETTY SAFE...
PLEASE? PRETTY PLEASE?
EXCEPT ...
WITHOUT MOKA...I DON'T CARE WHAT CLUB I'M IN.
HON-ESTLY...
WE'D LOVE TO JOIN, SENSEI! ♡
HUH...? WHA...?

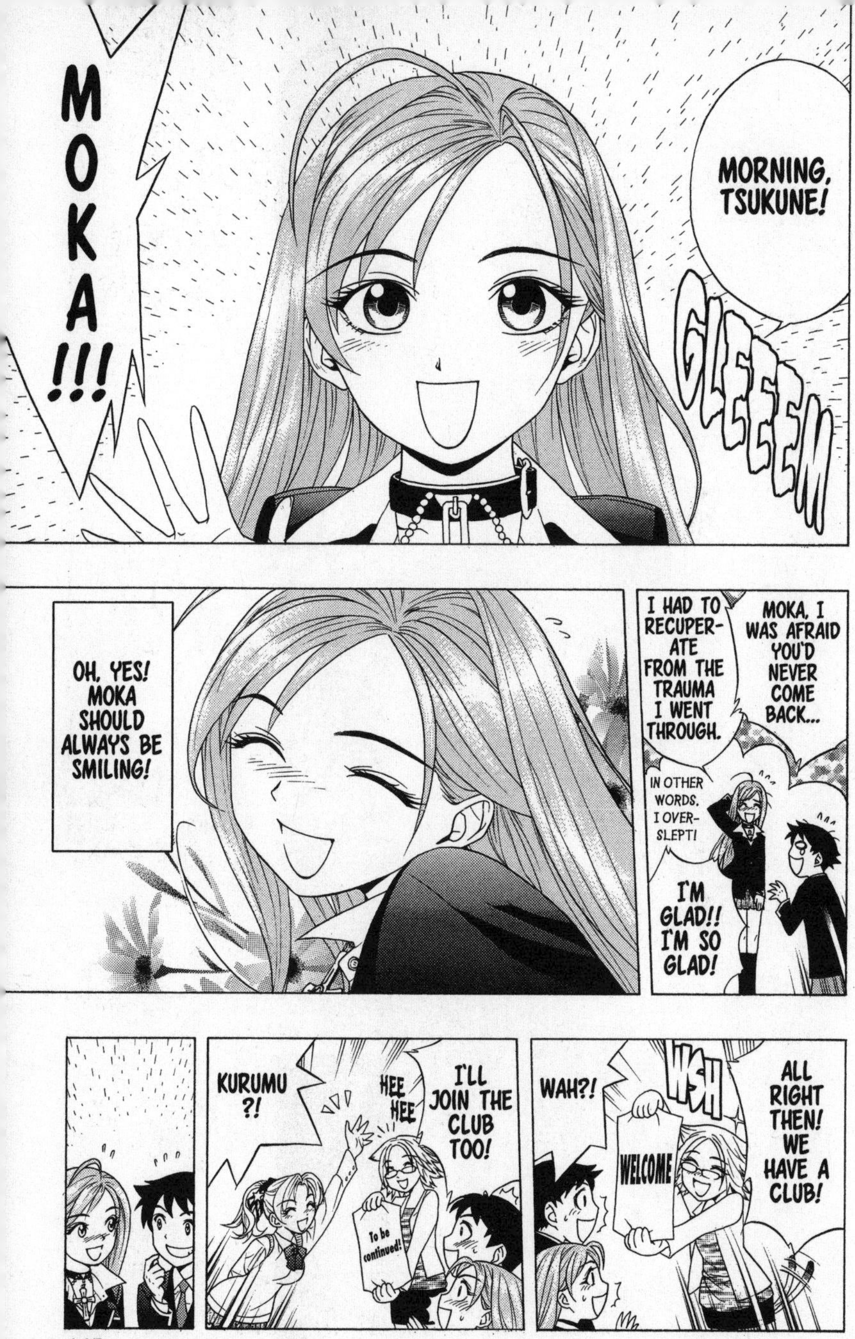

MORNING, TSUKUNE!
GLEEEEM
MOKA!!!
MOKA, I WAS AFRAID YOU'D NEVER COME BACK...
I HAD TO RECUPERATE FROM THE TRAUMA I WENT THROUGH.
IN OTHER WORDS, I OVERSLEPT!
I'M GLAD!! I'M SO GLAD!
OH, YES! MOKA SHOULD ALWAYS BE SMILING!
WSH
ALL RIGHT THEN! WE HAVE A CLUB!
WELCOME
WAH?!
I'LL JOIN THE CLUB TOO!
HEE HEE
KURUMU?!
To be continued!

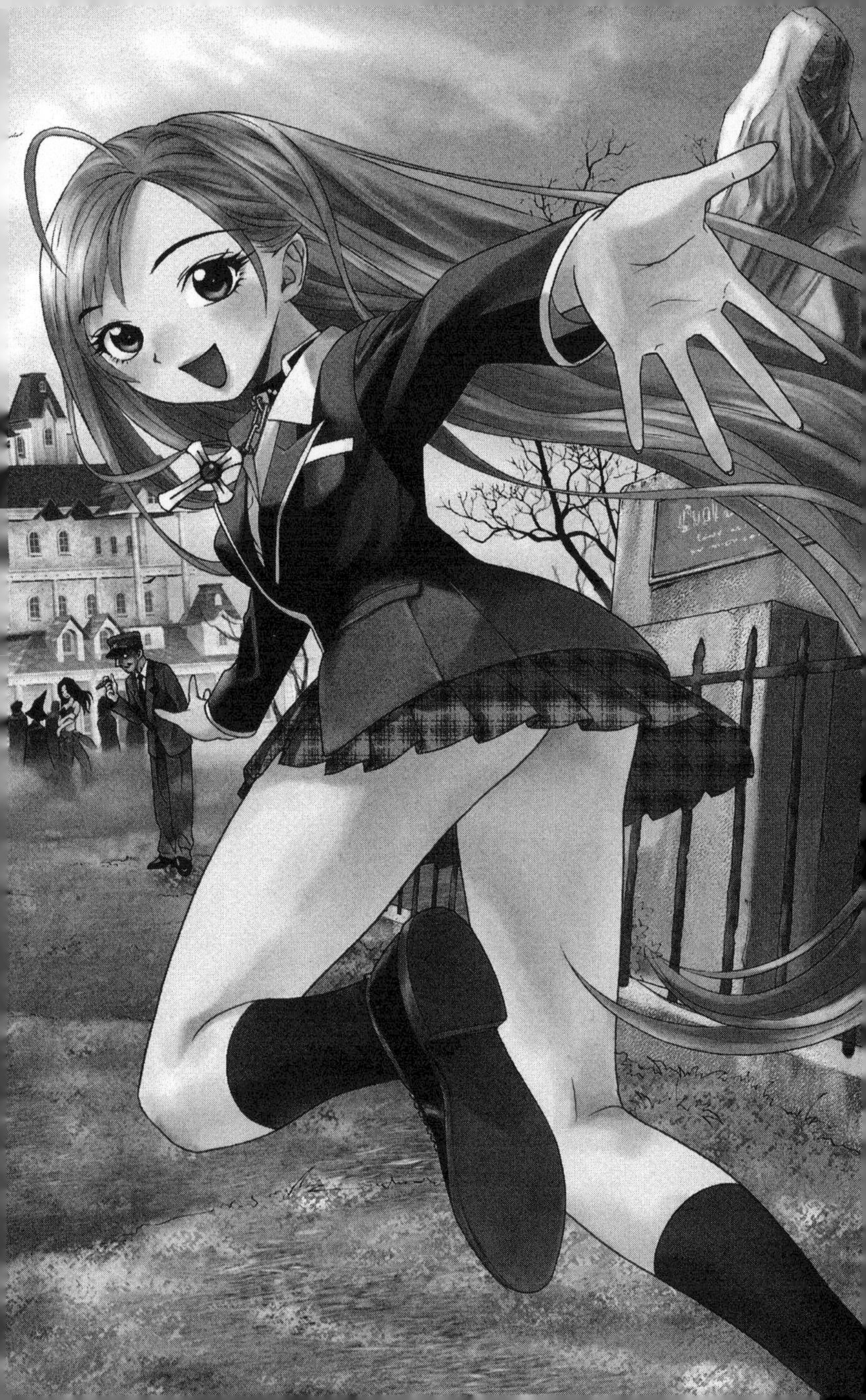

4: Coexistence

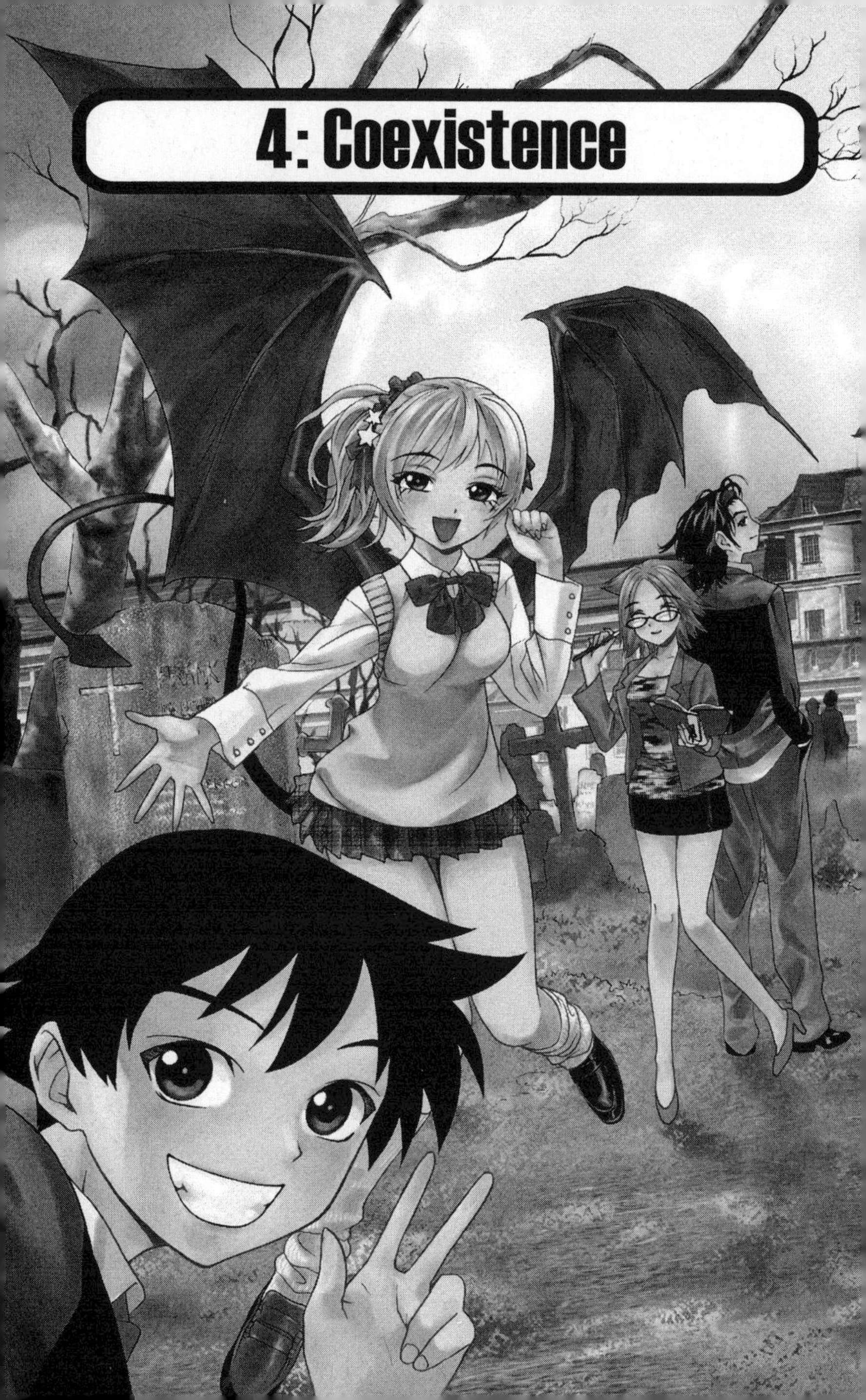

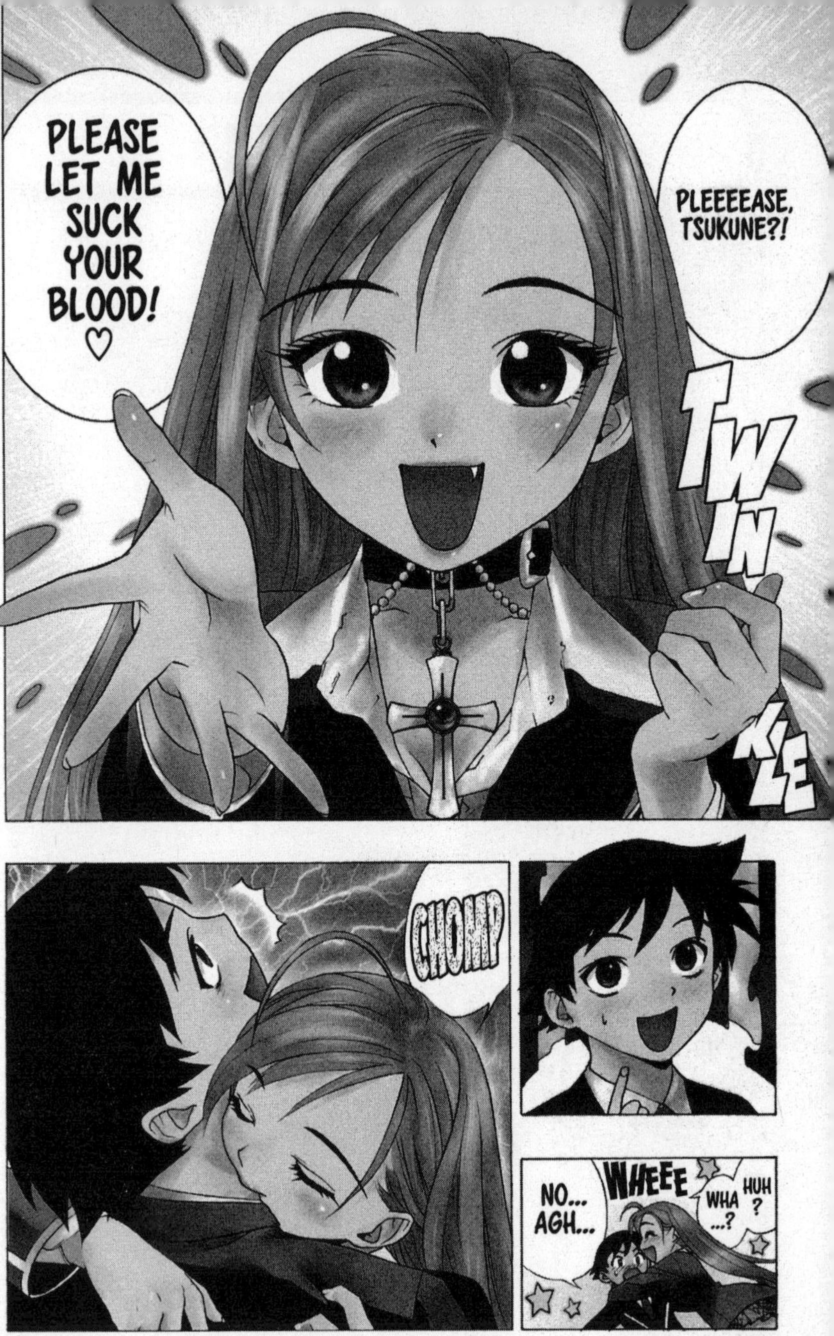
PLEEEEASE, TSUKUNE?!
PLEASE LET ME SUCK YOUR BLOOD! ♡
TWINKLE
HUH?
WHA...?
WHEEE
NO... AGH...
CHOMP

READ THIS WAY

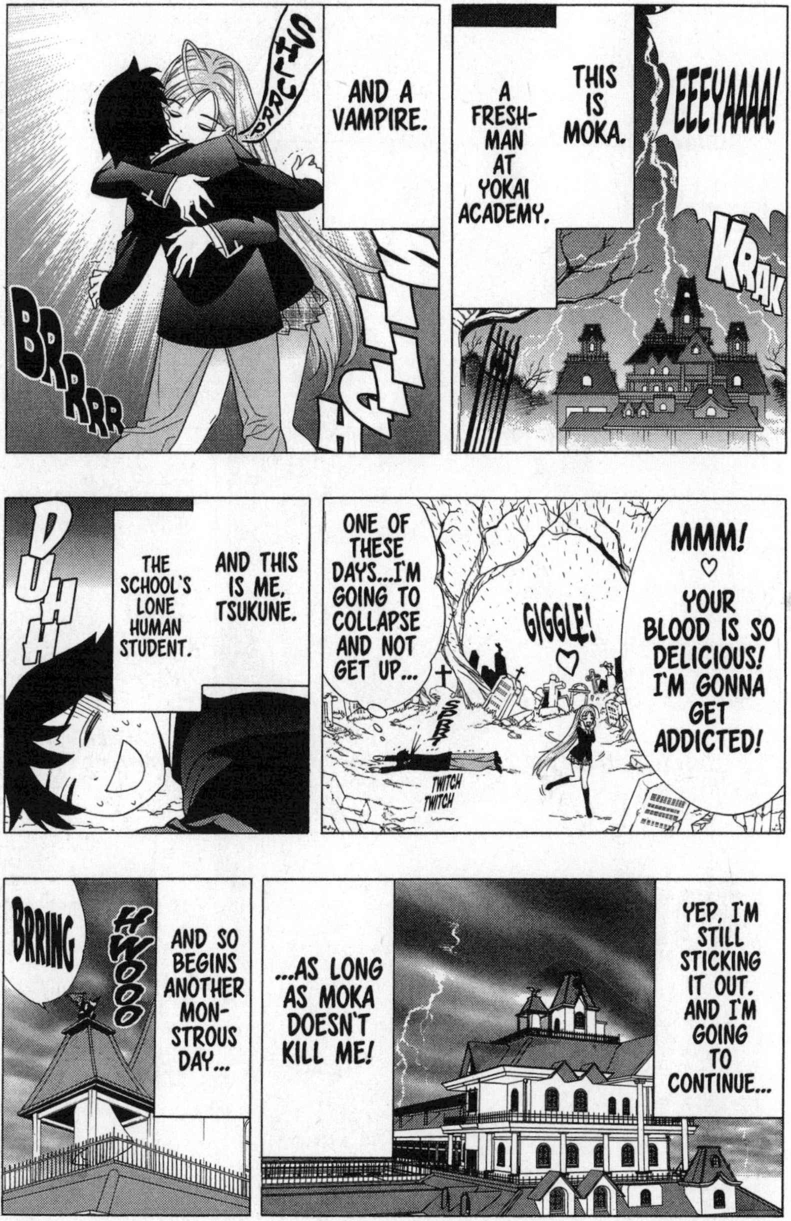
EEEYAAAA!
THIS IS MOKA.
A FRESHMAN AT YOKAI ACADEMY.
KRAK
SHLURRP
AND A VAMPIRE.
BRRRRR
MMM! ♡ YOUR BLOOD IS SO DELICIOUS! I'M GONNA GET ADDICTED!
GIGGLE!
ONE OF THESE DAYS...I'M GOING TO COLLAPSE AND NOT GET UP...
TWITCH TWITCH
DUHHH
AND THIS IS ME, TSUKUNE.
THE SCHOOL'S LONE HUMAN STUDENT.
YEP, I'M STILL STICKING IT OUT. AND I'M GOING TO CONTINUE...
...AS LONG AS MOKA DOESN'T KILL ME!
AND SO BEGINS ANOTHER MON-STROUS DAY...
HWOOO
BRRING

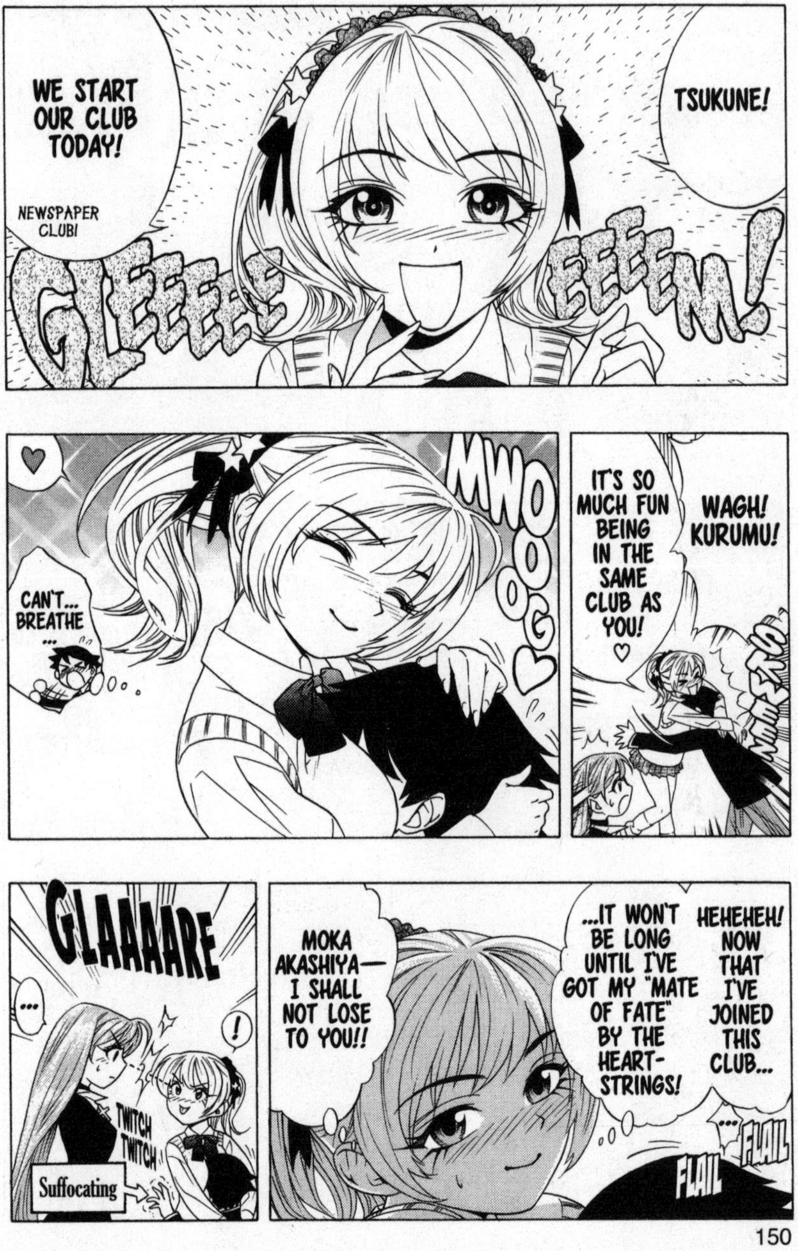
TSUKUNE!
WE START OUR CLUB TODAY!
NEWSPAPER CLUB!
GLEEEEEEEEEM!
WAGH! KURUMU!
IT'S SO MUCH FUN BEING IN THE SAME CLUB AS YOU! ♡
MWOOOOOG ♡
CAN'T... BREATHE ...
HEHEHEH! NOW THAT I'VE JOINED THIS CLUB...
...IT WON'T BE LONG UNTIL I'VE GOT MY "MATE OF FATE" BY THE HEART-STRINGS!
MOKA AKASHIYA— I SHALL NOT LOSE TO YOU!!
...
FLAIL
FLAIL
GLAAAARE
...
!
TWITCH TWITCH
Suffocating

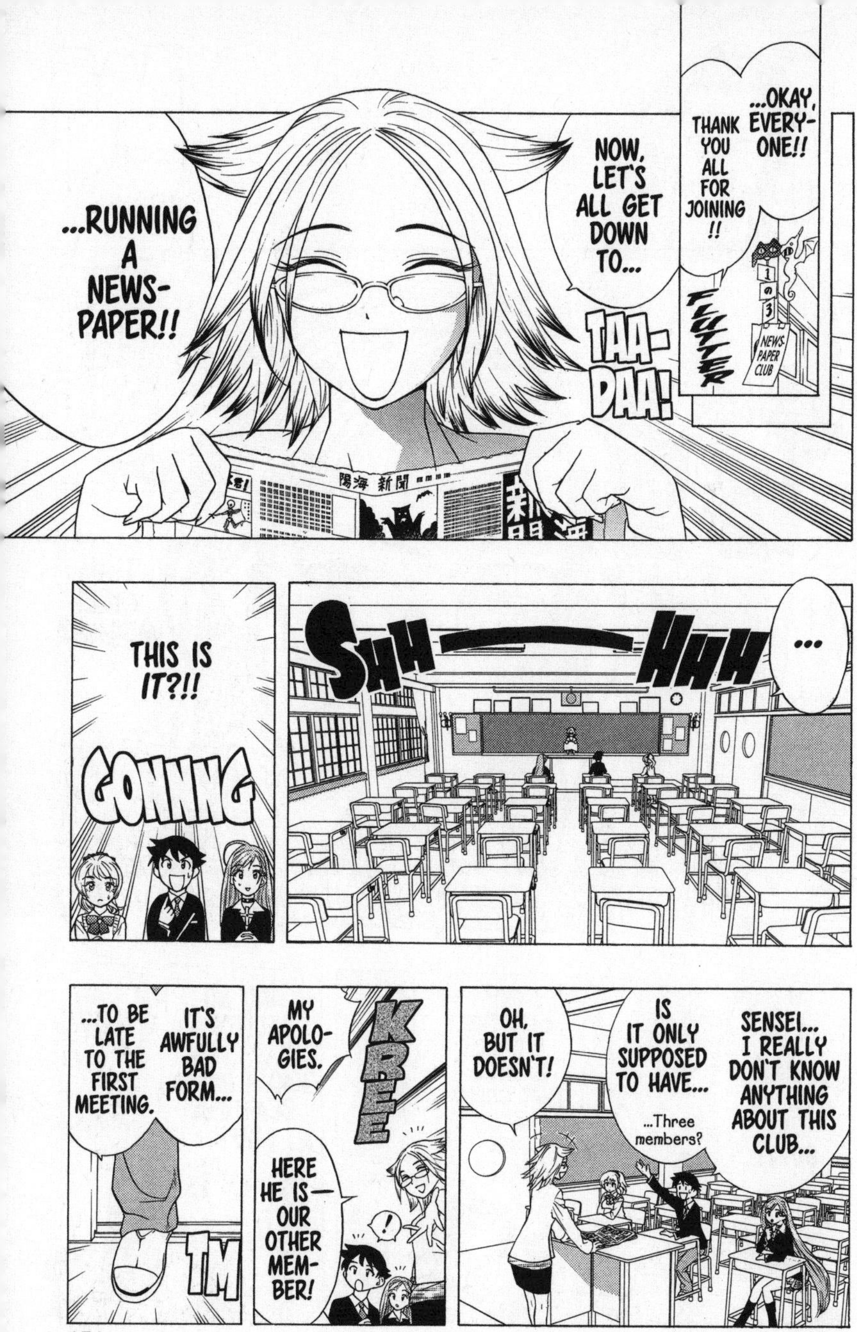

...OKAY, EVERYONE!!
THANK YOU ALL FOR JOINING!!
FLUTTER
1の3
NEWS-PAPER CLUB
NOW, LET'S ALL GET DOWN TO...
TAA-DAA!
...RUNNING A NEWS-PAPER!!
SHH——HHH
...
THIS IS IT?!!
GONNNG
SENSEI... I REALLY DON'T KNOW ANYTHING ABOUT THIS CLUB...
IS IT ONLY SUPPOSED TO HAVE...
...Three members?
OH, BUT IT DOESN'T!
KREE
MY APOLO-GIES.
HERE HE IS— OUR OTHER MEM-BER!
!
IT'S AWFULLY BAD FORM...
...TO BE LATE TO THE FIRST MEETING.
TM

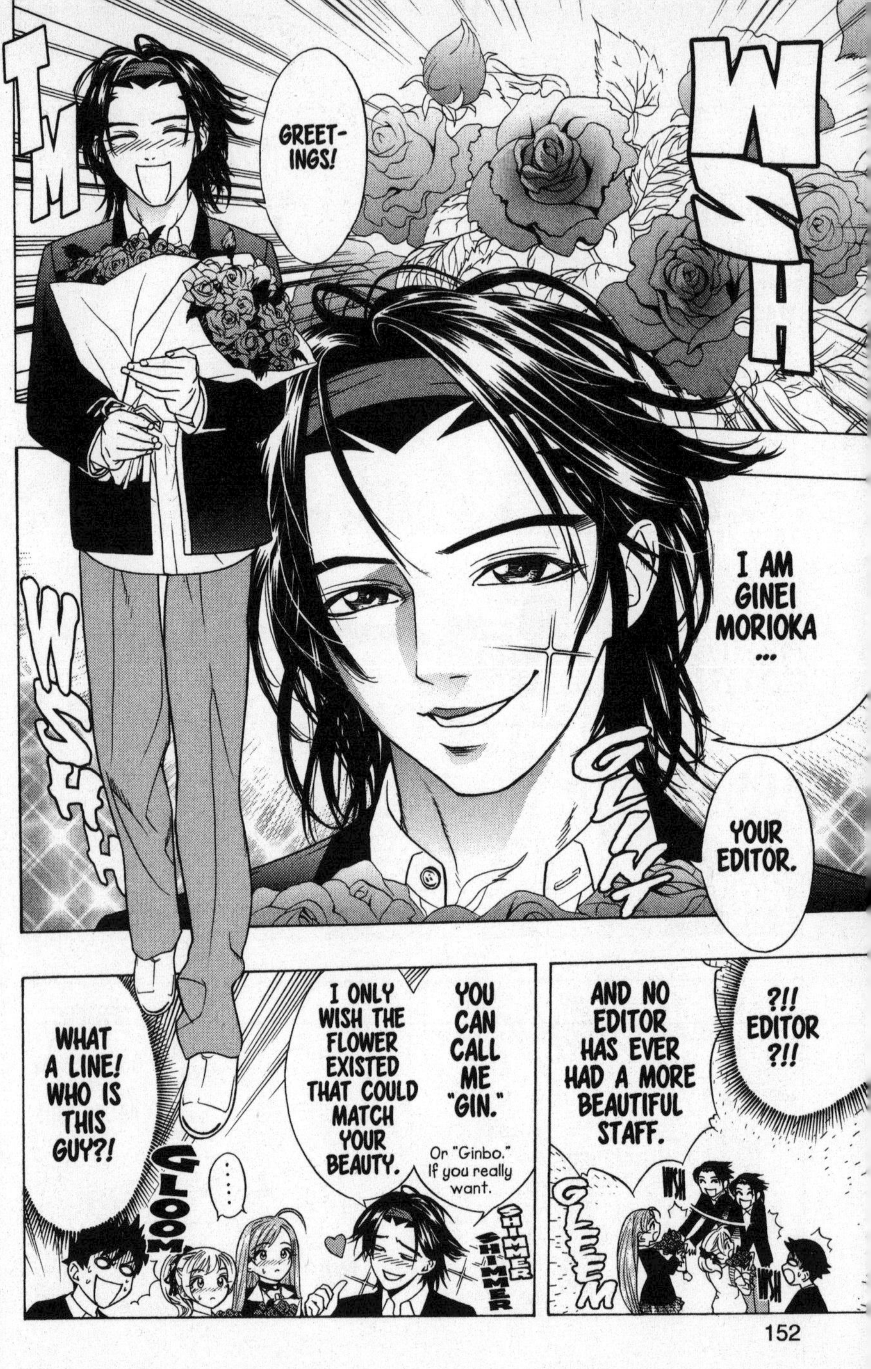
WSH
GREET-INGS!
TM
I AM GINEI MORIOKA...
YOUR EDITOR.
GLINT
WSH
?!! EDITOR?!!
AND NO EDITOR HAS EVER HAD A MORE BEAUTIFUL STAFF.
WSH
WSH
GLEEM
YOU CAN CALL ME "GIN."
I ONLY WISH THE FLOWER EXISTED THAT COULD MATCH YOUR BEAUTY.
Or "Ginbo." If you really want.
SHIMMER SHIMMER
......
WHAT A LINE! WHO IS THIS GUY?!
GLOOM

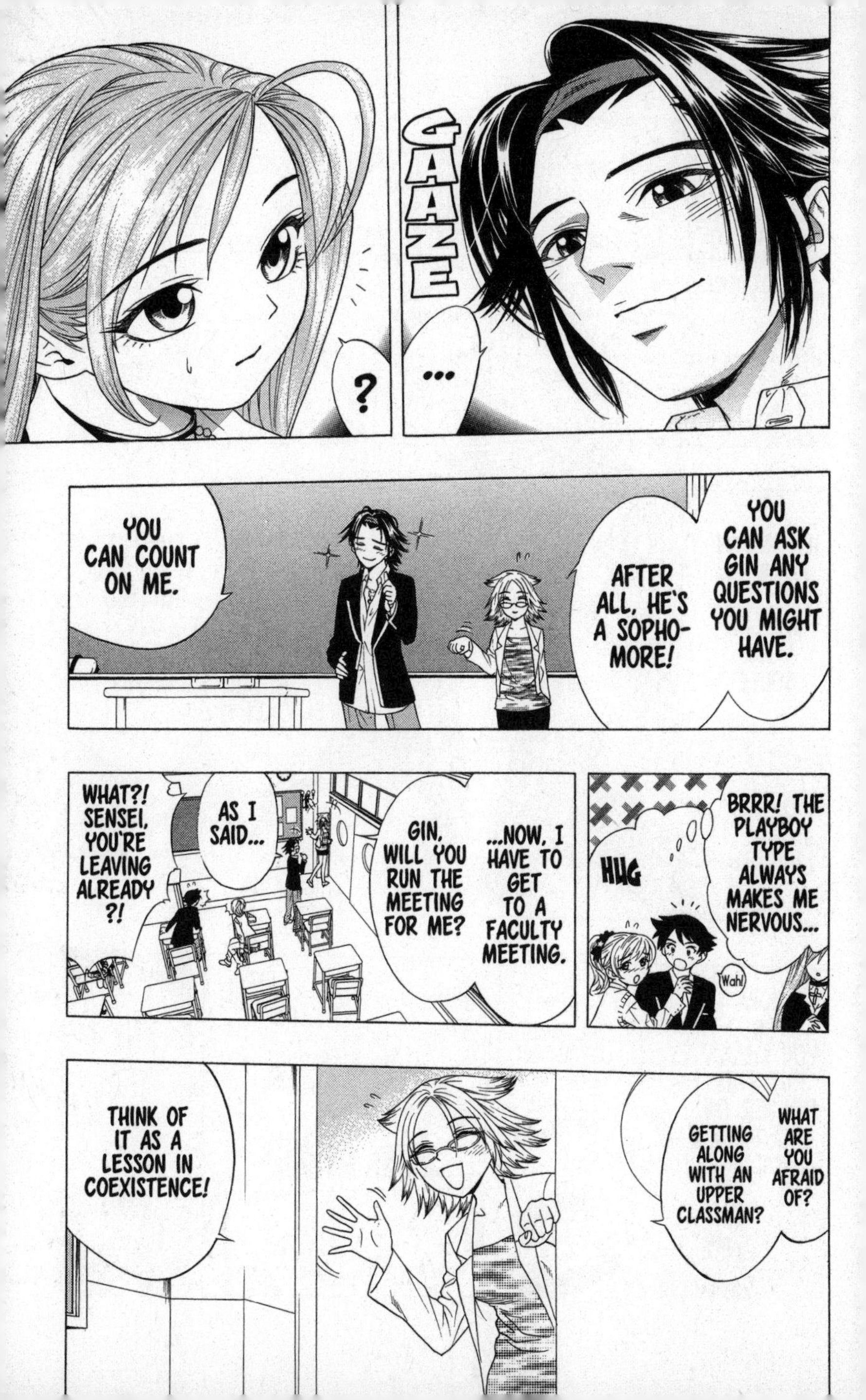
GAAZE
...
?
YOU CAN ASK GIN ANY QUESTIONS YOU MIGHT HAVE.
AFTER ALL, HE'S A SOPHOMORE!
YOU CAN COUNT ON ME.
BRRR! THE PLAYBOY TYPE ALWAYS MAKES ME NERVOUS...
HUG
Wah!
...NOW, I HAVE TO GET TO A FACULTY MEETING.
GIN, WILL YOU RUN THE MEETING FOR ME?
AS I SAID...
WHAT?! SENSEI, YOU'RE LEAVING ALREADY?!
WHAT ARE YOU AFRAID OF?
GETTING ALONG WITH AN UPPER CLASSMAN?
THINK OF IT AS A LESSON IN COEXISTENCE!

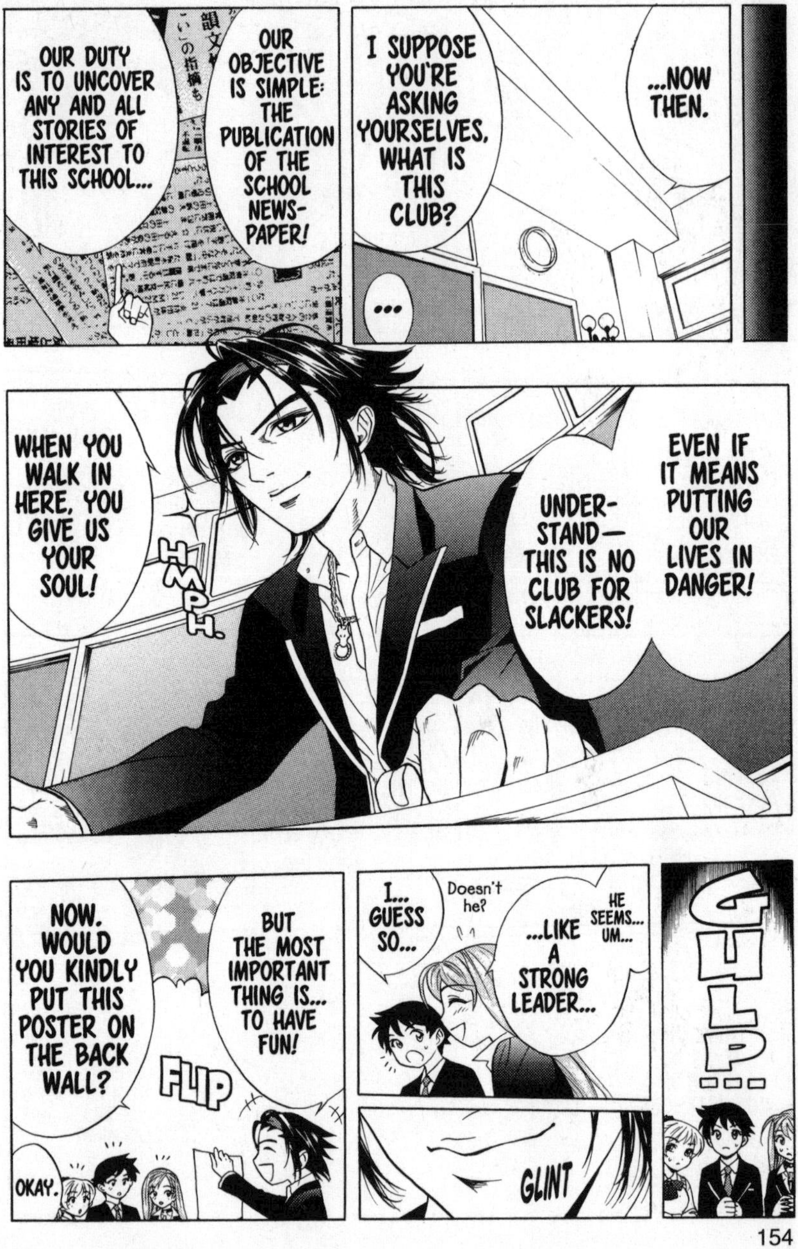
...NOW THEN.
I SUPPOSE YOU'RE ASKING YOURSELVES, WHAT IS THIS CLUB?
...
OUR OBJECTIVE IS SIMPLE: THE PUBLICATION OF THE SCHOOL NEWS-PAPER!
OUR DUTY IS TO UNCOVER ANY AND ALL STORIES OF INTEREST TO THIS SCHOOL...
EVEN IF IT MEANS PUTTING OUR LIVES IN DANGER!
UNDER-STAND— THIS IS NO CLUB FOR SLACKERS!
HMPH.
WHEN YOU WALK IN HERE, YOU GIVE US YOUR SOUL!
GULP...
HE SEEMS... UM...
...LIKE A STRONG LEADER...
Doesn't he?
I... GUESS SO...
GLINT
BUT THE MOST IMPORTANT THING IS... TO HAVE FUN!
NOW. WOULD YOU KINDLY PUT THIS POSTER ON THE BACK WALL?
FLIP
OKAY.

READ THIS WAY

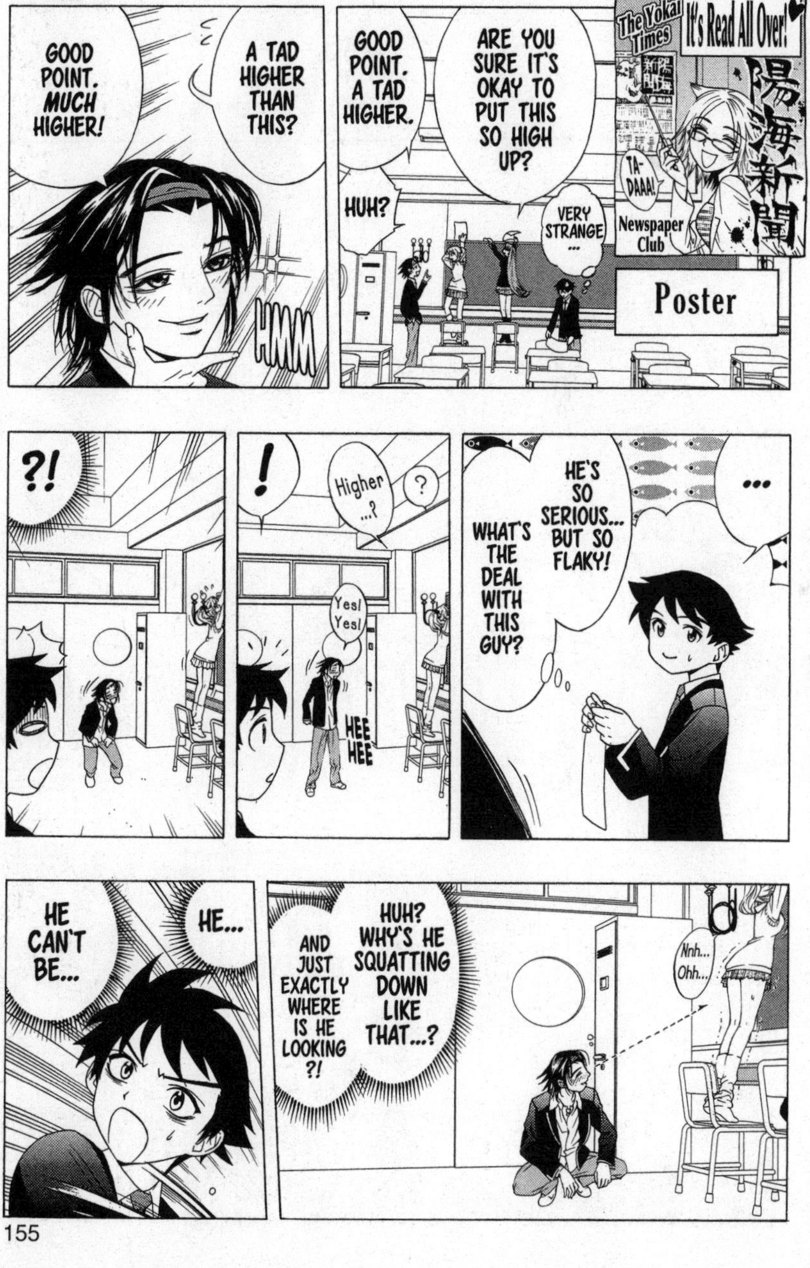
The Yokai Times
It's Read All Over!
陽海新聞
TA-DAAA!
Newspaper Club
Poster
ARE YOU SURE IT'S OKAY TO PUT THIS SO HIGH UP?
GOOD POINT. A TAD HIGHER.
VERY STRANGE...
HUH?
A TAD HIGHER THAN THIS?
GOOD POINT. *MUCH* HIGHER!
HMM
...
HE'S SO SERIOUS... BUT SO FLAKY!
WHAT'S THE DEAL WITH THIS GUY?
?
Higher ...?
!
Yes! Yes!
HEE HEE
?!
Nnh... Ohh...
HUH? WHY'S HE SQUATTING DOWN LIKE THAT...?
AND JUST EXACTLY WHERE IS HE LOOKING ?!
HE...
HE CAN'T BE...

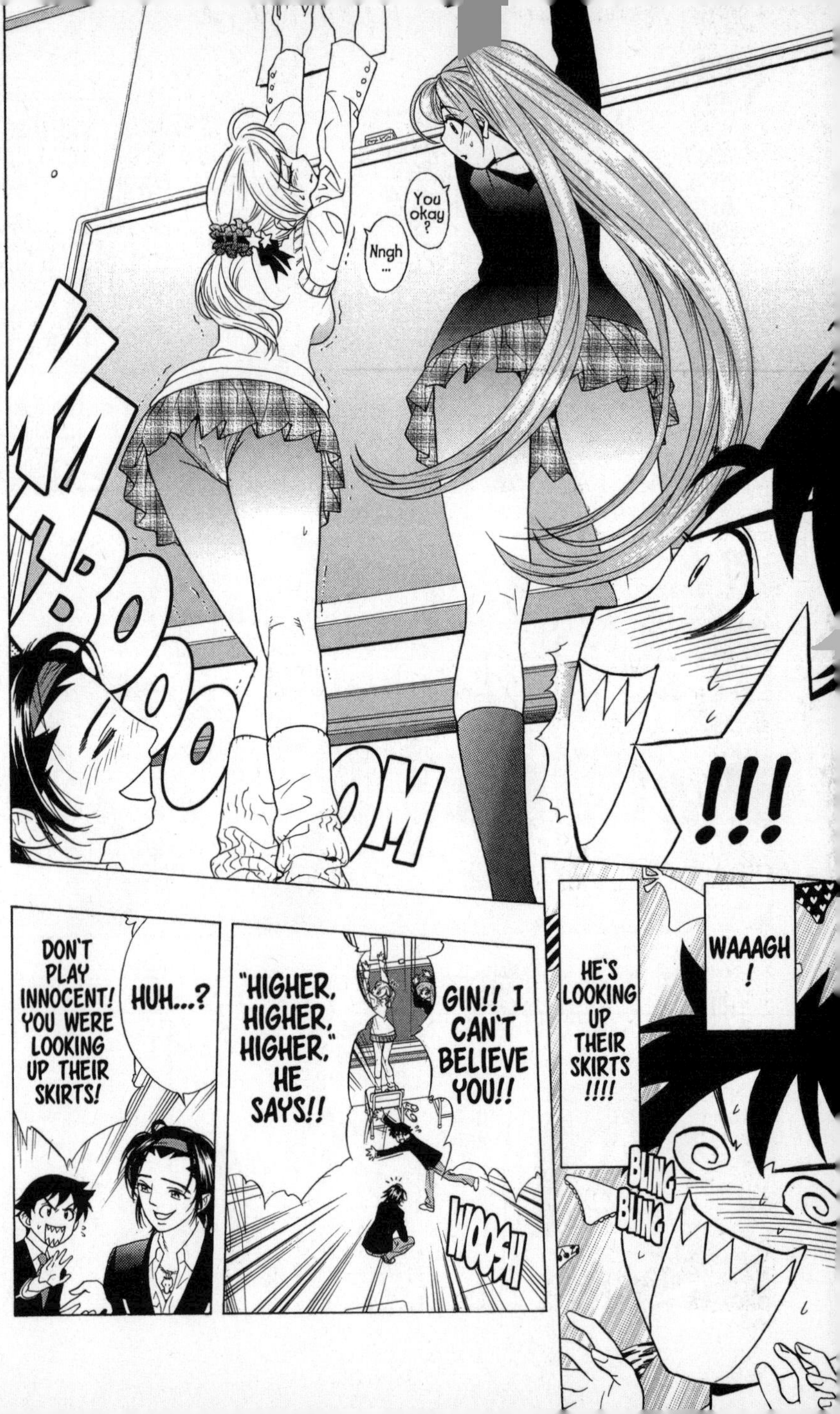
You okay?
Nngh...
KA-BOOOOOM
!!!
WAAAGH!
HE'S LOOKING UP THEIR SKIRTS!!!!
BLING BLING
GIN!! I CAN'T BELIEVE YOU!!
"HIGHER, HIGHER, HIGHER," HE SAYS!!
WOOSH
HUH...?
DON'T PLAY INNOCENT! YOU WERE LOOKING UP THEIR SKIRTS!

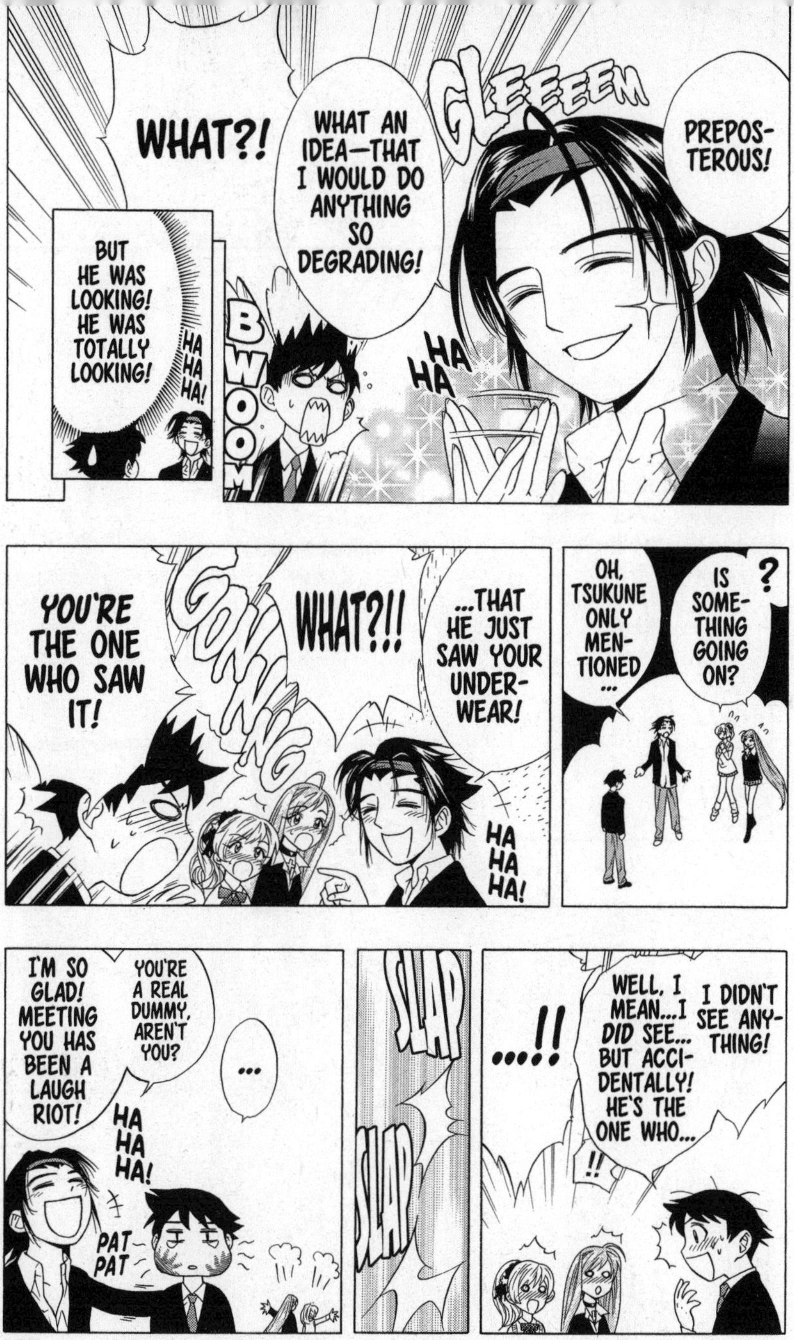
PREPOS-TEROUS!
GLEEEEM
WHAT AN IDEA—THAT I WOULD DO ANYTHING SO DEGRADING!
HA HA
BWOOM
WHAT?!
BUT HE WAS LOOKING! HE WAS TOTALLY LOOKING!
HA HA HA!
?
IS SOME-THING GOING ON?
OH, TSUKUNE ONLY MEN-TIONED ...
...THAT HE JUST SAW YOUR UNDER-WEAR!
WHAT?!!
GONNNG
YOU'RE THE ONE WHO SAW IT!
HA HA HA!
I DIDN'T SEE ANY-THING!
WELL, I MEAN...I *DID* SEE... BUT ACCI-DENTALLY! HE'S THE ONE WHO...
!!
...!!
SLAP
SLAP
...
YOU'RE A REAL DUMMY, AREN'T YOU?
I'M SO GLAD! MEETING YOU HAS BEEN A LAUGH RIOT!
HA HA HA!
PAT-PAT

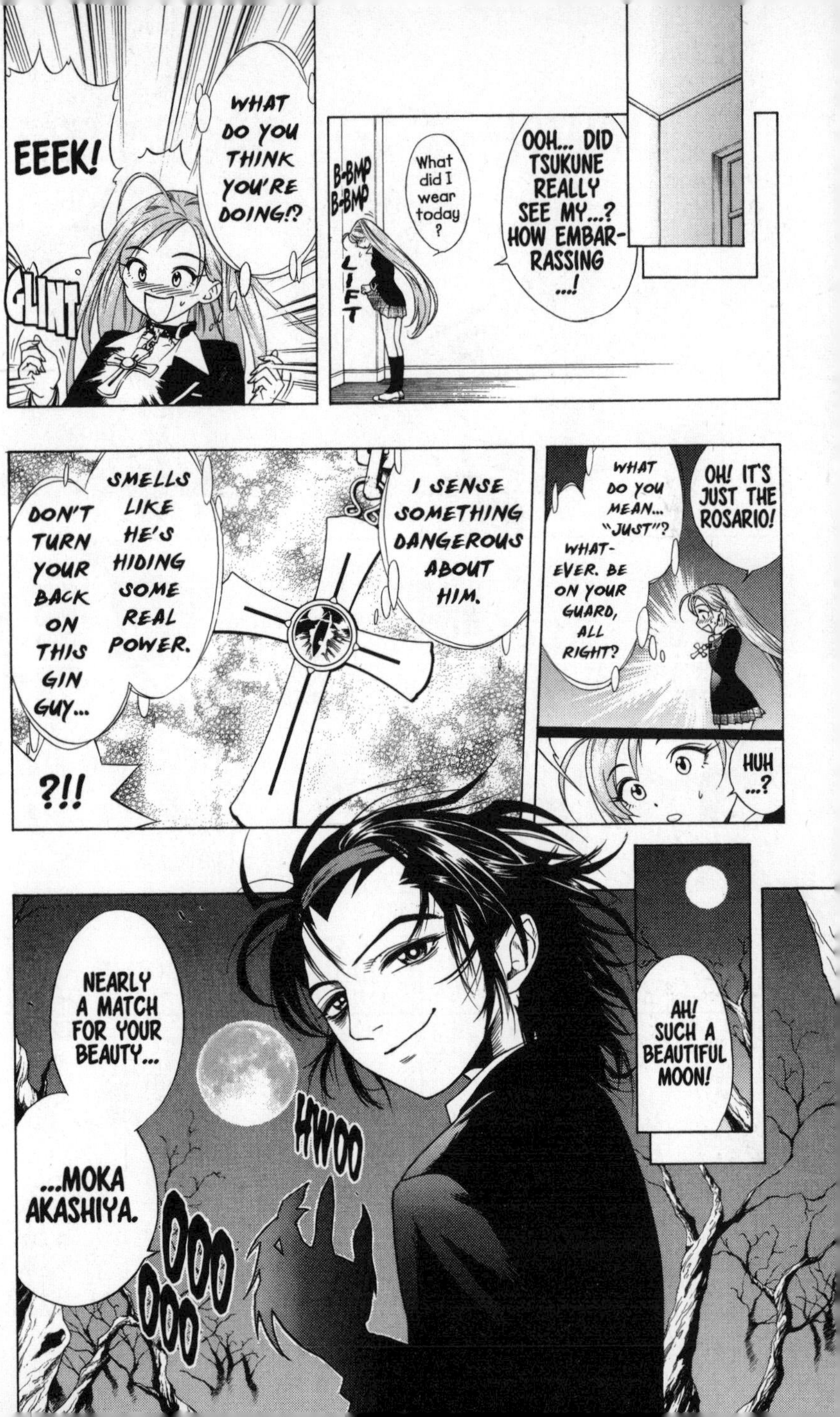
OOH... DID TSUKUNE REALLY SEE MY...? HOW EMBARRASSING ...!
What did I wear today?
B-BMP B-BMP
LIFT
WHAT DO YOU THINK YOU'RE DOING!?
EEEK!
GLINT
OH! IT'S JUST THE ROSARIO!
WHAT DO YOU MEAN... "JUST"?
WHATEVER. BE ON YOUR GUARD, ALL RIGHT?
HUH ...?
I SENSE SOMETHING DANGEROUS ABOUT HIM.
SMELLS LIKE HE'S HIDING SOME REAL POWER.
DON'T TURN YOUR BACK ON THIS GIN GUY...
?!!
AH! SUCH A BEAUTIFUL MOON!
NEARLY A MATCH FOR YOUR BEAUTY...
...MOKA AKASHIYA.
HWOOOOOOOO

READ THIS WAY

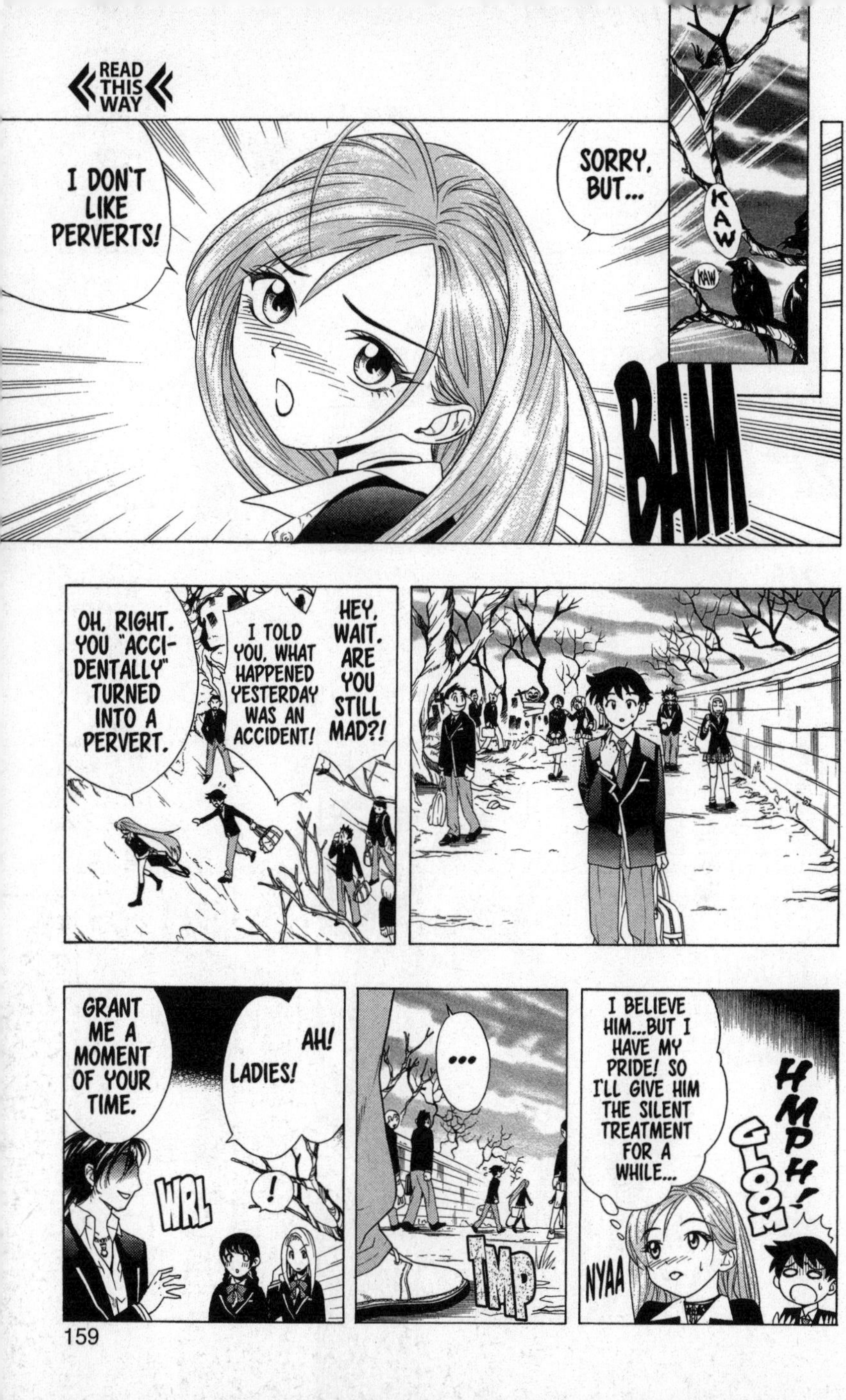

KAW
KAW
SORRY, BUT...
BAM
I DON'T LIKE PERVERTS!
HEY, WAIT. ARE YOU STILL MAD?!
I TOLD YOU, WHAT HAPPENED YESTERDAY WAS AN ACCIDENT!
OH, RIGHT. YOU "ACCI-DENTALLY" TURNED INTO A PERVERT.
I BELIEVE HIM...BUT I HAVE MY PRIDE! SO I'LL GIVE HIM THE SILENT TREATMENT FOR A WHILE...
HMPH!
GLOOM
NYAA
...
TMP
AH!
LADIES!
GRANT ME A MOMENT OF YOUR TIME.
!
WRL

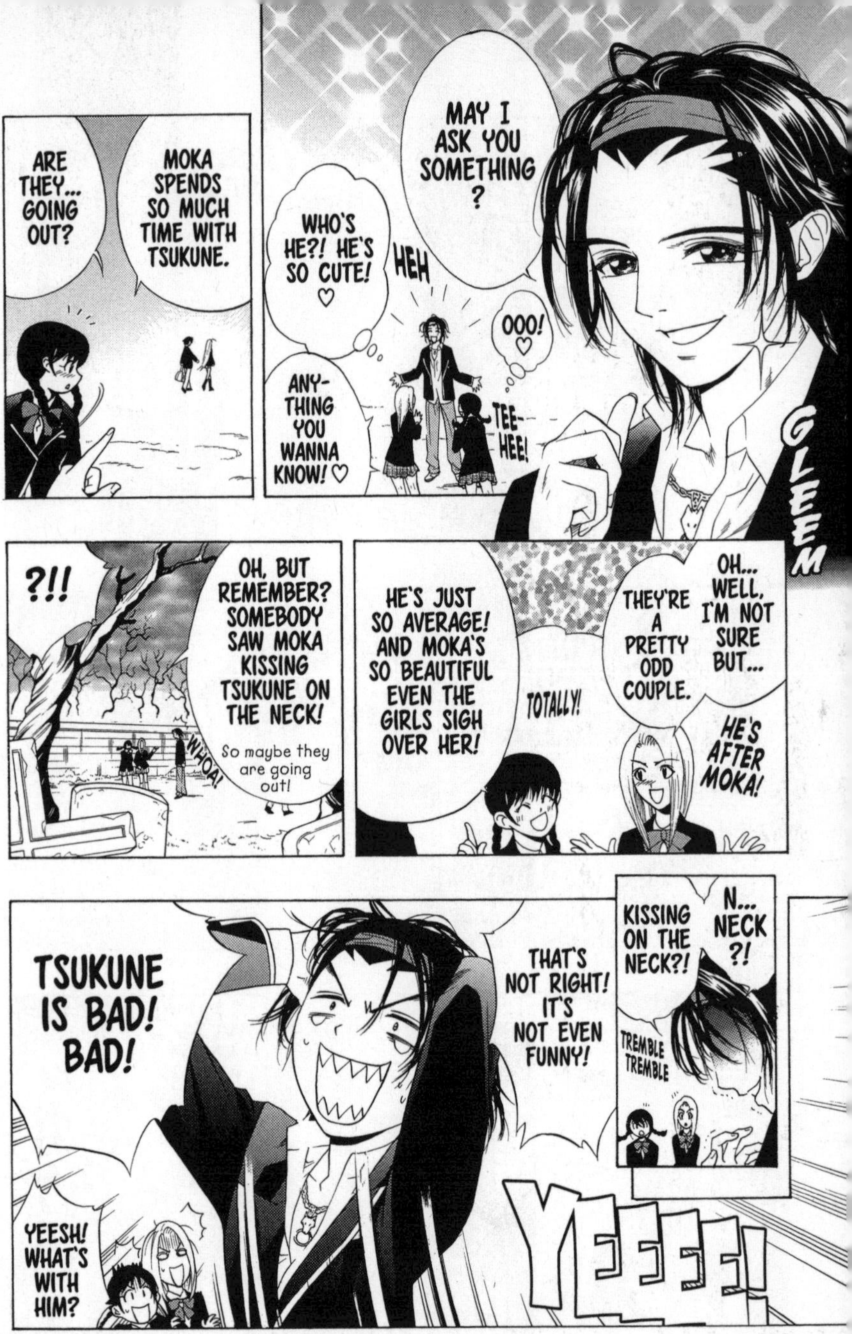
MAY I ASK YOU SOMETHING?
GLEEM
OOO! ♡
HEH
WHO'S HE?! HE'S SO CUTE! ♡
TEE-HEE!
ANYTHING YOU WANNA KNOW! ♡
MOKA SPENDS SO MUCH TIME WITH TSUKUNE.
ARE THEY... GOING OUT?
OH... WELL, I'M NOT SURE BUT...
THEY'RE A PRETTY ODD COUPLE.
HE'S AFTER MOKA!
TOTALLY!
HE'S JUST SO AVERAGE! AND MOKA'S SO BEAUTIFUL EVEN THE GIRLS SIGH OVER HER!
OH, BUT REMEMBER? SOMEBODY SAW MOKA KISSING TSUKUNE ON THE NECK!
So maybe they are going out!
WHOA!
?!!
N... NECK?!
KISSING ON THE NECK?!
TREMBLE TREMBLE
THAT'S NOT RIGHT! IT'S NOT EVEN FUNNY!
TSUKUNE IS BAD! BAD!
YEEEE!
YEESH! WHAT'S WITH HIM?

READ THIS WAY

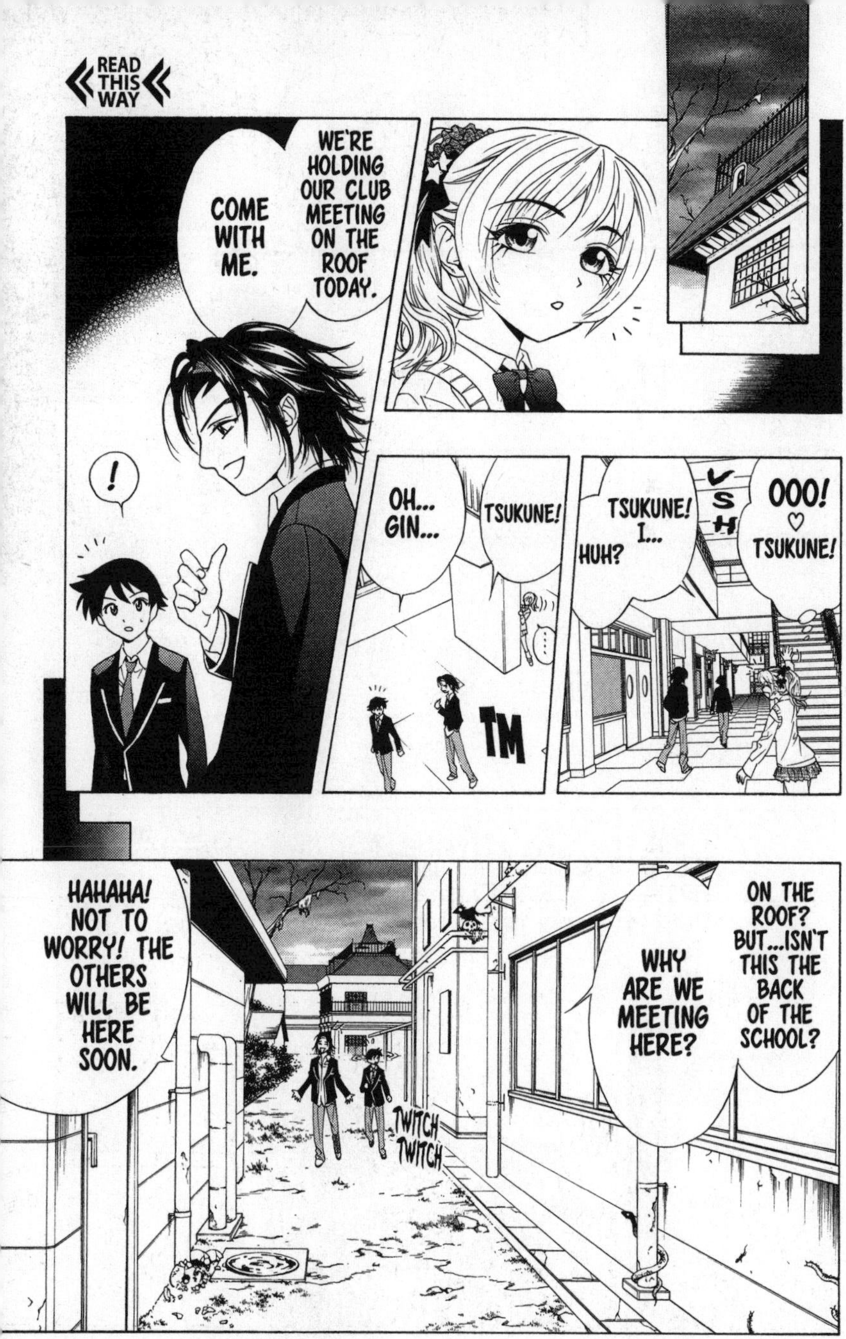
OOO! ♡ TSUKUNE!
VSH
TSUKUNE! I...
HUH?
TSUKUNE!
OH... GIN...
TM
WE'RE HOLDING OUR CLUB MEETING ON THE ROOF TODAY.
COME WITH ME.
!
ON THE ROOF? BUT...ISN'T THIS THE BACK OF THE SCHOOL?
WHY ARE WE MEETING HERE?
HAHAHA! NOT TO WORRY! THE OTHERS WILL BE HERE SOON.
TWITCH TWITCH

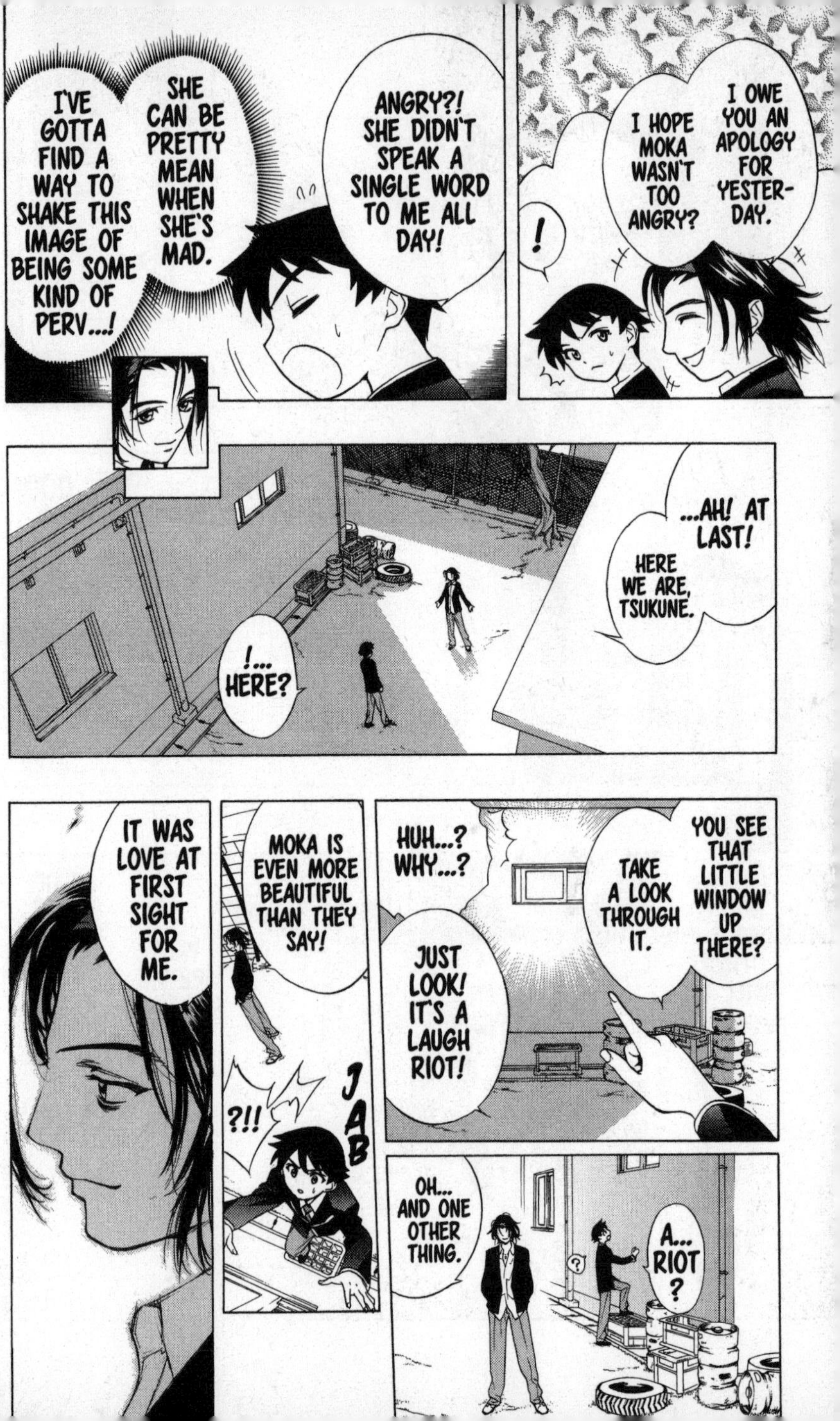
I OWE YOU AN APOLOGY FOR YESTERDAY.
I HOPE MOKA WASN'T TOO ANGRY?
!
ANGRY?! SHE DIDN'T SPEAK A SINGLE WORD TO ME ALL DAY!
SHE CAN BE PRETTY MEAN WHEN SHE'S MAD.
I'VE GOTTA FIND A WAY TO SHAKE THIS IMAGE OF BEING SOME KIND OF PERV...!
...AH! AT LAST!
HERE WE ARE, TSUKUNE.
!... HERE?
YOU SEE THAT LITTLE WINDOW UP THERE?
TAKE A LOOK THROUGH IT.
HUH...? WHY...?
JUST LOOK! IT'S A LAUGH RIOT!
A... RIOT?
OH... AND ONE OTHER THING.
MOKA IS EVEN MORE BEAUTIFUL THAN THEY SAY!
?!!
JAB
IT WAS LOVE AT FIRST SIGHT FOR ME.

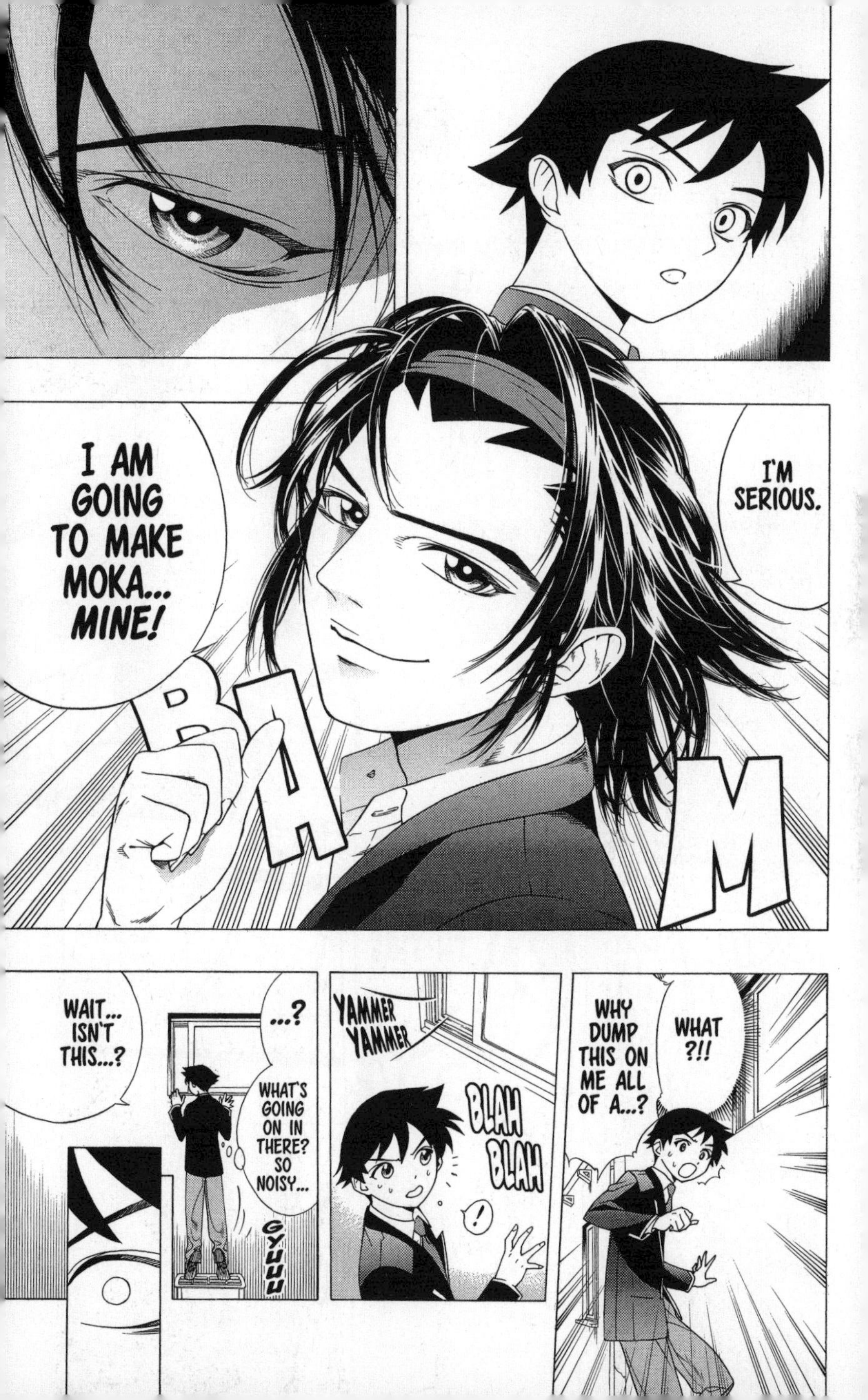
I'M SERIOUS.
I AM GOING TO MAKE MOKA... MINE!
BAM
WHAT ?!!
WHY DUMP THIS ON ME ALL OF A...?
YAMMER YAMMER
BLAH BLAH
!
...?
WHAT'S GOING ON IN THERE? SO NOISY...
GYUUU
WAIT... ISN'T THIS...?

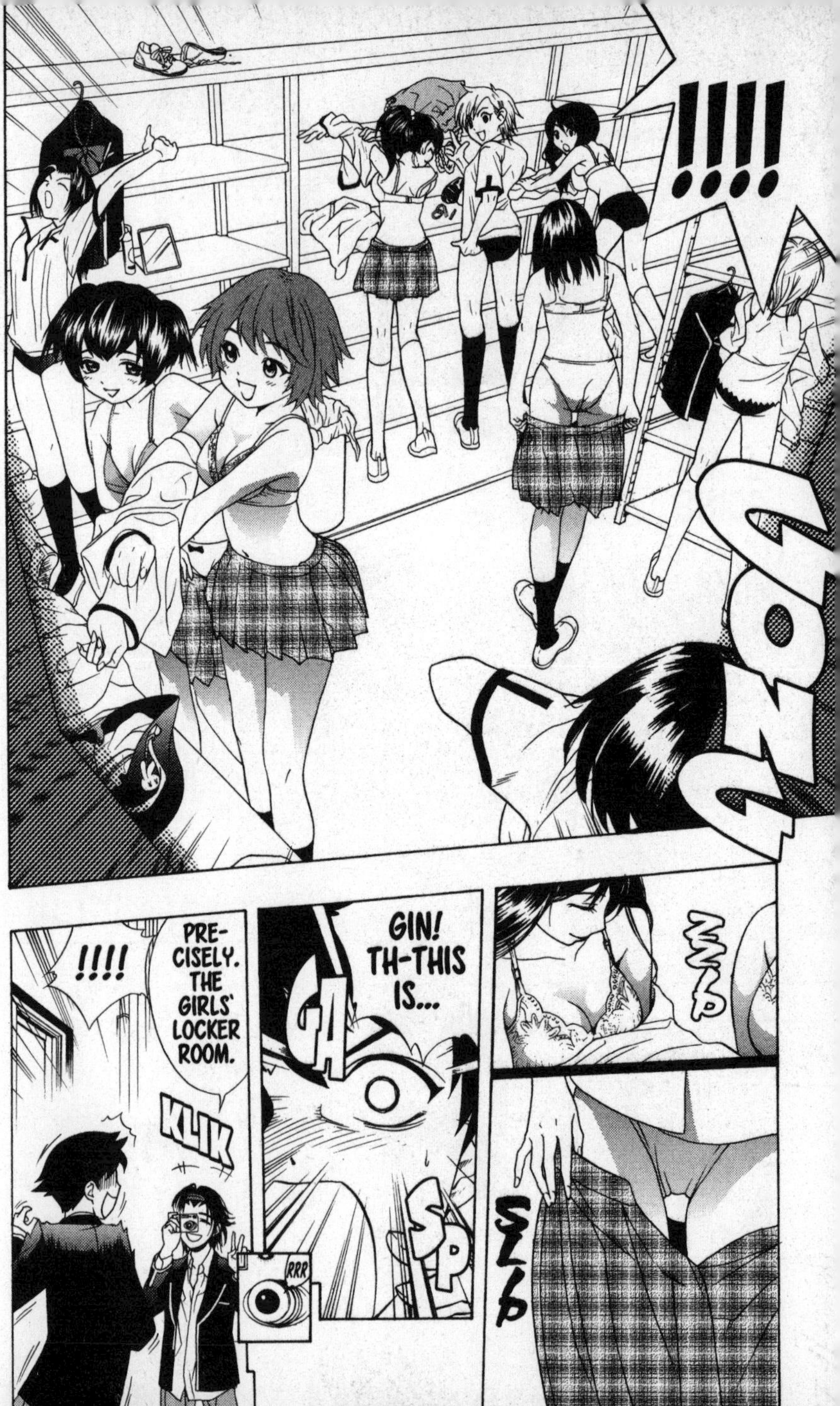
!!!!
GIN! TH-THIS IS...
GA
SP
RRR
SLIP
!!!!
PRE-CISELY. THE GIRLS' LOCKER ROOM.
KLIK

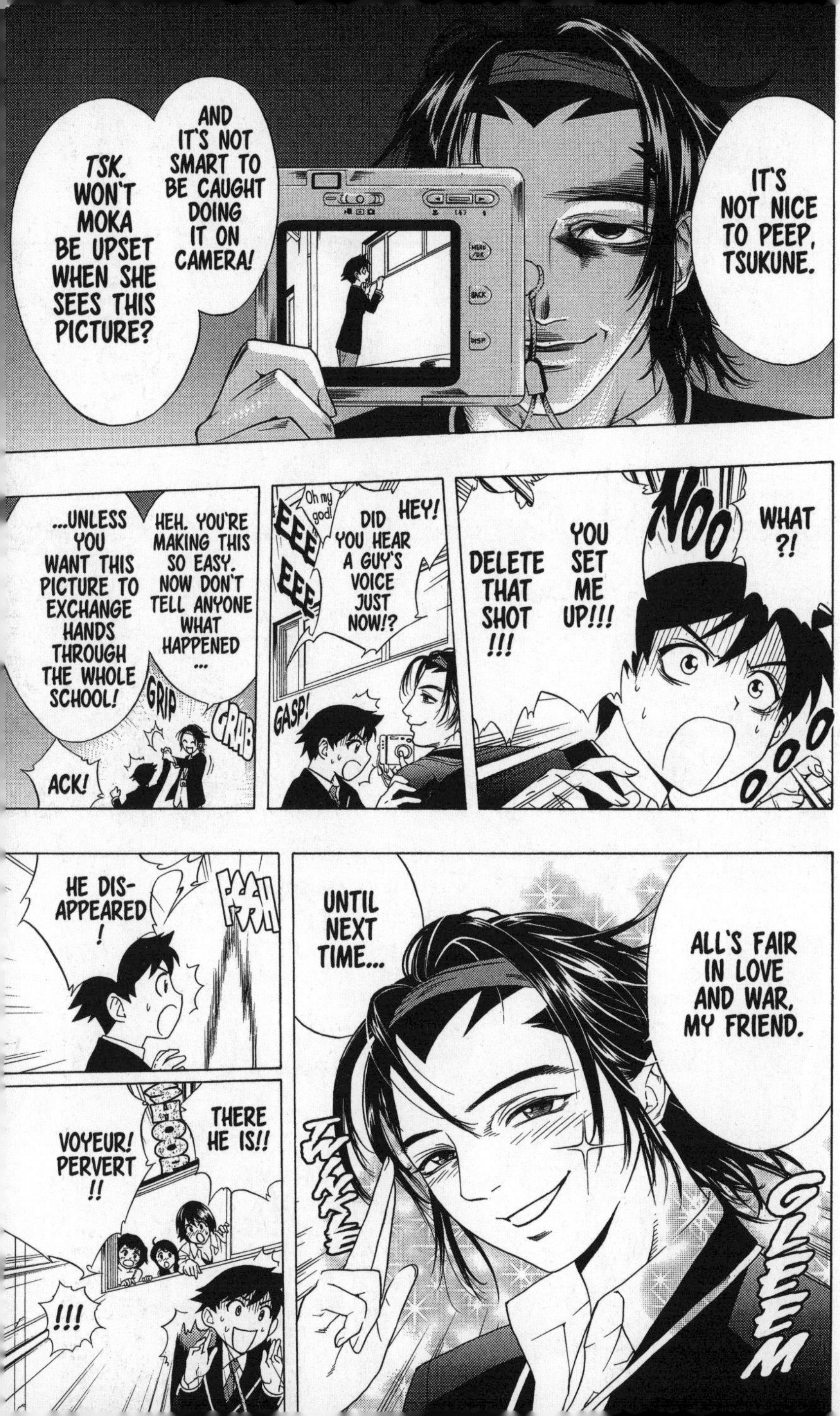
IT'S NOT NICE TO PEEP, TSUKUNE.
AND IT'S NOT SMART TO BE CAUGHT DOING IT ON CAMERA!
TSK. WON'T MOKA BE UPSET WHEN SHE SEES THIS PICTURE?
WHAT?!
NOOOOOO
YOU SET ME UP!!!
DELETE THAT SHOT!!!
HEY!
DID YOU HEAR A GUY'S VOICE JUST NOW!?
Oh my god!
EEEEEE
GASP!
HEH. YOU'RE MAKING THIS SO EASY. NOW DON'T TELL ANYONE WHAT HAPPENED...
...UNLESS YOU WANT THIS PICTURE TO EXCHANGE HANDS THROUGH THE WHOLE SCHOOL!
GRAB
GRIP
ACK!
ALL'S FAIR IN LOVE AND WAR, MY FRIEND.
UNTIL NEXT TIME...
GLEEM
HE DIS-APPEARED!
THERE HE IS!!
VOYEUR! PERVERT!!
!!!

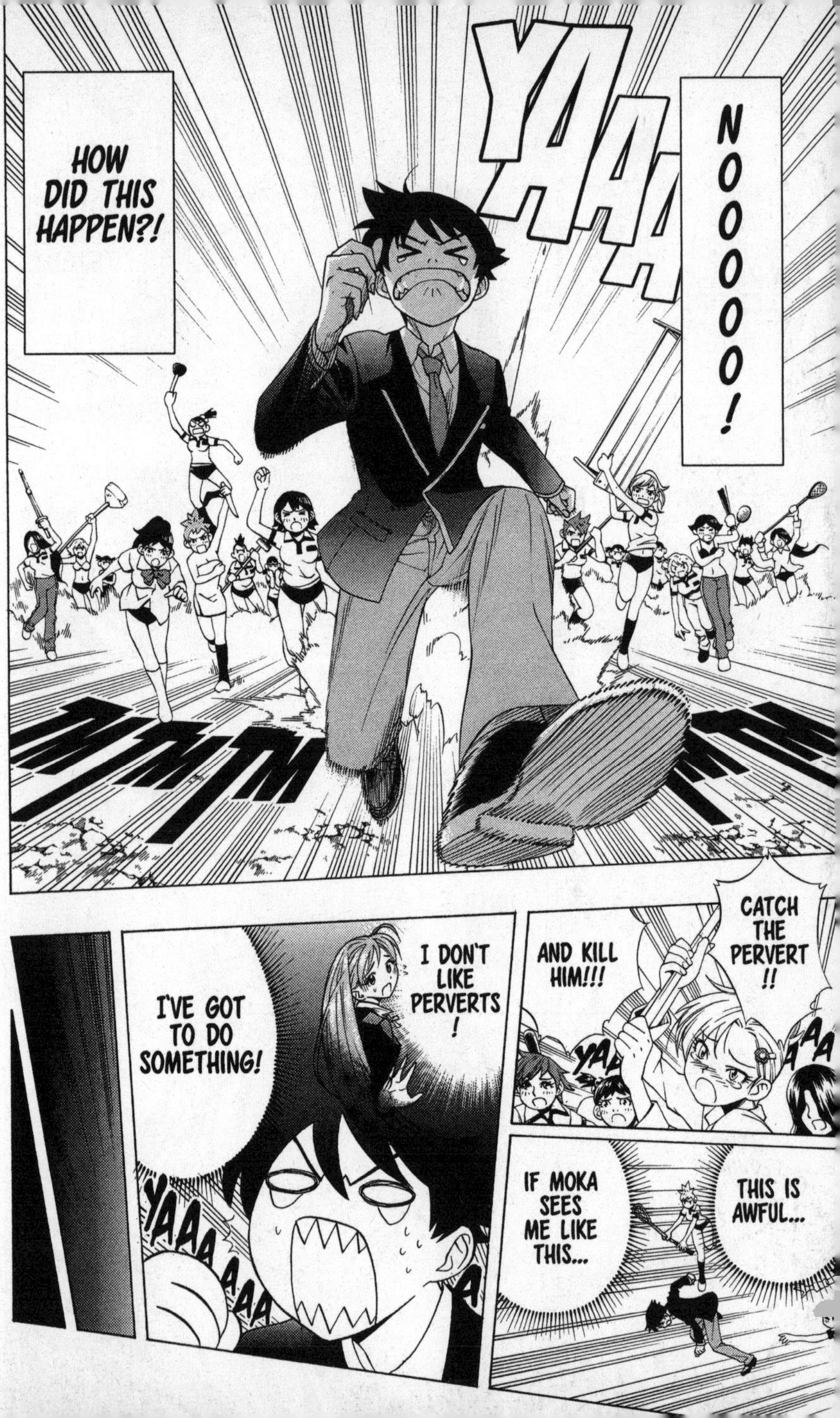
NOOOOOOO!
YAAA
HOW DID THIS HAPPEN?!
CATCH THE PERVERT!!
AND KILL HIM!!!
THIS IS AWFUL...
IF MOKA SEES ME LIKE THIS...
I DON'T LIKE PERVERTS!
I'VE GOT TO DO SOMETHING!
YAAAAAAAA

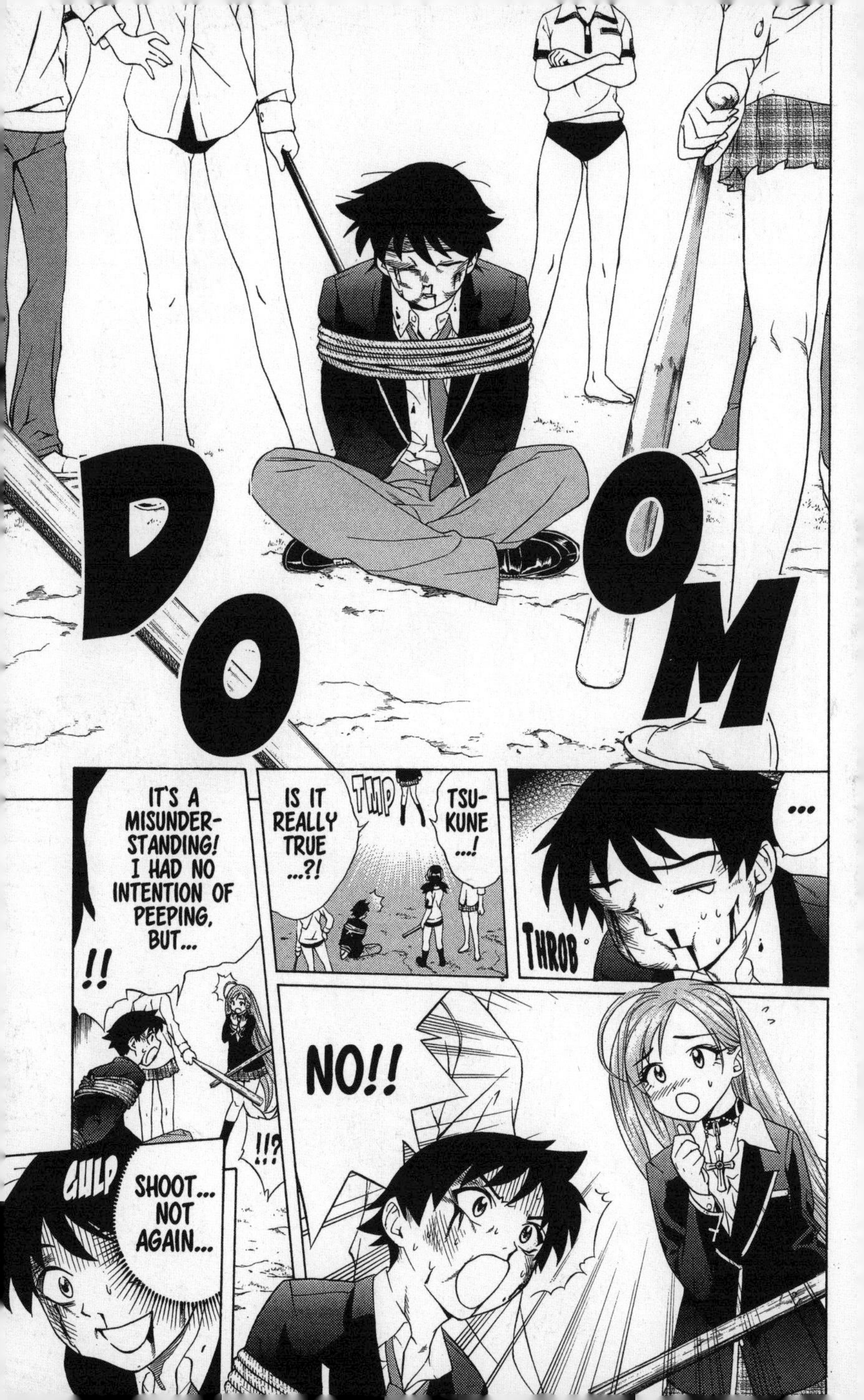
DOOM
...
THROB
TSU-KUNE ...!
TMP
IS IT REALLY TRUE ...?!
NO!!
IT'S A MISUNDER-STANDING! I HAD NO INTENTION OF PEEPING, BUT...
!!
!!?
GULP
SHOOT... NOT AGAIN...

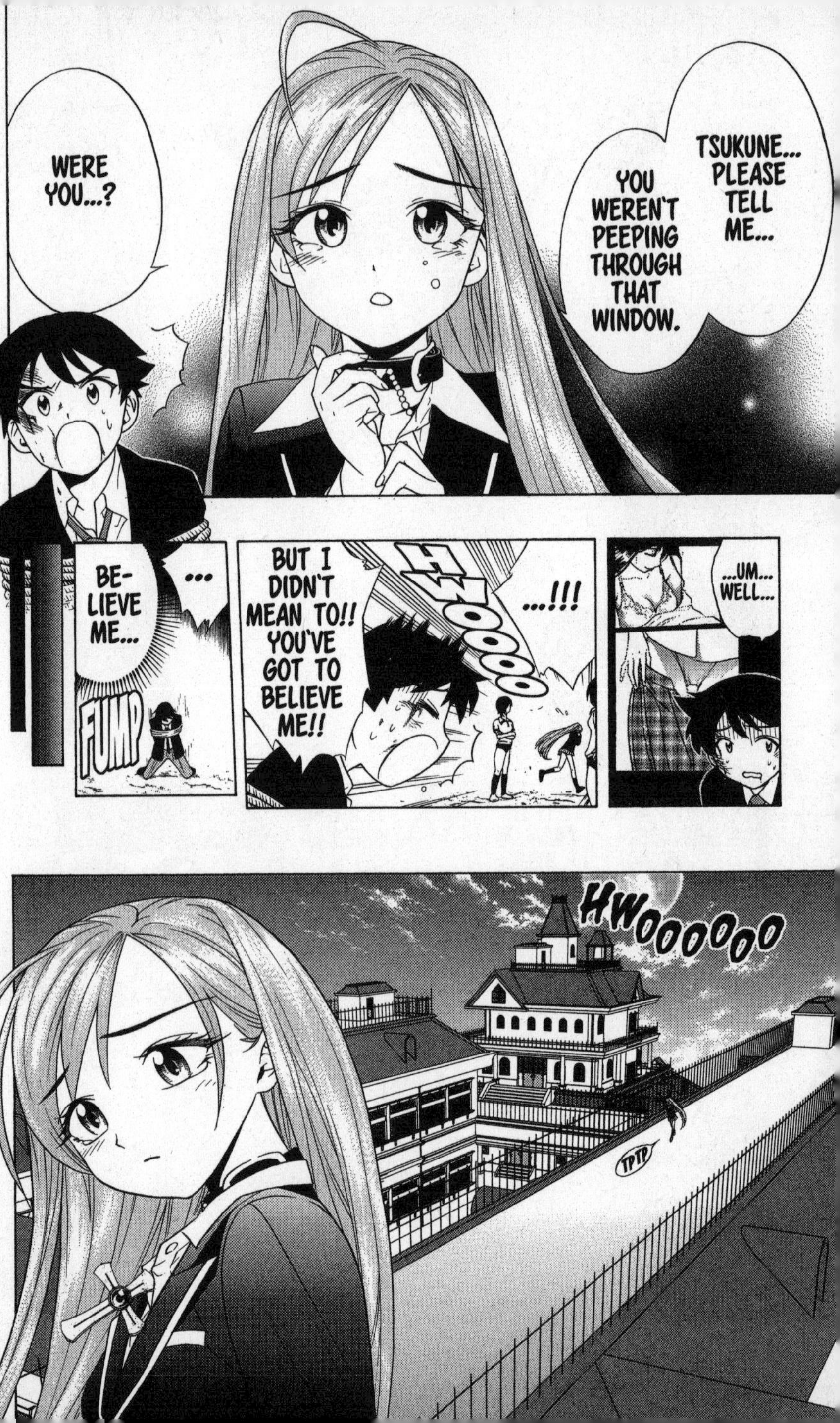

TSUKUNE... PLEASE TELL ME...
YOU WEREN'T PEEPING THROUGH THAT WINDOW.
WERE YOU...?
...UM... WELL...
...!!!
HWOOOOO
BUT I DIDN'T MEAN TO!! YOU'VE GOT TO BELIEVE ME!!
...
BE-LIEVE ME...
FUMP
HWOOOOOOO
TPTP

READ THIS WAY

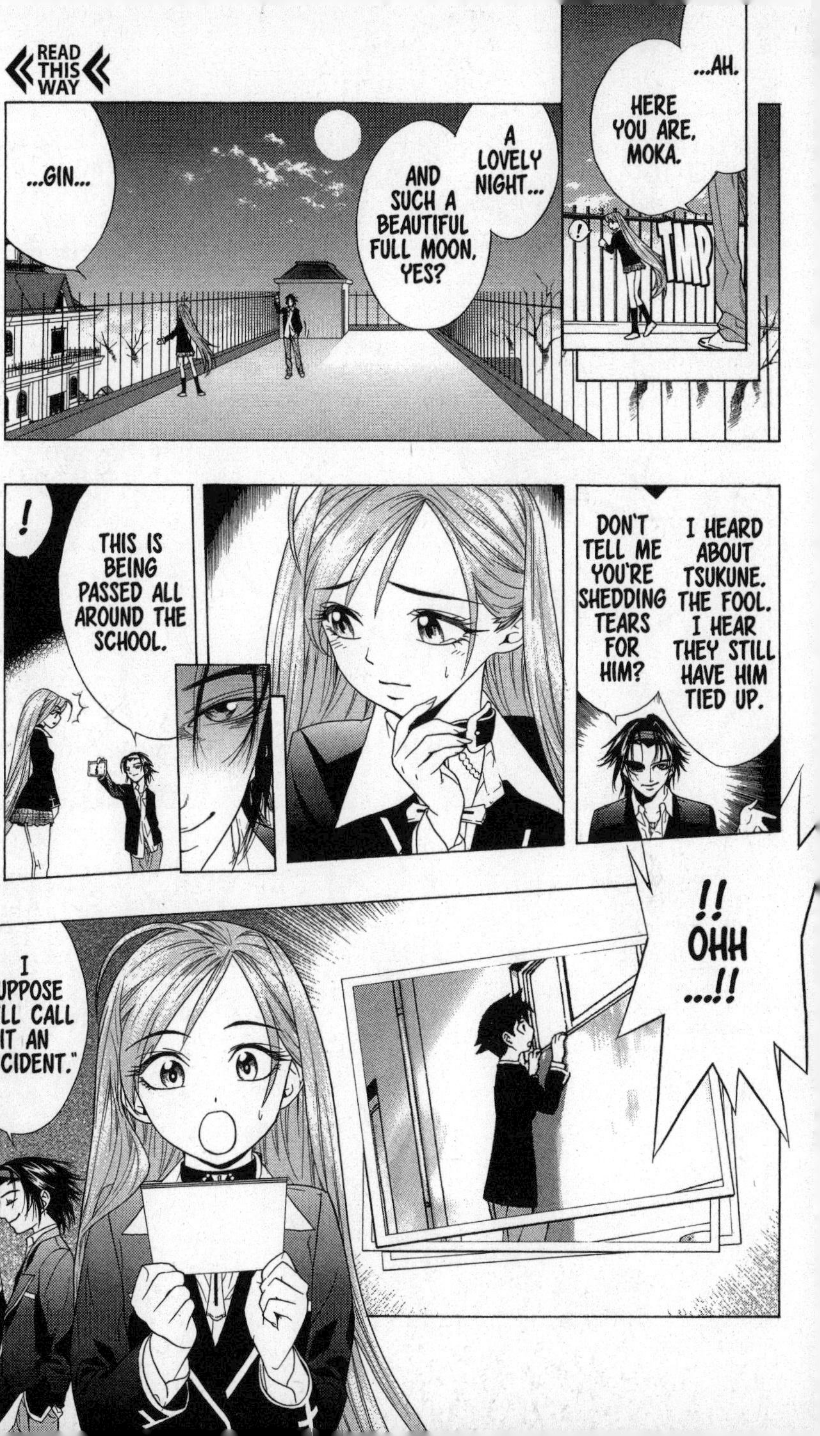
...AH.
HERE YOU ARE, MOKA.
!
TMP
A LOVELY NIGHT...
AND SUCH A BEAUTIFUL FULL MOON, YES?
...GIN...
I HEARD ABOUT TSUKUNE. THE FOOL. I HEAR THEY STILL HAVE HIM TIED UP.
DON'T TELL ME YOU'RE SHEDDING TEARS FOR HIM?
THIS IS BEING PASSED ALL AROUND THE SCHOOL.
!
!! OHH ...!!
I SUPPOSE HE'LL CALL IT AN "ACCIDENT."

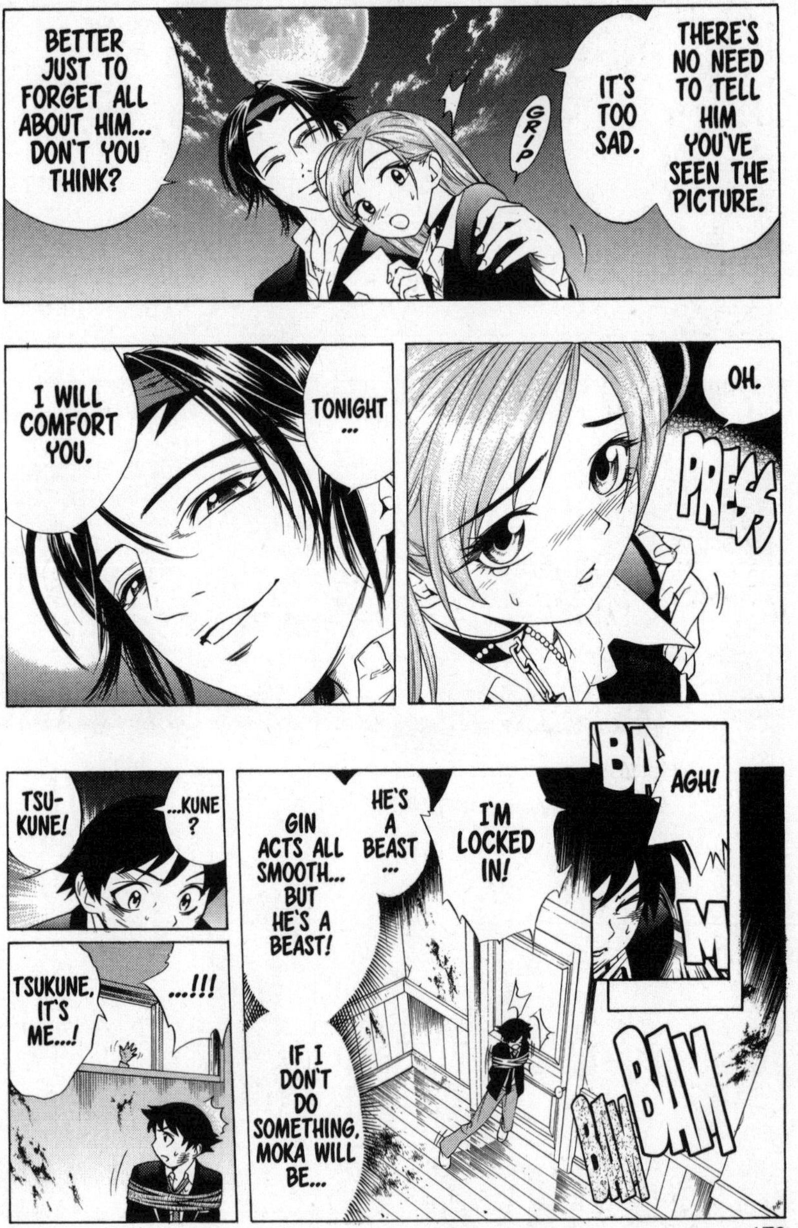

THERE'S NO NEED TO TELL HIM YOU'VE SEEN THE PICTURE.
IT'S TOO SAD.
GRIP
BETTER JUST TO FORGET ALL ABOUT HIM... DON'T YOU THINK?
OH.
PRESS
TONIGHT...
I WILL COMFORT YOU.
BAM
AGH!
I'M LOCKED IN!
HE'S A BEAST...
GIN ACTS ALL SMOOTH... BUT HE'S A BEAST!
IF I DON'T DO SOMETHING, MOKA WILL BE...
BAM BAM
...KUNE?
TSU-KUNE!
...!!!
TSUKUNE, IT'S ME...!

READ THIS WAY

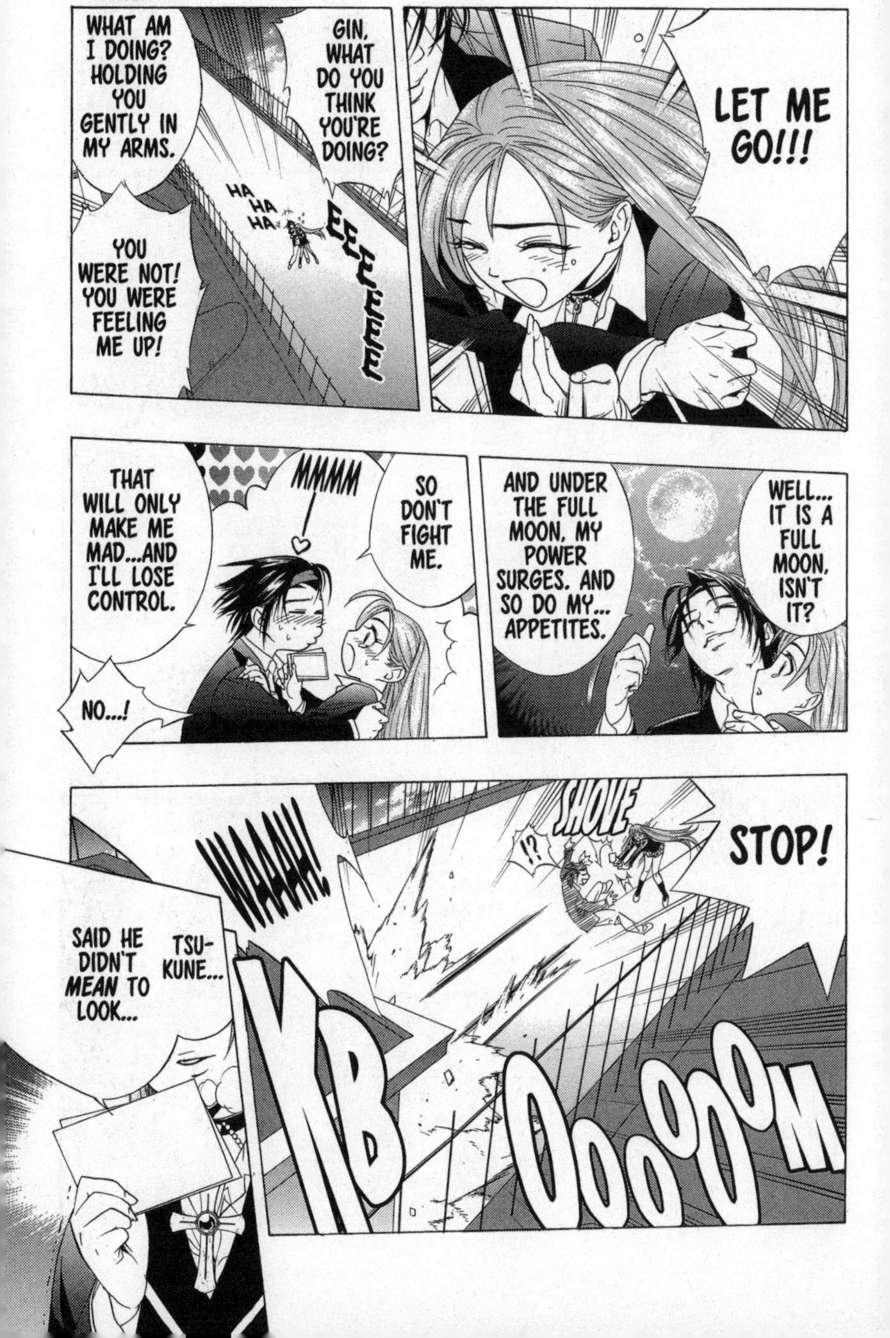
LET ME GO!!!
GIN, WHAT DO YOU THINK YOU'RE DOING?
WHAT AM I DOING? HOLDING YOU GENTLY IN MY ARMS.
HA HA HA
EEEEEEEE
YOU WERE NOT! YOU WERE FEELING ME UP!
WELL... IT IS A FULL MOON, ISN'T IT?
AND UNDER THE FULL MOON, MY POWER SURGES. AND SO DO MY... APPETITES.
SO DON'T FIGHT ME.
MMMM
THAT WILL ONLY MAKE ME MAD...AND I'LL LOSE CONTROL.
NO...!
STOP!
SHOVE
!?
WAAAH!
TSU-KUNE...
SAID HE DIDN'T *MEAN* TO LOOK...
KBOOOOOOM

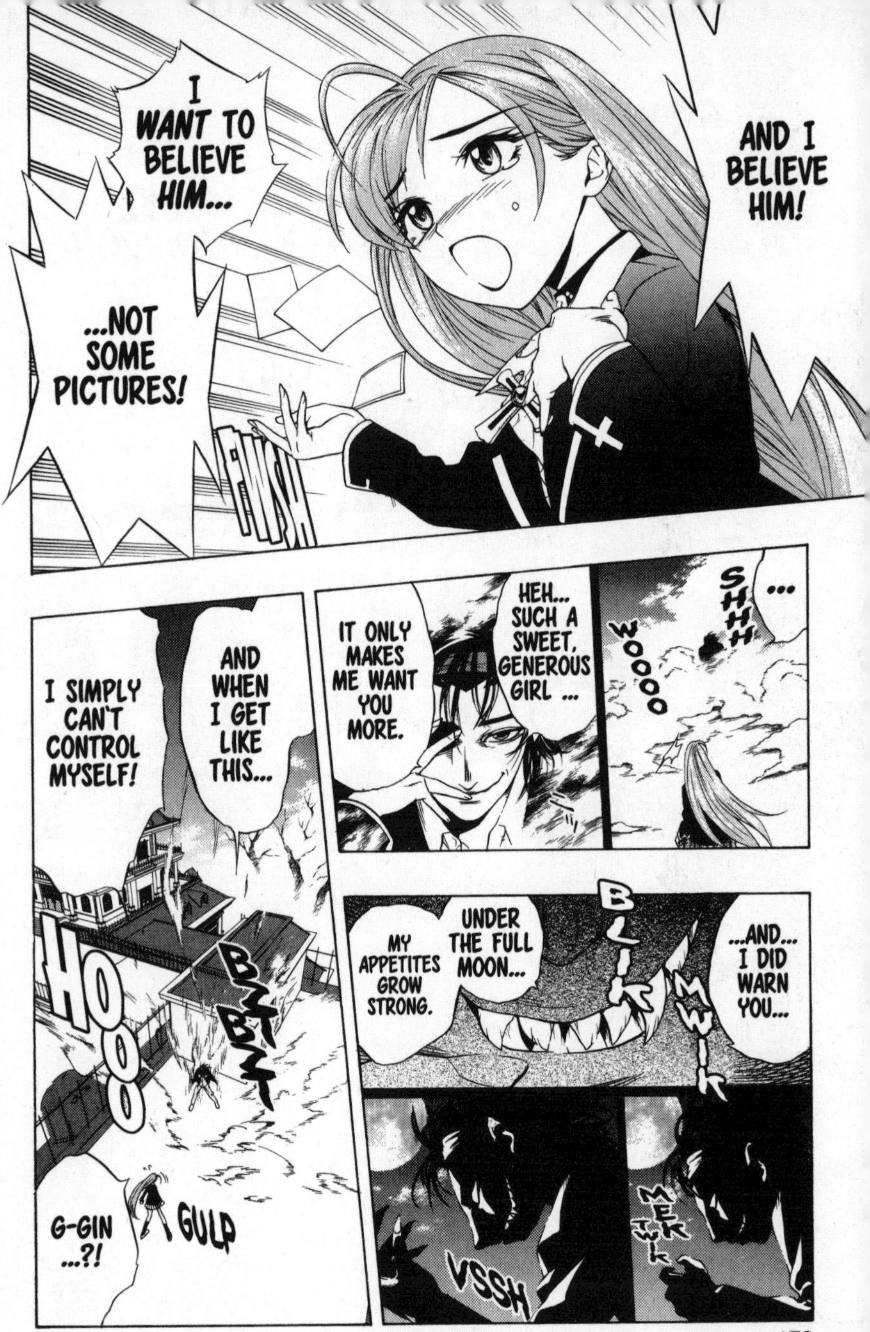
AND I BELIEVE HIM!
I WANT TO BELIEVE HIM...
...NOT SOME PICTURES!
...
SHHHH
WOOOOO
HEH... SUCH A SWEET, GENEROUS GIRL ...
IT ONLY MAKES ME WANT YOU MORE.
...AND... I DID WARN YOU...
MWIK
BLIK
UNDER THE FULL MOON...
MY APPETITES GROW STRONG.
MEK
TWIK
VSSH
AND WHEN I GET LIKE THIS...
I SIMPLY CAN'T CONTROL MYSELF!
HOOOOO
BZT BZT
GULP
G-GIN ...?!

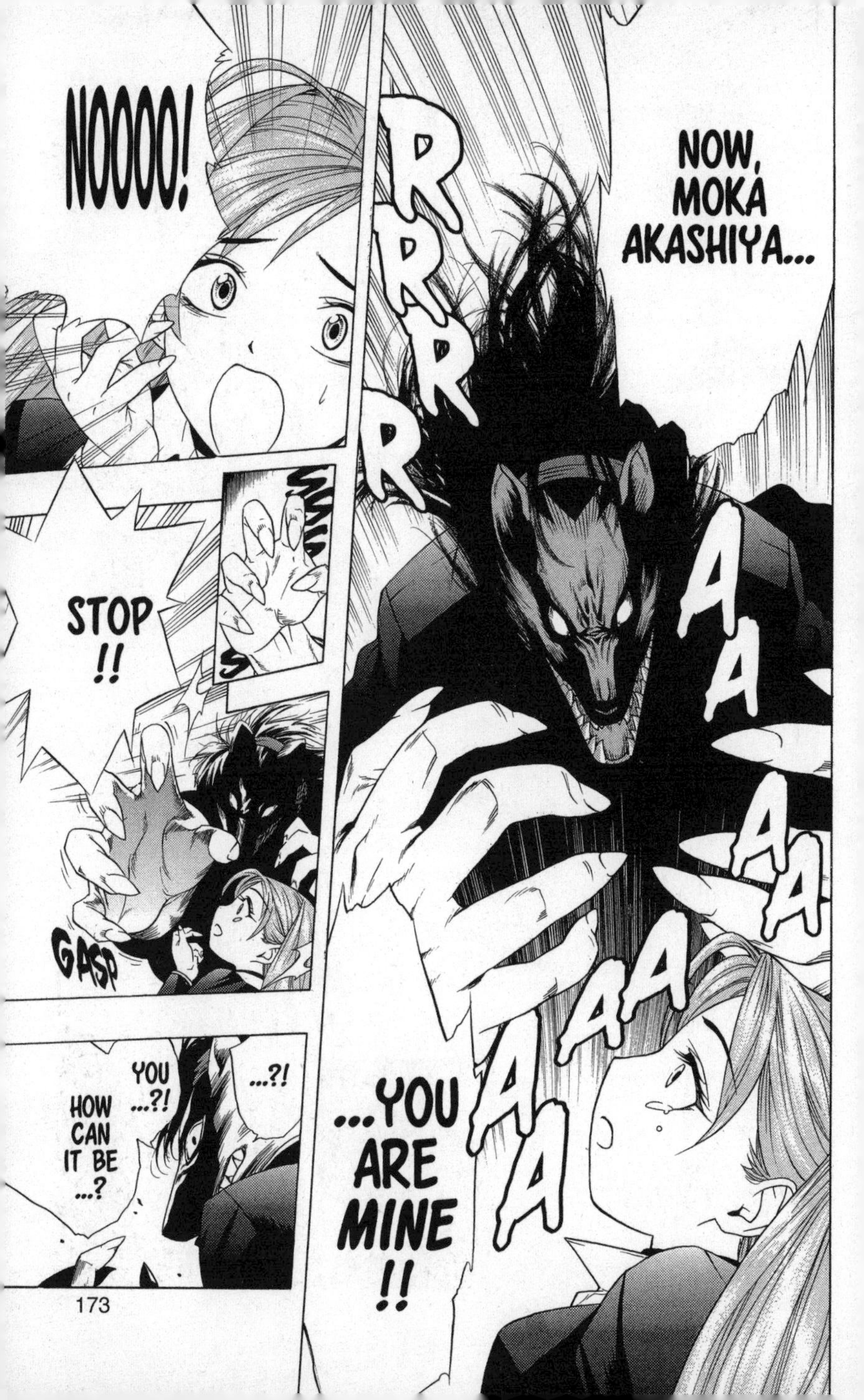
NOW, MOKA AKASHIYA...
RRRR
AAAAAAAAAAA
...YOU ARE MINE!!
NOOOO!
STOP!!
GASP
...?!
YOU ...?!
HOW CAN IT BE ...?

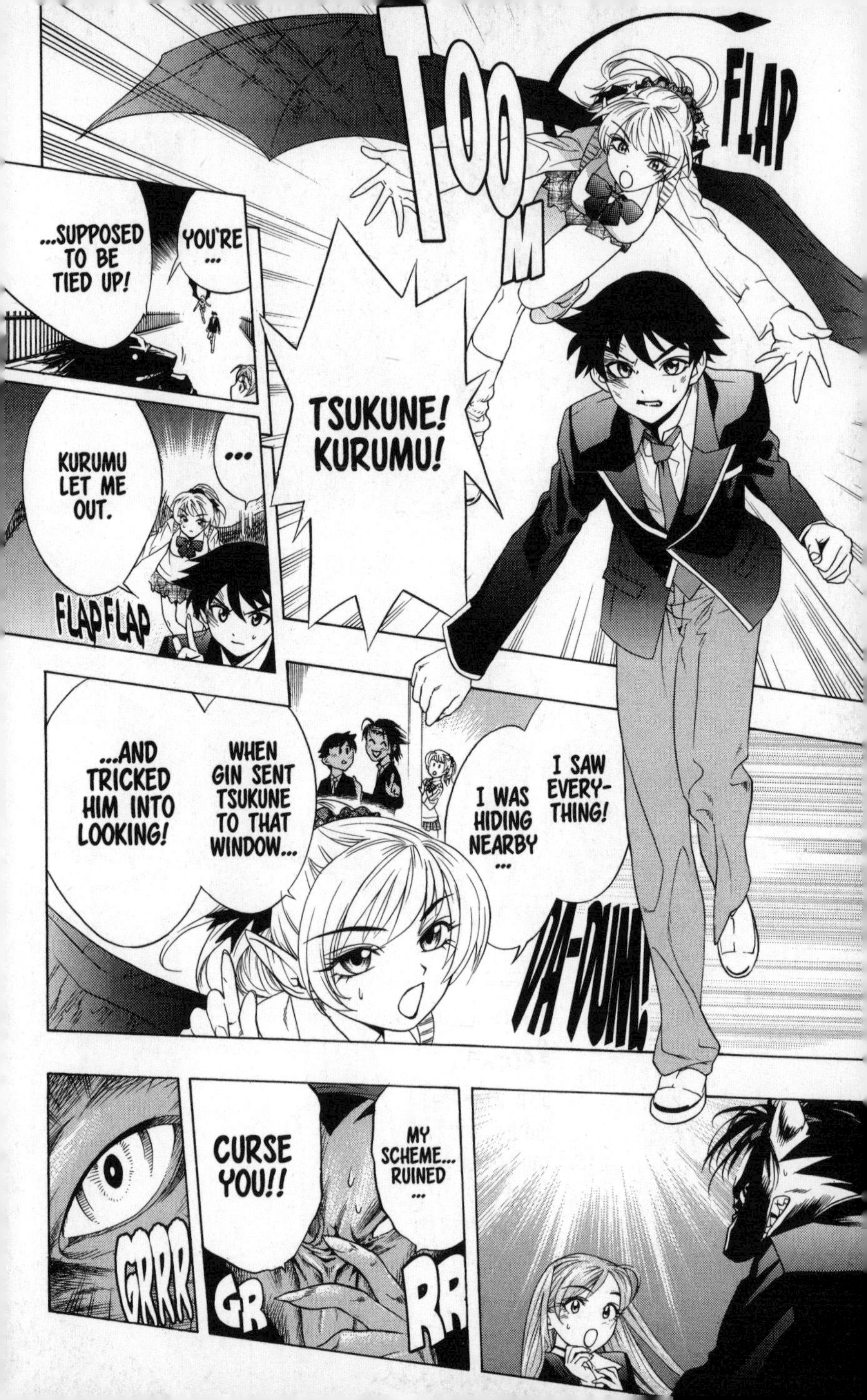

FLAP
TOOOM
TSUKUNE! KURUMU!
YOU'RE ...
...SUPPOSED TO BE TIED UP!
...
KURUMU LET ME OUT.
FLAP FLAP
DA-DUM!
I SAW EVERY-THING!
I WAS HIDING NEARBY ...
WHEN GIN SENT TSUKUNE TO THAT WINDOW...
...AND TRICKED HIM INTO LOOKING!
MY SCHEME... RUINED ...
CURSE YOU!!
GR
RR
GRRR

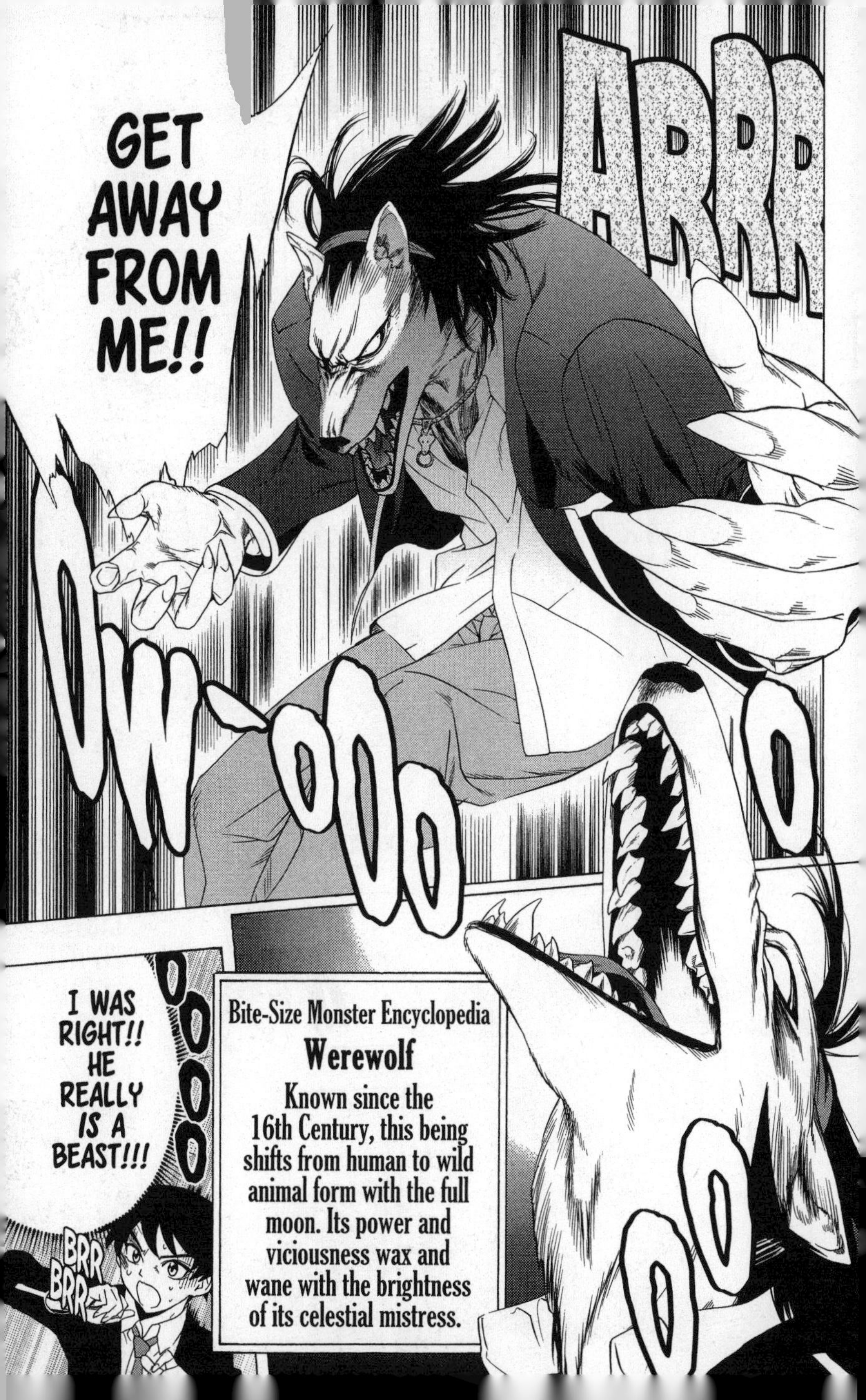
ARRR
GET AWAY FROM ME!!
OWOOOOO
Bite-Size Monster Encyclopedia
Werewolf
Known since the 16th Century, this being shifts from human to wild animal form with the full moon. Its power and viciousness wax and wane with the brightness of its celestial mistress.
I WAS RIGHT!! HE REALLY IS A BEAST!!!
BRR BRR

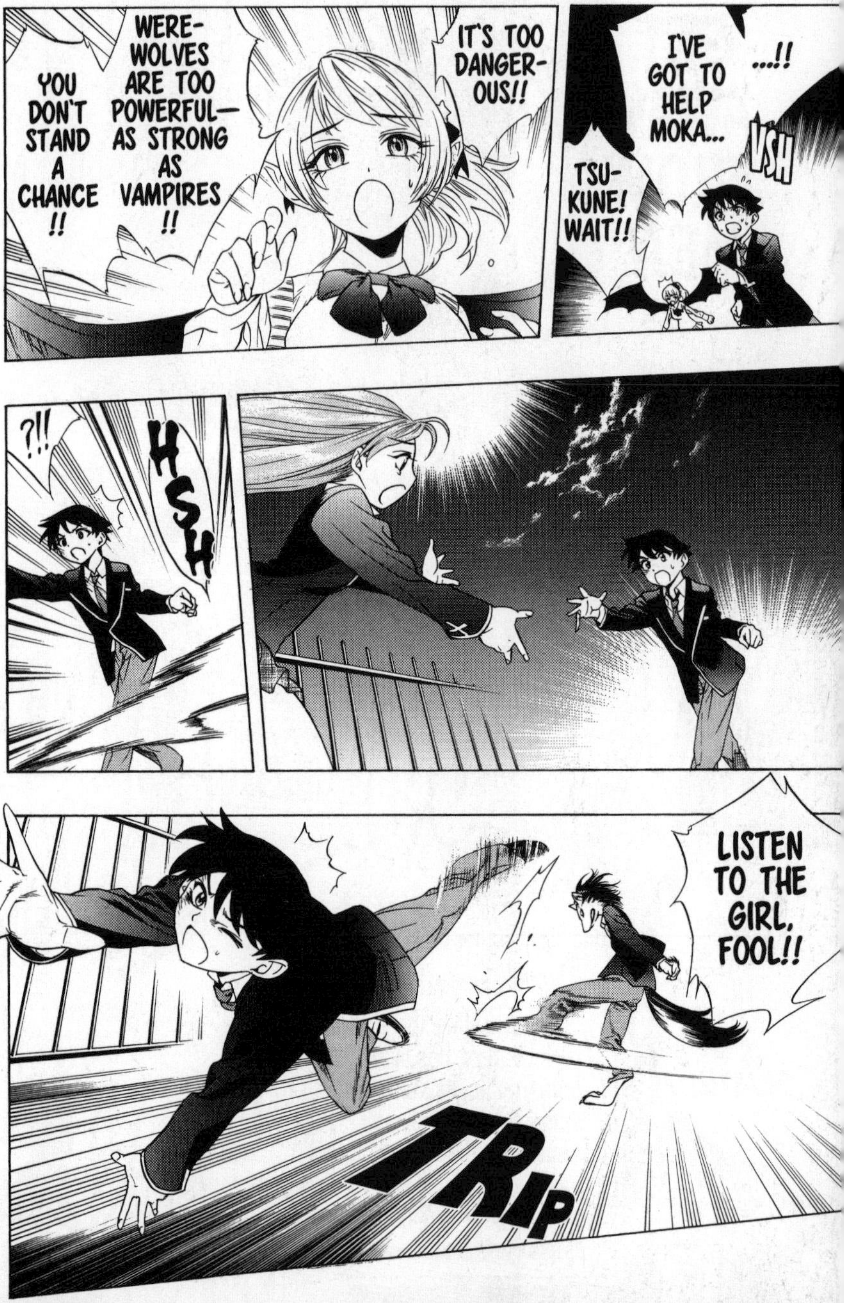
...!!
I'VE GOT TO HELP MOKA...
VSH
TSU-KUNE! WAIT!!
IT'S TOO DANGER-OUS!!
WERE-WOLVES ARE TOO POWERFUL—AS STRONG AS VAMPIRES!!
YOU DON'T STAND A CHANCE!!
HSH
?!!
LISTEN TO THE GIRL, FOOL!!
TRIP

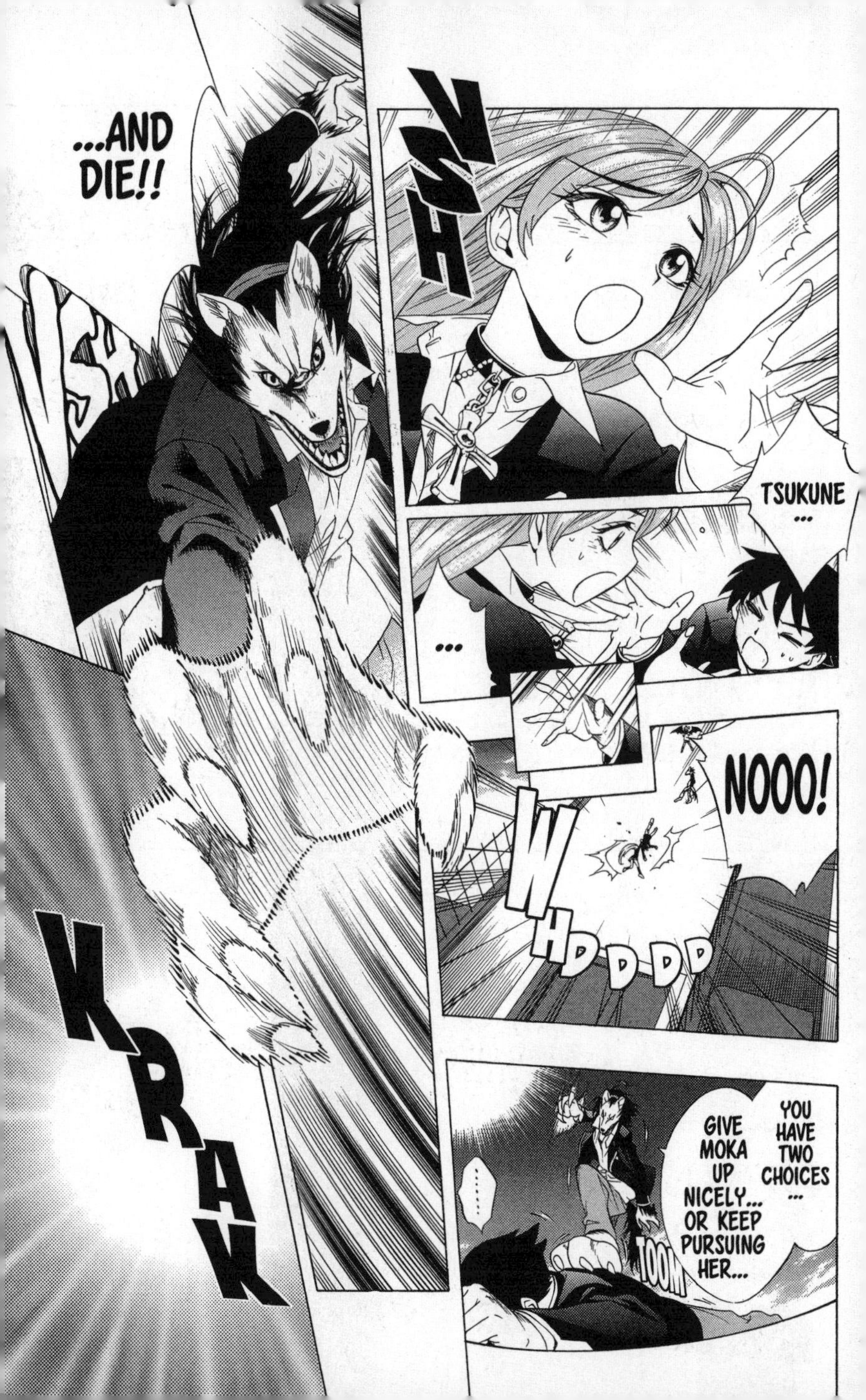
VSH
TSUKUNE ...
...
NOOO!
WHDDDD
YOU HAVE TWO CHOICES ...
GIVE MOKA UP NICELY... OR KEEP PURSUING HER...
TOOM
......
...AND DIE!!
VSH
KRAK

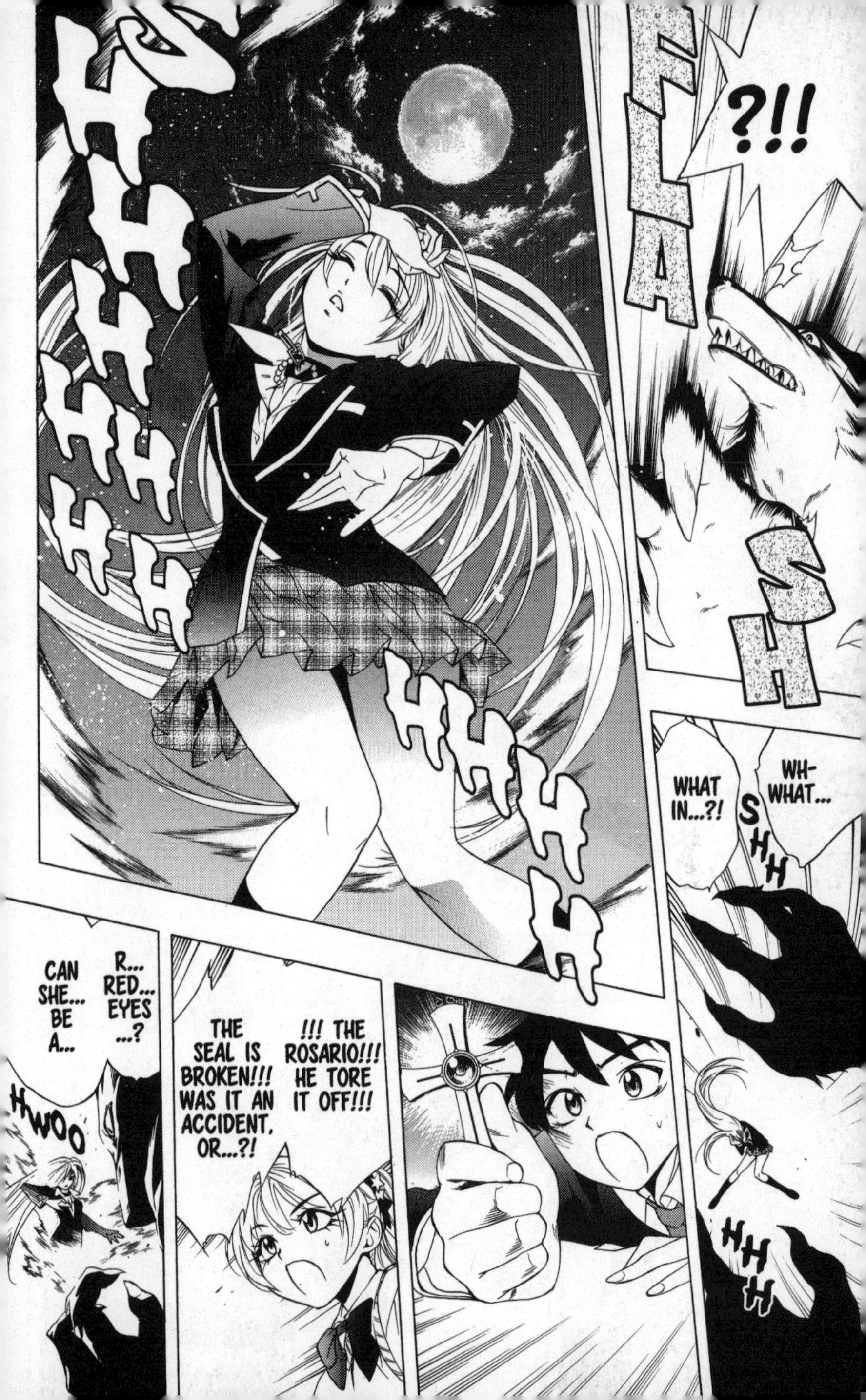
FLASH
?!!
WH- WHAT...
WHAT IN...?!
SHH
HHH
HHHHHHHH
HHHHHH
!!! THE ROSARIO!!! HE TORE IT OFF!!!
THE SEAL IS BROKEN!!! WAS IT AN ACCIDENT, OR...?!
R... RED... EYES ...?
CAN SHE... BE A...
HWOO

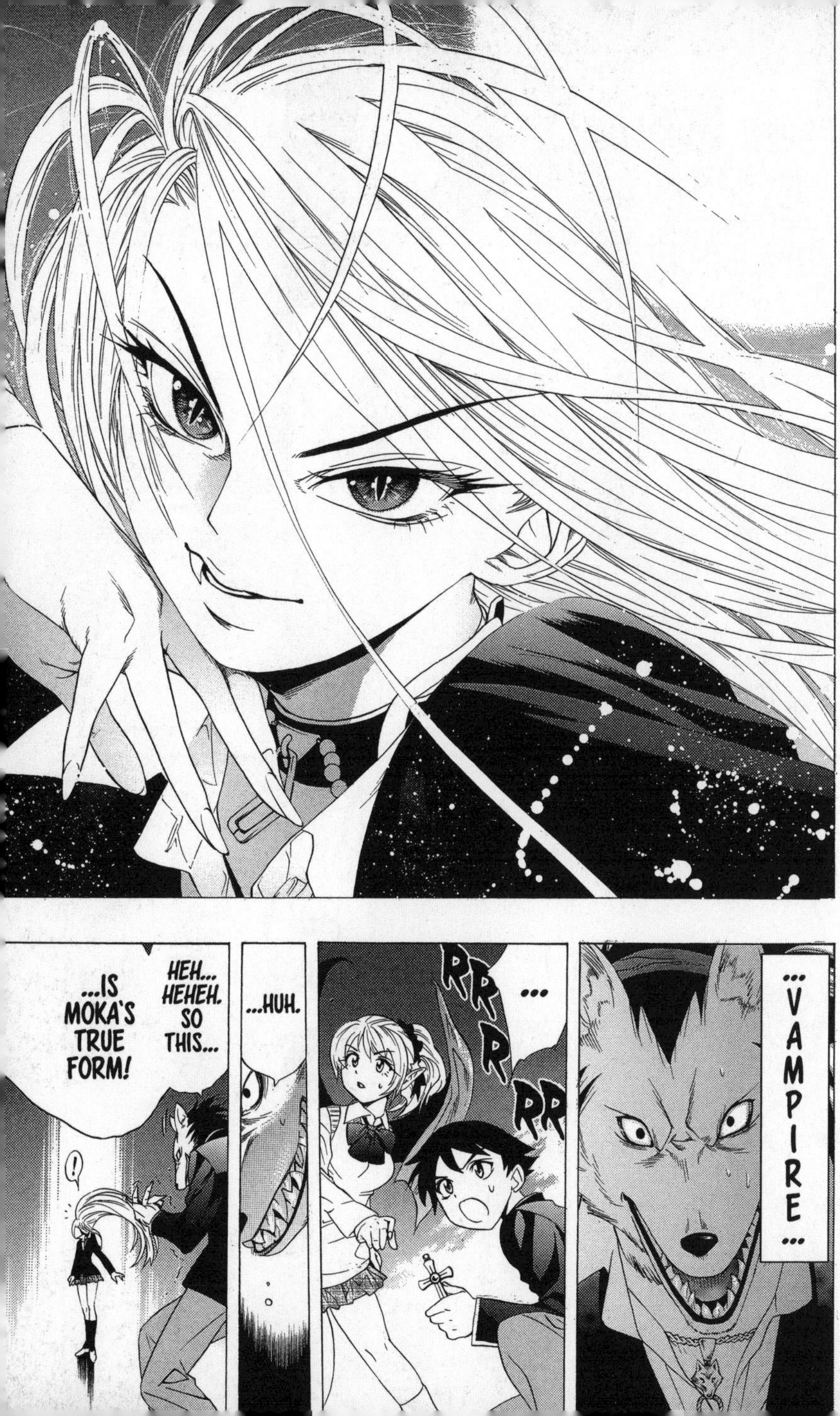
...VAMPIRE...
RRRRR
...
...HUH.
HEH... HEHEH. SO THIS...
...IS MOKA'S TRUE FORM!
!

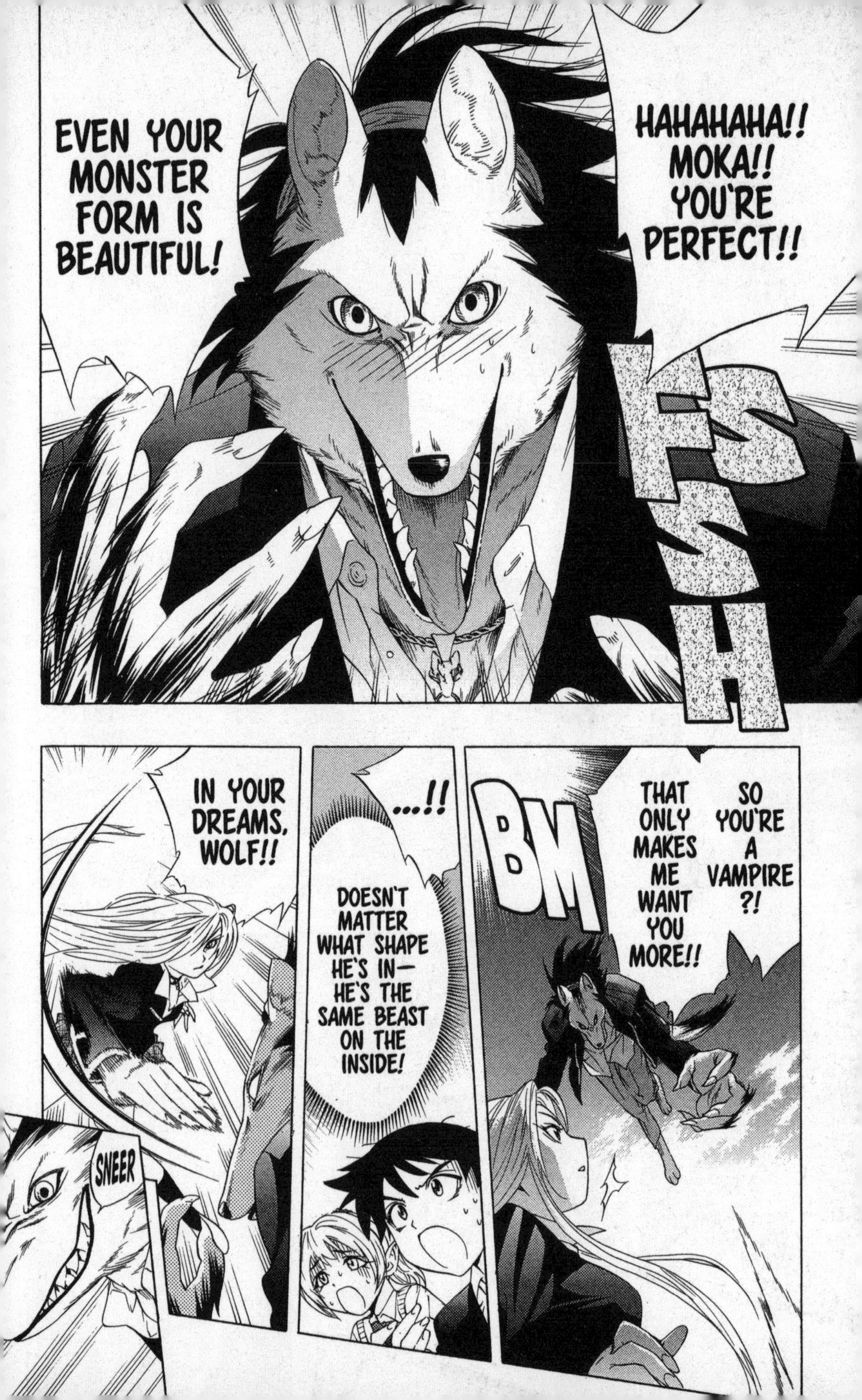
HAHAHAHA!! MOKA!! YOU'RE PERFECT!!
EVEN YOUR MONSTER FORM IS BEAUTIFUL!
FSSH
SO YOU'RE A VAMPIRE?!
THAT ONLY MAKES ME WANT YOU MORE!!
BM
...!!
DOESN'T MATTER WHAT SHAPE HE'S IN— HE'S THE SAME BEAST ON THE INSIDE!
IN YOUR DREAMS, WOLF!!
SNEER

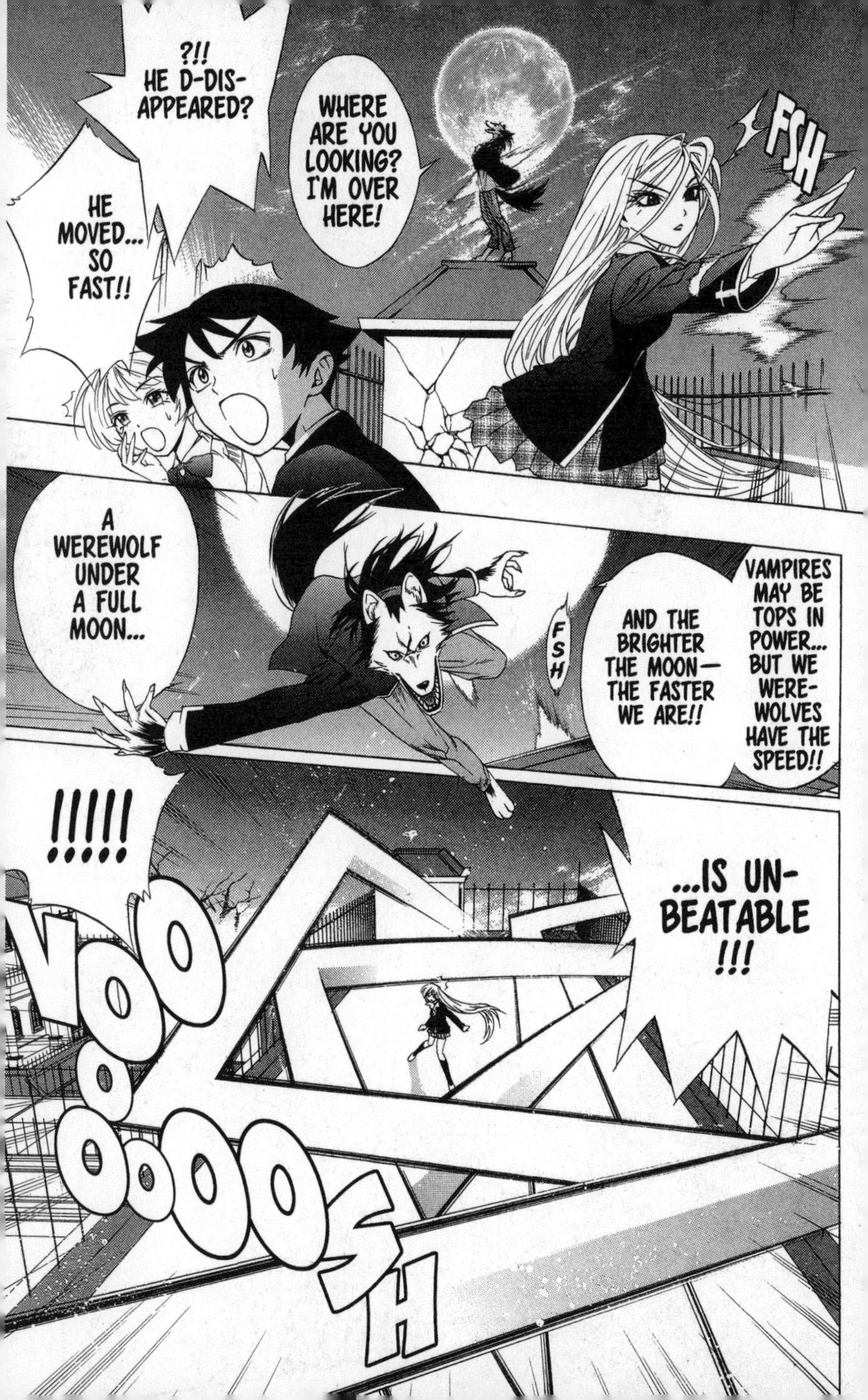
FSH
?!! HE D-DIS-APPEARED?
WHERE ARE YOU LOOKING? I'M OVER HERE!
HE MOVED... SO FAST!!
VAMPIRES MAY BE TOPS IN POWER... BUT WE WERE-WOLVES HAVE THE SPEED!!
AND THE BRIGHTER THE MOON—THE FASTER WE ARE!!
FSH
A WEREWOLF UNDER A FULL MOON...
...IS UN-BEATABLE!!!
!!!!!
VOOOOOOOOOSH

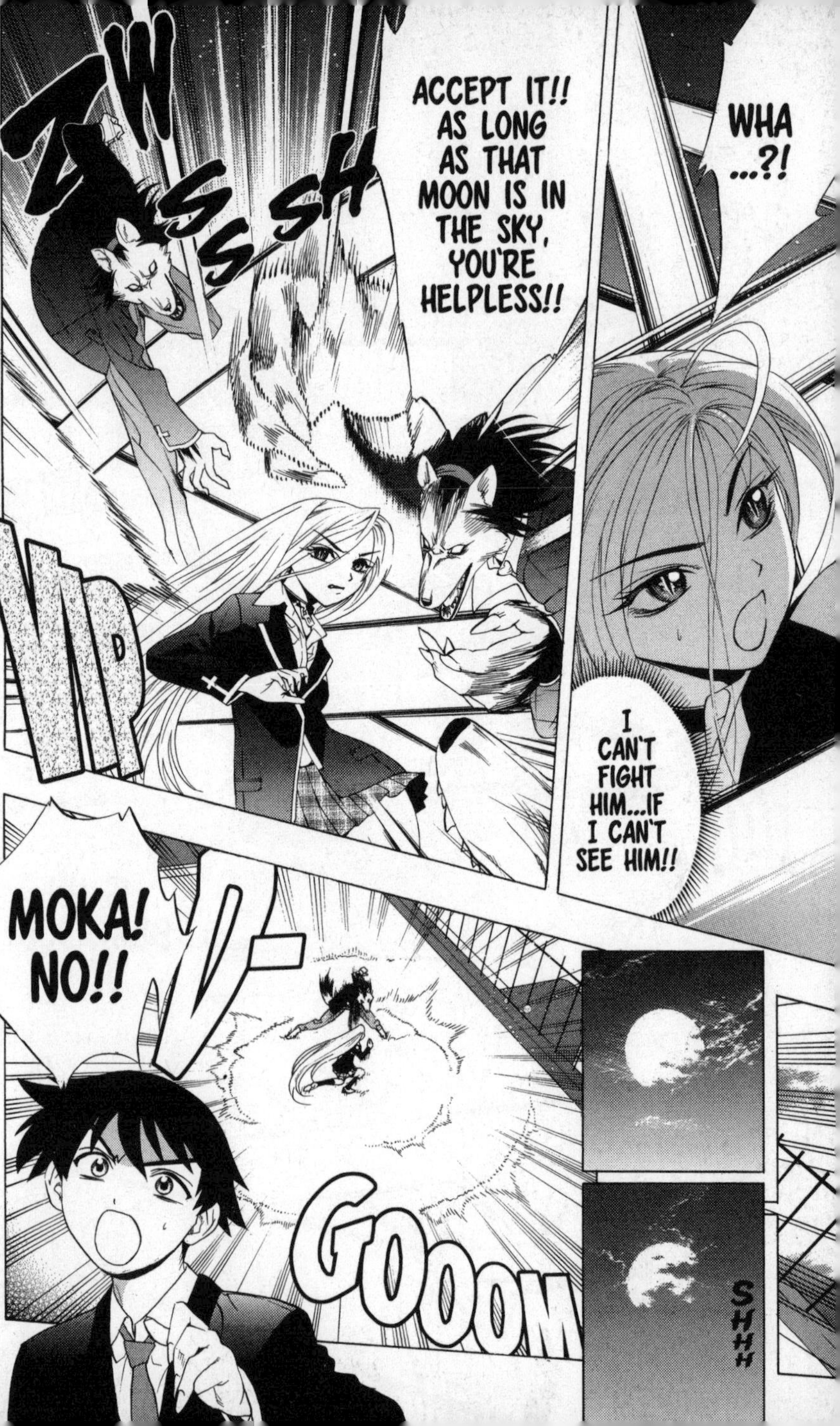
WHA ...?!
I CAN'T FIGHT HIM...IF I CAN'T SEE HIM!!
ZWSSSH
ACCEPT IT!! AS LONG AS THAT MOON IS IN THE SKY, YOU'RE HELPLESS!!
VIP
SHHH
MOKA! NO!!
GOOOOM

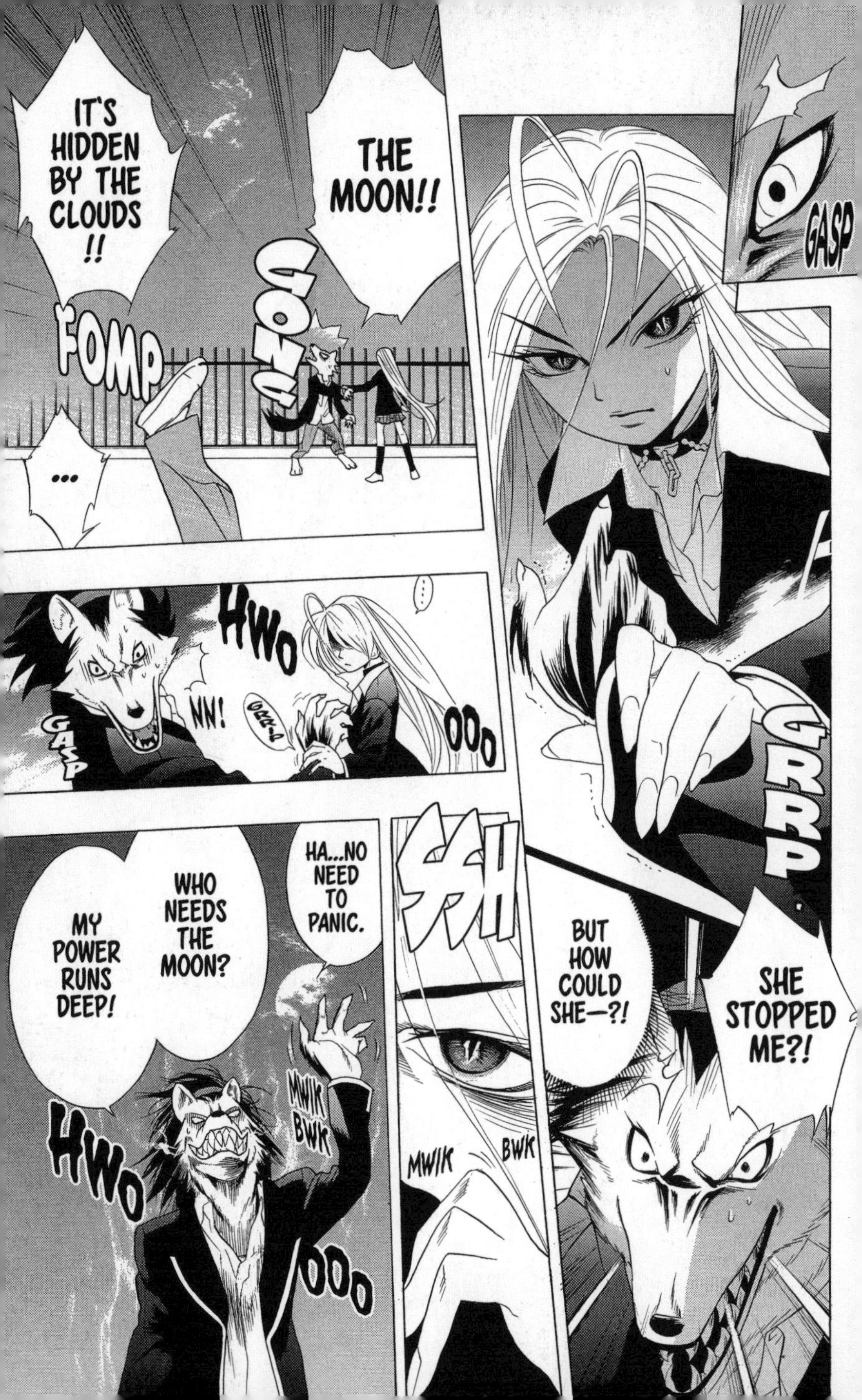
THE MOON!!
IT'S HIDDEN BY THE CLOUDS!!
GONG
FOMP
...
GASP
GRRP
HWO OOO
...
NN!
GRR-P
GASP
SHE STOPPED ME?!
BUT HOW COULD SHE—?!
SH
MWIK
BWK
HA...NO NEED TO PANIC.
WHO NEEDS THE MOON?
MY POWER RUNS DEEP!
MWIK BWK
HWO OOO

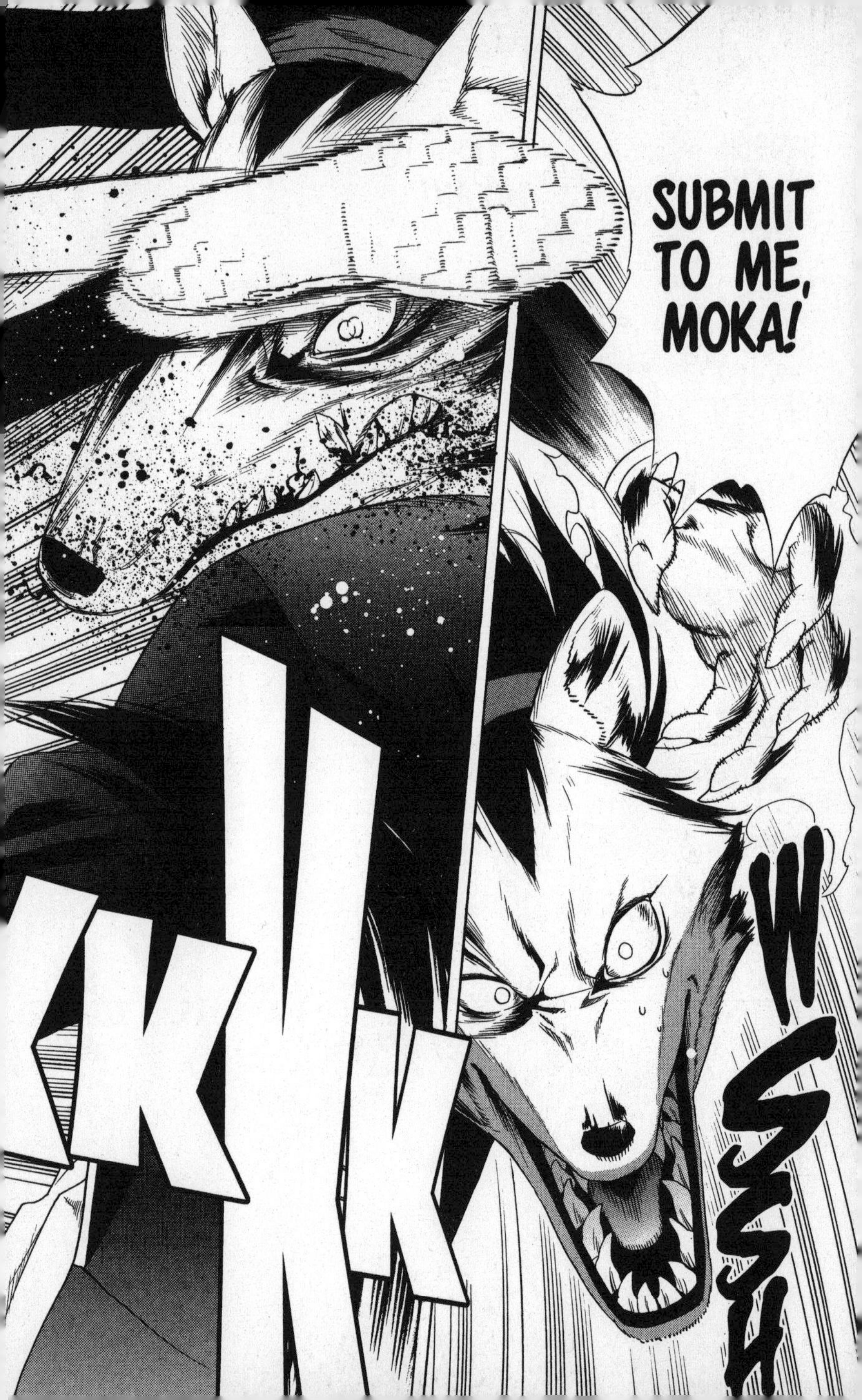
SUBMIT TO ME, MOKA!
WSSH
KKK

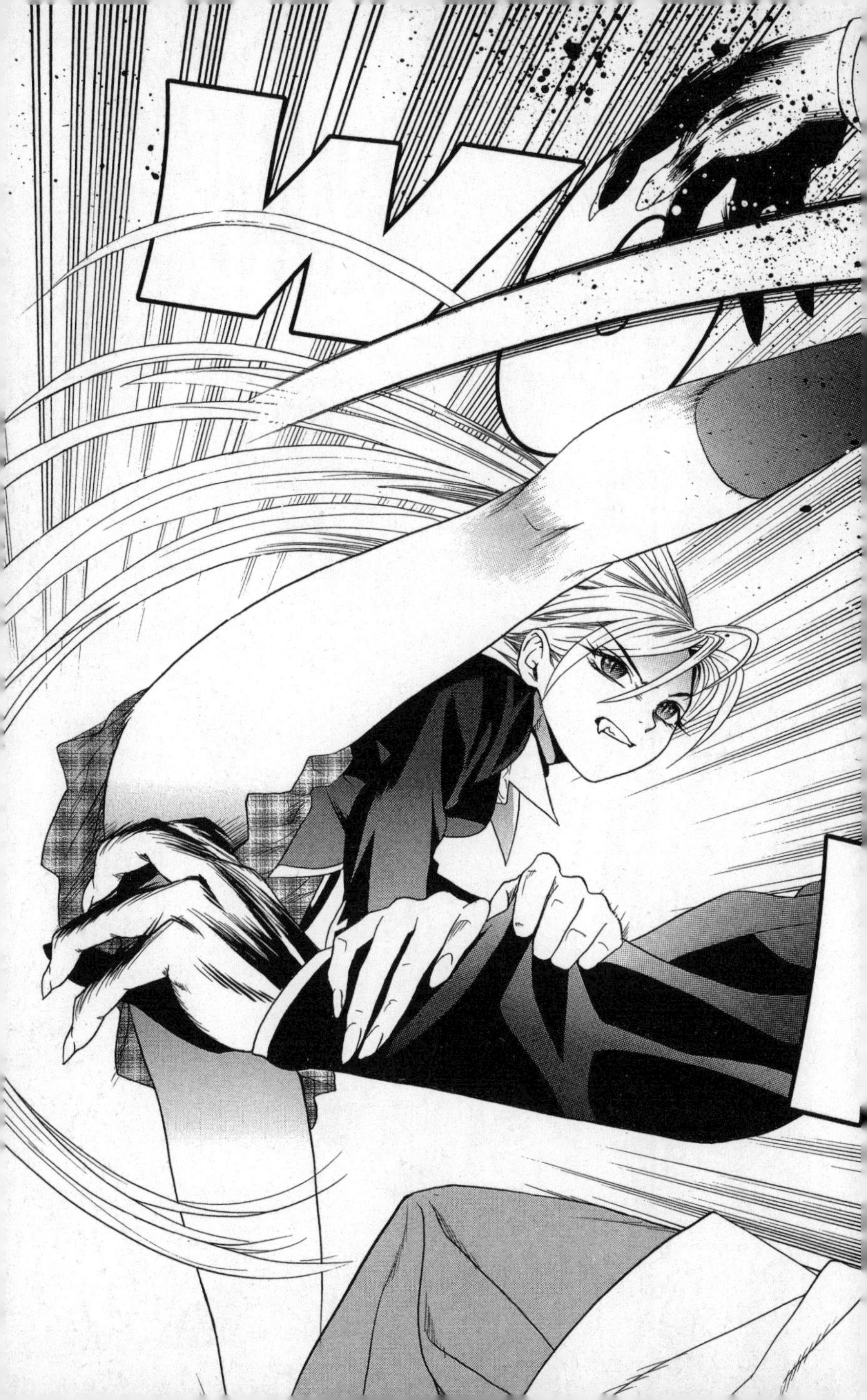

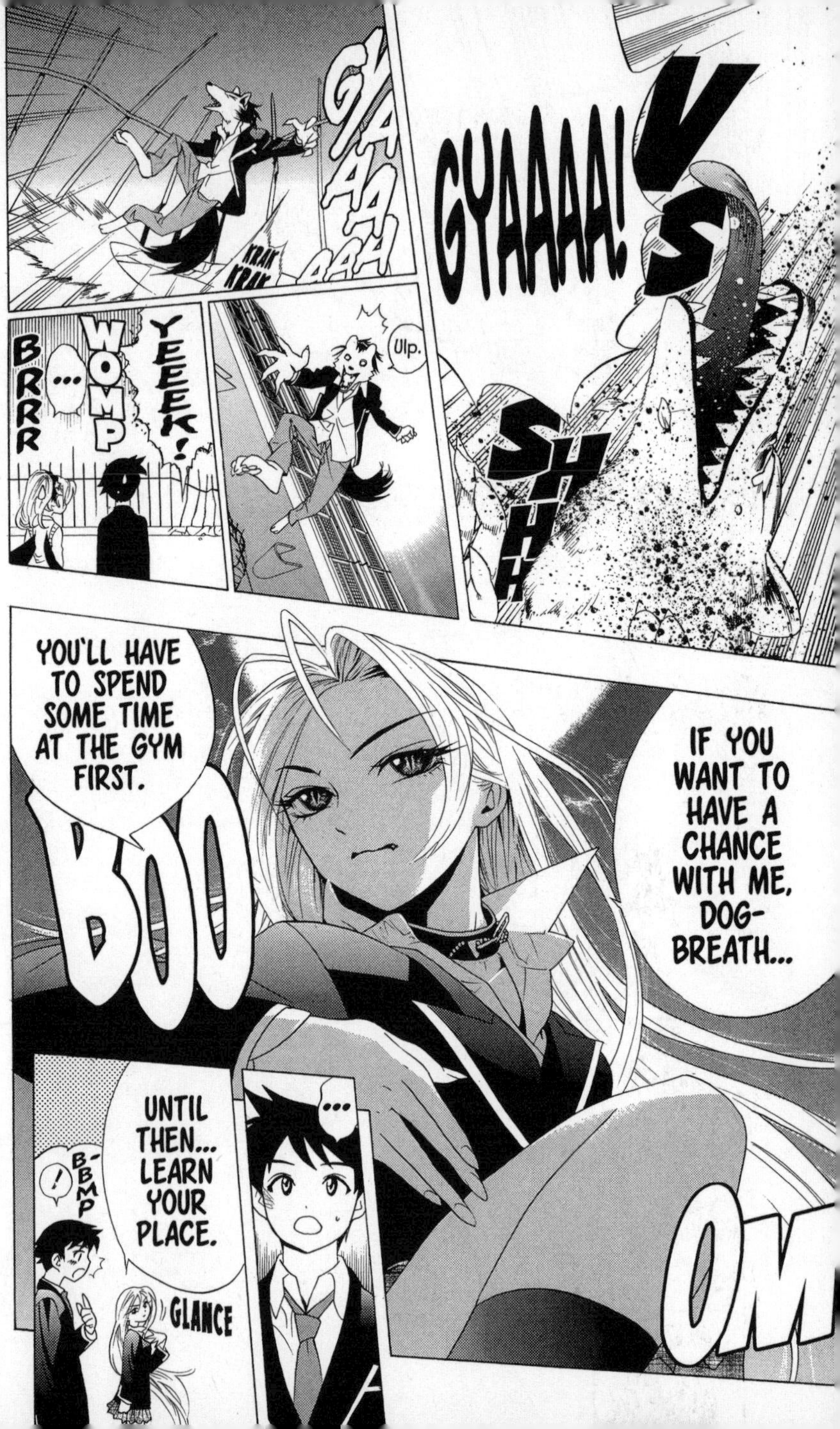
GYAAAA!
VSSHHHH
GYAAAAAAH
KRAK KRAK
Ulp.
YEEEEK!
WOMP
...
BRRR
IF YOU WANT TO HAVE A CHANCE WITH ME, DOG-BREATH...
YOU'LL HAVE TO SPEND SOME TIME AT THE GYM FIRST.
BOOOM
...
UNTIL THEN... LEARN YOUR PLACE.
!
B-BMP
GLANCE

READ THIS WAY

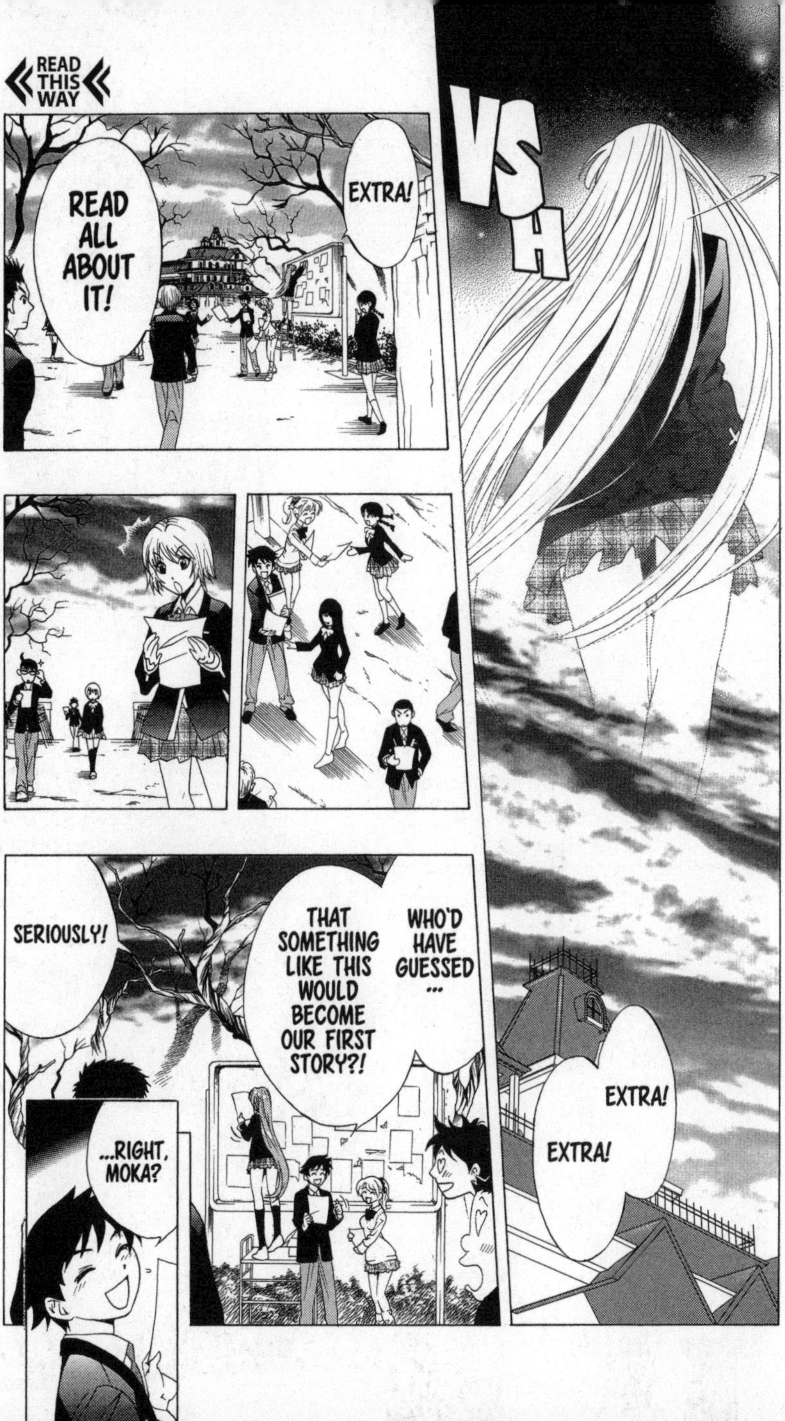
VS H
EXTRA!
EXTRA!
EXTRA!
READ ALL ABOUT IT!
WHO'D HAVE GUESSED...
THAT SOMETHING LIKE THIS WOULD BECOME OUR FIRST STORY?!
SERIOUSLY!
...RIGHT, MOKA?

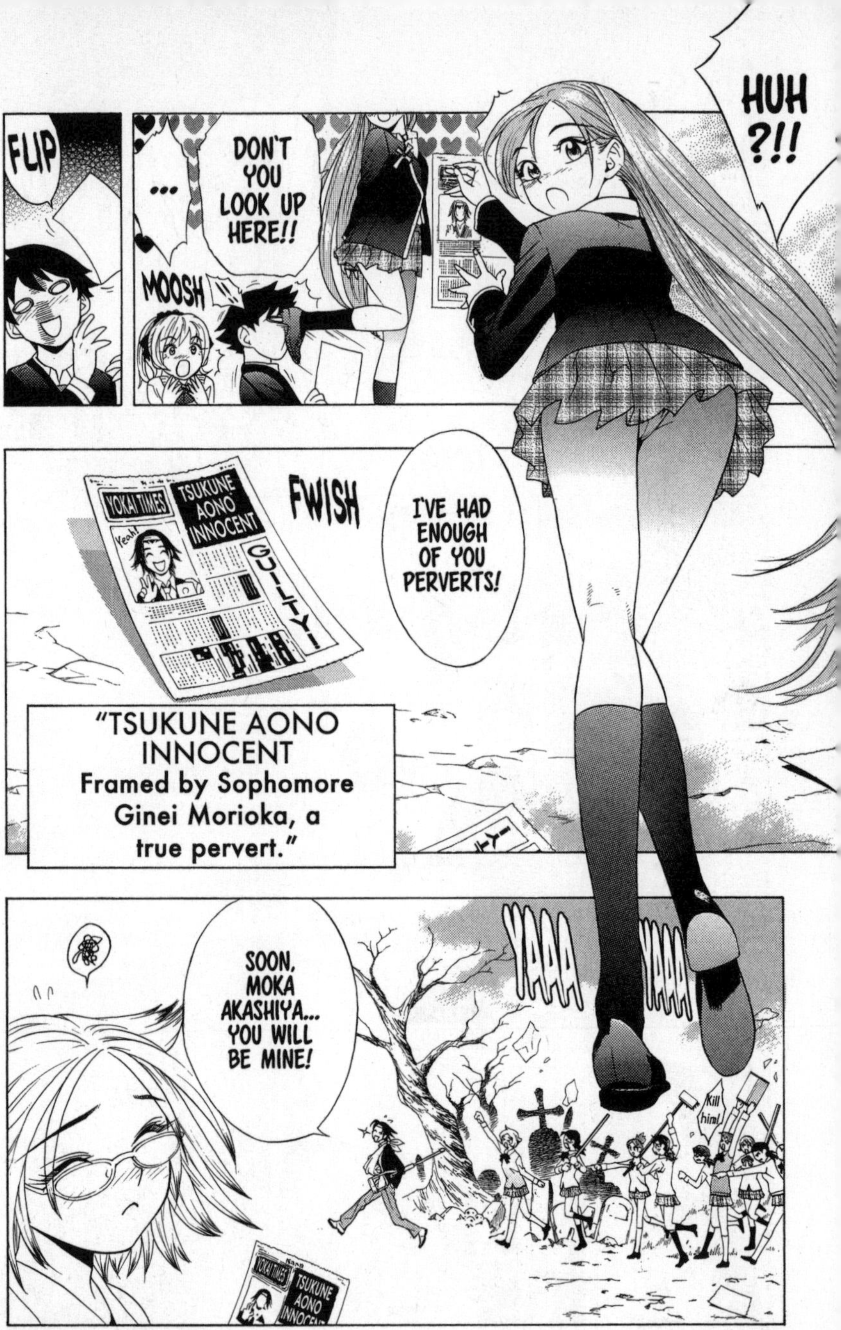
HUH ?!!
DON'T YOU LOOK UP HERE!!
...
MOOSH
FLIP
I'VE HAD ENOUGH OF YOU PERVERTS!
FWISH
YOKAI TIMES
TSUKUNE AONO INNOCENT
Yeah!
GUILTY!
"TSUKUNE AONO INNOCENT
Framed by Sophomore Ginei Morioka, a true pervert."
YAAA
YAAA
Kill him!
SOON, MOKA AKASHIYA... YOU WILL BE MINE!
YOKAI TIMES
TSUKUNE AONO INNOCENT

ROSARIO + VAMPIRE

Super Superficial End-of-Volume Theater

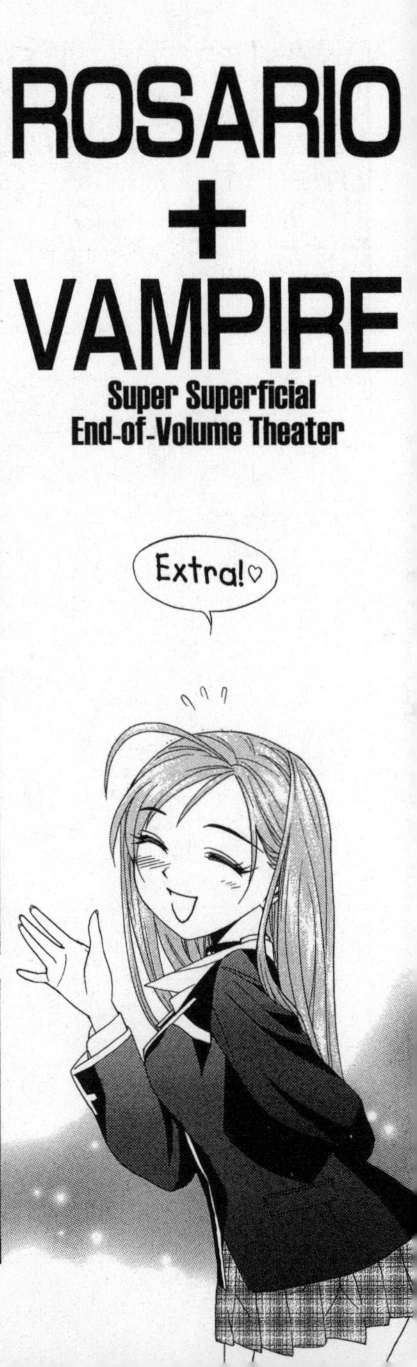
Extra!♡

• Moka •

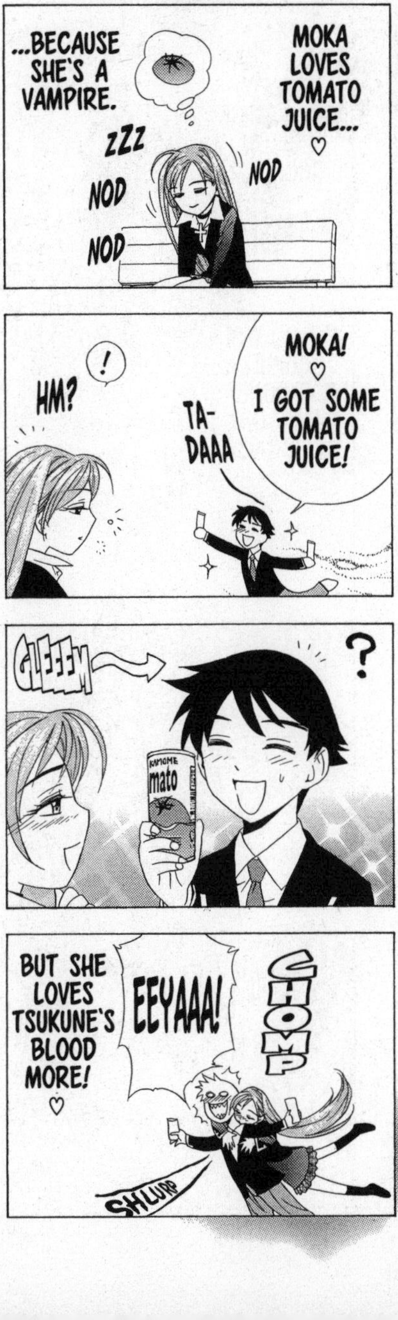
MOKA LOVES TOMATO JUICE... ♡
...BECAUSE SHE'S A VAMPIRE.
ZZZ
NOD
NOD
NOD
MOKA! ♡ I GOT SOME TOMATO JUICE!
TA-DAAA
!
HM?
?
GLEEEM
CHOMP
EEYAAA!
BUT SHE LOVES TSUKUNE'S BLOOD MORE! ♡
SHLURP

KURUMU

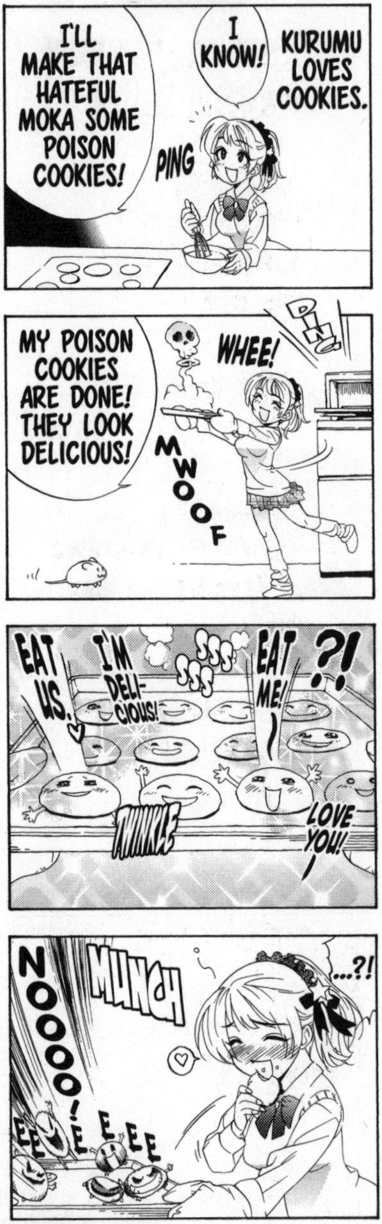
KURUMU LOVES COOKIES.
I KNOW!
PING
I'LL MAKE THAT HATEFUL MOKA SOME POISON COOKIES!
DING
WHEE!
MY POISON COOKIES ARE DONE! THEY LOOK DELICIOUS!
MWOOF
?!
EAT ME!
SSS SSS
I'M DELI-CIOUS!
EAT US.
LOVE YOU!
TWINKLE
...?!
MUNCH
NOOOOO!
EE E E EE

GIN

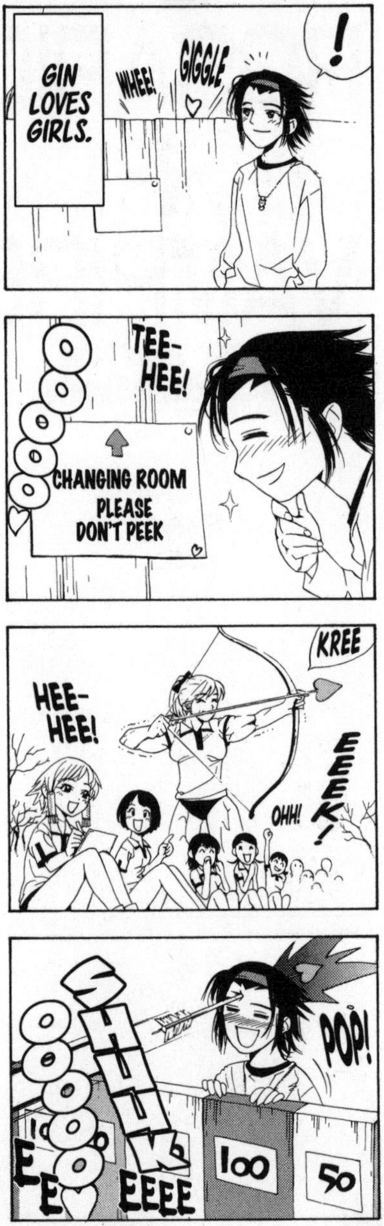
!
GIGGLE
WHEE!
GIN LOVES GIRLS.
TEE-HEE!
OOOOOO
CHANGING ROOM
PLEASE DON'T PEEK
KREE
EEEEK!
OHH!
HEE-HEE!
POP!
SHUUUK
OOOOOO
100
50
EEE
EEEE

• MS. NEKOME •

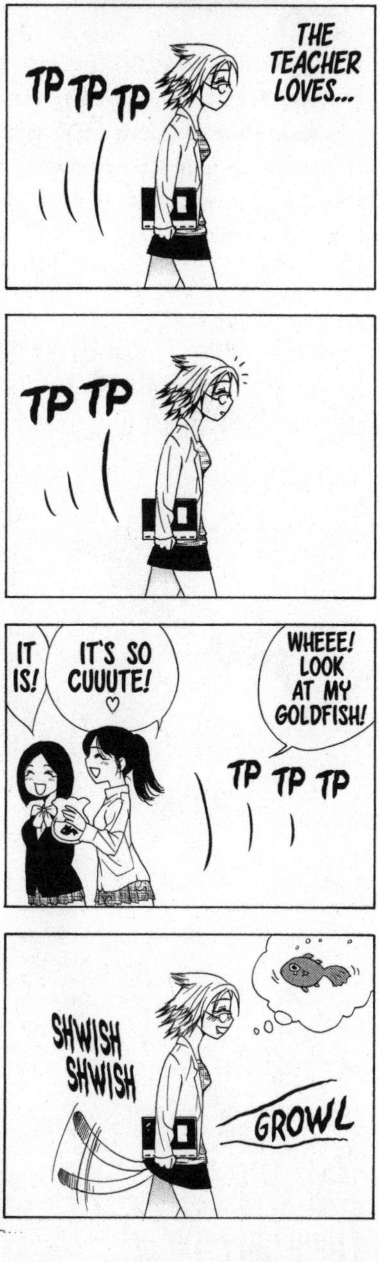
THE TEACHER LOVES...
TP TP TP
TP TP
WHEEE! LOOK AT MY GOLDFISH!
TP TP TP
IT'S SO CUUUTE! ♡
IT IS!
SHWISH SHWISH
GROWL

Rosario+Vampire
Akihisa Ikeda

Assistants:
Makoto Saito
Takafumi Okubo
Mio Isshiki

More assistants:
Ryuuji Ogaki (loves meat!)

3D modeling:
Takaharu Yoshizawa
Akihisa Ikeda & Raw Materials

Comic Strips:
Mika Asada

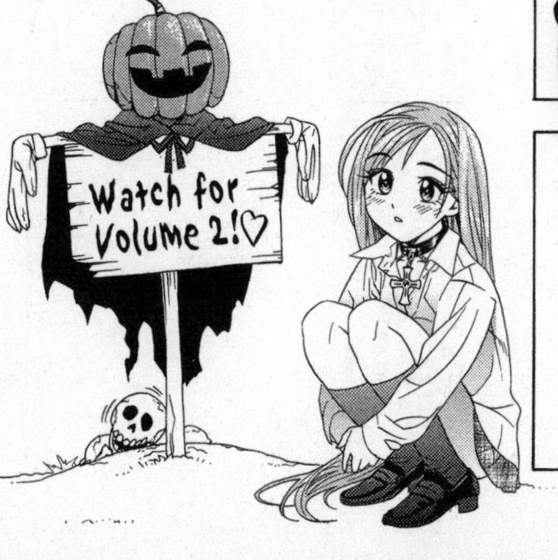
Watch for Volume 2!♡

Crypt Sheet for Volume 2: WITCHES!

QUIZ 2

HAVING A WITCH FOR A CLASSMATE CAN CREATE A HEX OF A VEXING SITUATION IF SHE…

a. casts spells stirring up all manner of mischief just to get attention

b. has no qualms about using magic to break you and your girlfriend up

c. becomes the target of a reptilian witchphobic hate group

d. all of the above

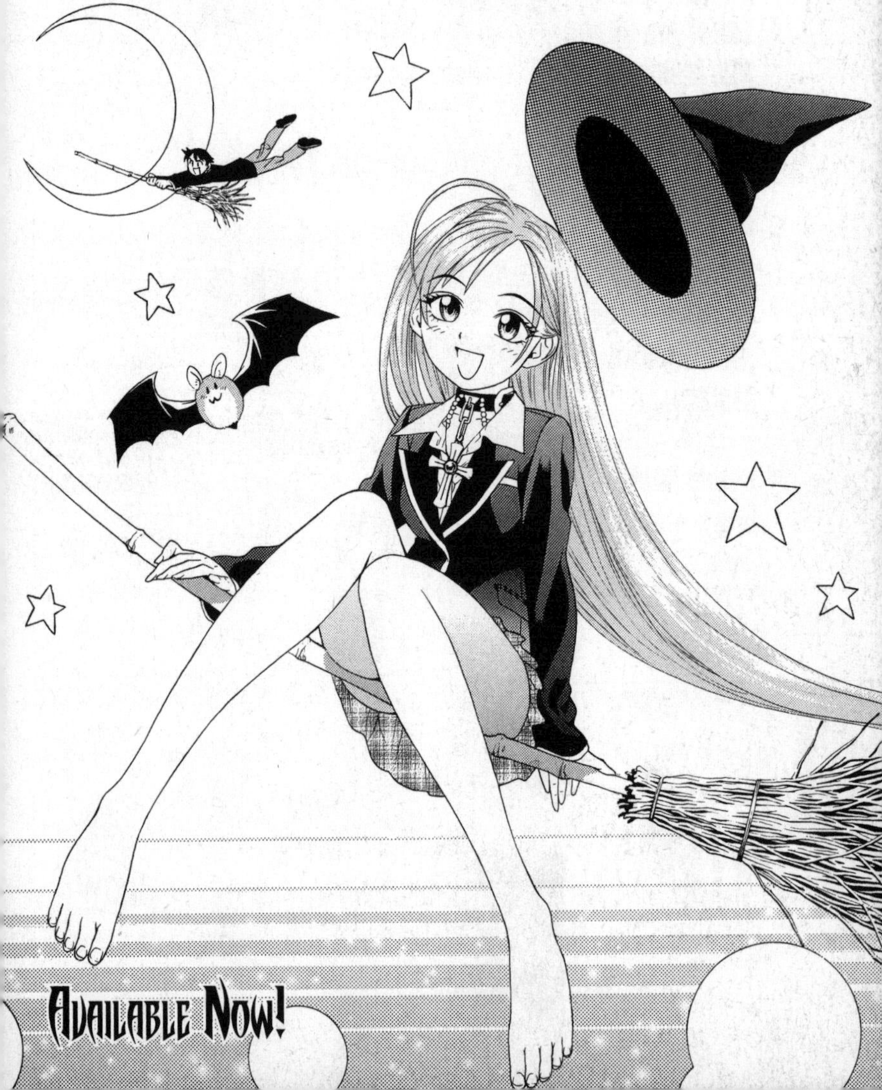

Available Now!

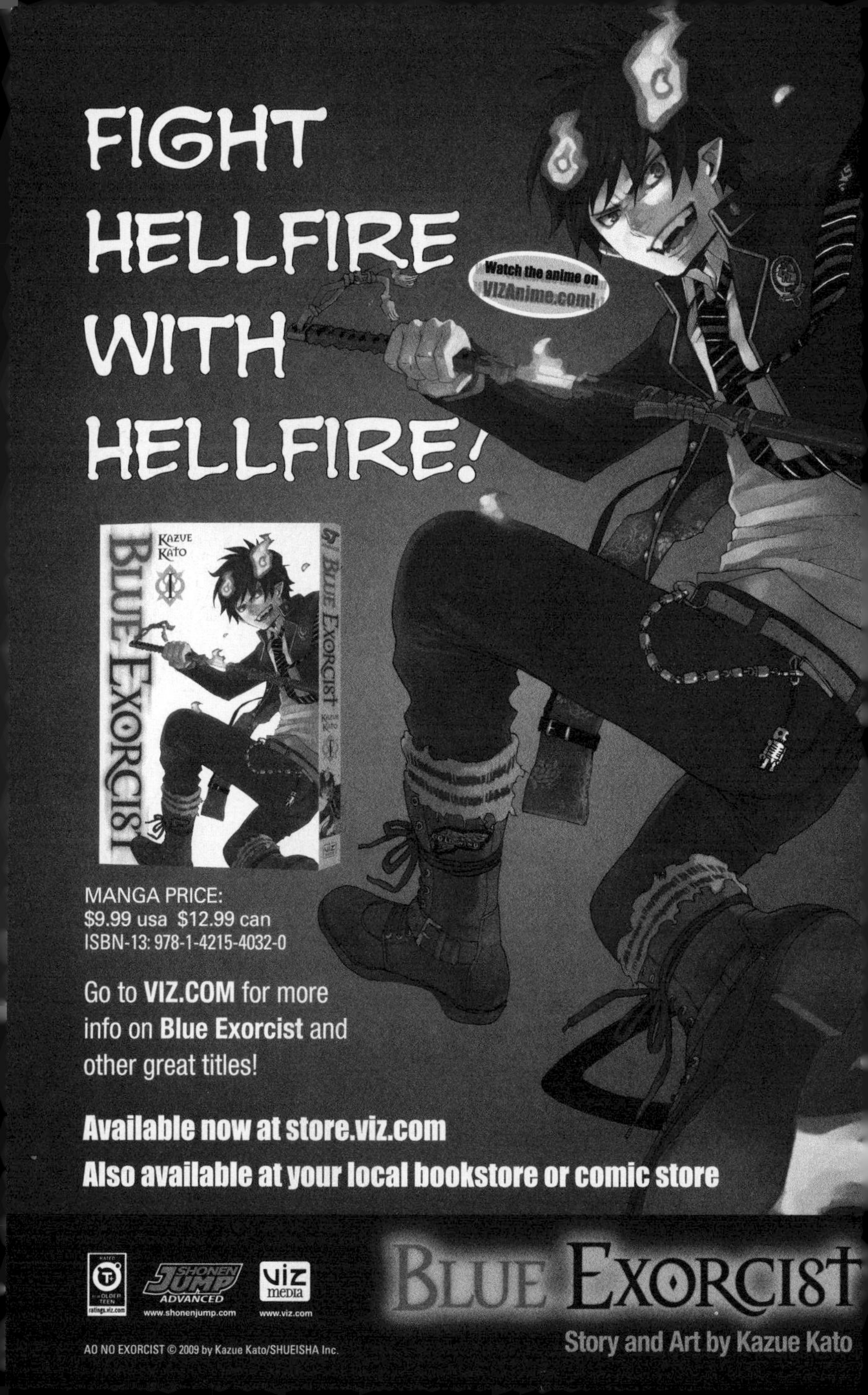
FIGHT HELLFIRE WITH HELLFIRE!
Watch the anime on VIZAnime.com!
KAZUE KATO
BLUE EXORCIST
MANGA PRICE:
$9.99 usa $12.99 can
ISBN-13: 978-1-4215-4032-0
Go to VIZ.COM for more info on Blue Exorcist and other great titles!
Available now at store.viz.com
Also available at your local bookstore or comic store
SHONEN JUMP ADVANCED
www.shonenjump.com
VIZ media
www.viz.com
BLUE EXORCIST
Story and Art by Kazue Kato
AO NO EXORCIST © 2009 by Kazue Kato/SHUEISHA Inc.

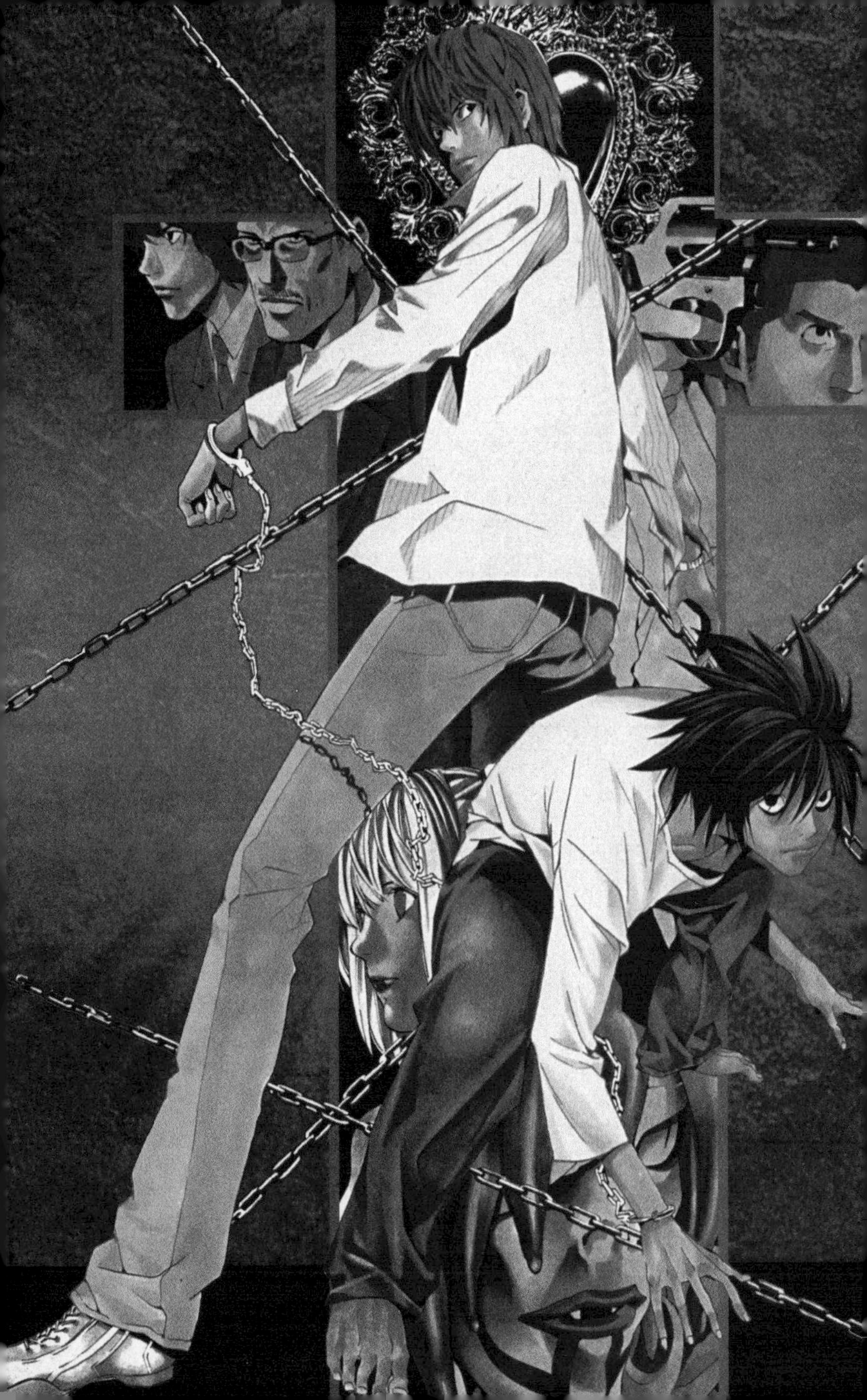

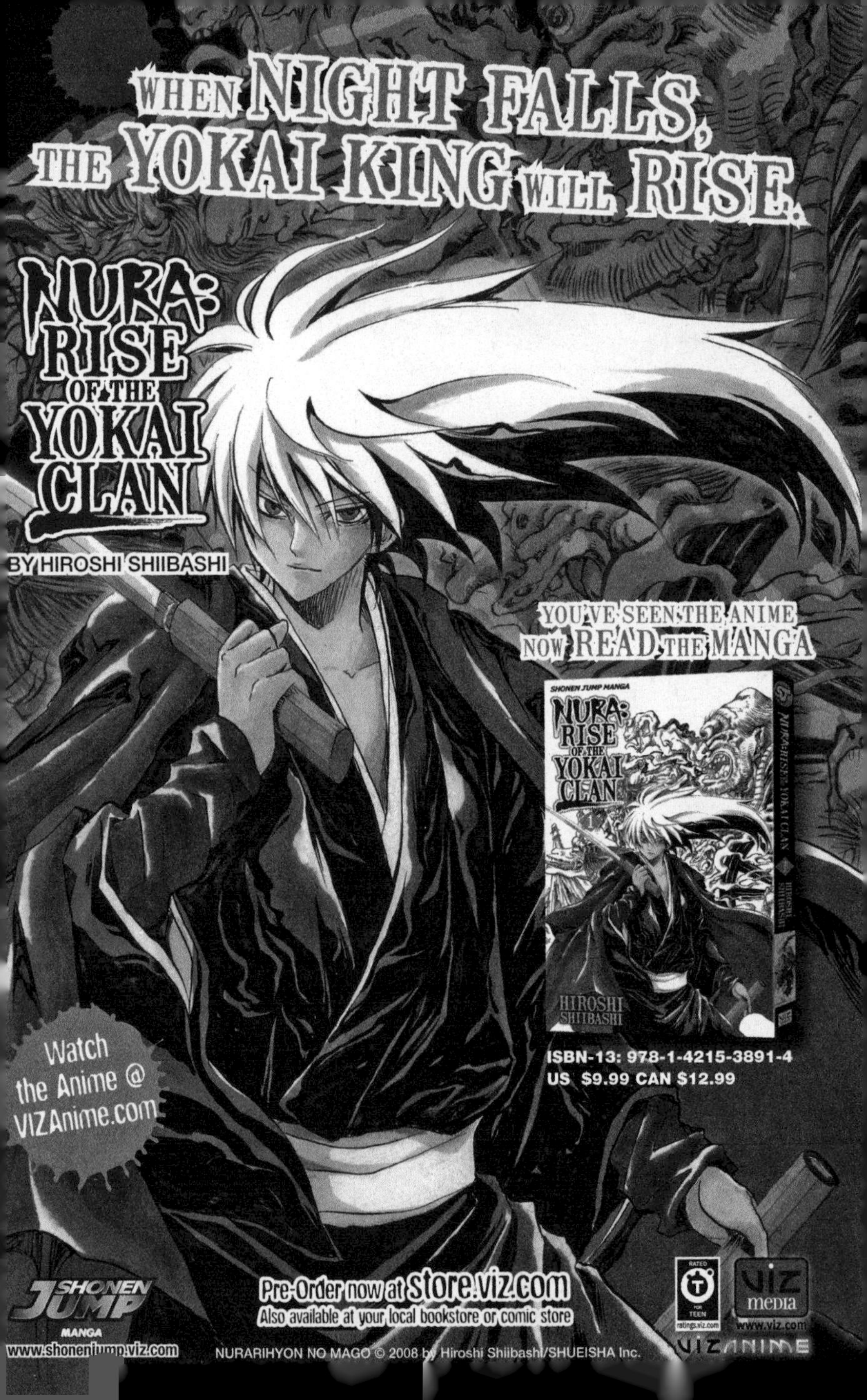
WHEN NIGHT FALLS, THE YOKAI KING WILL RISE.
NURA: RISE OF THE YOKAI CLAN
BY HIROSHI SHIIBASHI
YOU'VE SEEN THE ANIME NOW READ THE MANGA
SHONEN JUMP MANGA
NURA: RISE OF THE YOKAI CLAN
1
HIROSHI SHIIBASHI
ISBN-13: 978-1-4215-3891-4
US $9.99 CAN $12.99
Watch the Anime @ VIZAnime.com
SHONEN JUMP MANGA
www.shonenjump.viz.com
Pre-Order now at store.viz.com
Also available at your local bookstore or comic store
RATED T FOR TEEN
ratings.viz.com
VIZ media
www.viz.com
VIZANIME
NURARIHYON NO MAGO © 2008 by Hiroshi Shiibashi/SHUEISHA Inc.

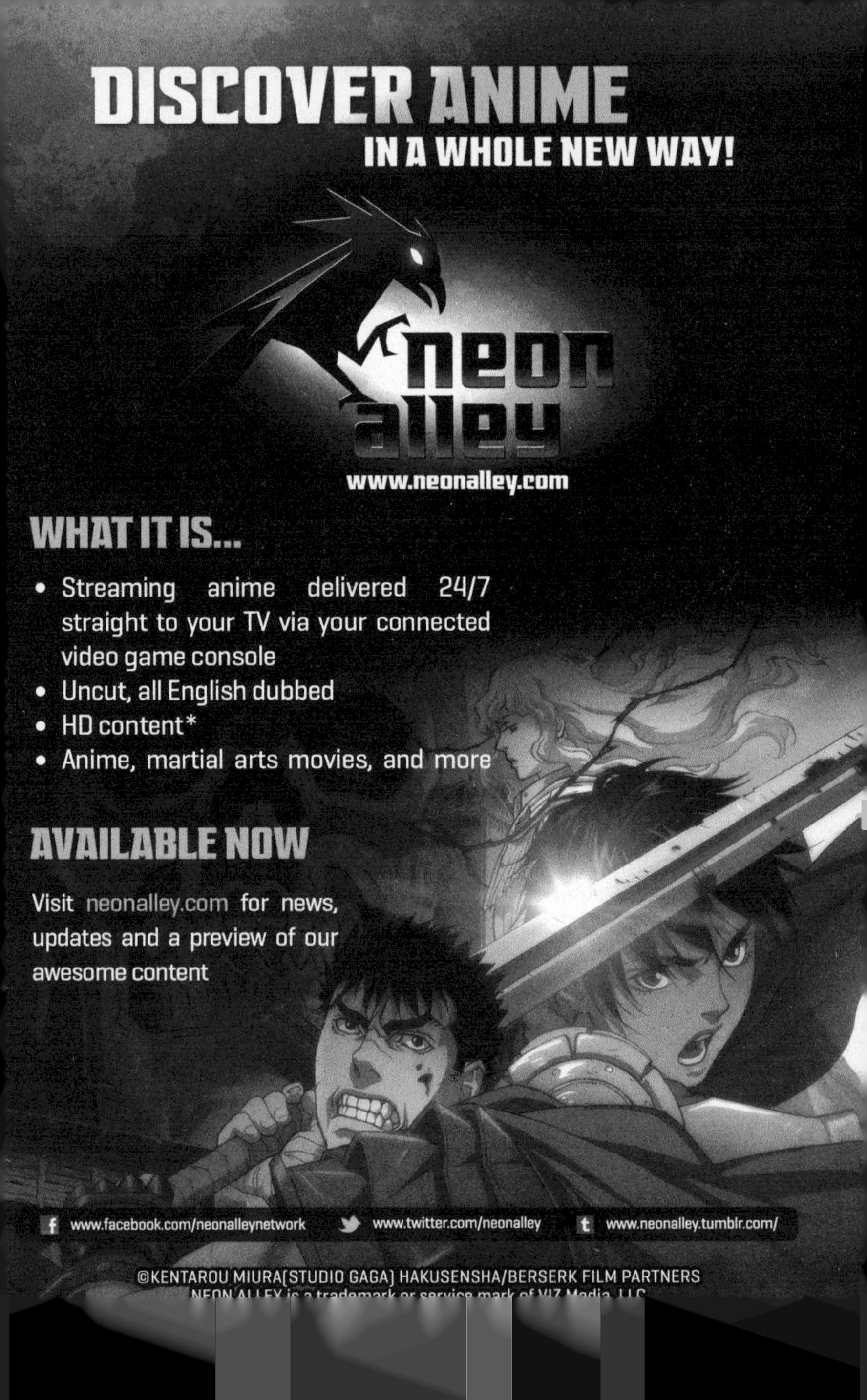
DISCOVER ANIME
IN A WHOLE NEW WAY!
neon alley
www.neonalley.com
WHAT IT IS...
• Streaming anime delivered 24/7 straight to your TV via your connected video game console
• Uncut, all English dubbed
• HD content*
• Anime, martial arts movies, and more
AVAILABLE NOW
Visit neonalley.com for news, updates and a preview of our awesome content
www.facebook.com/neonalleynetwork
www.twitter.com/neonalley
www.neonalley.tumblr.com/
©KENTAROU MIURA(STUDIO GAGA) HAKUSENSHA/BERSERK FILM PARTNERS
NEON ALLEY is a trademark or service mark of VIZ Media, LLC

The World's Greatest Manga
Now available on your iPad

Full of FREE previews and tons of new manga for you to explore

From legendary manga like *Dragon Ball* to *Bakuman*, the newest series from the creators of *Death Note*, the best manga in the world is now available on the iPad through the official VIZ Manga app.

- ## Free App
- ## New content weekly
- ## Free chapter 1 previews

You're Reading in the Wrong Direction!!

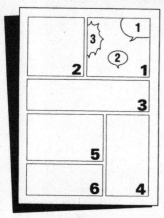

Whoops! Guess what? You're starting at the wrong end of the comic!

…It's true! In keeping with the original Japanese format, **Rosario+Vampire** is meant to be read from right to left, starting in the upper-right corner.

Unlike English, which is read from left to right, Japanese is read from right to left, meaning action, sound effects and word-balloon order are completely reversed… something which can make readers unfamiliar with Japanese feel pretty backwards themselves. For this reason, manga or Japanese comics published in the U.S. in English have sometimes been published "flopped"—that is, printed in exact reverse order, as though seen from the other side of a mirror.

By flopping pages, U.S. publishers can avoid confusing readers, but the compromise is not without its downside. For one thing, a character in a flopped manga series who once wore in the original Japanese version a T-shirt emblazoned with "M A Y" (as in "the merry month of") now wears one which reads "Y A M"! Additionally, many manga creators in Japan are themselves unhappy with the process, as some feel the mirror-imaging of their art skews their original intentions.

We are proud to bring you Akihisa Ikeda's **Rosario+Vampire** in the original unflopped format. For now, though, turn to the other side of the book and let the haunting begin…!

—Editor